Also by Judith Viorst

Poems

The Village Square
It's Hard to Be Hip Over Thirty and Other Tragedies of Married Life
People and Other Aggravations
How Did I Get to Be Forty and Other Atrocities
If I Were in Charge of the World and Other Worries
When Did I Stop Being Twenty and Other Injustices
Forever Fifty and Other Negotiations
Sad Underwear and Other Complications

Children's Books

Sunday Morning
I'll Fix Anthony
Try It Again, Sam
The Tenth Good Thing About Barney
Alexander and the Terrible, Horrible, No Good, Very Bad Day
My Mama Says There Aren't Any Zombies, Ghosts, Vampires,
     Creatures, Demons, Monsters, Fiends, Goblins, or Things
Rosie and Michael
Alexander, Who Used to Be Rich Last Sunday
The Good-Bye Book
Earrings!
The Alphabet from Z to A (With Much Confusion on the Way)
Alexander, Who's Not (Do you hear me? I mean it!) Going to Move

Other

Yes, Married
A Visit from St. Nicholas (to a Liberated Household)
Love and Guilt and the Meaning of Life, Etc.
Necessary Losses
Murdering Mr. Monti

Judith Viorst

Imperfect Control

Our Lifelong Struggles with Power and Surrender

A FIRESIDE BOOK
PUBLISHED BY SIMON & SCHUSTER

FIRESIDE
Rockefeller Center
1230 Avenue of the Americas
New York, NY 10020

First Fireside Edition 1999

FIRESIDE and colophon are registered trademarks
of Simon & Schuster Inc.

Designed by Bonni Leon-Berman

Manufactured in the United States of America

1   3   5   7   9   10   8   6   4   2

The Library of Congress has cataloged the Simon & Schuster edition as follows:
Viorst, Judith.
Imperfect control : our lifelong struggle with power and surrender
/ Judith Viorst.
p.   cm.
Includes bibliographical references and index.
1. Control (Psychology)   I. Title.
BF611.V56   1998
158.1—dc21   97-37302
CIP
ISBN 0-684-80139-6
ISBN 0-684-84814-7 (Pbk)

The author acknowledges with thanks
permission to reprint extended quotations from the following:

Margaret Wise Brown, *Goodnight Moon*. Copyright © 1947 by Harper &
Row, Publishers, Inc. Text copyright renewed 1975 by Roberta Brown
continued on page 445

in memory of
Kitty Gillman

Contents

Introduction

Control: The capacity to manage, master, dominate, exercise power over, regulate, influence, curb, suppress, or restrain.

Control is a rich and resonant word, a word that evokes strong feelings, a word that is familiar to the tongue, for it touches on lifelong concerns with power and helplessness, with freedom and limitations, with doing and being done to, with who's on top, with whether we see ourselves as someone who goes out and gets what we want or as someone who, for the most part, takes what we get. Control is a hard-edged word; it has—at least it seems to have—no poetry in it. It's something we want, need, seize, fear, lose, give up. In our feelings about our place in the world, in how we define ourselves, in our personal and professional relationships, we—consciously or unconsciously, positively or negatively—are constantly dealing with issues of control.

Do you think that control is always a negative concept? I'd like to persuade you of another view. Do you think that concerns with control do not apply to how you live or who you are? I'll argue that they apply both to me and to you. For when we can't walk one more step and yet we keep walking, when we learn something new by practicing every day, when we give ourselves over to blistering rage or to passion, when we fall off our diet and onto a crème brûlée, when we say we can't help what we do or resent what we do or deplore what we do and yet we still do it, when we force our nearest and dearest to do it our way, we are—though perhaps we don't know it, or perhaps we call it by another name—taking, or giving up, or abusing control.

We are constantly dealing with issues of control.

Control enough to shape our own fate—or are we shaped by our genes?

Control enough to master a skill, to work toward a goal, to finish what we start.

Control of our sexuality.

Control enough to manage on our own.

Control enough to hold ourselves up to certain moral standards and to hold ourselves responsible when we fall short.

Control within our marital relationships.

Control within our professional relationships.

Control of our adult children—don't they need us to tell them how to live their lives?

Control as something we sometimes surrender, either by choice or necessity.

Control in the wake of misfortune.

Control of our death.

Whether or not we believe we possess it, whether we rush to embrace it or claim to shun it, most of us want some control—sufficient control, sometimes total control—over ourselves, and over other people, and over the events with which we're involved.

Our feelings about control are expressed in our early sense of competence or powerlessness, in our power struggles during adolescence, in where and with whom and how often we make love, in how much aching regret and unfinished business we'll be dealing with when we die. Our beliefs about having control determine whether or not our small and large losses defeat us, how easily we quit, and how hard we try. Our strategies of control, when the point of control is to get our own way, include intimidation, recrimination, negotiation, the laying on of guilt, persuasion, flattery—and repetition, sometimes known as nagging. Our relinquishing of control may be a bitter failure, a facing of hard realities, or a willing, indeed eager, acquiescence.

Thinking about control can explain why "helpless" Kathy calls all the shots in the marriage; why Tom keeps losing job after job after job; why control-freak Vicky has to dine at precisely 7:00 P.M.; why criminals and other bad guys insist that, although they did it, and although they agree that it was wrong to do it, it isn't their fault. Thinking about control can explain why we let ourselves remain in a hopeless relationship; how an offer of help may be a power ploy; why persistence isn't invariably a virtue; and when we're allowed to enjoy the pleasure of saying, "This is not my responsibility."

In some of their definitions the word "control" and the word "power" are synonymous. I'll sometimes be using them interchangeably. I'll also be making the point—I'll be making this point repeatedly—that while most of us endeavor to mold the events of our lives to meet our personal needs, the control we exercise over ourselves, over others, and over what happens to us is almost always highly imperfect control.

In writing this book, I've drawn on the work of biological scientists, social scientists, psychoanalysts, philosophers, and others who, directly and sometimes very indirectly, examine the multiple aspects of control.* I've drawn, as well, on public reports and (with identities masked) on private case histories, and on the truths to be found in fiction and poems. In addition I've talked with children and parents, husbands and wives and lovers, victims and survivors, employees and bosses, focusing on people whose place in society and the economy allows for the possibility of control. And I've had some things to say about my own control concerns, both past and pending.

Don't look to this book for "Ten Easy Steps to Improving Your

---

* Information on all the source material and further elaboration on some of the points can be found in the "Notes and Elaborations" section.

Self-Control," or "How to Get Your Husband or Wife to Obey." I'm afraid you will have to seek elsewhere for prescriptions. But I'm hoping to persuade you that the ways we deal with control can enrich or diminish us, and can shape our relationships for good or for ill. I'm hoping to show why experiences you've known by other names can be called "control." I'm asking you to recognize (as I, with some shudders and sighs, have been learning to do) when the control we claim is too much or too little. And I trust that this recognition, this greater awareness, will enable us to make freer and wiser choices.

For I continue to believe that consciousness helps. I continue to believe that knowing where it is we're going really helps. I believe that constructive change begins when we're finally able to say, "There I go again," or *That's* what I'm doing." I also believe that by understanding how issues of control pervade our lives, we eventually may achieve a better balancing of power and surrender, better—albeit still imperfect—control.

Judith Viorst
Washington, D.C.

1

How Free to Be?

Humanity cannot be cut adrift from its own biology,
but neither is it enchained by it.

—*Not in Our Genes*

It seems foolish to speak of control when so many forces, inner and outer, have the power to sweep away our plans and dreams, when earthquakes and ice storms and plagues and wars, both literal and psychic, can undermine our dearest, most urgent intentions. Yet most of us behave as if we're the authors of our own fate, as if the ground is steady beneath our feet, as if we can rise every morning and enter into a life that we will be able to shape by our needs, our choices, our actions, and our will.

Most of us behave as if we do possess significant control.

We acknowledge, of course, that we have no control over natural disasters, over what are usually known as acts of God, though perhaps we will try to limit our exquisite vulnerability by setting up house far from storm-hammered coasts and faults in the earth. We're also prepared to acknowledge that we cannot impose control over the random Russian roulettes of life, though perhaps we will try to reduce the odds of being cut down by the madman with a gun by sedulously avoiding walks on the wild side. We'll furthermore grant that early events—events beyond our control—can give us, or deprive us of, a capacity to love and trust and hope, take pride in ourselves, feel concern for others. We'll even grant that a lifetime of diligent flossing and antioxidants may not keep us safe from periodontists or cancer.

But aside from cancer and gum disease and madmen and acts of God, and in spite of inadequate parents or social inequities, we continue to believe in our freedom to get where we're going, to be what we strive to be. Possessed of a view of an infinitely flexible, fixable self, a self unconstrained by fate or destiny, we place our trust in personal control.

And so I will promise I'll have that work finished three weeks from tomorrow, and swear to myself I'll be seven pounds lighter by May. And I draw up my daily list—I am devoted to making lists—of THINGS THAT I AM GOING TO DO TODAY, confident that before the day is done I'll have checked off almost every item. As for my larger ambitions, like mastering French, like achieving upper-arm definition, like learning to keep my mouth shut when there's something I'm bursting to say but shouldn't say, I believe that—though not yet achieved—they are surely achievable. Early in life I was taught—we're all taught—that where there's a will there's a way, which is why we keep making those New Year's resolutions, which is why we remain convinced (often in spite of compelling evidence to the contrary) that we really can do it and be it, that we're in control.

And if, in our striving to do and to be, we fall somewhat short of our goals, we still don't lose faith in our fixability—in our power to change and improve through determination and insight and effort and those courses and books that promise to teach us how . . .

. . . to take charge of our anger, our weight, our compulsive spending, our drinking, our time, our stress, our phobias.

. . . to overcome our shyness, our fear of flying, our fear of intimacy, our dependency.

. . . to acquire a good memory, a husband, a wife, a fortune, peace of mind.

. . . to improve our sexual pleasure, our intelligence, our character, our stomach muscles.

. . . to be in control.

But what do we mean by control when research has implicated our genes in everything from shyness to obesity? What do we mean by control when identical twins who have been reared in separate households display a host of eerily similar traits? What do we mean by control when serious scientists claim to have found a "happiness" gene, a "neurotic" gene, a "novelty-seeking" gene, and, yes, a "good mother" gene? What do we mean by control when no matter how hard we throw the apple, we find that it doesn't fall too far from the tree?

Dodie had done the right thing, she was sure, by giving up her infant for adoption. She wanted him to have a decent life. And he couldn't have a good life while she was still hooked up with Benjy, a so-called free spirit who warned her that he wasn't letting some baby cramp his style. Three years later, Benjy was dead, a ravaged junkie in search of a fix in an alley, and Dodie, with bitter regret, knew she'd made the wrong choice. Then twenty-five years later she picked up the phone and heard a strangely familiar voice saying that he was her son and wanted to meet her.

Dodie, unmarried and childless and lonely, thought for a while she was getting a second chance. Finding her son was surely a dream come true. In addition, she was shamelessly proud of his young Marlon Brando good looks, so much like his father's. But, like his father, he was a junkie too. And six months later he too was dead of an overdose.

How shall we understand the point of this story?

15

Must we interpret it genetically?

Does it mean we're compelled by our genes to behave in certain ways?

And, if it does, how free are we to be?

Behavioral genetics has revived the age-old nature-nurture debate, a debate that is—in essence—about control. For if our genes make us fat or depressed or aggressive or addictive or dumb or gay, we may have to find a new way to talk about choice and change, free will and responsibility. It's tempting, when confronting our failings, to comfort ourselves with the thought that they aren't our fault, that we should not be blamed, that our belly or beastly behavior doesn't derive from our character flaws but our DNA. Some of us, in fact, will passively settle for a state of genetic victimhood, willing to define ourselves as the helpless playthings of forces beyond our control. But most of us resist the idea that our genes are us, that we are enchained by biology. Most of us continue to claim free will.

"I am the master of my fate; I am the captain of my soul."

"Every man is the son of his own works."

"The fault, dear Brutus, is not in our stars, but in ourselves, that we are underlings."

"And you and me are free to be you and me."

Not quite.

For these declarations of freedom have been challenged by family, adoption, and twin research, especially the extensive research on identical twins raised separately from each other. Because their genes are the same and their environments—since an early age—dissimilar, these twins can help illuminate the influence of heredity on behavior.

It used to make sense to believe that identical twins who were raised together had similar traits *because* they were raised together, that, as a psychologist wrote in 1981, "Genes and glands are obviously important, but social learning also has a dramatic role. Imagine the enormous differences that would be found in the personalities of twins with identical genetic endowments if they were raised apart in two different families."

Ah, yes, it makes perfect sense—except it's wrong.

For substantial studies have shown that in a wide range of personality traits, in sexual orientation, in IQ, identical twins who are raised apart strikingly resemble one another. And even such characteristics as traditionalism and job satisfaction are also affected in part by heredity. As for personal quirks, consider these twins who meet for the first time as adults, and they're both wearing seven rings, or they both have the habit of reading magazines back to front, or they both drink their coffee sugarless, black, and cold.

What do these similarities do to our concepts of choice and freedom?

What do they do to our concept of control?

Genetics helps explain the similarities we see in identical twins who were raised in separate households. It also helps explain the dramatic differences we see in non-twin siblings raised in the same household. For differences may arise from what has been called the "nature of nurture," the child's *genetic* influence on experience, meaning that to some extent we're actively prompted by our genetic makeup to "elicit, select, seek out, or create" the specific environment in which we live.

A young boy enters the living room with a book, a deck of cards, and a jigsaw puzzle, and proceeds to finish the puzzle and build a house of cards, after which he curls up with *The Cat in the Hat*. His brother, in the same living room, sets a chair on top of the coffee table and stacks a couple of cushions on top of that, after which he uses this improvised ladder to climb on the mantelpiece and dive off. One has created a safe and cozy haven.

The other has created a danger zone. Prompted, it seems, by their very own specific genetic makeup, they have created two very different environments.

The nature of nurture also shows up in the way we "get" our mothers and fathers to treat us, which may be distinctly different from the treatment our brothers and sisters will receive. For if we're the cuddly type, our parents may give us more hugs and kisses than they give to our slow-to-warm-up, standoffish sister. And if we're the stubborn type, we may prod our parents to sterner treatment than they ever impose on our less contentious sibs. My younger sister, for instance, always regarded our dad as a softie because, whenever he scolded her, he'd stop the minute her big blue eyes welled with tears. I found him a much more tyrannical man because, from my earliest years, I'd respond to his scoldings by sticking out my chin and saying provocatively, "Go ahead and spank me—I am right." Because of genetic differences, non-twin brothers or sisters can experience the same family very differently, can grow up in the same house with the same mother and the same father and still, in effect, grow up in different homes, with different parents, in what has been described as a "nonshared environment."

The flip side of this, which might help explain the similarities of twins reared apart, is that their genetic makeup may dispose them to elicit, select, or seek out similar experiences—including similar treatment from their parents—even when they grow up with different parents.

Other research findings—studies of temperament—also ask us to ponder the power of genes.

For we do not enter the world a blank slate, without qualities. We enter the world temperamentally predisposed. Some 20 percent of us, says Harvard developmental psychologist Jerome Kagan, are born with a physiology so swiftly aroused, so sensitive, that everything unfamiliar or strange seems a threat. Some

40 percent of us, at birth, possess a far less excitable physiology and are thus—by nature—less fearful, more relaxed.

A portion of supersensitives will develop what Kagan calls an "inhibited" temperament, responding to new experiences with caution and restraint, distress and avoidance. A portion of less-excitables will develop, in contrast, an "uninhibited" temperament, comfortable with the unexpected and risky, fearless in the face of the unknown. Such very different reactions to new situations and new people may color our moods and behavior throughout our lives, making some of us poets, Albert Einsteins, Bashfuls, nerds, or people who carry umbrellas on sunny days, and making some of us parachute jumpers, masters of the universe, Candides, Madonnas, senators, or sociopaths.

The inhibiteds tend toward activities that let them control and limit the novelties and uncertainties of life.

The uninhibiteds are willing to put themselves into all sorts of situations where they're likely to confront unpredictable risks.

Discussions of temperament, present and past, always include these two types, though different labels may be used to describe them. Hippocrates called them melancholic and sanguine. Carl Gustav Jung called them introverted and extroverted. Parents and teachers today may simply call them shy and sociable, tense and happy-go-lucky, timid and bold. This isn't to say that there aren't as many temperaments as there are Baskin-Robbins flavors, but only that the inhibited and uninhibited temperaments are among the most familiar and best researched.

Few of us have temperaments that are undiluted examples of these extremes. And some of us have temperaments that combine, for instance, anxiety and aggression, or cautiousness and sociability. But all of us have surely encountered easy-to-recognize versions of Kagan's types. And many of us, I suspect, could broadly place ourselves (and also our mates and our children) in the basically inhibited or basically uninhibited category.

My youngest son, Alexander, for instance, arrived in this world a zesty and fearless adventurer—touching and testing and tasting and trying everything within reach, and (while we slept, unaware) climbing out of his crib and prowling perilously through the house. His reckless spirit, which over the years had us going steady with the emergency room, prompted him to drink turpentine, leap off tables, tumble from trees and canoes, walk on glass without shoes, find spaces his hand or his head could get into but not out of, and stand a stool *on top* of the jungle gym because he "wanted to make it go higher." I'd urge him to sit down and color, but he never wanted to color. Hanging by his fingers above some lethal twelve-foot drop was so much more fun. Looking back at his childhood of broken bones, smashed teeth, concussions, burns, and stitches, I often wonder how he, or I, survived the thrill-seeking nature he was born with.

Alexander is now an adult. He races in minitriathalons. He mountain-bikes, but always with a helmet. His annual Thanksgiving football game, once a regular source of holiday injuries, was long ago (thankfully) shifted from tackle to touch. Having learned some hard life lessons, he is currently finding ways to get his kicks without taking foolish risks. But while he is (mostly) looking before he leaps, and while (with one recent exception) he is no longer being rushed to the emergency room, he remains—in temperament—the avid adventurer I first met when he was a brand-new baby boy.

Current studies of alcoholism, manic-depression, drug addiction, obsessive-compulsive disorder, and schizophrenia also highlight the influence of genes, though that influence appears to be much stronger in certain complaints than it is in others. There seems to be, for instance, a substantial genetic basis for schizophrenia, a finding that has offered many guilt-tormented mothers vast relief. And while there is still much to learn about the highly publicized obesity gene, it too is assuaging guilt—the guilt of those who keep losing and gaining, again and again, the same thirty pounds.

The search for links between genes and crime has also produced some—forgive me—arresting findings. A study, for example, in the city and county of Copenhagen, Denmark, found that 22 percent of the biological sons of criminal fathers—sons whose adoptive fathers had clean records—wound up turning into criminals too. But when the adoptive fathers, not the natural fathers, were criminals, just 11.5 percent of the sons became criminals. These findings, which show *almost double* the number of criminal father-son pairs when the relationship is biological, seem to suggest some connection between a person's genetic makeup and criminality.

Other studies have correlated low levels of serotonin—one of the chemical messengers in the brain—with various kinds of criminal behavior, indicating some links between low serotonin, low self-esteem, aggressive impulsivity, and violence. And a Dutch-American research team has linked aggression with a mutated gene. More recently, it was discovered that when male mice lacked a gene that they needed in order to make NO— nitric oxide—they turned into "monster mice," attacking, chasing, biting, and killing normal male mice, and despite "substantial vocal protestations," mounting female mice to engage in "excessive and inappropriate" sexual overtures.

NO, the researchers speculate, may serve as some sort of brake on sexual and other violent aggression, turning those who lack this one brain chemical into vicious murderers and rapists. "What we might have here," says a member of the Johns Hopkins team that studied these monster mice, "is an example of serious criminal behavior that can be explained by a single gene defect."

. . .

We may or may not have genes that contribute to human criminal violence. We may or may not have genes that are making us anxious or reckless or manic-depressive or fat. But even granting the power of genes, we aren't prepared to believe that people can be reduced to their biochemistry. There is nurture as well as nature. There's our environment as well as our heredity. There's experience—and experience, as one researcher put it, "can push genetic constitution around."

For most of the time it is clear that nature and nurture work on each other. They interpenetrate. Nature and nurture are rarely an either/or. Indeed, they're so tightly entangled that it would be futile to try to separate one from the other. Passionate disputes may arise over where the emphasis falls, over whether we're more the product of nature or nurture. But it's widely understood that we are indisputably influenced by both.

"Just as there is no organism without an environment," write scientists R. C. Lewontin, Steven Rose, and Leon Kamin, the authors of a book called *Not in Our Genes*, "so there is no environment without an organism. Neither organism nor environment is a closed system; each is open to the other."

It's true that the color of our eyes is 100 percent determined by our genes, that other than wearing contact lenses we can't environmentally alter our eye color. It's also true that certain diseases are caused by specific genes; this has been termed OGOD—one gene, one disorder. But even our height is just 90 percent genetically determined; the remaining 10 percent is the result of our nutrition—our environment. As for behavioral traits, the Minnesota Center for Twin and Adoption Research tells us that genes (in a given population; *not* in any particular individual) account for only some 50 percent of the total variation in personality, while environmental effects account for the rest.

Environment has an impact.

Our destiny isn't written in our genes.

Though nature may indeed set its stamp upon us, nature is just where we start—not where we end up.

For we don't, at birth, possess a definitive *temperament*. We simply start with certain *proclivities*, proclivities that our subsequent experiences sometimes heighten, sometimes mute. These experiences determine whether tendency becomes temperament. They also play a crucial role in how a particular temperament is expressed.

For instance, we who possess an uninhibited, fearless temperament may feel less guilty and anxious about breaking rules, for among the fears that are minimized is the fear that helps to keep others in line—fear of punishment. In one kind of home environment, where our rule-breaking ways are chastised and rechanneled, we might develop the sort of leadership qualities that help us become the governor of the state. In another kind of environment, where aggressive behavior is tolerated and commonplace, we might develop the sort of asociability that eventually leads us into a life of crime.

"The psychopath and the hero," says psychologist David Lykken, a student of temperament, "are twigs of the same branch." The difference, he says, has to do with our experience.

Or perhaps we're among those people who possess an inhibited temperament, quick to react with guilt and anxiety. If so, we may have to struggle with "a natural urge" to be glum, to be a worrier. If our mother is overanxious and overprotective, her concerns are likely to fuel our own anxiety, increasing our feelings of fearfulness and ratcheting up our level of tension and stress. But research shows that inhibited children securely tied to loving, accepting mothers can "learn to be kind to themselves and back off a little in a stressful situation . . . until we can't even see the stress response anymore."

Environment has an impact.
We aren't the slave of our genes.
Most of the time.

But then there's the story of Amy and Beth, identical twin baby girls adopted soon after their birth into two different households. By the end of the first year of life, each girl had begun to develop problems. By the age of ten they were having serious problems, characterized by, among other things, hypochondria, fear of the dark, and fear of being alone, plus difficulties with learning and with their peers, plus poor integration, significant immaturity, and a disturbing "quality of shallowness." If either girl had been studied without her sister, it was observed, her doctors would have concluded that her problems were the product of her environment. They might have gone even further and offered the following clinical speculations:

> If Beth had only had the dominant features of Amy's family—the confrontative mother, the strong father, the successful brother, the value of academic achievement—or if Amy had only had the dominant features of Beth's family—the overly accepting mother, the evenly attentive father, the less successful brother, the lack of concern about education—how much better each of them would have fared!

This all might have sounded persuasive, except that *both* twins displayed the same set of disabilities, which thus would have to be seen as genetically based. It's clear that the family environment, that two different family environments, can't always overcome the power of genes.

Psychologist Kagan echoes this view, noting that even the most *benign* environment is sometimes defeated by heredity. He regretfully observes that a very small group of inhibited children —no matter how dearly cared for and loved they might be— will probably suffer throughout their lives from bouts of the most terrible anxiety. So although he says that, in temperament, "the power of genes is real but limited," he also seems to be saying that there are times when the power of genes may be nonnegotiable.

Stephen, I suspect, would surely agree.

Stephen, a sophomore in college, has just informed his mother that he is gay. He is trying to listen patiently to her questions.

"What I mean is, is this something you're just going through? Just a stage? Is it something you've chosen? I mean . . . are you *angry* at us? Or maybe especially at me? Are you trying . . . I don't know . . . to *rebel* against the sort of life we live? Trying not just to be . . . oh . . . bourgeois, or something?"

Stephen replies to his mother. "God. Something I've *chosen!* I don't think this is anything that *anyone* would choose in this society. I didn't plan this . . . I didn't wake up one day and think it would really be *interesting* to be gay."

The concept of "sexual preference," which suggests some sort of negotiable lifestyle choice, has been supplanted in recent years by the more imperative "sexual orientation." For it's difficult to talk about choice when male sexual orientation appears to be so stubbornly immutable. And it's difficult to talk about choice when the current research indicates that biology helps determine whether that sexual orientation is straight or gay.

One study, for instance, found that in pairs of male identical twins, where one of the twins was already known to be gay, 52 percent of the co-twins were gay. In contrast, just 22 percent of fraternal co-twins were gay, and only 11 percent were gay among pairs of unrelated adopted brothers.

The theory here is if gayness is significantly genetic, then identical twins (who have the same genes) should most often share the identical sexual bent, with fraternal twins (who share half their genes) taking second place and nonrelated brothers coming in third.

Which is precisely what the study showed.

Another important study of the possible biological causes of gayness took a look at brain anatomy, finding that the part of the brain that governs sexual urges—the hypothalamus—is much smaller in gays than in heterosexual men, and raising the question of whether this quite striking difference in size might play a role in influencing gayness. More recently, a widely publicized study by geneticist Dean Hamer, examining the DNA of gay brothers, presented compelling evidence that something called a "gay" gene might exist, that a proclivity toward gayness may sometimes be passed from mothers to sons on the X chromosome.

(I should mention that the phrase "gay" gene, like "happiness" gene or "obesity" gene, is—though admittedly catchy—imprecise. To the degree that human behavior is said to be genetic, it is *polygenic*, caused by *many* genes. Thus Hamer's gay gene, if it does exist, would most likely be only one of many genetic contributions to gayness.)

A father who had rejected his two gay sons for religious reasons was able to warmly welcome them back in the fold only after he'd read about Hamer's gay gene. He was ready to forgive them because they weren't *choosing* to be the way they are. But many of the researchers, Hamer included, believe that nurture can influence gayness too, that once again—in intricate and variable ways—nature and nurture work on one another. At one end of the spectrum, there may be people whose gayness is mostly due to their genes, while those at the other end may be gay almost entirely because of their personal history. We need to know, however—and that father with the two gay sons should know—that even those whose gayness is more the prod-

26

uct of nurture than nature may have just as little choice about what they desire, and just as little capacity to change.

We need to know that nurture, like nature, sometimes has the power to set unyielding limits upon our control.

Indeed, in all our behavior, not only in sexual orientation, we must consider the limits imposed by nurture. We must understand that some life events can be almost as determining as the genes that determine the color of our eyes. Some life events, in fact, can actually alter our biology, can rewire the circuitry of our brain.

Nurture, like nature, can be very powerful.

It can give us, as we'll see in the next chapter, our sense of who we are and what we can do, providing us, if we're lucky, with the fundamental developmental right stuff. But if we're not so lucky, our nurture can damage us profoundly, and sometimes that damage cannot be repaired. Sometimes our life experiences, our environment, our nurture, can sear our soul indelibly and forever.

Indeed, it is simplistic to think that nature is the part that can't be changed and that nurture is the part of us that is fixable. It's simplistic to think that nurture is the part of us that's under our control. For a two-year-old can't protect herself from being beaten or raped or locked in a closet. A three-year-old can't protect himself from the loss of the person he most loves and needs. Such early childhood experiences, experiences that are out of our control, can shape our future feelings with the force of a message from our DNA.

Nurture is powerful.

Though not everyone who has lived through a childhood in hell is doomed to suffer irreparable damage, extremes of neglect or brutality may very well be the cause of enduring impairment. Though not every child whose parent dies young experiences

27

such a death as a lifelong catastrophe, some find all future rela-tionships stamped by that loss. And though we imagine high drama when we think of traumatic events—a father's beatings, a mother's psychotic break, Citizen Kane being torn away from his "Rosebud"—far less flamboyant experiences (a father's in-trusiveness, a mother's indifference) may mark us, and mark us for life, in ways that therapies can only mute, not mend.

Nurture can be very, very powerful.

Freud said that we could change ourselves by making the unconscious conscious, by bringing into awareness the conflicts and fears and needs that prompt us to do what we do. The great transformations wrought by psychoanalysis and therapy prove that this is true—but it's not *always* true. For sometimes, al-though we become a lot better at working with what we've got, we've still—alas—got it.

I could give you a brilliant analysis of the early-childhood events that compel me to be not only on time but early. A friend of mine, just as brilliantly, can point to his past experiences to explain why he works—is compelled to work—a seventy-five-to-eighty-hour week. Because of my hard-won insights, I never (well, rarely) berate my husband anymore when his lack of ur-gency makes us ten seconds late. Similarly, my friend, because of *his* insights, is actually now able—when pressing family matters arise—to cut back on his work. Yes, both of us, thanks to our understanding of why we do what we do, can behave much better than we used to behave, but the feeling we feel remains exactly the same—a panicked pounding in our chests (when I'm late, when he's working less) that recapitulates our old child-hood anxieties, that hasn't vanished and probably never will.

Not everything, despite our efforts, is fixable.

There are people, for instance, who live their whole lives con-vinced that they are fundamentally flawed, that they aren't the kind of child their mother wanted, enduring a sense of defec-tiveness that subsequent experience cannot dispel. Analyst Michael Balint offers the valuable concept of the "basic fault" to understand some of these women and men, ascribing to failures in their early nurturing experiences "a legacy of permanent defectiveness . . . beyond the capacity of analysis to repair."

There are life events that may mark us inescapably.

This view has its extremists—those environmental determinists who ignore or dismiss the role that nature plays, arguing that we human beings are born "a blank sheet on which experience can write without restriction." This view admits no freedom from the pressures of the environment and sees us, instead, as "virtually a slave of it," resulting in a life that isn't our fault, creation, or responsibility.

Like biological determinists, environmental determinists take a fundamentally fatalist view. Like biological determinists, who see us as the prisoners of our genes, environmental determinists see us as the prisoners of our childhood.

Either way, we are told that we are prisoners.

Either way, we are told that we are determined by events beyond our control.

Determined? Beyond our control? Then what about the question of human freedom? What about the question of free will?

Charles Darwin, who believed that our heredity and environment *together* determine all feelings, thoughts, and actions, confessed in one of his notebooks that "one doubts [the] existence of free will." That being the case, he concluded, we deserve neither credit nor blame for whatever we do. Two tenets of psychoanalysis also subscribe to this pessimistic view: one, that whatever we do or think is strictly determined by what has happened before, and, two, that we are driven, primarily, by our instinctive needs and unconscious impulses. Together these concepts argue on behalf of determinism. Together these concepts suggest that our belief in free will is merely an illusion.

29

There are, however, philosophers who argue for "soft" determinism—a notion of freedom compatible with determinism. There are analysts who hold this position too. Psychoanalyst Robert Waelder, for instance, writes that our future is not preordained, that the forces that go into shaping us are only *"pressures"*—not an immutable destiny. And analyst David Rapaport, whose definition of freedom is "the acceptance of the restraints of the law," declares that we can, within those restraints, make free choices.

Though we love control, we may have to settle for that.

But it seems reasonable to insist that, aside from infants and the severely mentally ill, all of us—in spite of bad genes or bad childhoods—ought to be held accountable for our actions. It seems reasonable to insist that while such "pressures" as childhood abuse or a genetic predisposition to impulsivity may make it much harder for us to do right or do well, we must—if we do wrong, mess up, fail others, fail ourselves—be held accountable. We may be entitled to sympathy for the bad cards we've been dealt. We may very well ask, "Could you, with these cards, have done better?" But it nonetheless seems reasonable, *and valuable*, to insist that we are responsible for the choices that we make.

Discussing the so-called "Doctrine of Necessity," philosopher John Stuart Mill once observed that man's "character is formed by his circumstances; . . . but his own desire to mould it in a particular way is one of those circumstances." He also wrote that if, in fact, we have the desire to form and to change our character, "we should know that the work is not so irrevocably done as to be incapable of being altered."

We can't always alter the nature or the nurture that might mark us with black depression or heart-pounding panic or surges of rage. We can't always control the feelings that we feel. But between our feelings and actions lies the power of our will to choose the ways in which we'll express those feelings. Between our feelings and actions lies our power to be free, to take control.

"The self is not a thing carved on entablature," says Alice Flett Downing, recalling the beginning of her own metamorphosis. At the age of nineteen, she tells us, "I was on the verge of becoming a certain kind of person, and then I changed. . . ."

Alice's transformation began on a summer morning when she woke up early in her parents' home and "looked straight up at the ceiling where there was a long circular crack shaped like the hunch in an old crone's back. . . . That selfsame crack had been there ever since I could remember, since earliest childhood. It was the first thing I saw in the morning and the last thing at night, this menacing inscription in plaster that roofed me over with dread. Not that I feared the witchlike configuration. . . . No, what I dreaded about the ceiling crack was its persistence. That it was always there. Determined to accompany me. To be a part of me."

Although she has never done anything like this before, Alice locates a ladder in the basement, a spatula in the kitchen and, in the garden shed, a box of plasterer's putty, which she mixes and spreads over the ceiling crack. After the plaster dries, she sands it smooth. Later that day she paints the entire ceiling, adding a second coat just before bedtime. She then lies down in the dark, dizzy with happiness.

"In one day," she says, "I had altered my life: my life, therefore, was alterable. This simple axiom did not cry out for exegesis; no, it entered my bloodstream directly, as powerful as heroin; I could feel its pump and surge, the way it brightened my veins to a kind of glass. I had wakened that morning to narrowness and predestination, and I was falling asleep in the storm of my own will."

• • •

Sir Isaiah Berlin, the philosopher, says that if our belief in freedom is an illusion, it is what he calls a "necessary illusion." Real people in the real world, he observes, don't behave as if they lack free will. And analyst Ernst Lewy adds, rephrasing Voltaire's famous observation about God: "If free will and responsibility did not exist, they would have to be invented."

Whether or not it's illusory, we must act and expect to be judged as if we have the power to make free choices. Acknowledging that our control is highly imperfect, we still must take responsibility. And though we aren't as flexible and as fixable as we'd dreamed, though something less than the sky may be our limit, though none of us can entirely escape our history and heredity, we still must live as if we're free to be.

2

The Taste of Control

There is hardly a single point of excellence belonging
to human character which is not decidedly repugnant
to the untutored feelings of human nature.
—John Stuart Mill

All those qualities that we call human derive from
the possibility within every human being of
acquiring control over the instinctual self.
—Selma Fraiberg

To live as if we're free to be, we need to learn to tutor our untutored feelings. We need to interpose our will between what we desire and what we do. But it takes a while to accept the on-the-face-of-it preposterous point of view that self-control may be the royal road to freedom, allowing us to become not only civilized but competent, allowing us to master ourselves—and the world.

Jan, age two and a half, was banging her teaspoon on her high chair while ceaselessly and shrilly demanding dessert. Annoyed by the noise, her mother, heading down to the freezer to fetch her some ice cream, said irritably, "Have a little patience." On her return from the basement Jan's mother found her little girl in what seemed to be the middle of a convulsion. Her face was bright red, her body was rigid, her fists were clenched, her eyes were fixed in a stare, in addition to which she didn't appear to be breathing. Letting the ice cream drop from her hands and screaming, "What's the matter?" Jan's mother hurried to her daughter's side. Whereupon Jan unclenched her fists, stopped holding her breath, and replied, "I'm having patience."

This story is told by the peerless child psychoanalyst Selma Fraiberg, whose point is to show how extraordinarily difficult it can be for young children to fight against their own urgent wishes. It gives us a vivid picture of the struggles that we, in our early years, engaged in as we learned to manage, master, dominate, regulate, influence, curb, or restrain our impulses, as we slowly learned to exercise control.

It's hard to learn patience. It's hard to learn that we cannot get what we want whenever we want it. It's hard to deprive ourselves, to deny and delay. Though most of us, as we grow up, acquire increasing amounts of self-control, we enter this world in pursuit of gratification. Far too soon the powerful care-taking grown-ups in our lives not only restrict our pleasures but expect us to begin restraining ourselves:

Telling us to quit screaming even though we need to have dessert RIGHT NOW. Stopping us from touching ourselves down there. Making us desist from the joys of poking fingers into electric sockets, from the thrill of removing the stuffing from our stuffed bear, from the relief of relieving ourselves when and where we choose to, from the satisfaction of giving a vigorous pinch on the upper arm to our brand-new sister. We're a bundle of imperatives—Eat! Explore! Excrete! Eliminate that kid!—but the people in charge are getting in our way. The constraints they impose upon us and require us to impose upon ourselves introduce us to the taste of control.

Some two hundred years ago a German pedagogue named Sulzer urged that parents control their children "from the very beginning by means of scolding and the rod." Willfulness and wickedness appear in the first year of life, he warned, when children

> see something they want but cannot have; . . . become angry, cry, and flail about. Or they are given something that does not please them; they fling it aside and begin to cry. . . . The moment these flaws appear in a child, it is high time to resist this evil so that it does not become ingrained through habit and the children do not become thoroughly depraved.

In the second and third years of life, Sulzer said, parents must devote themselves to instilling "a strict obedience" in their children, which might, he conceded, be hard to achieve because "it is quite natural for the child's soul to want to have a will of its own." Nevertheless, he noted:

> It is essential to demonstrate to them by word and deed that they must submit to the will of their parents. . . . One of the advantages of these early years is that then force and compulsion can be used. . . . If their wills can be broken at this time, they will never remember afterwards that they had a will.

Though "force" and "the rod" are no longer recommended by child-raising pundits, the violent abuse of children—as our daily headlines attest—is still with us today. So are the other

35

abuses of power, nonphysical but equally coercive, which intimidate or humiliate or manipulate young children to obey. But the fact is that even the kindliest parents begin opposing our will somewhere toward the end of our very first year, when instead of remaining primarily preoccupied with nurturing they develop this annoying new interest in discipline. If our parents are good-enough parents, they understand that our capacity for control is initially inefficient and undependable. If our parents are good-enough parents, they will take their cues on discipline not from Herr Sulzer but from Selma Fraiberg:

> We satisfy, as far as possible, all needs of the tiny infant because he is completely dependent and has no means of controlling his own urges. But as the child's physical and mental equipment matures he is able more and more to take over the regulation of his own body needs and to control his impulses. As his readiness for self-control gradually reveals itself, we increase our expectations for him and alter our methods accordingly.

And so they start imposing on us their standards of good and bad, of right and wrong. We find ourselves encountering a host of prohibiting "don'ts" and approving "do's." Our shame and "guilt" when we breach the "don'ts" and our pride when we do the "do's" help to lay the foundation for what will later become our superego—our conscience.

Conscience has been described as the installation of our parents in our mind, the internalization—the taking in—of their moral prohibitions and their ideals. Conscience has been described as the force that keeps us from doing wrong though no one would know. Classic psychoanalysis says that this conscience develops around age five or six, and that only then—when we toe the line out of fear of our *inner* judges—can we be seen as capable of guilt. But something that looks a lot like guilt is apparent in us much earlier, though perhaps we only feel guilty if we get caught. And current studies suggest that those parental do's and don'ts begin to be internalized, start becoming a part of us, somewhere in the course of our second year.

An eighteen-month-old girl sits near some video equipment, repeating "no, no, no" to herself, and not touching it. Another stares at, and reaches toward, forbidden objects placed upon a table, then—smiling with pride at not grabbing them—walks on by. In both of these situations there are adults in the room, but Julia, thirty months old, is all alone, torn between an ardent desire to play with a bowlful of eggs and a sharp awareness that this is not allowed. Julia, however, comes up with an ingenious resolution of this conflict between her wishes and mom's rules: Dropping the eggs one by one on the floor, she scolds herself every time another egg smashes. "NoNoNo," she says aloud. "Mustn't dood it."

It's clear that a grown-up's presence is needed to help these young ladies restrain themselves from doing what they deeply long to do. It's clear that the rules in their heads are not really *theirs*. But eventually, out of varying proportions of love and anxiety, they'll learn, as we do, to make those rules their own. Eventually, without an outside authority on the premises, they'll come to display the inner controls which characterize that powerful force called conscience.

Our conscience enforces its standards and restrictions, now *our* standards and restrictions, by making us feel guilty when we do wrong. Indeed, in order to spare ourselves the misery of guilt, we avoid doing wrong in the first place—we control ourselves. We control our urges to seize what we want and our urges to kill what we hate by repressing them, by shoving them out of awareness. Or we settle for a substitute. Or we settle for a spoonful instead of a plateful. Or sometimes we use reaction-formation—we bury a not-nice impulse and claim that we feel the exactly opposite impulse—although, as this little poem indi-cates, our buried wish may not be all that buried.

I love love love my brand-new baby sister.
I'd never feed her to a hungry bear.
I'd never (no! no! no!)
Put her outside in the snow
And by mistake forget I put her there.

I'd never want to flush her down the toilet.
I'd never want to drop her on her head.
I'm only asking if
She by mistake fell off a cliff
The next time we could get a dog instead.

Repression, substitution, reaction-formation, and other tactics restrain us from bad behavior, from behavior that's harmful to others—and to ourselves. Our natural impulsivity, our "immod-erate pursuit of immediate pleasures," is tempered as well by our learning how to wait. For we cannot be in control of our-selves unless we can defer our gratifications. We cannot be in control of ourselves unless we are able to have a little patience.

It's sobering, therefore, to see myself in the hotel-lobby mirror, having just talked with the reservations clerk, and to realize that my red face, rigid body, clenched fists, fixed stare, and lack of discernible breathing are not the signs of convulsion but of the fact that my room won't be ready until four o'clock.

It's sobering to observe how hard it can be, at any age, to have self-control.

Some notes from New York:

December 25: A man in a Mercedes pulled a gun on the driver of a Chevrolet, shooting him in the face because the victim had cut him off at one of the toll lanes of the Triborough Bridge.

December 9: A man shot and killed an employee of an East New York video store after the victim refused to refund the quarter the shooter had lost in a pay telephone.

August 24: Two teenagers killed the owner of a Brooklyn candy store because he complained that they hadn't paid for their Snapple.

April 8: A gunman driving a car in Crown Heights shot the driver of a special-education school bus, apparently because the school-bus driver was taking too long unloading the kids at the corner.

March 25: A teenager shot a bodega owner in Brooklyn because he was dissatisfied with the ham-and-cheese hero sandwich he had been served.

January 7: The owner of a Bronx deli shot one teenager in the buttocks and killed another after they complained that their order—one gyro, one slice of pizza, and one beef patty—was taking too long.

Some notes from elsewhere:

Boston: An insurance executive charged with murder allegedly tore out his wife's heart and lungs and impaled them on a stake after she chided him for having overcooked ziti, a form of pasta.

Chicago: Two boys . . . dropped a five-year-old to his death from a fourteenth-floor apartment because he would not steal candy for them.

Stockholm: A man was charged with killing his wife because she was using the vacuum cleaner while he was engaged in watching TV.

And in Honolulu: A man attending an anger-management class was beaten to death by his anger-management counselor.

It's more than sobering—it's downright chilling—to see how hard it can be to have self-control.

But control is not only a host of no no no's, of shouldn'ts and don'ts, of prohibitions. Control is not only constraint; it is also mastery. Control is effective action, the exhilarating achievement of becoming the person in charge of our self and learning how to manipulate our environment.

From the moment we arrive in this world, we actively manipulate our environment by what we do and what we don't take in—shutting our eyes if the lights are too bright or moving our eyes to track an intriguing object or turning our head away from a too-loud noise. Our first job in life is to gain some control over our motor and autonomic systems, which frees us to pay more attention to the ooohs and coos of that person who is cuddling us. And through our emerging ability to respond to her, to elicit her responses, and to build upon the responses we have brought forth, we discover the satisfactions of controlling our emotional environment.

"Sometimes I want to be jiggled or tickled or patted or burped or rocked . . . ," says the teeny tiny hero of a charming children's book by Amy Schwartz. And "sometimes I want to ride in my Snugli . . . my stroller . . . my swing or my sling. . . ." And "sometimes I just want to be left to my own devices."

We quickly learn how to make such wishes known.

This learning process begins in our early experiences with our mother, when together—in an ever more nuanced give-and-take exchange—we build a rewardingly synchronized relationship. Holding and rocking, feeding and soothing, encouraging and accommodating, our mother adapts to our rhythms and our needs, while we—with our wriggles and trills and smiles and other communications of contentment—let her know that she is doing just fine.

Of course, our mothers—most mothers—are primed to receive our communications and eager to reply responsively, their attunement intensified, as the following song, "First Baby," describes, by the fact that they've fallen madly, deeply in love:

> I hadn't expected
> To feel so connected
> To someone I'd only just met.
> Could this be love at first sight?
> You bet! You bet!

> I would have insisted
> I could have resisted
> The charms of your coo and your cry.
> But who is this fool for love?
> It's I. It's I.

> You're a paragon of sweet perfection
> From your fuzzy head to rosebud toes.
> My love for you is like an insurrection
> That occupies my heart and grows and grows.

> I never predicted
> That I'd stand convicted
> Of totally turning to mush
> Over your toothless grin
> And peerless tush.

Nor did I assume
You could fill every room
With six pounds, eight ounces of boy.
And such joy! Such joy! Such joy!
And so much joy!

Although I always knew that you'd be cared for,
Although I dreamed of holding you some day,
I find myself completely unprepared for
The feelings that are sweeping me away.

Swept by such feelings, our mothers—most mothers—are eagerly alert to our slightest cues. But our fathers, often equally loony with love, can also be taught, *by us,* to tune in to our needs, taught to respond to the eloquent movements of our baby bodies with exceedingly exquisite empathy. At a very young age, according to psychoanalyst Stanley Cath, we know how to get our messages across, relying upon an already extensive repertoire for "eliciting competent, loving caretaking not only from female but also male adults."

When the care we seek from our parents is sufficiently in sync with what they provide, not only they but *we* develop a burgeoning sense of personal effectiveness, a sense that we are able to make things happen. Thus our earliest feelings of mastery are experienced through the contentment of our bodies, a contentment we have helped to bring about, a contentment which tells us, long before we can think such thoughts or put such thoughts into words, "I'm a teeny tiny baby and I know how to get anything I want."

"Human infants," writes psychologist Martin Seligman, "begin life more helpless than infants of any other species. In the course of the next decade or two, some acquire a sense of mastery over their surroundings; others acquire a profound sense of helplessness." Which category we wind up belonging to, he argues, depends on our personal history, and how early and how often and how intensely we experience either impotence or efficacy. He also argues that maternal deprivation—the lack of a steadfast mothering presence—is a powerful source of early, deep, and repeatedly confirmed feelings of helplessness.

For without such a mothering presence, there is no real give-and-take exchange, no real synchrony. There is no one to reliably respond to our shrieks and smiles, our gestures and movements, no one to give us a sense that what we do matters, makes a difference in what happens. Dr. Seligman believes that an infant who has an absent or unattuned mother suffers not only from a lack of love. That infant also suffers from "a particularly crucial lack of control."

Sometimes attunement fails because our parents lay upon our unique, special nature what Fraiberg has characterized as "ghosts in the nursery," ghosts of past relationships that stand between us and them and interfere with their knowing who we are. It's quite common for our parents to endow us, to some degree, with positive qualities, qualities that they value and reward, qualities that are consciously or unconsciously tied to cherished former attachments. But sometimes what they endow us with is drastically at odds with our own nature. And sometimes it is negative and destructive.

And so we are seen as tyrannical (because our mother's brother bossed her around), or endangered (because an uncle had died of cancer), or selfish and judgmental (because our mother's mother was selfish and judgmental). And sometimes we are seen as angry and bad because the ghost our mother projects on us is her own young self as "a terrible little girl."

When we infants are seen as these ghosts, we become the recipients of the emotions that they evoke—the resentments ("He thinks I'm his slave") or the anxieties ("He'll die if he doesn't eat") or the feelings of rejection ("She's looking daggers at me"). Our overtures, cues, and expressions of need may be constantly missed or misread, and we will suffer from a crucial lack of control.

And then there are babies like Monica, who was born with a gastric defect to a mother too depressed to respond to her needs and who, as Winifred Gallagher tells us in her fine book *I.D.*, "couldn't forge the connection between the effort of going for it and the pleasure of getting it." As an infant, Monica's tries for attention and even her cries for help went unrewarded, teaching her very early that endeavors to get what she wanted and needed would fail. Not having learned that persistence paid off, she lacked a sense of efficacy that in later life was expressed by "a certain inertia. . . . Rather than driving her circumstances," says Gallagher, "she was often carried along by them." She too had endured a crucial lack of control.

Without a responsive mother we may wind up believing that taking action is meaningless, that we can't affect events, that we are helpless. Without a responsive mother the early competence-building relationship is derailed. Such discouraging encounters stand in stark contrast to experiences of synchrony, where we gain an I-can-get-what-I-need sense of efficacy—and a trusting expectation of ease and good feelings.

This trust—this "basic trust," as analyst Erik Erikson terms it in his classic discussion of the "Eight Ages of Man"—includes both trust in our mother and the confidence "that one may trust oneself." Erikson links basic trust to hope, and hope to two kinds of faith that propel us to engage in the human world. One is faith "in the kindness of the powers of the universe." The other is "faith in the goodness of one's strivings."

By our second month of life, our successful strivings to in some ways control our environment enormously—and discernibly—delight us. In an experiment with three groups of eight-week-olds, each infant was provided with a special air pillow that responded to the pressure of its head by closing a switch. In one group—let's call it group A—a mobile of colored balls, hanging over each infant's crib, spun for one second whenever the pillow was pressed. In group B the mobile also spun, but its spinning did not depend on the infants' actions. Group C, given a stabile, not a mobile, experienced neither movement nor control.

The infants of group A, having learned that they could control the movements of the mobile, demonstrated their knowledge by greatly increasing the number of times they pressed the pillow. The others did not. Group A was also the only group whose infants—three or four days into the experiment—were, each and every one of them, smiling and cooing.

Controlling our surroundings clearly brings pleasure. And so, with increasing purposefulness, and awesome determination, we strive—through our first year of life—to expand our mastery, to broaden our control.

It may not come easily.

Just look, if you please, at this baby, who is trying to get himself up on his hands and knees. He rises and falls and rises and falls, repeatedly. Exhausted by his efforts, the poor kid flops down on the floor and consolingly sucks his thumb while he recovers, whereupon he resumes his struggles until—it takes him thirty-five minutes!—he makes it.

Many psychologists, watching such early and eager pursuit of—and vast pleasure in—mastery conclude that they are observing a drive (or instinct or motivation) that has to be fundamental to human nature. They call it by various names: an "exploration drive," a "need for activity," a "manipulative drive," an "instinct to master," a "will to conquer," a "striving for superiority," "Funktionslust," or—this is developmental psychologist Robert White's term—an "urge toward competence."

White argues that this competence urge "is directed, selective, and persistent" and that "it satisfies an intrinsic need to deal with the environment." What is the goal of such dealings? White replies that our goal, our reward, is a feeling of having an impact, "a feeling of efficacy"—a feeling which, he says, includes "a theme of mastery, power, or control."

It also includes the pride and glee of knowing that we can do it and that we have done it.

Watching the pleasure my own three sons took, when they were baby boys, in their (to them) remarkable achievements, watching their loopy grins and sparkling eyes, watching them revel in their conquests and triumphs, I almost could hear what (if they could speak) they'd have said:

I'm banging these two big blocks together. Am I great, or what?

I just figured out how to climb up these steps. What a genius!

I put this ball in the box, and I dump it out, and I put it back, and I dump it out again. Oh, wonderful me!

Psychoanalyst Ives Hendrick observes that the "instinct to master" is hedonistic in aim, producing "primary pleasure" when it "enables the individual to control and alter his environment." Psychiatrist Andras Angyal adds that human life is "a process of self-expansion," a process in which it "assimilates more [and more and more and more] of the environment [and] transforms its surroundings so as to bring them under greater control."

This self-expansion process, which begins in infancy, involves us in active and continuous learning, with our rattle-shaking and peek-a-boo-ing and "hustling things about," our explorations and "joy in being a cause," tutoring us in the management of our environment. "Helpless as [an infant] may seem until he begins to toddle," White observes, "he has by that time already made substantial gains in the achievement of competence."

• • •

We have indeed.

As our first year draws to an end, we have learned to grab and drop and bang and handle objects, to sit and stand and crawl and perhaps to walk. Our power to make things happen has increased and goes on increasing, most gratifyingly. Our need to explore our surroundings and to investigate the alluring things it contains is sometimes almost as urgent to us as hunger, and it frequently propels us into perilous and calamitous pursuits. Necessary restrictions (designed to save our life, the house, and our mother's sanity) are received with all the outrage at our command. And sooner or later we're off and running on our own two feet, miniature masters of the universe.

For the next several months, we explore our world and practice and hone our skills, impervious to the bumps on our road to mastery. Our bruises and knocks, our stumbles and falls, our setbacks and frustrations cannot discourage us from pursuing our aims, cannot slow us down as we push and pull and climb and carry and drag and drop and squeeze anything and everything we can get to. Besotted by a blissful belief in our magical omnipotence, we are under the illusion that our mother's enormous powers are ours to share and that these powers—*our* powers—give us complete control of our body and the world. The end of this illusion will confront us with some hard-to-take realities. The end of this illusion will precipitate what is called the rapprochement crisis.

This crisis arises when, between our sixteenth and twenty-fourth months, we become aware of our separateness from our mother and confront the scary fact that we're far less powerful, far more vulnerable, than we had imagined. We're alarmed at being what feels like on our own in a great big world, and yet the world is what we want to explore. And so we struggle to reconcile our wish to cling to Mommy with our I-want-to-do-it-

47

myself urge toward autonomy. In resolving this conflict we'll have to find an optimal distance between us and our mother, a distance neither too close nor too far away, a distance that allows us—unimpeded by feelings of helplessness and hopelessness— to continue our explorations of the world.

In Erikson's terms we have to resolve the conflict between our yearnings for autonomy and excessive, crushing feelings of shame and doubt, shame and doubt that arise from a "sense of loss of self-control and of foreign overcontrol." We need our parents' "foreign" controls to keep us from careening over a precipice. We need them to help us when we're scared or stuck. But if our every venture is greeted with "stop" . . . "watch out" . . . "beware," our zestful curiosity, our confidence in our compe- tence, may be stifled. If all goes well, however, our parents will hold and protectively care for us while also letting us go and letting us be. If all goes well, we'll reach age two eager to keep on striving to manage and master some portion of our universe.

We'll also reach age two with a magnificent new tool for controlling both ourselves and the world around us. That tool is language—the words to name the objects that surround us, the words to say what we want and how we feel.

The naming of objects—Mama, cookie, blankie—is in itself a form of mastery, the possession through language of pieces of our world. And when the language we use lets us summon our mother, who gives us a cookie or finds our blanket, our sense of mastery explodes and expands. Fraiberg also speaks of the bedtime soliloquies of the child, who—talking aloud to herself alone in the dark—repeats the *names* of people and objects to substitute for the *actual* people and objects as a way to ease her anxiety and establish some control over her circumstances.

A version of this soliloquy is offered in the picture book *Good- night Moon,* where a drowsy rabbit bids good night to the special objects that occupy his universe:

Goodnight room
Goodnight moon. . . .
Goodnight bears
Goodnight chairs. . . .
Goodnight clocks
And goodnight socks. . . .

Drifting off to sleep, the rabbit—thanks to his naming of names—remains in reassuring command of his world. So do the boys and girls who hear this story. And, when they awaken the next morning, the possession of language continues to give them control.

" 'Baby Beluga'!" commands my grandchild Miranda, and her mommy flips on the tape deck and plays that tune. "Grandma Judy, dance!" commands Miranda, and I leap from my chair and start bopping around the room. "Daddy, hold me now!" commands Miranda, and her daddy stops in his tracks to hold her tight. "Papa, make a girl!" commands Miranda, and my husband—Miranda's grandpa—whom I've never seen draw a picture in all his life, sets earnestly to work with an orange crayon. Four adults are doing the bidding of one twenty-two-month-old, a toddler empowered by the power of words.

And then there's two-and-a-half-year-old Jake, sitting with his grandma and watching—yet again—his *Snow White* video. Previous experience has acquainted him with that terrifying moment when the envious, murderous stepmother, with cackles and shrieks and bubbling potions and skulls, turns herself into a hideous black-cloaked hag. And so, at the very first sign of this alarmingly spooky scene, he loudly orders his grandma: "Fast-forward Fast-forward!" Later, however, the stepmother-hag receives her full comeuppance, tumbling off a precipice to her doom, a gaudy and garish doom complete with raging thunderstorm and hovering buzzards. Jake, beaming with gratification at these perfectly just deserts, again calls on language to get himself what he needs. Turning to his grandmother, he issues another order. He says: "Replay!"

The poet Louise Glück addresses the child's discovery of the power of words in a tender little poem entitled "The Gift":

> Lord, You may not recognize me
> speaking for someone else.
> I have a son. He is
> so little, so ignorant.
> He likes to stand at the screen door, calling
> *oggie, oggie,* entering
> language, and sometimes
> a dog will stop and come up
> the walk, perhaps
> accidentally. May he believe
> this is not an accident?. . .

The use of language gives us a sense of control of our outside world. It also gives us some control of our feelings, allowing us to put into words that which, before we have words, we simply act out.

"I'm having a terrible, horrible, no good, very bad day," announces Alexander, who used to deliver this message by punching out walls.

"It's scary to see those aminals," says Lindsay, her words replacing the ear-splitting shrieks with which she used to inform folks of her anxieties.

And when Cody declares that he's "sad and mad" because his best friend Drew "was mean to me on the swings in the playground today," he has found a mode of expression that does not involve being mean, in turn, to his younger brother. Putting our feelings into words is an enormous achievement of self-control.

The acting out of emotions will often plunge us into big trouble, trouble that language can help protect us from, giving us time to judge the situation, to look—and think—before we leap. It's true that our early efforts at using words to restrain ourselves are merely invocations—and not always, as egg-breaking Julia reminds us, successful ones—of our parents' warning *hot*s and *break*s and *no*s. But eventually these prohibiting words become internalized, become more effective. Eventually language will help to create our conscience.

The language we use at around age two is heavy on verbs like "want," "eat," "get," and "go," and also on personal pronouns—"my, "me," "mine." We see ourselves as actors in our own dramas. And in our third year our sense of self, our individual "I," begins to become consolidated and stable. We also begin acquiring a stable inner image of our mother that remains with us when she isn't in-the-flesh there and that helps us, in her absence, to feel secure enough—at three, at four, at five—to go about our business at greater distances and for longer stretches of time.

As we go about our business there's another Eriksonian crisis to deal with—the conflict between initiative and guilt. We wish to assertively use our growing mental and physical powers. We wish to undertake, plan, and attack a task. But sometimes our parents meet our endeavors with harsh rebukes that discourage all risk and all daring. And sometimes our goals involve us in acts of coercion and aggression that fill us with guilt. And sometimes our guilt is so strong, our budding conscience so cruel and primitive and uncompromising, that we overcontrol and overconstrict ourselves, says Erikson, "to the point of self-obliteration." The trick here is to acquire a reliable moral sense without derailing our efforts to act with purpose and direction, to take the initiative. The trick here is to acquire a capacity for guilt that doesn't crush our joyful pursuit of mastery.

51

• • •

The development of our moral sense requires us, of course, to control our impulses. So does the pursuit of mastery, for accomplishments of every sort demand the capacity to postpone our wish for instant gratification.

Consider, for instance, the "marshmallow test," which psychologist Daniel Goleman describes in his best-selling book *Emotional Intelligence,* calling it "a microcosm of the eternal battle between impulse and restraint, id and ego, desire and self-control, gratification and delay." Four-year-olds are offered this deal: They may, if they wish, eat a marshmallow immediately. Or, if they can restrain themselves until the tester returns, they then will be permitted to eat *two.* Some four-year-olds, not surprisingly, grabbed the single marshmallow almost as soon as the tester left the room, while others—valiantly fighting off temptation—held out for the fifteen or twenty minutes until the tester returned, winning their well-earned two-marshmallow prize.

Evaluated in adolescence, the two-marshmallow children were measured against their one-marshmallow peers and found to be more confident, more competent, more assertive, more reliable, and less likely—when faced with difficulties—to quit, not to mention more eager to learn, better able to concentrate and to achieve higher scores on the SATs. In addition, they continued to be far better at self-control, better at deferring gratification.

The marshmallow test connects all sorts of attainments—social, emotional, intellectual—with keeping our eyes on the prize, with resisting impulse. It suggests that if we can, at four, impose some restraint on our passionate marshmallow yearnings, we've got a pretty good shot at winning that prize, at reaching our goals, at achieving mastery.

By the time we start elementary school there is plenty that we two-marshmallow kids have mastered. In a mere five years we've developed impressive skills. We can get where we want on our own two feet. We can say what we need to say. We can hang in there until we reach a bathroom. We've acquired a conscience whose standards we strive toward, whose rules we try to obey. And we've grown more realistic about what powers we actually do and do not possess.

We've also learned that control has two meanings: constraint (the delay and denial of gratification) and mastery (the gratification that comes from feeling effective and in charge).

And we've also learned that constraint (not wetting our pants) and mastery (the use of the potty) often turn out to be a package deal.

The learning process has not always gone smoothly.

For as we've acquired the taste of control we've engaged in many small and major control wars, in many child-versus-grown-ups battles of will, during which—with wails and tears and tantrums and acts of overt and covert defiance, and every theme and variation of "NO!"—we fought against the restraints our parents imposed on us.

We fought, at eight or nine months, to all-by-ourselves put our food in our mouth, and also in our lap, on our head, on the floor. We fought when they changed our diaper, snapped on our bib. We fought to get up and get out to where all the action seemed to be, rattling the bars of that prison they called our crib. We fought, once we'd learned to walk, over how fast to run and how high to climb and where was the line between safety and suffocation. We fought through the Terrible Twos and the Trying Threes and the Fresh-Mouthed Fours and the Fresher-Mouthed Fives, giving our parents plenty of aggravation.

We even knew about psychological warfare.

Nick, age five, refuses to wear the jacket that his mother says he must wear. It's cold outside, she tells him. It's warm, says he. She reasons. He won't. She cajoles. He won't. She threatens.

He won't. She issues a command. Nick maintains his position obstinately. And after several more minutes of utterly fruitless negotiations, Nick's mother (I'll mention no names, but her initials are J. V.) totally loses it.

"Sometimes," she screams at her five-year-old, pounding the kitchen table, "sometimes I think that you argue just to argue."

Nick has no comment.

"Sometimes," she continues, her voice growing louder, "sometimes I think you just argue to see if I'll crack."

Nick still has no comment.

"Sometimes"—she's at top volume now and pounding the table hard—"sometimes I think you push me and push me and push me and push me and push me just to turn me into this raving maniac."

The faintest of triumphant smiles plays across Nick's lips. He turns to his mother and calmly replies, "Sometimes."

Another triumph of child over mom was related to me by Megan, the winner's sister, who described how "my mommy got so mad she yanked the plate off the table and all the potato puffs flew up in the air."

She then explained why her mom did a thing like that.

"Well, she told my brother to eat the potatoes and Mike said, 'Later.' And then she told him to eat the potatoes and Mike said, 'Soon.' And then she told him to eat the potatoes and Mike said, 'In a minute.' And then he told her, 'How can I eat them? They're cold.' "

Using all the weapons that we have at our command, we fight to be the boss of our body and soul. We fight for our pleasure and power. We fight against the inroads of civilization. And our parents—with their superior strength, their armory of punishments, their negotiations, their explanations, *their* temper tantrums—fight back.

Often their acts of control—a smack on the hand, a "Stop that!

54

Now!"—are unmistakable. But sometimes they control us in sneakier ways: Insisting that we don't feel what we feel—"Of course you love your baby sister." Insisting that we don't want what we want—"You'd rather have carrots than candy, now wouldn't you?" Persuading us—with a glance, a shrug, a sigh, a tone of voice—that *their* wishes are *ours*. It's hard, in such situations, to know what we feel, to know what we want, to know what we know, especially if we have parents who, without ever having read him, follow the instructions of Jean-Jacques Rousseau, who advised adults to always allow a child to "think he is the master, but always be it yourself." Rousseau explained:

> There is no more perfect form of subjection than the one that preserves the appearance of freedom; thus does the will itself become captive. The poor child, who knows nothing, can do nothing, and has no experience—is he not at your mercy? Are you not in control of everything . . . ? His tasks, his games, his pleasures, his troubles—is not all this in your hands without his knowing it? Doubtlessly, he may do as he wishes, but he may wish only what you want him to.

Some of us may have mothers who have found, in their mothering role, the power that has eluded them all of their lives, their self-esteem buoyed by their function as "the mother who always knows best, who knows what to do and how to do it, who knows what is right, what is good, and what is of value." Such a mother, dependent and weak in all of her other relationships, thrives in her newfound omnipotent-caretaker role, a role that depends, however, on our always remaining powerless and inadequate.

Except, there's a complication. Along with her need for us to be powerless and inadequate is the opposite need—that we must do her proud, that we must provide her with a sustaining

55

sense of superiority by growing up to be Ms. or Mr. Wonderful. Her double-bind message—"Succeed for me but fail for me"— may leave us torn between failure and success, and may leave us enraged and depressed at being so cripplingly and completely controlled by our mother.

There are lessons to be drawn, and we will draw them, from our early encounters with control, lessons that will be shaped by what befalls us, and how our nature responds to what befalls us, and the ways in which the subsequent experiences of our lives mitigate or underscore what befalls us. There are lessons to be drawn, but what seems to be the same event can teach different people very different lessons.

We may, for example, have parents who regard all expressions of anger as unacceptable, leaving us so afraid of letting our hostile feelings surface, of even acknowledging them, that we tamp ourselves down, bland ourselves out, restrict our emotional range, become devitalized. Or else, having never been taught by them to manage and to modify our anger, we could find ourselves—when our buried feelings erupt—explosively, sometimes violently, out of control.

Though parents will differ widely on whether anger ought to be tightly controlled or "let out," no one disagrees about the eventual need to control certain bodily functions. Learning to use a potty—submitting our body's imperious needs to the world's demands—may be even more of a challenge than learning patience.

"Can I please wear diapers today?" a very newly toilet-trained three-year-old asks her mommy. "I want to relax."

Control of our bladder and bowels requires a certain maturing of our central nervous system, and some interest on *our* part in keeping clean and dry. It's a process that works best when we are ready for it. Trouble arises, however, when our parents demand too much control too soon or respond to our loss of control with harsh reprisals, leaving us with anxious concerns about being shamed or whipped should we have an "accident." Our concerns might find expression in a vigilantly regulated life designed to ward off the risks of the unexpected. On the other hand, it's possible that Charlie Brown's playmate Pigpen—and his messy, dirty, disorderly adult counterparts—are in part the products of a determined stand against overzealous toilet training.

There are mothers, by the way, who never completely surrender control over their children's elimination functions. One man tells me that every letter that came from his mother while he was in the army expressed her ardent hope that he was "regular." And another man, age forty-five, embarking on a long auto trip with his mom, was stunned to hear her ask, as he was about to get in the car, "Wouldn't you like to peepee before you leave?"

Over-the-top intrusiveness will certainly shape our feelings about control.

An intrusive mother does for us what we want to, ought to, need to do for ourselves, rushing in to monitor our every breath and act, rushing in to wipe us and wash us and warn us, rushing in to prop up our castle before the blocks tumble down and to finish our words before they're out of our mouth, rushing in to assist and correct and protect us. Hovering so ceaselessly and anxiously, she challenges our conviction that, yes indeed, we can make it on our own. Unable to relinquish us, or her power over us, she insists on controlling all aspects of our experience.

Perhaps the lesson we take from this is that acts of independence could be fatal, that safety resides in other people's control. Or perhaps we're compelled to embrace what we fear, to set ourselves up for disappointment and danger, out of an I'll-show-her need to disdain control. Perhaps the lesson we learn is that control is really caring, just another way to say "I love you."

Or perhaps we conclude that if ever again we let anyone get too close, he—or she—is going to try to control us.

A thirtyish woman recalls, "My mother always used to tell me, 'I know you better than you know yourself.' She figured that made it okay to run my life. But I wouldn't want a husband —I wouldn't want *anyone*—knowing, or even thinking they knew me, that well. It was hard enough getting out from under my mother."

When our early encounters with power are not just intrusive but humiliating and hurtful, we may acquire the habit of compliance, of placating those in authority to protect ourselves from any further harm. Or we may instead repudiate our frightened, helpless selves and do unto others what others once did unto us, engaging in a tactic that is known as identification with the aggressor. Or we may, for the rest of our days, attempt to undo our former powerlessness by acquiring the accoutrements of power—high office or celebrity or wealth and all the goodies that money can buy. Or we may deny our powerlessness—and our need for anyone's help—by a boastful I'm-the-greatest grandiosity or a secret Clark-Kent-into-Superman fantasy life.

We may also, like this therapy patient described by the psychologist Althea Horner, try to undermine anyone who offers us help or reminds us of our dependency.

> I hate being needy. It's a set-up for pain. It makes me furious to need your empathy—the humiliation and powerlessness. I want to be able to rescue *you*, to . . . seduce you into needing me. That way I will be able to feel in control.

In nontherapeutic relationships, this resistance to emotional dependence may compel us to attack those on whom we depend —criticizing, denigrating, trying to reduce or destroy their power. The kindest of helping hands, the most compassionate expressions of concern may merely remind us of our power-lessness. To value this help, to want this help, to accept this help is equated with surrendering to a malevolent control.

As adults we may replay with those around us—and most clearly with our children—the patterns of control laid down in our childhood. Or maybe we run like hell in the other direction. If, for instance, our parents ruled us with a heavy hand, we may raise a child without limits or restraints, picking him up whenever he cries, sparing him any distress, providing him with instant gratification. But while we may think we're escaping the strict authority of our past, we—unaware—may be arranging to repeat it. We may find ourselves again living under authoritarian rule—except that the person who's ruling us now is our very own demanding, tyrannical child.

But despite the risks of permissiveness, we who as children were strictly overcontrolled may be determined not to control our own kids. "In her righteous reaction against . . . the constraints and tyrannies, the scoldings and browbeatings and punishments she had suffered in her childhood," says playwright George Bernard Shaw of his mother, ". . . she carried domestic anarchy as far as in the nature of things it can be carried." Noting that this oppressed young girl grew up to be a woman "incapable of unkindness to any child, animal, or flower, or indeed to any person or thing whatsoever," he concludes that he was "badly brought up" because his mother was "so well brought up."

I cannot say if GBS, genius though he was, was damaged by his mother's "domestic anarchy." But there's general agreement today in the child-development field that too little parental control is as bad as too much. And in interviews I once held with boys and girls in kindergarten through second grade, almost all of the children agreed with the experts.

Indeed, there was only one child among those I asked to define a "good mommy" who thought a good mommy shouldn't exert restraint. Everyone else conceded that a good mommy was obliged to make some rules.

"You need them," said Peter. "It's dangerous out there."

"Cars could run over you," Lily explained, "and matches could burn you up, and a tiger could stand on your back and chew off your hair."

What kind of rule could a mommy make to keep the tigers from chewing off her hair?

"She makes up a rule not to jump in their cage at the zoo."

The children also accepted the fact that good mommies made rules about bedtime, "or else you are grouchy and kicky and bitey next day." And though they had dreams of the freedom to eat "a hundred ice creams, more if that's what I want," they also said a "good mommy is supposed to know" this isn't a great idea—and "supposed to not let you."

The experts have fancier words to explain why it's bad for these children—and bad for us, as children—to be raised with insufficient parental control.

Too little control is bad because, when we're overwhelmed with anger and aggression, we need someone to stop what we can't stop ourselves. We need some outside assurance that our primitive, runaway feelings will not pull down the house, will not wreak destruction.

Too little control is bad because, when we're charging forth to manage and master our universe, we need to be protected from going too far. We need some outside assurance that we can stretch and strive without falling down so hard that we will never be able to get up again.

There's too little control when our parents fail to step in to restrain and rescue us. There's also too little control when our parents fail to insist that we restrain ourselves.

Selma Fraiberg points out that if we're still allowed—at six and seven and eight—to indulge in screaming or tantrums or verbal or physical abuse to get what we want or express our distress at not getting it, we're likely to be not only an obnoxiously ill-behaved child "but a child whose intellectual development is slowed down." She notes that when we're permitted to use these very primitive means of expressing feelings, "there will be less incentive to develop the higher mental processes, to reason, to employ the imagination creatively."

But even at an earlier age we need to be introduced to *some* control. We need to be able to tolerate *some* frustration. We need, as one psychologist put it, to learn "to wait for what will come in good time." The all-giving mother, who gives us whatever we want whenever we want it, allows us the illusion—long, long after it is time to let it go—that we're in control of everyone and everything. We will move into the wider world poorly equipped to handle the frustrations and limitations that reality must inevitably impose on us.

Parents who believe that love should have no strings attached may also be exerting too little control. For if they give love, whatever we do, why not do whatever we damn please? Growing up with no price to pay for disregarding their rules and prohibitions, we may very well acquire a sense of entitlement, seeking friends and lovers who, without any quid pro quo, will (like our all-understanding, ever-forgiving mom and dad) keep us supplied with unconditional love.

"Parents tend to underestimate the enormous power their loving approval wields over the young child," says psychoanalyst Erna Furman. It matters because we love our parents, need their love, feel desolate when we lose it, and will do, she says, "anything to bring it back." That "anything" takes the form of learning to do what they approve of and to abstain from actions they deem to be wrong, to submit to their control, which—in the best of situations—is prompted and implemented by their love.

For it seems that neither control without love nor love without control is the best way to help us to gain self-control and mastery. A study of child-rearing practices—and the impact of these practices several years later—makes the case for "a warm and affectionate bond combined with consistent and judicious discipline." The study found that children whose parents had raised them in the "authoritarian mode"—that is, cold and aloof and very controlling—were most likely to be passive and withdrawn, while children whose parents had raised them in what was called the "permissive mode"—loving and warm but lax about rule-enforcement—tended to lack self-reliance and self-control. But the children whose parents had raised them in the "authori*tative* mode"—characterized as controlling but also rational and communicative and warm—were most often the most self-reliant and self-controlled, especially when their parents had taken the time to explain the reasons for their rules.

I imagine those three different parenting modes playing out in families something like this:

Authoritarian: Hit your brother again, and I'll break your knee caps.

Permissive: Does hitting your brother make you feel better, darling?

Authoritative: You can't hit your brother because hitting hurts, and we don't believe in people hurting people.

I'd like to think that I raised my sons primarily in the authoritative mode, but I think that there's also a place for what I'll call end-of-discussion authoritarian, that sometimes it's fine to say, "You have to do it because I'm the parent and you're the kid." Judiciously used, this approach teaches something that children (and adults) must understand: that sometime—though it seems outrageous, unreasonable, and unfair—we have to surrender to another's control.

• • •

Both kinds of control—both mastery and constraint—are initially learned in the bosom of our family, in the context of our relationship with parents who are more or less loving and beloved. We learn through their teachings and preachings but we also learn through their actions—by what they do as well as what they say. We learn through their praise and scolding, their punishments and rewards, their smiles and frowns. We learn the power they have over us, and the power that we possess—the power to be effective, to make things happen, to plan and take action, and the power to resist and to restrain (although imperfectly) the clamorous urges of our uncivilized heart.

In the bosom of our family we first learn about yes and no, can and can't, should and shouldn't. We learn about winning and losing, active and passive, taking over and giving in. Walking into the world that lies beyond our own front door, we already know the bittersweet taste of control.

3

Taking Possession of Ourselves

Teenager to parent: "It's my hair and I have a right to
wear it any way I want."
Parent to teenager: "Like hell you do!"
—*Talking with Your Teenager*

In that period of rapture and rupture, anguish and excess
known as adolescence, we find ourselves feeling literally possessed. Our once-reliable bodies are now budding, bleeding,
tumescing, expanding, erupting, and in other ways running
amok without our having the slightest say in the matter. Our
once-clear "Hi, I'm So-and-So" persona is now in such a state
of flux that we may decide that we're suffering from multiple
personality disorder. We did not choose this dismaying disequi-
librium. It descended upon us and quickly took over our life.
Somewhere around the age of thirteen we found ourselves possessed, like some victim from *Invasion of the Body Snatchers*.

We are not in control.

And as if that were not bad enough, we have to contend with mothers and fathers who fail to recognize that we have outgrown them. They get in our way and our face with their rules and curfews and the kind of helpful advice that hasn't been relevant since we were two and a half. We don't mind the room and board they provide, or the clothes and allowance and use of the family car. We don't even mind that they're there— just in case we should need them. But they somehow fail to grasp that not only our hair but our everything else belongs to us to do with as we choose. Even those moms and dads who insist on quoting *The Prophet*'s "your children are not your children" seem to believe that, to some extent, we're theirs—their thing, their possession.

They seem to believe that we're subject to their control.

During our teenage years we struggle to wrest control from the forces that possess us. During our teenage years we—most of us—struggle to take possession of ourselves.

But what happened, it seems fair to ask, to that apparently self-possessed kid who was last seen moving into the wider world? What happened to us between kindergarten and puberty? What happened was an expansion of our mental and motor abilities, which allowed us to master a host of higher pursuits—to learn to spell c-a-t, do back flips, program the VCR, make tuna-fish salad. What happened was that lull before the storms of adolescence known as latency.

Latency coincides with Erik Erikson's fourth age of man, our next life crisis—the conflict of industry versus inferiority. This is when we start gaining "big people" skills. We receive systematic instruction, we acquire habits of work, we plan and complete things, we broaden our aspirations. And our learning not only occurs at home but in classes, in Cub Scouts, at dance recitals, on soccer fields, where we find the opportunities to develop the physical, mental, and social know-how that allows us to live in the world beyond our family—and to drastically expand our realm of control.

The major task of latency, which extends from six or seven to ten or eleven, is learning to be competent out in the world. Indeed, it seems that all throughout history children who reach age seven are treated as having arrived at a special new stage. For instance:

During the Middle Ages, seven-year-olds were thought to be old enough to be sent away to become Pages of the Court.

During the time of the Guilds, seven-year-olds were considered ready to be apprenticed.

According to English Common Law, a child who has reached age seven is deemed capable of criminal intent.

And according to the Roman Catholic Church, the "age of reason" is age seven.

And so, somewhere close to seven, with the major growth spurt of infancy behind us, and the growth spurt of pubescence yet to come, we too must become life's pages and apprentices. We are, or should be, ready for the challenge.

Our brain, whose volume was only 10 percent of an adult brain's volume when we were born, has increased to over 90 percent by age seven. (The rest of the growth occurs in the next nine years.) Evidence suggests that there is major growth in the areas of the brain—the frontal areas—most associated with socialization. We have also reached a new level in our cognitive development, the so-called "concrete operations" stage. This means, among other things, that we can form categories and recognize, for instance, that apples, bananas, peaches, and plums, but not Fords, belong to a category called "fruit."

By seven we possess both the gross motor skills that we need for various athletics and the fine motor skills that allow us to print and draw. Our abilities in language allow us to formulate thoughts and express them, and even to play with words through humor and puns. Our capacity to grasp the rules of the game and then to create our own rules and games allows us to enter into "the culture of childhood." And our ability to separate —at least some of the time—from our parents allows us to turn our face from home and to learn new ways of being and thinking and doing.

And competing.

Toward the end of his kindergarten year, our son Tony returned from school and proudly announced, "I learned to tie my sneakers." "That's wonderful," we said. "How did you learn it?" He explained to us that Patrick Dowling marched to the front of the class and successfully tied *his* sneakers that very morning. "Oh," we replied. "So you said to yourself, 'If Patrick Dowling can do it, I can do it.' " Tony, shaking his head, set us straight as to one of the primary motivaters of mastery. "No," he explained. "I said, 'If they can clap for Patrick, they can clap for me.' "

Note: I can't discuss competition without some mention of sibling rivalry, our fierce competition for our parents' love, for our wish to be Number One Child can often spur us to, along with civil war, impressive accomplishments. One route to these accomplishments is a process known as de-identification, the parceling out of the achievement turf, with one sib becoming athletic or scientific and the other becoming artistic or bilingual, in an effort to gain an uncontested—and so-called "fair"—portion of parental love. (Though we shouldn't forget that "fair," as defined by us siblings, is giving our brother or sister one-third, not one-half, of whatever it is that we have to share.)

Yes, competition—for clapping, for love—can be a spur to achievement. Achievement, in turn, can fill us with great pride, though sometimes, as this poem called "Good-Bye, Six—Hello, Seven," describes, our pride may be colored with a touch of anxiety:

I'm getting a higher bunk bed.
And I'm getting a bigger bike.
And I'm getting to cross Connecticut Avenue all by
myself, if I like.
And I'm getting to help do dishes.
And I'm getting to weed the yard.
And I'm getting to think that seven could be hard.

As mastery increases, pride prevails.

Jack, age eight, confides that, with some assistance from his best friend, "I've just learned how to spell most of Mississippi."

Kate, age nine, informs me that "I clear the plates after dinner and take a shower without even being told."

Candice, a Texas fourth-grader, writes, "You know what? I've started to check out books with twenty or thirty chapters. And I keep reading and learning about the world, probably forever."

If the major task of latency is learning to be competent in the world, the major risk is concluding that we are not, that out here in the society of the clever and the powerful and the adept, we can't compete, we do not measure up. Physical problems, emotional problems, learning disabilities, chaotic or fractured homes, terrible schools can contribute to failures from which it is hard to recover. Confronted by a task that we can't deal with, we may conclude that we'll *never* be able to deal with it, that there's nothing we can do, that there's no point in trying. This reaction, called "learned helplessness," derives from an environment in which important events are beyond our control, leading us to conclude that it is useless to try to control *any* events.

In experiments with animals and humans, experiences of uncontrollability (like inescapable exposures to electric shocks or loud noises) undermined the subjects' capacity to help themselves—even when escape from the shocks or loud noises became available to them. Furthermore, these feelings of being helpless impaired their incentive to endeavor to control other sorts of events, or to believe that they could in fact control them.

"Men and animals," notes psychologist Martin Seligman, "are born generalizers. . . . The learning of helplessness is no exception: when an organism learns that it is helpless in one situation, much of its adaptive behavioral repertoire may be undermined."

Children who are convinced that they are helpless, that they are lacking control and mastery, will perform badly in learning situations. Consider the sad story of young Victor:

> Victor was a slow starter when reading instruction began in kindergarten and first grade. He was eager, but just wasn't ready to make the connection between words on paper and speech. He tried hard at first, but made no progress; his answers, readily volunteered, were consistently wrong. The more he failed, the more reluctant to try he became. . . . By second grade, although he participated eagerly in music and art, when reading came around he became sullen. His teacher gave him special drilling for a while but they both soon gave up. By this time he might have been ready to read, but simply seeing a word card or a spelling book would set off a tantrum of sullenness or of defiant aggression. This attitude began to spread to the rest of his school day. He vacillated between being dependent and being a hellion.

Getting the lowest grades in the class, always being picked last when they choose up teams, being rejected or bullied by our peers, we feel ourselves to be powerless and inferior. If these feelings of inadequacy persist we may fail to develop what psychologist Althea Horner calls "intrinsic power, . . . a deep sense of one's ability to be in the world as a person of worth to others and to himself as well."

Without intrinsic power we will depend on, or be scared of, the power of others.

Without intrinsic power we will either be helplessly yielding to, or fearfully fending off, others' control.

But when latency goes well, we lay the foundation on which will rest all of our future academic learning. We learn the ways of the world, and we take pride in what we are able to do and achieve. With a conscience that is both stringent enough to keep us out of big trouble and mellowed enough to allow us to stretch and dare, we can strive without overcautiousness or lawlessness. And our strivings include a better, though still imperfect, understanding of what we can and what we can't control.

How, in the years between five and thirteen, do the boys and girls in that age group define control? Here are some answers:

- a five-year-old girl: "Like when you're going fast and you pull over to control your bike."
- a five-year-old boy: "When you drive a car, pushing on the gas pedal."
- a five-year-old boy: "Control is when you control your arms."
- a six-year-old girl: "Something you can do whatever you want with."
- a six-year-old girl: "When you're mad at somebody and you don't hit them. If they punch you then you say don't do that and you don't punch them back. You control yourself."
- a six-year-old boy: "When you're steering a car or a motorcycle, by your hands."
- a ten-year-old boy: "Like my sister; she was acting wild when I was the babysitter and I had to get her under control."
- a ten-year-old boy: "Power; you have power, like if you're in control of a plane."

- a thirteen-year-old boy: "Being able to take charge of a situation."
- a thirteen-year-old boy: "When you make something turn out the way you want it to."

Defining control (as that last boy did) as causing something we want to happen to happen, researcher John R. Weisz explores our developing understanding of control. His studies suggest that our judgment of how much control we possess in a given situation is based, in part, on how we assess the issues of contingency and competence.

By "contingency" he means the degree to which people's actions or attributes can have an impact on a desired outcome. (Blowing on the candle will make it go out. Blowing on the dice won't help either us or anyone else to come up with a seven.) By "competence" he means the degree to which a person can manifest the attributes or actions that are required to produce a desired outcome. (Blowing on that candle, for instance, will make it go out only if we can blow hard enough.)

The younger we are the greater is our belief that events dependent on luck or chance—noncontingent events—can nevertheless be influenced by us. The younger we are the higher and more inaccurate are our estimates of our own competence. It's not until adolescence that we can combine information on competence and contingency to figure out how great or how small are our chances of controlling this or that outcome. And it's not until adolescence that we relinquish our belief that noncontingent events really can't be controlled, that there's really nothing we can do to make that roll of the dice come up with our number.

We relinquish such beliefs, but not completely.

For even in late adolescence—even, in fact, in late middle age —we harbor certain illusions about control. And sometimes, in the hope of controlling events that are essentially uncontrol-

71

lable, we engage in silly or superstitious behavior. In studies of gambling, for instance, various researchers have found that many gamblers behave as if the dice were actually under their control, throwing them softly when they need a low number, throwing them harder when they need a high number, insisting on a moment of silence in order to concentrate on the number they want. As social psychologist Shelley Taylor persuasively argues in *Positive Illusions,* "Any situation in which a person confronts options, develops strategies, and devotes thoughts to a problem"—no matter how pointless such endeavors may be —"is vulnerable to an illusion of control."

The illusion that our essentially pointless behavior can make things happen just as we wish. The illusion that it can hold bad things at bay.

Which is why, to avert disaster, I will never sing before breakfast, or walk under ladders, or put a hat on a bed. And which also is why I'm unable not to act on my superstitions, even when I must make a public fool of myself. I recently sat at a conference table surrounded by women and men I hoped to impress. When asked how my children were doing, I said, "Pretty good." And then I had to get up, because the table and chairs were stainless steel and plastic, and I desperately needed to find something made of wood—I found a cabinet—so I could knock on it.

(In case you didn't know this, knocking on wood, when you've said things are good, is somehow supposed to protect them from turning bad.)

Do I really believe that knocking on wood will prevent bad things from happening? Do I really believe in such magical control? My answer is, "Certainly not!" But my answer is also, "Why take a chance? Especially when I'm talking about my children."

Yes, even when we are heading toward the far shore of middle age, we're vulnerable to illusions of control.

Still, latency is when we begin to grasp the concepts of competence and contingency. We begin to tailor our actions to what is doable, and specifically to what we ourselves can do. We may also start to understand (not I, but maybe you) that we don't accomplish much by knocking on wood. We start to shed some illusions about control.

Some of us also begin to acquire constructive control techniques to deal with events that are frightening or painful, techniques that can help us reduce our stress by giving us some semblance of control. An eight-year-old boy describes his distraction technique:

"I can get through most anything as long as there's something to count—like those little holes in the squares on the ceiling at the dentist's. When I got sent to the school office for getting into trouble, I saw all the Principal's freckles. The whole time he was giving it to me, I started at the top of his face and counted his freckles all the way down."

(Adults also use distraction techniques as a way of controlling stress. I, for instance, can mute the claustrophobic effects of an MRI procedure by listing, as I lie in the narrow tunnel, all of the fifty states, alphabetically. And I've often calmed myself down when I've been stuck in an interminable traffic jam by reciting all of the poetry I know.)

Another useful control technique is reinterpretation. This too is nicely described by an eight-year-old boy:

"As soon as I get in the dentist's chair, I pretend he's the enemy and I'm a secret agent, and he's torturing me to get secrets, and if I make one sound, I'm telling him secret information, so I never do. I'm going to be a secret agent when I grow up, so this is good practice."

Indeed, it was such good practice and such an effective control technique that this boy could get carried away playing secret agent. On one occasion, in fact, when his dentist asked him to rinse out his mouth, he snarled—both to his own and his dentist's amazement—"I won't tell you a damned thing."

As we move through our latency years, as we sharpen our concepts of what we can and can't control, as we learn—when facing a tough situation that we can't control—how to at least control the way it affects us, we're acquiring skills that will serve us throughout our life. It's true that at ten, at eleven, at twelve, we may still indulge in impossible dreams of glory, in fantasies of triumph far beyond our own, or anyone's, control. And it's true that if our parents divorce, or a brother or sister falls ill, we may still—out of an untamed sense of omnipotence—hold our oh-so-powerful selves to blame. But we're now, for the most part, rooted in reality. Our feet are, for the most part, on the ground. We seem to be well on our way—we latency girls, we latency boys—to becoming our own mistresses, our own masters.

Then puberty strikes.

In a poem about a tart and thorny fruit plant called the gooseberry, poet Amy Clampitt slyly paints a picture of the teenage years, noting that the gooseberry is "an outlaw or pariah even" and that its virtues

> take some getting
> used to, much as does
> . . . having turned thirteen.
> The acerbity of all things green
> and adolescent lingers in
> it—the arrogant, shrinking,
> prickling-in-every-direction thorn-
> iness that loves no company except its,
> or anyhow that's what it gets:
> bristling up through gooseberry ghetto sprawl
> are braced thistles' silvery, militantly symmetrical
> defense machineries.

Prickly? Defensive? Something of an outlaw or a pariah? Somewhere between the ages of eleven and fourteen, we steady, agreeable, easy-to-get-along-with latency kids may indeed begin to resemble Clampitt's gooseberry.

And why not? The hormones flooding our system have dramatically undermined our equilibrium, plunging us into a sea of raging emotions. The reflection in our mirror has dramatically revised our body image, making us over into Beauties and Beasts. And these inner and outer changes have forever fractured our self-as-child identity, leaving us with a serious case of who-am-I, or what Erikson calls an identity crisis. Hyper and horny and hairy, burning with incomprehensible lusts, driven to despair by minimal breasts, insufficient height, or the anguish of acne, we struggle with painful confusions and bewildering complexities from which we were sheltered during our latency years.

We also—most of us—struggle to affirm and assert our autonomy, which means we're no longer willing to define ourselves as "daughter" or "son" or "child." Indeed, our passionate need to establish the right to a life of our own, our need to loudly proclaim "I'm mine, not yours," is so urgent and so powerful that even a parent's request to "please pass the butter" can feel like an attack on our very being.

"Pass the butter—what am I, your slave?"

"Pass the butter—why are you always picking on me?"

"I'm sitting here thinking that people all over the world are starving to death—and all you can say to me is pass the butter?"

In our struggle to disengage from the attraction and the authority of our parents we may find ourselves rebelling against requests to pass the butter and everything else they request/ expect/demand from us. We chafe at their prohibitions. We close our ears to their sermons. We roll our eyes at their cautionary tales. And we scoff at their presumptuous we-were-young-once-too assumptions that they understand our feelings, that they've had the same experiences, that they've been through what we are going through.

How can parents think that they have a clue to what their children are going through?

Says Frances, sixteen: "There's no way to compare when they were our age. It's so different."

How can parents think that what they know is in any way relevant to their children?

"I can understand," says Darcy, thirteen, "that she doesn't want me making the same mistakes, but I'm not her."

How can parents think that they can stop their children from checking out drugs and sex, from driving too fast or with pals insufficiently sober, from hanging out with friends who range from unsuitable to unspeakable, from courting disaster?

Mother: "At least while they're having sex they can't be driving the car a hundred miles an hour."

Daughter: "Why can't they?"

Analyst Joseph Noshpitz observes that "the acquisition of a mature body is a heady thing, a seductive evocative experience that leads one to want to use that body, to do things with it. . . . Excitement, thrills, novelty—every kind of stimulating experience beckons invitingly, and the avid youngster responds," diving into the off-limits quarry pool, climbing the stony face of the dangerous mountain, plunging—in spite of urgent parental warnings—into hair-raisingly high-risk situations.

"My parents try to prevent a lot of things from happening," says Ted, seventeen. "Like, 'What happened to me, I don't want to happen to you.' I think parents should realize that the only way to learn is by things happening to you."

How can we learn if they won't relinquish control?

A mother issues a global warning to her precious daughter: "Whatever you're thinking of doing, darling, don't." But the whole delicious, perilous world is calling to her, to us—and we've got to do it.

76

• • •

We've also got to do some things that are not on our conscious agenda: the accomplishment, as we move from early to middle to late adolescence, of what experts have portentously named the developmental tasks of adolescence. These growing-up accomplishments include:

Consolidating our sexual identity.

Finding tender, romantic, and sexual love beyond the confines of our family.

Modifying—still further—our still-harsh superego, our conscience, and developing a personal moral value system.

Resolving our identity crisis and figuring out who we are, what we want, where we're going.

There are two other major tasks, and they seem to book-end the complex course of our adolescence. The first is the scary and painful task of breaking away from mother, from father, from childhood. The second is coming home again, dressed now in the clothes of an adult.

Analyst Hans Loewald offers some fascinating thoughts about why these growing-up tasks are so deeply disrupting— stirring up guilt and fear in us and provoking intense resistance from our parents. "In the process of becoming and being an adult," he writes, "significant emotional ties with parents are severed. They are . . . actively rejected, fought against, and destroyed to varying degrees. . . . In an important sense, by evolving our own autonomy, our own superego . . . , we are killing our parents."

I don't want you doing this for me.

I can do it myself.

Your services—thanks, but no thanks—are no longer needed.

Loewald maintains that this parricide is "more than symbolic. . . . Not to shrink from blunt language, in our role as children of our parents, by genuine emancipation we do kill something vital

77

in them—not all in one blow and not in all respects, but contributing to their dying."

And we may feel guilty or anxious without knowing why.

While for most of us, the fear of killing our parents by taking control is buried far out of reach of our awareness, some of us are quite clear about the stakes, especially if we have parents who want to control not only our actions but also what we think and feel and believe. "There was an issue of loyalty to Mother," one woman told psychologist Althea Horner. "You had to be loyal in your thinking and think the way she did, so you just didn't think. If you insisted on your view, it would be like killing her, stealing her power, annihilating her adulthood. Just thinking was destructive."

And yet, despite our ability to break our parents' hearts, to steal away their power, to annihilate them, Loewald says that emancipation demands the usurpation of their authority, arguing that "without the guilty deed of parricide, there is no individual self worthy of that name." Taking over our parents' power and competence, claiming responsibility for ourselves, are, writes Loewald, developmental necessities.

"No offense, Mom," said my son Alexander, just on the brink of thirteen, when I came to his room to hug and kiss him good night. "No offense," he repeated, very kindly, "but you've really got to stop tucking me in at bedtime."

Parents may feel joy and pride in their children's growing independence and accomplishments. They may nonetheless find the loss of their roles, the take-over of their functions, hard to take.

In her fine novel *Lovingkindness* Anne Roiphe writes:

> What do we know about mothers and daughters? If there is a recurring myth of matricide and usurped power, who tells that story? If mothers and daughters form a unit that crackles and splits and sends particles

out into the universe, particles of hate, revenge, and passion, where do we hear it? Mothers are not afraid of their daughters (except for the wicked queen in "Snow White"). Our power is so oblique, so hidden, so ethereal a matter, that we rarely struggle with our daughters over actual kingdoms or corporate shares. On the other hand, our attractiveness dries as theirs blooms, our journey shortens just as theirs begins. We too must be afraid and awed and amazed that we cannot live forever and that our replacements are eager for their turn, indifferent to our wishes, ready to leave us behind.

A mother confesses: "My daughter is so beautiful, and everywhere we go everyone says how beautiful she is. Sometimes I want to say, 'Hey, what about me over here?' "

A father confesses: "My son uses my car. He takes my shaving cream; he drinks my beer; he wears my socks. He even beats me at tennis. If I were a little more uptight, I'd feel like my position was being threatened."

Consciously and unconsciously, our parents may envy our juiciness and potency, resentful that we are blossoming as they are more or less fading, resentful that they are being demoted to has-beens. And if they are feeling threatened or jealous or envious, if they *are* a little more uptight, they may tighten the screws and heighten their control over us.

"I'm my father's only girl," Joy, eighteen, complains, "and . . . there's no reasoning with him. I'll tell him, 'Dad, I'm going on a date and I'll be home by twelve.' He says, 'You're not going out with any strange boy I don't know!' Then when he meets them he'll dream up some excuse why I can't see them. He's impossible."

The contrast between the physical powers of waxing adolescent and waning adult is one of the features of family life that, a study of parent-child strife concludes, makes intergenerational conflict inevitable.

Conflict is also promoted by the rapid rate of sociocultural change that barrages parents and children with new information. Since adults will take in the new ideas more slowly than adolescents, a gap is likely to open up between them. This is, of course, the generation gap.

"My father never gives me a chance," says Robert, age sixteen, "to explain to him the kind of music I like. . . . All he does is scream and say, 'Turn it off!' So I turn *it* and *him* off."

Also making for conflict is the collision between the idealism of youth and the often hard-bitten realism of adulthood, producing (from the teenagers) cries of "How can you be so cynical!" and (from the parents) "How can you be so damn dumb!"

The immaturity of an adolescent, writes psychoanalyst Joseph Noshpitz, "frequently leads him to take stands and make assertions that are at best illogical and which to the adult ear may sound downright ridiculous. The resultant critical interactions . . . are emotionally costly to everyone. Many a young person resorts to attitudes of pitiless defiance and even of arrogance in insisting on some valued position," whose value may mostly depend on its ability to drive his parents up the wall.

My friend Cecilia, for instance, describes what she sighingly calls her son's The Real Me phase, during which he refused to say "Thank you" unless he truly felt that he was grateful, and insisted on giving his honest opinion ("It makes me want to puke") when asked about matters like "How do you like my new haircut?" Along the same lines, he insisted on showing up at church on Easter in cutoffs, a torn T-shirt, and thong sandals because God—at least, he explained, the God *he* believed in—ignored superficialities (like how a person was dressed) and only cared about The Real Me.

Idealism versus realism and immaturity versus experience are major sources of conflict between generations.

Bracketing all of these conflicts is the tension that arises from the fact that parents have more power than children, which includes the power to give or withhold the privileges we seek and to impose their will—arbitrarily, autocratically.

"You'll do what I tell you to do because I'm older, because I'm your father, because I said so, because that's the way I want it to be," is Superior Power's response to the perennial adolescent question, "Why?"

"My parents can never compromise," Ann, age fifteen, complains. "It's always what they want to do. They say, 'When you're eighteen and out of school, you can do what you want to do. But as long as you're under my roof, you'll do what I want you to do.' No discussion. I'm not allowed to ask any questions or say what I think. It actually makes me feel like I'm unwanted. Like shit. Like what am I here for?"

It's true that some parents may keep their children dependent and diminished because they cannot bear to relinquish their power. Others overcontrol because, reflecting popular views, they see adolescents stereotypically. Melinda, sixteen, recalls a woman who stopped her and her friend Wanda in the street to say, "If you're going to be sluts, use protection." The woman had mistaken a weight gain produced, Melinda explained, by an excess of milkshakes for the early signs of unwed pregnancy. As though, Melinda sighed, "we all get pregnant. . . . We all do drugs, we all drink."

"Our adolescents," goes one complaint about the inadequacies of modern youth, "now seem to love luxury. They have bad manners and contempt for authority. They show disrespect for adults and spend their time hanging around places gossiping with one another. . . . They are ready to contradict their parents, monopolize the conversation in company, eat gluttonously, and tyrannize their teachers."

Ah yes, kids today are not at all what they used to be. Except that this complaint was made some 2,500 years ago—by Socrates.

Child analyst James Anthony argues that stereotyping adolescents—as delinquent, irresponsible, hypersexual, simple-minded, self-indulgent—contributes to the conflict between generations, "causing parents to respond to their adolescent children as if they were embodiments of negative ideas rather than real people."

But even when parental controls derive from a caring concern rather than power-tripping or stereotyping, the benevolence of their intentions doesn't make their interference any more palatable.

They claim that it's their duty to guide and protect us.

We claim that it's our right to control our own lives.

One way to take control is to prevent our parents from knowing what's going on, choosing—like Abby, age fifteen—to "keep things to myself or talk to my friends."

Willa, eighteen, concurs. Her parents, she says, "want to know who, what, where, why and lots more than I have any intention of telling them."

For telling them runs the risk of inspiring sermons. Says Randy, thirteen: "My father gives me an hour lecture if I bring something up to him. So I don't bother." And telling them runs the risk of being force-fed parental advice—and if it's not taken, says Ralph, eighteen, "they get furious." And telling them runs the risk of getting their parents very upset. "There's no way I'd admit to my parents that I smoke pot," says fourteen-year-old Karl. "They'd have a heart attack." And though sixteen-year-old Debbie would like to be honest with her mother, she fears that if she told the truth she'd be running the risk that her mother "would look down on me."

Why expose ourselves to sermons, advice, guilt, disapproval, and, of course, punishment?

Why not present a compliant face, cover our tracks, keep our mouth shut—and do as we please?

It's actually not that difficult to lead a double life, one former "very wild teenager" recalls. "I would be out drinking at sixteen and seventeen and coming home ripped out of my mind. And my folks would be in bed and shout out, 'You home?' And I'd say, 'Yeah, Good night.' Then I'd go throw up or pass out on my bed."

But sometimes we get caught.

And sometimes we cannot conceal our acts of defiance.

And sometimes we most emphatically don't want to.

Like Robin, thirteen, who appeared one day with a yellow and pink and thoroughly butchered punk haircut—and a look in her eye that said, "I did this for you, Mom."

In challenging our parents, in our sporadic or ongoing struggles for control, we have our choice of various forms of rebellion: From usurpation (demanding what *they* have, *now!*) to repudiation (rejecting whatever they value). From covert operations (what my parents don't know won't hurt them) to up-yours confrontations (try and stop me). And from low-stakes provocations (not doing our homework, neglecting our chores, bad manners, a messy room, coming home past our curfew) to high-stakes provocations (delinquency, drug abuse, and other risky business).

I once knew a girl whose mother had started, the second that she hit puberty, to keep her under strict sexual control. "I don't want you doing this—you'll end up pregnant." "I don't want you going there—you'll end up pregnant." "I don't want you hanging around with him or her, with this crowd or that—you'll end up pregnant."

When the time finally came for this girl to rebel against her mother's control, she knew exactly where she wished to end up.

Some of us, determined to fiercely fend off our parents' control, may form what are known as "spite and revenge attachments," attachments to people our mothers and fathers find

83

alien or repugnant, attachments established—consciously or unconsciously—in order to rupture the parent-child relationship. We may also arrange to connect ourselves to gangs or cults or exotic ideologies, acquiring what psychologist Althea Horner has called "illusory power." The illusion is that we're in control because we've spurned the authority of our parents. The reality is that we're simply submitting to another authority, that we've given over control to our gang, cult, group.

Eating disorders—especially anorexia nervosa—are also enlisted in the fight for autonomy, as teenage girls (and to a much much smaller extent) teenage boys assert their independence by endeavoring to take control of their bodies. Anorexia is self-starvation—to the point of emaciation and sometimes death—accompanied by a distortion of body image that makes the anorectic insist that she's still too fat when she's clearly wasting away. This dangerous eating disorder makes its debut during adolescence and serves as a powerful instrument of control—as a way for adolescents, in the face of a deep sense of powerlessness, to control themselves, their families, and their lives.

Helen describes her self-starvation, begun at age fourteen and continued—with just a few slips—for some fifty years, maintained by minimal eating and by exercising four full hours a day. "Being thin is the most important thing in my life," she explains. "I enjoy living because I keep my weight down." Approaching her sixtieth birthday, Helen expresses some regret at having so few accomplishments to look back on. But she's able to console herself with the reassuring thought, "Well, I've stayed thin."

The adolescent anorectic, writes psychiatrist Regina Casper, "believes her thinness to be her own accomplishment, borne through prolonged deprivation, hunger, sacrifice, and against her parents' protests." Her restriction of food allows her to stop feeling helpless, allows her to feel self-determined and in control.

• • •

Whether we are starving ourselves or arranging to flunk twelfth grade or hanging out with skinheads or piercing our body parts, our parents almost never accept our challenges to their authority without argument. Indeed, they have plenty to say—and not always in calm and measured tones—on the superheated subjects of what we're ingesting, whom we're seeing, and the ways in which we're destroying our bodies and minds. They have plenty to say—but we are prepared not only to defend ourselves but to attack.

For one of the strongest weapons in our battle with the older generation is a recently acquired cognitive skill—the ability to perform what has been termed "formal operations." This is the kind of reasoning that allows us to think about thinking; to think not only literally but symbolically; to understand that "a rolling stone gathers no moss" is a figure of speech, not a comment on stones; to analyze and theorize, philosophize and conceptualize —and also to invidiously compare our actual parents with our idealized image of what parents should be.

This is the kind of reasoning that enhances our control by turning us into highly effective debaters.

A worn-down father storms from the room in the midst of an argument with his teenage daughter, a once-enchanting child who is using her handy new cognitive skills to icily attack him for not letting her take the car and (while she's at it) for cowardice and shallowness and hypocrisy and various other fatal flaws in his character.

"Just because you're not raising your voice," he screams at the top of his, as he makes his exit, "doesn't—goddamn it to hell!—mean that you're right."

Another mighty weapon in the kids-versus-parents control wars is that of running, or moving, away from home. As a threat it can sometimes force parents, scared to death of losing their kids, to make all sorts of against-the-grain concessions. When acted upon, it can leave a rent in the fabric of the family that is difficult, sometimes impossible, to mend.

It can also leave all those involved with a deep sense of loss.

Kelly, who first began running away in her freshman year of high school and who currently lives in a house with several other estranged-from-their-family daughters and sons, speaks with vast aggrievement about her parents' regulations and expectations.

"They criticized all the people I hung out with. They made me come home at eleven o'clock at night. My dad expected straight A's and that I should always be his perfect little girl. My mom kept shoving religion down my throat. They wouldn't let me be what I wanted or make my own decisions. I finally couldn't take it anymore."

Although she is out of the house and in control—she says—of her life, her anger at her parents bubbles and boils. Although she says "They meant well. They did their best. They cared about me," she can't imagine making up any time soon. And although she claims that she has no regrets and is so much happier now, happy isn't the way she sounds to me, for she also says that she would tell others in her situation, "Stay home. Don't rush it."

She adds, "I grew up so fast. I kind of regret growing up so fast. I feel a little gypped. I'm just seventeen."

"There are few situations in life which are more difficult to cope with," writes Anna Freud, "than an adolescent son or daughter during the attempt to liberate themselves." This may well be true. But if our struggle to break away is hard on our mothers and fathers, let it be understood that it's hard on us too. It's hard because the fights are often bruising. It's hard because we feel guilty for giving them grief. It's hard because, in pulling away, we're losing as well as gaining. It's hard because, although we're of the belief that we gotta do what we gotta do, we want —often desperately want—their love and approval.

Liberation is also hard because our urge for autonomy is accompanied by our yearnings to be cared for. Consciously or unconsciously, occasionally or constantly, alternately or at the very same time, we want adulthood's privileges along with the cozy comforts of being a kid.

> Mother, Mother!
> as a gemlike undergraduate,
> part criminal and yet a Phi Bete,
> I used to barge home late.
> Always by the banister
> my milk-tooth mug of milk
> was waiting for me on a plate
> of Triskets.

Like Sebastian of *Brideshead Revisited,* we want to guzzle champagne while we cling to our teddy bear. Like nineteen-year-old Pam, we want to be free to make love while our mother makes our dentist appointments. Like poet Robert Lowell we want to stay out as late as we please and know that our crackers and milk—and our mom—will be waiting.

Adolescence is a time of aching ambivalence, a time of both wanting to have—and surrender—control.

Sometimes the future we contemplate looks hard and cold and unwelcoming while our past seems bathed in a rosy nostalgic glow. Sometimes adulthood's burdens seem too hard to bear. What if we don't have the wherewithal to control this life we so eagerly want control of? What if our parents believe us when we tell them to leave us alone—and then we call for help and they aren't there?

We need to try to make it without them there.

Until I asked her to please stop doing it and was
    astonished to find that she not only could
but from the moment I asked her in fact would stop
    doing it, my mother, all through my childhood,
when I was saying something to her, something
    important, would move her lips as I was speaking
so that she seemed to be saying under her breath the
    very words I was saying as I was saying them.

It's endearing to watch us again in that long-ago dusk,
    facing each other, my mother and me.
I've just grown to her height, or just past it: there
    are our lips moving together,
now the unison suddenly breaks, I have to go on by
    myself, no maestro, no score to follow.

How are we going to make it without a maestro, a score to
follow? How are we going to make it if they're not there?

Some of us, in a panic over how and whether we'll make it,
may choose to remain in a state of arrested development, fearing
decisions, avoiding commitment, keeping all options open,
playing at life, preferring to stay in the twilight zone of perpetual adolescence to taking control.

Or if the price of autonomy is our parents' anger or hurt or
withdrawal of love, we may back off from claiming our right to
a life, accepting the roles that they choose for us, living by the
rules that they impose on us, preferring the goodies we get
because of our well-behaved-child compliance to taking control.

"He was such a powerful figure in our household," says Marianne, the only child of a brilliant, charming, elegant, and fiercely
controlling father. "He told me where I could go and who I
could go with and how I should act and what I should wear,
and even what music to listen to. He told me I couldn't go to a
coed college." And though she chafed against his constraints,

and feared his raging outbursts when he was crossed, she basically did what he wanted because "there were so many, many rewards for toeing the line. He fostered my mind. He was proud of me. He saw me as superior, as special." And so, if her compliance was the price she had to pay to keep this terrific high-standard man's approval, she paid it—and, after college, continued to pay it, moving back home to her small midwestern town and her father's undiminished authority.

Eventually, in her mid-twenties, Marianne somehow slipped away to San Francisco. But it took her many more years before her psychological distance equaled the distance she'd moved geographically. Her father's yeas and nays, his critical standards, his disapproval weighed on her life through marriage and parenthood. It took her many more years to feel fully free of his control, to finally leave home.

Some of us leave home and enter into the wider world harboring an unconscious rescue fantasy. Disguised as autonomous women and men, we are in fact secretly hoping that someone or something—good fortune, kind people, beneficent circumstances, special privileges—will turn up and help us master the tasks of living. We wait to be saved by a spouse, or a different job, or a move to a "better" part of the world, or even by some change in the way we look. We do not take control of our life because we keep hoping our life—and we—will be rescued.

Some of us, unwilling or unable to take control, never grow up.

In a good-enough adolescence, our mothers and fathers will neither abandon nor engulf us but will gradually give us more and more control, restraining us when we need and even want to be restrained, and supporting us as we separate and forge— from our pieces of self—our own identity.

In the crisis of identity that seems to be one of the hallmarks of adolescence, we struggle to create an authentic self, connecting our private and public selves, balancing our separate and loving selves, linking what we are now with what we once were and what we hope someday to be. By the close of adolescence we possess a unique this-is-me-and-no-other self, a self not imposed by others but truly our own. And even though that self may be more in tune with our parents' values than seemed possible during the height of our control wars, we feel that we've actively chosen to be what we are.

Our choices may be subject to revision.

Our future may be unnervingly obscure.

Our control of our body and psyche may be imperfect.

But we have taken possession of ourselves.

As we venture forth to meet, and to make, our destiny, we could turn for inspiration to James Joyce's "soulfree and fancyfree" young artist who, declaring that "I do not fear to be alone . . . or to leave whatever I have to leave," enters his future crying "Welcome, O life!"

Or else we could turn to Dr. Seuss, who—in his rousing *Oh, the Places You'll Go*—urges us onward with these bracing words:

> You have brains in your head.
> You have feet in your shoes.
> You can steer yourself
> any direction you choose.
> You're on your own. And you know what you know.
> And YOU are the guy who'll decide where to go.

4

The Power of Sex

Every step along the way you have to ask. . . . If you
want to take her blouse off, you have to ask. If
you want to touch her breast, you have to ask. If you
want to move your hand down to her genitals, you
have to ask.

—Antioch College rules

Men rule the world.
Penises rule the men.
Who rules the penises?
We do, darling.

—Nicky Silver, *The Food Chain*

We head out into the world equipped with some sense
of who we are, or aspire to be. We joyously and nervously—
ambivalently—confront our adult freedoms. Among the powers
we've come to possess (as well as to be possessed by) is the
power of our sexuality, which offers us (and threatens us with)
multiple opportunities for control.

And loss of control.

Back when I was a girl, the sexual warnings went like this:

"Men can't help it. They're animals. That's why women have to be in control."

And, from North Dakota, "Lose control, and you will bring disgrace on the family."

And, from northern New Jersey, "If you lose control and give him what he wants, he's going to talk about you in bars."

And, from practically everywhere, "If you lose control and give him what he wants, he won't respect you in the morning."

And, my personal favorite, delivered by my mother at the end of her heart-to-heart about unchecked passion, "I never in my life heard of one decent woman who wasn't a virgin when she got married."

Back when I was a girl, young women thought a lot about sexual control.

It seems they still do.

"I had been thinking about everything, including sexuality, in terms of control," muses Katie Roiphe in her 1993 book, *The Morning After.* "So did most people around me. Whether it was getting it, keeping it, needing it, wanting it, sex always seemed to come back to control. Control was not just a vocabulary. It was at the heart of our actions, the way we felt and thought about sex. Most people I knew, myself included, measured their behavior with some internal barometer of control, the dial wavering between extremes of release and extremes of self-restraint. I knew it hadn't always been like this. In the sixties and seventies, sex was about expression and orgasm, at least in theory. . . . But these days even the wildest, most carefree of hedonists I knew framed their adventures in terms of control lost."

What do we mean when we talk today about sexual control? We mean that, instead of simply letting sex happen, we take conscious charge of our sexuality. This includes deciding if we want, or don't want, sex. And selecting the person with whom we want to have it. And choosing which sex acts we will, or won't, engage in. And exerting sufficient restraint, over both ourself and our partner, to ensure that we are protected from sexual risks.

From our preadolescent gropings to something that might be described as mature sexual love, the issue of control—and of surrendering control—is intricately intertwined with sex.

"We wouldn't just jump into bed," says Shannon, a sensible single young woman, explaining her view of control in the age of AIDS. "We'd talk about it first. We'd ask about each other's previous partners. We'd agree that in the beginning he'd use a condom. And we'd both get tested for HIV before we'd be willing not to use a condom."

Such sexual control makes a great deal of sense, we would all agree, at a time when losing control could leave us dead. But as Meghan Daum, twenty-something, considers herself and her friends, she concludes that these oh-so-responsible words are far more often preached than they are practiced. Though urged "to keep our fantasies on a tight rein," though warned not to "lose control of the whole buggy," she says that when it comes to claims of practicing safe sex, "there is a lot of lying going around."

She says that "we're all but ignoring" the crisis warnings. And she says that we "vow to protect ourselves, and intend (really, truly) to stick by this rule," and then "we don't because we just can't, because it's just not fair, because our sense of entitlement exceeds our sense of vulnerability." Deluged with information about the AIDS virus and convinced (well, sometimes convinced) that they could actually contract this dread disease, she and her friends, she tells us, nonetheless "blow off precaution again and again."

And after having engaged in what, in retrospect, looks a lot like risky behavior, and after having endured some utterly terrified I-am-going-to-die sleepless nights, they go to the clinic to take the test that will tell them whether their loss of control was fatal.

And long for those good old days, when it was safe to dispense with sexual control.

Perhaps there actually was a brief time, during the height of the sexual revolution, when we tried to shed our concerns about control, when women as well as men were into the joys of uncensored sex, when restraint was an embarrassment not a virtue. Perhaps, between the Pill and AIDS, there was a sexual window of opportunity when everyone—male *and* female—was said to be doing it, cheered on by John Updike's faithless *Couples* and Erica Jong's "Zipless Fuck" and Hollywood's *Bob & Carol & Ted & Alice*. During this time *John & Mimi*, a sexual memoir published under the authors' real names, detailed (orifice by orifice) the delights of open extramarital sex, including sex with "the three of us being together," sex with "Mimi and Ava . . . discovering each other's bodies," and sex "with other couples where we split up, go to different parts of the house, then all get back together for coffee and cake." The tenor of that time, a time of seemingly boundless sexual possibility, is conveyed by the authors' pride in their "free marriage" and by their earnest convictions that soon "there will be nothing unusual about this book."

But even during those throbbing years, I recall a young wife sobbing to me on the phone, "He says it's good for us to be having sex with other people, but it hurts me so much when he does. It hurts me so much." I recall a single woman complaining, "We first have to go to bed. Then, if he sticks around, we get acquainted," adding with a sigh, "I sleep with guys who don't even know my middle name." Despite all the brave sixties talk about the values of doing away with sexual jealousy and the benefits of engaging in casual sex, open infidelity and see-yaaround one-night stands tore up a lot of hearts and souls and relationships.

It seems they still do.

For even without the onset of AIDS, the sexual revolution could not free our sex lives from issues of control, or from the related stubborn fact that our sexual encounters are weighted—and probably always have been weighted—with quite different meanings for women and for men.

This old Calvin Coolidge story helps capture those meanings:

> Mrs. Coolidge . . . , on a presidential tour of a chicken farm, noted approvingly a rooster copulating with a hen. "Does he do that often?" she asked. "Oh, several times a day," said the farmer. "Please tell that to the President," she directed pointedly. Coolidge turned to the farmer. "Always with the same hen?" he asked. "No, all different," was the response. "Please tell *that*," Coolidge said, "to the First Lady."

Why is having sex (still known in certain wistful circles as "making love") so emotionally different for females and males? Some of the answer lies in our developmental history of separation and gender identification.

For boys, as they develop, dare not identify too closely with their mothers. Girls can. Girls grow into womanhood by taking on the womanliness of their mothers. Boys who take on too many of their mothers' characteristics will not—or, at least, are afraid they will not—become men. And so little boys must pull away, farther than little girls need ever go, from their intense connection with their mothers. They distance themselves, hold back, hold women at bay. And although the emotional closeness that little boys once shared with their mothers may remain a forever-yearned-for paradise lost, it also remains a fearful threat to their manhood and their masculine sexuality.

"Attached, dependent, reengulfed, entrapped, smothered, eaten up alive, effeminized, merged, fused," writes analyst John Munder Ross, "—these are but a few of the words clinical experts have used to describe a son's fear of sinking back into the psychological symbiosis and sexual ambiguity of his earliest days." With fears like that, small wonder that a fellow disavows his feminine side. With fears like that, small wonder that he is at ease with what has been called "unconnected lust."

D. H. Lawrence had some thoughts on this matter:

> I wish I knew a woman
> who was like a red fire on the hearth
> glowing after the day's restless draughts.
> So that one could draw near her
> in the red stillness of the dusk
> and really take delight in her
> without having to make the polite effort of loving her
> or the mental effort of making her acquaintance.

For women, however, connectedness is basic to their feminine identity. The development of their "I" does not depend, as it does with men, on definitively breaking away from their "we." Indeed, women's sense of self is so strongly linked to their investment in caring relationships that some of them—when a close relationship ends—will say, "I not only lost him; I also lost me." With their fear of separation overshadowing any fears of being submerged, small wonder that women insist on intimacy. Small wonder that women find it a whole lot harder to cast off control and give themselves over to unconnected lust.

Thus men, in far greater numbers than women, enjoy recreational sex, sex divorced from love or long-term commitment. (The figures—33 percent of the men and 18.7 percent of the

96

women—dramatize their striking disparity.) This gap between what men want and what women want from sex has always made sex more complicated for women. And while the sexual revolution has somewhat legitimized recreational sex for both sexes, many women still believe that they *give* something to a man when they have sex with him, while many men still believe that when they have sex with a woman they *take* something from her.

While a man is not supposed to "take" what a woman does not wish to "give," men often feel—or claim to feel—confused. Should I keep trying? Isn't she asking for it? Does she really mean "yes" when she's saying "no"? Indeed, when it comes to sex there are opportunities for major misunderstandings, for signals to be truly mixed or radically, disturbingly misconstrued.

The authors of *Sex in America*, a survey of sexual practices and beliefs, find that a very high number of women—22 percent—say they were forced by a man to do something sexual. In contrast, a very low number of men—only 3 percent—report having forced a woman to do something sexual. Attempting to make some sense of these dramatically different statistics, the authors have proposed the following view: That "most men who forced sex did not recognize how coercive the women thought their behavior was." That "some men may have thought they were negotiating for sex, while the women who were their partners thought that they were being forced."

"Do you mean that if I grab a woman's crotch, that could be rape? That's unfair!"

"Well, I had consent and then she changed her mind."

"As far as I'm concerned you can change your mind before, even during, but just not after sex."

"With this new definition of rape, we could end up in prison for not satisfying a woman sexually!"

"She got herself raped."

97

Presumably, if every man applied the Antioch rules—"Can I touch you down here now?"—every woman could be in control of her sex life, her "yes" or "no" or "not until the third date" averting communication failures. No woman could claim she was carried away by passion. No man could claim she didn't make herself clear. Nothing would happen without explicit double-checked are-you-sure-you-mean-it consent. This Q and A approach presumes that women are always certain of what they want sexually, that they're never torn between a yes and a no, that they're clear on precisely how far they want to go, that their desires are unambivalent. But what about, "I really shouldn't be doing this, but don't stop," or "I know that this is bad, but it feels so good"? What about the wish to not be responsible? And what about my friend Trudy, who rather abashedly tells this story on herself:

"I invited him up for coffee, but I told myself—and him—that I only meant coffee. I definitely had no intention of going to bed. But before we'd gone out that night, I'd changed the sheets, and sprayed them with a little cologne. I'd put a bottle of Chardonnay in the fridge. And I'd also—although, as I say, I had no intention of going to bed—put in my diaphragm."

Did Trudy's friend make some moves on her? He did.

Did Trudy resist his moves? She did, and she didn't.

Did he get somewhat insistent with her? He did.

Did she finally have sex with him? She did.

Did she or didn't she want to have sex? Yes.

I think Trudy's story helps explain why the women and men in that survey gave such disparate reports about forced sex. But I also think their answers may reflect something more complex than misunderstood cues. For although the *Sex in America* men overwhelmingly claim that they do not find forced sex appealing, there are other studies that tell a quite different story.

Consider, for example, these responses to a survey of 114 male undergraduates:

"I like to dominate a woman"—91.3 percent.

"I enjoy the conquest part of sex"—86.1 percent.

"Some women look like they're just asking to be raped"—83.5 percent.

"I get excited when a woman struggles over sex"—63.5 percent.

"It would be exciting to use force to subdue a woman"—61.7 percent.

Another survey, designed by the Columbia Psychoanalytic Center for Training and Research to study sexual fantasies and behaviors, found that the number of males who fantasized forcing sex on their partners was 44 percent. In contrast, only 10 percent of the women who were surveyed said that they had fantasies of forced sex, suggesting that women and men come into the sexual situation with drastically different levels of aggression.

Must we conclude then that men—the lovely men who are reading these words; husbands and fathers and brothers and sons and friends—are intrinsically beasts? Psychoanalyst Ethel S. Person says no, challenging "the popular cultural notion that male sexuality is by its nature aggressive." She argues instead that male sexual aggression is secondary, not primary; that it serves to defend against sexual anxieties; and that it is these anxieties, engendered by male developmental experiences, that predispose the majority of men to concerns about sexual power and control.

In other words, men aren't basically beastly. They're frightened.

Some of their anxieties derive from their suspicion—no, their *certainty*—that out there in the world are guys who possess superior sexual skills and equipment. And right they are—or were—for each of these men was once a small boy comparing his miniature penis to his dad's awesome one, a comparison that confronted him with the humiliating fact that he didn't have what it takes to beat out his dad. A lot of men, says Person, clearly never seem to recover from "this literal sense of genital inadequacy"—this blow to their self-esteem, to their self-love, to their narcissism that may leave them with a lifelong case of penis envy.

"My penis," three-year-old Tim tells his mom, "is as big as daddy's penis. No, it's bigger." It makes a lot of sense, once you start thinking about it, that boys—and men—could suffer from penis envy.

A front-page story in *The Wall Street Journal* addresses the male obsession with penis size, reporting on the emergence of a new cosmetic specialty—penile enlargement, a.k.a. phalloplasty. Despite alarming tales of infections, scarring, lumpiness, impotence, even death, this surgery—which promises to make a patient's penis longer and wider—is raking in profits. Says Frank Whitehead, a satisfied customer, "I never felt comfortable or confident about myself before. . . . Now [when] I go into business meetings, I'm thinking, 'If you guys had just half of what I have.' "

(This operation sounds dramatically creepier to me than anything women do to enlarge their breasts, but I think it's sad that both sexes suffer from the misguided belief that bigger is better.)

In addition to size concerns, a man's developmental history includes the awkward arousals of adolescence, erections and emissions that make it plain that his penis possesses a life of its own. The tragedy of the young man is "having a gun and ammunition, but no control," a condition, says Person, which makes achieving mastery of his penis a high priority. This teenage lack of control, with its public declarations of sexual excitement, not only produces anxiety and shame. It can also leave a grown man with enduring concerns about other kinds of control deficiencies—like premature ejaculation and impotence.

In some men's sexual history, experiences with an overpowering mother produce extreme, and unconscious, fears of engulfment, fears that can lead to their seeing all of their subsequent sexual partners as dangerous "mothers" who'll eat them up alive. These fears can be assuaged by their inability to sexually perform—if I don't go inside, or I climax real fast, so the unconscious logic goes, she cannot engulf me. But the price they pay for their safety is the anguish of recurrent difficulties with failed erections or swift ejaculations.

But even without an overpowering mother, men worry a lot about sexual inadequacy. And even a certified stud may find himself tormented by a number of anxious questions: Is my penis too small? Can I get it, and keep it, up? Will I be able to satisfy her? Will she reject me?

"According to my experience," says psychoanalyst Karen Horney, "the dread of being rejected and derided is a typical ingredient in the analysis of every man."

"According to my experience," says a psychotherapist who prefers to be nameless, "if a man doesn't feel adored, he feels as if he has a small penis."

Noting that sexual fantasies are often the mirror image of sexual fears, Dr. Person points out that among the most common male sexual fantasies—perhaps more common than those about domination—is the fantasy of the lusty, perpetually lubricated, I-gotta-have-it woman, a woman who is wildly hungry for sex, a woman so ready and willing that she would never turn a man down or find him unsatisfying. A variation on this theme is the popular fantasy of lesbian sex—two women making love with the fantasizing male either watching or joining in. This fantasy offers anxious men an "overabundance of women," women whose only function in life is sexual, women whose appetites and availability promise these men that they'll never be rejected or humiliated.

These fantasies are what Person calls "compensatory mechanisms," masking men's deep concerns about being powerless, inferior, not in control.

While fear of female rejection will be largely resolved in the course of normal development, male worries about control of both the partner and the penis always remain a universal "fault" line. This fault, this vulnerability, may find expression only through these fantasies, but sometimes a man seeks more concrete "compensations." Sometimes his concerns about, and need to have, control are directly expressed through his penis—through phallic power.

Consider, for instance, Aaron, a phenomenal charmer and playmate, a good-looking, fun-loving, fortyish neurosurgeon, a man who makes fantastic love to the woman in his life, thereby making her feel exquisitely special. But the problem is that Aaron has *two* women in his life, and though they now know of —and have even met—each other, he somehow has sweet-talked each of them into remaining in their "very special" relationship. Indeed, he may even—if his seductive persuasive powers prevail—exert sufficient control to someday talk them into having three-way sex.

For these macho men, the key to phallic power resides in their proficiency as lovers, a proficiency based on the stereotype of "a large, powerful, untiring phallus attached to a very cool male, long on self-control, experienced, competent, and knowledgeable enough to make women crazy with desire." Such a cool male—so the story goes—can turn even a shy or proudly self-contained woman into a meltingly submissive sex slave, one who happily sings to her man, "I've got you under my skin," or "I'd sacrifice anything, come what may, for the sake of having you near," or, more ominously:

> So taunt me and hurt me,
> Deceive me, desert me,
> I'm yours 'til I die . . .

—sentiments that can turn phallic power dangerous.

For if sexual proficiency can give men control through their power to give pleasure, that power—so the story goes—can also be corrupted and abused. Indeed, psychoanalyst Rollo May seems to see all Don Juans as potential victimizers, arguing that the macho male sterotype is so "heavily invested with assertion and activity" that the "image of the tireless seducer differs only in style and degree from that of the rapist."

Having known—although not biblically—a few tireless seducers, I believe that, like rapists, their interest is power not sex. But I don't think they differ only in style and degree. For that statement seems to suggest that women are putty in the hands of forceful men. That statement seems to suggest that even when the sexual force is just verbal, not physical, women can't be expected to have control.

Certainly one of the hotly debated issues in certain circles is over the definition of "real" rape, over the question of when a woman is fully accountable for her sexual actions and when she is to be viewed as a sexual victim. The assault of a man on a woman using weapons or threats of violence in order to achieve his sexual ends tends to make for a clear-cut case of real rape. But is it rape—is it date rape—when a woman surrenders her body to a man who plies her with liquor or with drugs, to a man who psychologically intimidates her, to a man who exploits her low self-esteem by threatening "I'll break up with you if you don't"? Is she the victim of date rape if the evening was a blur or if—at the moment of orgasm—he calls her by another woman's name or if—the next day or next week or even next year—she passionately wishes she hadn't done it?

Those who, like me, are resistant to such broad definitions of rape say that these broad definitions diminish women, portraying them as passive, innocent, helpless, and weak-willed, lacking the character—and the control—to stand against the pressure of male peers. They also object to the tacit implication of female sexlessness, the suggestion that women don't hunger, as men do, for sex. This portrait of women as helpless, as sexless, as urgently needing protection from the nasty incursions of males—both strangers and friends—is, so the critics argue, and I agree, a denial of who women are and what they've achieved.

A denial that women have sexual control.

But those who believe that all of us are living in what they collectively call a "rape culture" insist that every woman (no matter how take-charge she may be) suffers from fears of sexual assault, fears that constrict her life by making her censor the way she dresses and talks and behaves, and by making her feel that independence is risky. They also maintain that along with the more incontrovertible definitions of rape, date rape can be legitimately defined as "conniving, coercing, pushing, ignoring efforts to get you to stop" and "getting her so drunk that she loses the ability . . . that one needs to give consent."

But what do they mean when they talk about getting her drunk? How come a woman doesn't get *herself* drunk?

Says David Danon, a sophomore at Brown University, "Women have all the power here on sexual conduct. . . . It's very dangerous for us."

Others, citing U.S. rape statistics—97,464 female rapes in 1995 —say that it's very dangerous for women.

The fact that *"some* men rape," according to journalist Susan Brownmiller in her pioneering study of the subject, "provides a sufficient threat to keep all women in a constant state of intimidation." And although some women have falsely cried rape, with devastating results—the lies of Potiphar's wife put Joseph in prison; the lies of some Southern women got black men lynched—Brownmiller scorns "the deadly male myths of rape":

That complaints about rape are the product of hysteria or vengeance.

That a woman can't be raped against her will.

That "a rape usually is . . . a woman who changed her mind afterward."

That every woman, like Dominique in *The Fountainhead*, really

104

longs to be raped and experiences "the act of a master taking shameful, contemptuous possession of her" as "the kind of rapture she had wanted."

> I've been raped . . . I've been raped by some red-headed hoodlum from a stone quarry. . . . Through the fierce sense of humiliation, the words gave her the same kind of pleasure she had felt in his arms.

Says Michael Kimmel, professor of sociology: "Escalating a sexual encounter beyond what a woman may want is date rape."

But if Sigmund Freud had met Dominique he might have concluded that rape is what women want.

Most women, however, in spite of Dominique, do not want forced sex. Most women, in spite of the victim-poetry of Sylvia Plath, don't subscribe to the view that "Every woman adores a Fascist, / The boot in the face, . . . " Most women, in spite of the superheated diaries of Anaïs Nin, don't have a "secret erotic need" to be violated. Nor, in spite of the theories of psychoanalysts Sigmund Freud, Helene Deutsch, and Marie Bonaparte, do women possess a "primary, erotogenic masochism" (Freud) and "a deeply feminine need to be overpowered" (Deutsch) and a vaginal sensitivity that is based (according to Bonaparte) on "immense masochistic beating fantasies."

According to early theorists, internalized female aggression led to a girl's intense feminine masochism, heightened by penis envy (she couldn't have one) and her oedipal defeat (she couldn't have Daddy), plus "anticipation of, as well as experience in, menstruation, defloration, penetration and parturition" —all of which were presumed to hurt like hell. Disappointed, damaged, cheated, inferior, and subject to bodily pain, girls—so these theories asserted—became resigned masochists, a state

105

that, according to Deutsch, was a "woman's anatomical destiny" —normal, desirable, realistic, and necessary.

Modern psychoanalysts regard these startling theories of female development as unsubstantiated and antiquated. They reject the idea of a "normal" feminine masochism. They say they see no evidence that women find a particular pleasure in pain. Indeed, it has been said that the masochistic woman caricatures femininity.

In other words, the answer to Dr. Freud's perplexed question "What does a woman want?" is not submission, humiliation, and suffering. Nor is her willing sexual surrender a masochistic surrendering of control.

Another antiquated claim is that women have a weaker sexual instinct—and that this is why men insist and women resist. But the fact that a woman turns a man down cannot be read as proof that she lacks an equal enthusiasm for sex. It may simply mean that she has a different agenda.

Kimmel makes the point that while women today want and feel entitled to sexual pleasure, they continue to be pressed—by men's determination to "put it in," to score—into the unwanted role of "asexual gatekeeper," the ones who decide "who enters the desired garden of earthly delights, and who doesn't." Confronted by what Kimmel colorfully calls "the incessant humming of male desire," a woman has to practice discrimination. And a woman—no matter how sexual—who seeks something more than unconnected lust will want to keep control of her agenda by exercising her privilege to say "no."

No, I don't know you well enough.

No, we don't really care about each other.

No, I have no interest in one-night stands.

No, not without a commitment from you.

No, not without some jewelry from you.

No, not unless there's something—something more, that is, than sex—in it for me.

Women may indeed be just as sexual as men, and some evidence suggests they may even be more so. But in spite of their carnality and their capacity for prolonged and multiple orgasms, they seem less compelled, less controlled by their desires.

For many women sexual pleasure, despite a strong libido, isn't the only prize they pursue in bed. For many women sexual pleasure, even if they adore sex, is not the main point. There are plenty of women—I'm not talking here of those who do this professionally—who use a man's desire for them to convert their bodies into negotiable currency. There are plenty of women who, in concert with men, participate in a sexual barter system:

> Illiterate, tattooed Baines lusts after the mute, school-marmish Ada. He has her piano. She wants it back. "Do you know how to bargain?" he asks, and then he explains: "There are things I'd like to do while you play," and if she will let him do them, she can earn her piano from him, key by key.

> "Lift your skirt," he begins. And then, on the next day, he commands, "Undo your dress. I want to see your arms." Later he offers to give her four keys—no, *five!* Ada fiercely insists in emphatic sign-language—if she will only lie next to him in bed. And after that she assents to his "I want to lie together with no clothes on" in exchange for ten precious piano keys.

This barter takes place in a haunting little movie called *The Piano*, at a time when a woman like Ada had no other currency, at a time when men controlled the world and women controlled them by controlling the penis. But trading sex for material goods has certainly not been restricted to bygone, women-are-chattel, prefeminist eras. There are plenty of women today who get what might otherwise be very-hard-to-get benefits by taking control of the sexual agenda, by exchanging sex for what they want from their men.

A letter to Ann Landers from a woman who signs herself "Been There and Back" describes, quite unabashedly, her utilization of the sexual barter system:

> Even the dumbest wife knows that the only way to get anything extra out of a husband is to nail him when he feels romantic. Any wife who tries to get a new vacuum sweeper or a new rug out of the old man by explaining that she *needs* one is out of her mind.

Is this wife really any different from the fictional Lorelei Lee who, only a few decades earlier, cut the same deal—though for somewhat higher stakes?

> I mean it seems to me a gentleman who has a friendly interest in educating a girl. . . . would want her to have the biggest square-cut diamond in New York. I mean I must say I was quite disappointed when he came to the apartment with a little thing you could hardly see. So I told him I thought it was quite cute, but I had quite a headache and I had better stay in a dark room all day and I told him I would see him the next day, perhaps. . . . But he came in at dinner time with a very beautiful bracelet of square-cut diamonds so I was quite cheered up.

Sex in exchange for vacuum cleaners or diamonds or pianos, for rent or for a walk-on part in a movie—there will always be women who alchemize men's desire for them into some kind of gold. With different degrees of explicitness about the deals they are making, and with partners who may or may not know they're making a deal, married women and single women and courtesans and virgins use sex as their means of getting goodies from men.

Not all of these goodies, however, are quite so material in nature. Sex can yield other benefits as well. Some women choose to trade sex for shelter, security, and safety—"It's a very cold world out there." Some women trade sex for experience—It's "like taking an advanced-placement course in life." And others give sex in exchange for some substitute mothering or fathering —"I swear," says Suzette, "he's like a father to me"—using men's desire for them to meet cuddle-me, take-care-of-me, little-girl needs.

There are plenty of women who feel that the only real power they have in this world, their only lever for exercising control, is men's desire for them.

When sex is a means of exchange, copulation is bound to be preceded by calculation. There also are sometimes bound to be some serious miscalculations, especially for women who engage in the riskiest trade of them all: sex for love.

Seventeen-year-old Tracy went to bed with her boyfriend, Mark, not out of physical passion but out of love, hoping that the surrender of her virginity "would make things better. . . . Make the relationship stronger." Her strategy failed, for soon Mark grew restless and started seeing her less, and soon he had returned to his previous girlfriend, a girl who, Tracy said bitterly, "made herself available to him whenever he wanted her . . . [and] really kissed his ass, and . . . did oral sex and stuff." Her expectations, writes researcher Sharon Thompson, that sex could "generate caring and love; cure all instead of end all; save a faltering relationship" and serve as a "lasso that would give her control of him once she got it around his neck" were sunk by a drastic shift in supply and demand.

For among the American girls who turned eighteen between 1967 and 1969, almost 75 percent were still virgins, having successfully stood their ground against the kinds of lines that "guys give girls . . . to break down their resistance":

"What are you afraid of? Don't be a baby. It's part of growing up."

"If you really loved me, you would."

"It's very painful for a guy to be in this condition and not get relief."

"It will be good for your complexion."

"I have never wanted anybody the way I want you."

"It would be awful if you died in an accident without experiencing the greatest thrill of all."

"Sex is a great tension-breaker. It will make you feel relaxed."

"You have the body of a woman. Mother Nature meant for you to have sex."

And, mining my long-gone girlhood, I would like to contribute this, from a boy who had seen too many World War II movies: "I'll keep it a secret—even if they torture me."

And one more, from a lad known less for his charm than for his efficiency: "Aw, come on—let me do it. It won't take long."

In spite of such irresistible lines, and in spite of raging hormones, most teenage girls up through the sixties said "no" to intercourse. But the sex revolution had come and was here to stay. Between 1979 and 1981, writes Thompson, who interviewed 400 teenage girls about their sex lives, more than half of the girls who, during this time had turned eighteen, had gone all the way. Furthermore, in this new world order, sex was acknowledged to be as pleasing and normal for girls as it was for boys, which meant that having sex was something a girl did for herself, not for her fellow. With a girl's consenting to intercourse no longer perceived as a sacrifice, as a gift for which a boy was obliged to pay, her "yes" (which for many girls was still a complicated "yes") lost much of its power as a bargaining chip.

"See, the reason they can't really understand why a girl says no," Tracy lamented, "is because so many girls say yes."

It's true that in more virginal times a girl who had sex risked losing the man she loved because, having had her, he might cease to respect her, though she hoped sex would lead to matrimony rather than to the conclusion, "Why should I buy the cow when I get the milk free?" It's also true that, even today, girls are concerned with being seen as sluts. And yet, with so much free milk around, it's harder for girls—and much harder for older women—to market their sexual selves as a precious commodity. Those who hope to trade sex for love are going to run the risk of becoming, like woeful Tracy, one of love's victims.

I'm not suggesting, however, that the longing for a sex-and-love connection is always the province—and the sole risk—of girls, that girls are potential fools for love and boys keep a score card where their hearts ought to be. Romantic passion, the melding of soulful love and hot desire, strikes Romeos as well as Juliets, putting them at risk and introducing them (welcome to the club) to possessiveness, jealousy, longing, loss, and heartbreak.

Listen to David:

> I tried to turn my thoughts toward my own help-lessness, my inability to get on with life, to begin again. But the truth was that I had no will and no intention to begin life again. All I wanted was what I'd already had. That exultation, that love. It was my one real home; I was a visitor everywhere else. . . . It would have been better, or at least easier, if Jade and I had discovered each other and learned what our being together meant when we were older. . . . It was diffi-

cult to accept, and it was frightening too, that the most important thing that was ever going to happen to me, the thing that *was* my life, happened when I was not quite seventeen years old.

As girls become women and boys become men, all of us learn that sex is a power that we can possess—or be possessed by, a power derived from beauty or youth, firm flesh and dewy skin; from the aphrodisiac aspects of wealth, celebrity, social status, achievement, influence; from the arcane lovemaking skills that enable courtesans to rule over kings in the bedroom; or from the blood-stirring magic wrought by the shadow of a smile or the way he wears his hat or sings off-key. It's a power that we can succumb to, falling off the edge of the earth into mindless sensation, reveling in the ecstasies of the flesh. It's also a power that we can turn into a weapon, observes psychologist Althea Horner, "a weapon used by the self to control others."

Men can control women sexually because, if one doesn't say "yes," they'll find one who will.

Women can control men sexually because it's they who decide if it's "yes" or "no."

Men can control women sexually because they're physiologically able to rape.

Women can control men sexually because, if they choose to, they can call anything "rape."

Men can control women sexually because they get sex from women by giving them goodies.

Women can control men sexually because they get goodies from men in exchange for sex.

Contemplating this list, we may conclude that—when it comes to sexual power—women and men have only imperfect control.

• • •

There are, nonetheless, some inequities which may give the sexual-power edge to men.

For the *Sex in America* survey points out that as single women age, it becomes increasingly harder for them to find partners, both because there are fewer available men and also because these men often choose younger women. A statistic:

For single white women with college educations between ages thirty-five and thirty-nine, there are—*for every hundred of them*—only *thirty-nine men* who are either their age or older and who are also single and white and college-educated. Using the same criteria, the demographers conclude that there are two hundred women for each of these hundred men.

As for the tendency of older men to choose younger women, consider this statement from a taxicab driver, a paunchy and balding man whose teeth are terrible and whose age is sixty-eight. After telling writer Susan Jacoby that he would never date a woman his own age, he goes on to say:

> You think that's unfair, right? Well, it is unfair. I don't want to go out with women in their sixties. I'll tell you why—their bodies are just as flabby as mine. And, see, I don't have to settle for that. I've got a good pension from twenty-five years in the fire department on top of what I make driving a cab. Gives me something to offer a younger woman. Oh, I know they aren't going out with me because I'm so sexy-looking. A woman my age is in a tougher spot. See, she's got no money and no job. The way I figure it, you've got to have something else to offer when the body starts falling apart.

Unfair though it may be, the sexual marketplace is tougher for older women. This is true for some of the very best women I

113

know, divorced and widowed women with warmth and charm and wit and intelligence, and balance and a seasoned sense of things, attractive women who—in their fifties and sixties and seventies and even in their eighties—have playfulness and passion and excellent teeth. Not all, but most, of these women want a man to have and to hold but few, if any, men knock at their door. And while none that I know would settle for that boor of a taxicab driver, most of them, longing for love but aware of the harsh realities of the sexual marketplace, are willing to settle.

They are ready and willing to settle, but no one is asking.

Yes, age creates inequities that give the sexual-power edge to men. Furthermore, at every age, as we've already learned, more women than men are out there looking for love. More women than men are seeking not recreational sex or unconnected lust but sex within the context of a relationship.

From the "Strictly Personals":

Creative, Intelligent, Amusing—And attractive . . . 40s, nonsmoker, seeks a witty, accomplished, caring, thoughtful man . . . *ready to share a lasting future.*

Attractive, Caring And Athletic Lady—*Looking for committed relationship.*

LI Lady—56, very attractive, glamorous, classy . . . seeks attractive, successful, romantic male *for long-term relationship.*

Ravishing, Romantic Redhead—a size 4
Seeks lifelong companion, lover, more.

I don't know how many answers these poignant self-advertisements drew, but I know exactly how many my friend Meg received. Her "Beautiful, bright, professional woman searching for short-term lover to mend broken heart" included

114

an irresistible phrase—"short-term"—a phrase which, she is certain, was responsible for the deluge of responses (seventy-five of them!) from fear-of-commitment men all over Manhattan.

The authors of *Sex in America* conclude: "When women bitterly complain that the men they meet are not interested in long-term commitments, their laments have a ring of truth. . . . When men note that their girlfriends are always trying to lure them into making a commitment . . . there is a good reason for it." There seems to be this vast gulf between what men and women want. And yet . . . And yet . . .

And yet, despite his resistance to her need for commitment, her wish for some love with her sex, women and men still fashion loving connections. The recreational view of sex doesn't seem, in the long run, to prevail. Love never quite conquers all, but at its best it can calm concerns about control. Reciprocal sexual love can free us from sexual power games and put an end to the sexual barter system.

Remember Baines and Ada from *The Piano*?

> As Baines falls in love with Ada, their sex-for-piano-keys negotiations break down. "It's making you a whore," he says, "and me wretched." He tells her, "My mind has seized on you. I can think of nothing else. I am sick with longing. So if you come with no feeling for me, go . . . go . . . go. Get out. Leave."

She doesn't leave.

After great travail, Baines and Ada settle down with each other. Last seen, they were living together happily. If the trip from piano-key passion to sweet domesticity sounds like a comedown, consider this striking news from *Sex in America:* Those in the survey "most physically pleased and emotionally satisfied were"—does this surprise you?—"the married couples."

• • •

A little boy asks his mommy and daddy to tell him how babies are made. They answer with anatomical correctness, droning on and on about the penis and vagina, the egg and sperm, until he interrupts their very tedious explanation with an impatient "Okay, but . . . is it fun?"

Shaking off their solemnity, his parents smile at each each other. Last night's remembered pleasures shine in their eyes. After a moment, they turn to their son and give him their heart-felt reply: "Oh, yes, it's fun."

But while sex can be fun, can be ecstasy, can be the ultimate intimacy, can be the most perfect blending of body and soul, and while marriage may be the best place for regular sex and for a satisfying sex life, sex is still a common marital problem. It's a problem, in part, because—along with intimacy and ec-stasy and fun—the marriage bed can also be the source of sig-nificant conflicts over various troublesome issues of control.

Control of how often we do it.

Control of what we do.

Control of ourselves.

Control is surely the issue when it comes to sexual frequency. Who is the marriage partner who decides how often a husband and wife have sex? If he wants to do it every night, and she only wants to do it once a week, what happens when it's always his—or her—way? When partners have dramatically different levels of desire, which partner prevails?

"I never refuse my husband," says Leona, who thinks it's her duty to have sex.

"I don't want to do it unless I mean it," says Ruth, who thinks it's dishonest to "accommodate."

"I let him have as little sex as he wants," says Caroline, who fears she'll embarrass her husband by asking for more.

"I'd never impose myself on her," says Edward, who also wants more, but whose wife is often inclined to feel imposed on.

Leona and Edward and Caroline—and Ruth's husband—live with the fact that their spouses control how frequently they do it. But other wives and husbands are far more troubled by what they perceive as excessive demands for—or refusals of—sex. The partner who is too often turned down may feel angry, deprived, rejected, or "like an animal." The partner who often refuses may feel guilty or pressured or psychologically forced. Not asking for sex when we want it, or engaging in sex when we do not want it at all, is sometimes healthy compromise, sometimes catastrophe. And sometimes, as Edith reports, it is simply exhausting.

Edith's husband, Brent, is a man of voracious sexual appetite, who wants sex every day—and wants it several times a day whenever possible. Edith, who holds the view that "a wife should make her husband omelettes even if she herself isn't hungry at all," is feeling worn out from all of her omelette-making. And so, while her sex-driven husband keeps on wanting to have sex with her, all poor Edith wants is a good night's sleep.

Lest we should think, however, that the husbands always want it while their sexless wives are always turning them down, this letter to Ann Landers from "Zero Self-Esteem in Chicago" should set things straight:

> My husband no longer finds me sexually attractive. For the past several years, he has made love to me only when I've asked. . . . I've tried discussing the problem. . . . I've begged, remained silent and cried. He told me a while back that a woman shouldn't be aggressive, so I decided to wait for him to make the first move. I'm still waiting. Next month, it will be two years since we've made love.

Another woman writes, "It was humiliating for me to ask him to make love to me, but I did. He told me he was tired and rolled over and went to sleep." A woman who signs herself "Mad" observes that "it is not normal for a man who is thirty-eight years old to be too tired for love, no matter how hard he works at his job." And "Lollypop" inquires, "Where do all the tired men come from? When I was single, I never ran into a man who was too tired for anything."

How couples handle the issue of initiating and refusing sex, say sociologists Philip Blumstein and Pepper Schwartz in their valuable book *American Couples,* can reveal an enormous amount about their relationship. It "can tell us the degree of power or dependency each partner has, and the many ways in which partners use sex to control each other."

The conventional marital pattern is (still!) for husbands—more often than wives—to initiate sex, while wives—more often than husbands—do the refusing. When the roles are routinely reversed, problems ensue, problems having to do with fears that the husband may be "abdicating his maleness" or with fears that the wife is "becoming the man of the family." The conventional pattern prevails because initiating sex is equated with dominance, and dominance is equated with being male. It also prevails because being rejected sexually feels less insulting to husbands than to wives. The reason for this? When a wife says "no," her husband can attribute her refusal to her (hypothetically) lower sex drive. But since a man is (hypothetically) ever ready for sex, his refusal to have sex with his wife is perceived as a specific rejection of *her.*

(The reality, need I remind you, is that a man isn't always up for having intercourse, which may be another reason why he does the asking.)

Given all the above, it's quite understandable that sexual equality tends to be "an elusive balancing act." But when balance is achieved, it brings good news. Husbands and wives, say Blumstein and Schwartz, are happier with their sex life when they are equally free to ask and refuse. They are happier with their sex life when they are equally sharing sexual control.

As for control of what we do, of what sex acts we engage in, *American Couples* offers this interesting finding: The less power that a wife has in her marriage, the more often she's on the bottom during intercourse. The reason for this seems to be that the person on top has more freedom to control the moves, thus being on top is associated with dominance. Thus, too, when the marital power is more equally divided, the wife will more often get her turn on top.

Oral sex—cunnilingus and fellatio—is also endowed with images of control, with some wives and husbands refusing to give it, or deeply resenting giving it, because "it" is seen as submissive and even demeaning. It's true that there are women and men who regard getting oral sex as a proof of their power. On the other hand, there are women and men who say they find tremendous power in giving it.

One husband puts it like this: "When I'm going down on her, I feel like I'm controlling her. . . . She's less in control."

One wife puts it like this: "Sometimes when I'm going down on him, I feel powerful. . . . The giving of pleasure is a powerful position."

Another wife, however, makes the nice point that oral sex can offer a sense of power to both partners. "I think he likes it so much," she says, speaking of cunnilingus, " . . . because it's the only time he controls me." But then she adds that his doing it makes her feel like an "all-powerful . . . real woman." She says, "I feel domineering when he's going down on me."

Sometimes a wife engages in uncongenial sexual acts because she, in some way, is under her husband's control. Audrey, for instance, submits to her husband's demands for anal sex because he has made it clear that, if she won't, he'll find a more compliant partner. Cassie, intimidated by her husband's complaints that their sex life is getting boring, is wrecking her back having sex on the shower floor. And Martha, at her husband's request, strikes porno poses for him while dressed like a whore in heavy makeup, stiletto heels, and a garter belt, consenting to this (for her) not especially gratifying sex because he controls the purse strings and rewards her with an enormous clothing allowance.

(One theory of why men demand that their wives dress up in costumes or uniforms, or submit to assorted perversions for their pleasure, is that they're engaged in an unconscious act of revenge, that they are re-creating—in *reversed* form—an earlier relationship where they'd been a helpless child subjected to the aggressive control of others.)

Men also, of course, may be pressured into sex acts they don't like, as demonstrated by Mr. D from Nevada, a man whose school-teaching, church-choir-singing lover insisted to him that she couldn't be sexually satisfied unless he wore his motorcycle helmet in bed. "Just how kinky is this?" a clearly concerned Mr. D inquired of Ann Landers. "I hope to marry the woman and would not like to carry on this way forever."

The control of what we do sexually can sometimes become a problem when a husband resents a wife for "constantly giving me all these touch-me-here instructions" and when, in turn, his wife resents his ignoring these instructions, his "not really giving a damn about my needs." Though women today may feel freer to come out and directly ask for what they want, a man who is insecure sexually (or whose wife is indefatigably explicit) may perceive her do-it-a-little-slower-and-ever-so-slightly-to-the-left-dear directions as insulting and demanding and . . . overcontrolling.

How often we have sex and what we do when we're in bed can surely be laced with concerns about control. So can our anxieties about losing ourselves in sex, our anxieties about totally letting go. Some women, accustomed to carefully presenting themselves to the world, to always looking attractive and composed, are afraid that uncontrolled passion will expose them in some cruelly unflattering light, will show what they're "really like," will humiliate them. Some of these women, quite capable of having thoroughly gratifying orgasms as long as they are home alone with their vibrators, cannot have orgasms with a sexual partner, even when that partner (and maybe especially when that partner) is their husband.

Bea also cannot have orgasms with her husband who, she complains, wants it too often and has too small a penis. At least, that's why she thought she couldn't come. But she's starting to understand that she holds back out of fear that her husband will try to control her, just as her mother did and still tries to do. And she's also starting to understand that her quite uncontrolling husband is not—and has no wish to be—her mother.

Eve's fear of being swept away by an "unacceptable" passion goes back to her father's sexual intrusiveness—and also to the forbidden desire she felt for her father and guiltily fended off. Today, in her marriage bed, Eve still equates unchecked desire with grave danger, a danger she avoids by never ever allowing herself to have an orgasm.

There are wives, and husbands as well, says psychoanalyst David Scharff, who fear "becoming a hostage . . . through sexual intimacy," who unconsciously fear that receiving sexual pleasure from their spouse will leave them trapped, swallowed up, or taken over. Some couples who come into treatment because bad sex is hurting their marriage may find that the marriage gets *worse* as the sex improves, that for one or both partners the body's surrender to sexual delights threatens a loss of control that feels intolerable.

In Erikson's classic "Eight Ages of Man," he characterizes the fifth stage of our development as a time when we start to consolidate our identity. In the sixth stage, the stage he calls intimacy versus isolation, he says that we acquire the capacity to fuse our identity with our beloved's. The fear of losing ourselves in sexual intimacy and orgasm can lead us to pull away from such experiences. And if we're afraid that passion can make us excruciatingly vulnerable, we are correct. But we cannot know what Lawrence calls "the wild orgasms of love," "the wild chaos of love," unless we risk dissolving the boundaries of self. We cannot know the wild ecstasy of passionate sexual love unless we risk surrendering control.

But when to surrender, and when to hold back?

When to do what, and how frequently?

How to decide if it's right to do—and with whom?

How to surrender abandonedly, while also behaving responsibly?

How to bring sex and love into the same room?

When to follow, without hesitation, our unmistakable appetites, going wherever our body demands that we go?

And when, out of cold calculation, self-preservation, self-respect, good sense, or anxiety, to ignore our body's "yes" and just say "no"?

Confronting the powers of sex we may, like Roiphe and her friends, find ourselves constantly wavering between extremes of release and self-restraint, struggling "with the desire to be wild and not wild, to be careful and not careful, to be free and not free." The sexual control that we possess and exercise over ourselves, and our lovers, will be—can be—no more than imperfect control.

5

Who Controls
the Couple?

It is almost impossible in our times to think about
love, sex, intimacy, or marriage without thinking
about power.

–Michael Vincent Miller

Abandoning ourselves to sexual passion, temporarily giving up control, is one of the greatest pleasures of married life.
But such surrender is a sometimes thing. For many of us, in the
marriage bed, still want to exert control over how much, and
what kind of, sex we engage in. And outside of bed, in the
other rooms of our marriage, control issues may arise with an
intensity and a frequency that astound us.

For when we choose a partner to love and to live with, words
like "control" and "power" do not leap to mind. Equal? Of
course we're equal, we—should anybody ask—would blithely
say. We would furthermore add that were we ever to find ourselves in conflict over which of us was going to get our way,
we'd resolve the matter civilly and equitably. Awash in romantic

sentiment, we enter a marriage or other long-term commitment unprepared for the power struggles ahead, unprepared for the fact that—out in the open or subterraneanly—we'll each be wanting, seeking, taking control.

Some of us want partial, and some of us want plenty, and none of us get perfect, but we're all concerned with having sufficient control.

We're concerned about having sufficient control over how the money is spent, and whether or not we go to the beach on vacation, and which of us is taking the car today.

We're concerned about having sufficient control over the lives of our partners—over what they do, wear, think, and say.

We're concerned about having sufficient control over our time and agenda, over when we are two and when we are one.

We're concerned about having sufficient control over the running of the marital enterprise.

We're also concerned, sometimes deeply concerned, about being controlled.

"On the basis of family life," writes Phyllis Rose in *Parallel Lives*, "we form our expectations about power and powerlessness, about authority and obedience." We bring all those expectations, and their concomitant resentments and fears and needs, into the new relationship we're creating. But we're often unaware of how our past has shaped our feelings about seizing or surrendering control. And we're often unaware, when power issues begin to emerge, that we're repeating—with our mate— our own early history.

I won't let anyone tell me what to do.

I'll do whatever you want if you swear not to leave me.

Your piece of pie is bigger than my piece of pie.

This is mine—all mine—and I'm not sharing.

Though we don't come out and speak these words, though we may not even recognize what we're feeling, our old autonomy battles, fearful dependencies, and sibling rivalries are replayed in our marital struggles over control.

"Marriage and other adult intimacies," writes therapist Michael Vincent Miller, author of a provocative book called *Intimate Terrorism*, "resurrect earlier periods of crisis in the relations between self and other, from the infant's first intimations of separateness from its parents to the adolescent's efforts to consolidate a secure identity yet remain closely connected with others."

In a psychologically perfect world we and our partner would come to each other unburdened by the need to jockey for power, free of former experiences of dominance and submission, free of the fear of being submerged or abandoned. We wouldn't have to overcontrol to make up for feeling powerless in the past. We wouldn't be linking love to abject obedience. We wouldn't be viewing our mate as a father abrogating our freedom or a grabby sister invading our precious turf. But even in the best of all worlds, a lasting love relationship encroaches on our personal control, demanding that we give in, give up, give over to another powers we might prefer to keep for ourselves. Even in the best of love relationships, we will struggle to balance power and surrender.

"Can't you just *obey?*" I only half-jokingly will say to my husband, Milton, when there's something I want him to do and he—too often, much too often—doesn't want to do it or wants to do it an entirely different way. "Must we have a discussion on this?" my husband will exasperatedly say, when there's something he wants me to do and I resist. "Why," I once moaned when we were having one of our testy exchanges over whether to pay off the mortgage (or was it what kind of vinegar to use in the salad?), "didn't both of us marry much more pliable, unopinionated people?" "Because," my husband replied, "if we'd married people who went along with whatever we wanted, we wouldn't respect them."

125

I know two couples who seem to find the power-surrender balancing act fairly painless. I've almost never seen them disagree. She tells him, "I really don't care one way or the other." He tells her, "Whatever you want is okay with me." They don't hold ferocious opinions on every subject. They rarely feel this is how it *has to* be. (I haven't yet decided if these couples are mature or simply passionless.) There are also those happy pairs —like John Stuart Mill and Harriet Taylor—whose power needs are perfectly complementary, whose longing "for the surrender of will," as Phyllis Rose shrewdly puts it, has been gratified by marrying "someone controlling." But many of us will find it surprisingly hard to allow our power to be diminished. And for some of us the surrender of certain powers may be experienced as a defeat, a humiliation, an intolerable vulnerability, a threat to our safety, a threat to our very self.

"Love makes us anxious . . . ," says Miller. "One has to lean a good ways out of the self in order to love another, and that always feels dangerous." It will feel especially dangerous if we have endured, in our past, experiences of abandonment or betrayal. But even without such experiences, "the anxiety of loving" will stir up concerns about power and control.

What's mine to decide?

What's yours to decide?

When do we make joint decisions?

Who's really in charge?

Who controls the couple?

A successful marriage, writes psychiatrist John Toews, requires us "to share intimately with the marital partner while at the same time maintaining and enhancing individual autonomy." Does this sound hard to you? It sounds hard to me. It's hard because autonomy means being free of other people's control, means independently making choices and being responsible for the choices we make. Intimacy, on the other hand, is all about commitments to other people, about shared decision making, interdependence. Comparing these two definitions, these two quite admirable—but often conflicting—states, we can see the potential for a whole lot of trouble. We can see how our inability to reconcile connection and separateness can lead, as Toews points out, to "interminable arguments, loss of all ability to negotiate constructively, and major battles"—as well as plenty of minor ones—"over issues of dominance."

Husband (leaving on business trip) to wife: "I'll see you tomorrow."

Wife to husband: "Call me when you get there."

Husband to wife: "I'll probably be too busy."

Wife to husband: "You can find time to call me."

Husband to wife: "I'll be home in twenty-four hours."

Wife to husband: "I really want you to call me."

Husband to wife: "Who the hell are you, my mother?"

All of us must deal with our ongoing conflict between autonomy and intimacy, a conflict both inside ourself and with our partner. But though this is everyone's conflict, it appears to be widely agreed that men (because of their history) tend to pursue autonomy over intimacy while women (because of their history) do the reverse. Each of these pursuits has its limitations and its benefits, its special strengths and its vulnerabilities. But it seems to me that men's emphasis on autonomy over intimacy gives them a power advantage in love relationships.

In *American Couples*, Blumstein and Schwartz discuss what is called the "principle of less interest," according to which "the person who loves less in a relationship has the upper hand because the other person will work harder and suffer more rather than let the relationship break up. This partner's greater commitment hands power to the person who cares less." Extending this thought, I'd like to suggest that, because of their greater concern with maintaining intimacy, wives—more often than husbands—may "work harder and suffer more" to preserve the relationship. And because of this greater willingness to accommodate and compromise, to choose harmony over having things their own way, wives may cede significant power to their husbands.

Judith Wallerstein, coauthor of *The Good Marriage,* describes her own daughter's reaction when offered a tenured position at a big university, a position that would require her to uproot herself and her husband, who was also an academic and whose fast-track career would be put on hold if they moved.

" 'Mom,' she explained, 'with all the equality that Ed and I have, some things are more equal than others. When women think of moving the family because of a job they want, they think about how it will disrupt the lives of their children and husband. Women take responsibility for the happiness of every-one in the family and feel guilty about uprooting them.' She sighed. 'I don't think it's fair, but it's still true. Men expect that the women and children will adjust to the moves they make. And we do.' "

Taking responsibility for the happiness of the family often requires deferring *my* needs to *ours.* Even in modern marriages, women do this—and *choose* to do this—more often than men.

For even modern marriages have need of a general manager. That manager is almost always the wife. And the kind of control she exercises may not be for power purposes, for the narrow purpose of having things her way, but for the purpose of helping the family run smoothly. Indeed, as I look around me, I find that in almost all of the families that run smoothly, the wife is doing a great deal of orchestrating.

She's mentioning to her husband that it would be nice if he called his mother to say that he wished her good luck with her colonoscopy. She's suggesting that he please not raise his eyebrows and clear his throat when his overweight daughter takes a large piece of cake. She's reminding all of the children that next Wednesday—one week from today—is their father's birthday. And she's mentioning to her oldest son that when he's playing tennis with his dad, he doesn't have to play such a killer game. A nudge, a reminder, a word to the wise, a recommendation to tone it down or apologize: her antennae are constantly out to prevent hurt feelings or to soothe someone's rotten mood. In the larger interests of intimacy and harmony, many women, without engaging in power plays, routinely engage in familial control.

Yet in spite of women's greater concern with maintaining domestic intimacy, *American Couples* presents this anomalous finding: that wives—as they grow older—want more time away from their husbands, while husbands—as they grow older— want more time together. This apparent contradiction starts to make sense, says linguistics professor Deborah Tannen, if we think of how hard it is to be the greater accommodater in the marriage. Indeed, it may be so strenuous to be constantly trying and trying to make things work that wives have much more of a need than men to seek a respite from the delights of togetherness.

A number of wives have told me how much they enjoy— when their husbands are out of town on a business trip—the pleasure of putting their preferences first, of deciding when to eat and sleep, whom to see and where to go, of controlling their schedule. They savor the freedom of suiting themselves instead of vigilantly maintaining harmony, of "going ahead and doing it without first wondering if it's okay with him." In other words, they like retrieving—if just for a little while—the power to unconnectedly, unconcernedly, unfamilialy have it *their* way.

For though women tend to be the more accommodating partner in the marriage, this doesn't mean that they don't wish to have their own way. Nor does it mean that they're martyrs or saints. And it certainly doesn't mean that they are always the

129

partner with less power. When women and men pair off, one of the pair—through some combination of nature and nurture— may clearly be stronger or weaker than the other. One (and this could be the husband) may be needier, more emotionally dependent. One (and this could be the wife) may be more at ease with running things, with taking charge. External factors— like who makes more money, or who is more attractive, or who comes from a "better" family background—can also help determine whether we feel we're in a position of weakness or strength. But weak or strong, man or woman, if we're in a close relationship we're "each wanting something from the other," says Miller, and "wanting to control the terms of getting it." Weak or strong, man or woman, we can't be in a close relationship without attempting to exercise control.

Struggles over control are very often focused on money. Even when cash is not scarce, disputes will arise. As Blumstein and Schwartz point out in *American Couples*, intimate partners "must decide what money, if any, is to be personal, what money is to be shared, who will manage the books, how much consultation is appropriate when purchases are made." And when, as they often don't, they don't agree on how the money should be handled, they have to deal with the question of which of the two has the greater control, the final say. Here is some intriguing, and sometimes surprising, information on the tricky relationship between money and power:

—In married, cohabiting, and gay couples, money bestows power, giving the higher earner the final say. Lesbian couples, however, are a "notable exception" to this rule, and Blumstein and Schwartz have a theory on why this is so. They suggest that "because women historically have not earned much money, they may be unaccustomed to using wealth to 'throw their weight around.' Men on the other hand have a long tradition of feeling they have the right to exercise control if they have proved their worth by being financially successful."

—When a wife grants her husband the power to have the final say about money, she may be unconsciously granting him other powers. She may be tacitly saying that the money he earns also gives him the final say in matters having nothing to do with finances, making him "likely to be in charge of most important decisions in the family."

—In marriages where a husband or wife believes that it is better for the man to be the provider in the household, the husband has more of a say in major decisions. A wife who subscribes to this male-provider view grants the greater power to her husband even "if she is employed full time" and *even if "she earns more money than he."*

—Though the wife of a "male provider" may decide what to spend on furniture, food, and clothes, those rights have been assigned to her by her husband. But in handing over control, he is only allowing her to act for him as his agent. Her possession of these rights should not be seen as "a sign of a more fundamental power."

—There are more fights among married couples than there are among cohabiting, gay, and lesbian couples about the ways in which the money is managed. One reason is that in marriage, "property and assets are usually commingled," making for more frequent consultations. Furthermore, even when the male provider "lets" his wife make major purchases, he always retains the right to "evaluate her performance and find it wanting."

—When both spouses work, a wife is more reluctant than a husband to pool incomes. There are several reasons for this, say Blumstein and Schwartz, "and they are all related to power." When a wife has her own account, for instance, her husband need not be aware of how much money she spends and where she is spending it. A woman who had been married before recalls, "I had to explain why and almost ask forgiveness for spending any money. And now that I've got . . . my own account and stuff, I know that I'm responsible for it and nobody else is. If I goof up, that's my problem. I don't have to rationalize or explain. I just do it."

A wife may also dislike pooling funds out of concern that her smaller contribution will totally vanish into the family "pot," with her husband still retaining the final word on how that family pot gets spent. Still, pooling is more prevalent among couples where the wife is the lower earner, says a study by psychiatrist Ann Ruth Turkel, while the separation of income is more common when the wife earns the same or more.

Looking at two-career couples, Dr. Turkel identifies four money-management styles: two pooled, two separate. In the pooled system, all of the money goes into a common pot, with sometimes the wife and sometimes the husband making the larger financial contribution. In the separate money system, there is still a common pot for basic expenses, with the husband and wife contributing either an equal amount to that pot or an amount that is proportionate to income. All of these systems, says Turkel, have plenty of room for arguments: What, exactly, is a "basic expense"? Why isn't he—or she—earning more money? How, when a wife and a husband choose to separate their money, do they handle the fact that, after each has contributed to the pot, one may be much richer than the other, allowing her, for instance, to buy Armani while he can only afford Montgomery Ward? And, when a wife and a husband pool funds, how do they handle discretionary income if they have very different spending philosophies—if, for instance, she thinks he's a tightwad and he thinks she thinks money grows on trees?

—When a wife has no separate money and her husband has the last word on how the discretionary income is to be spent, she may resort to less-than-straightforward tactics to acquire a secret slush fund of her own.

"Nate," says one such wife, "is tightfisted. It's the most unflattering part of his personality. I don't try and meet him head-on. It's not that I don't think I can get my way; it's what I have to go through to do it. I don't like to see that part of him. So I'm more the politician. I skim a little off the top! . . . Oh, I'll tell him the groceries cost more than they did, or something like that. Nothing spectacular, but it gives me a little breathing room."

Carrie adds: "And when I buy something expensive, I always pay part by credit card and part with the cash he doesn't know I have. It saves all kinds of discussions about, 'I can't believe you spent that for a lampshade.' "

—Straight or gay, cohabiting or married, couples have better relationships when the partners feel they have equal control of the money. "If either partner is *too* dominating," say Blumstein and Schwartz, "conflict occurs."

As long as one partner wants and the other possesses the power to give or to withhold, the partner who runs the money tends to dominate. That partner has traditionally been the man. But sometimes, despite the husband's breadwinner role, it is the wife who is the powerhouse, and the husband who depends on her for everything. Often, in such situations, the wife may take pains to conceal her power, and her husband may collaborate in the deception.

Sylvia, speaking of her husband, Zach: "He's so good to me. I don't know how I could have managed in life without him. I mean he's everything. I simply can't get along when he's not with me."

Zach, speaking of Sylvia: "She's really the boss in the family. . . . I couldn't manage without her to make up my mind for me. It doesn't bother me at all. But don't say anything to her about it. She likes to act as though I'm the bigshot."

Though Sylvia's emotional power far outweighs her husband's financial power, some of her younger sisters may possess both. More and more wives are working full-time and some are becoming equal—or higher—earners. Indeed, in 1996 26 percent of full-time working women were making more than their working husbands did, but whatever the size of their salary many more women now claim a larger financial say. "They do not want to dominate their men," say Blumstein and Schwartz, "any more than men want to be dominated. But they want enough power so that . . . the relationship does not always operate on their partner's terms."

For many couples, money is the primary source of conflict because of its very direct connection to power. But our sex life, our children or parents or friends, our jobs or household chores, our personal habits or tastes, our religion or politics are only a few of the dozens or maybe hundreds of other issues over which control wars can be fought. These wars aren't always won by the strong; the weak also have their strategies for obtaining significant measures of control. Indeed, weak or strong, there are many ways for women and men to get what they want from each other. Researchers have identified these different control techniques, or what some have called "taxonomies of power." Can anybody look through them—I couldn't—without admitting, "This one sounds like me"?

Manipulation, says Webster's, means "to manage or control artfully," getting what we want "by shrewd use of influence." We manipulate to obtain what we want without engaging in win-lose confrontation. We manipulate to be given what we can't—or would prefer not to—take for ourselves. Manipulation is said to be a tactic of the weak, often (though not invariably) unsavory and fraudulent and unfair. But all of us who have ever, before presenting a request, bided our time, set the scene, prepared a nice dinner, made sure that our mate was in a good mood have practiced the subtle art of manipulation. And while some may call this "sneaky" and "underhanded," others insist it's the civilized form of control.

"If you get your way as a result of having demanded it," says Tannen, "the payoff is satisfying in terms of status. You're one-up because others are doing as you told them. But if you get your way because others happened to want the same thing, or because they offered freely, the payoff is in rapport. You're neither one-up nor one-down but happily connected."

Status is an I'm-in-charge autonomy matter. Rapport is a connection, intimacy matter. To the extent that women are more invested than men in intimacy, in rapport, they may prefer to avoid making blunt demands. One of the ways to avoid this is to manipulate.

Not that husbands don't know how to manipulate. In Arlie Hochschild's *The Second Shift,* a study of the division of labor in two-job marriages, she talks about the "leisure gap" that exists between women and men, with women putting in more time than their husbands on a "second shift" of housekeeping and child care. In discussing the different male strategies for maintaining this inequity, Hochschild notes: "Many men praised their wives for how organized they were, how competent in planning." Although she grants that these compliments appeared to be sincere, she makes the point that they were "convenient" too, that "appreciating the way a wife bears the second shift can be another little way of keeping her doing it."

Both women and men can manipulate by using shrewd or crude flattery ("*You're* the one who should do it—you do it so well"). Or by letting our wishes be known ("I really need a few things from the store, but I'm so tired") without explicitly making a request. Or by setting up a third party to pass on a message ("It's hard for your wife not to have her own car") rather than delivering it ourselves. Or by gently reminding our spouse, when announcing, "My mom wants to come and visit us over

Easter," that we are owed a big one ("Weren't your folks down here from Thanksgiving straight through Christmas?").

We would never come out and say, "You owe me a big one." When our power ploy of choice is manipulation, our style is *artful* management and control.

Supplication is also perceived as a tactic of the weak. We control by pleading, "I need you to do this for me." We're helpless, we're inadequate, we're suffering, we're sick. If our needs aren't met, we might even be suicidal. In view of my desperate condition, so the supplicant's message goes, how can you possibly ask me to do so-and-so, how can you fail to give such-and-such to me?

Josh has some kind of allergy that always seems to flare up when they visit his in-laws. Daniel, whenever he vacuums, wrenches his back. Kathy, a non-career mother, nonetheless requires full-time help with the baby because otherwise she might have a panic attack. And if her husband questions this or any other demand, she might start having that panic attack immediately.

Josh gets to skip a lot of trips to his in-laws.

Daniel's wife gets to do the vacuuming.

And Kathy, the poor delicate thing, almost always gets whatever she wants.

And so does Nicole, whose fragile psychological condition has turned her psychiatrist husband into her nursemaid, devoting career and character to keeping her afloat and ultimately being destroyed by her needs. And so does Florence, whose husband—another nursemaid—is solemnly warned "that if she became excited over anything or if her emotions were really stirred her little heart might cease to beat." How sick, really, are these women? Florence, of Ford Madox Ford's *The Good Soldier*, is an outright fraud, using her "heart condition" to keep her husband (but not her lovers) out of her bed. As for Nicole, the exquisite Fitzgerald heroine of *Tender Is the Night,* she certainly was at one time desperately ill. But later? "I think Nicole is less sick than anyone thinks—" says one resentful observer; "she only cherishes her illness as an instrument of power."

Phyllis Rose talks about "the plot of female power through weakness," noting that the "suffering female demanding care has often proved stronger than the conquering male." But I have also seen men who, claiming that conflict is "churning" their ulcer or "raising my blood pressure—you're going to give me a stroke," have used their weakness to dominate their wives.

"As a mode of influencing human behavior," writes psychoanalyst Mortimer Ostow, "the display of vulnerability, weakness, and suffering is well known and often exploited." The person running the show may be Poor Little Me. But it sometimes takes a while for husbands or wives to understand that they are under the tyranny of the weak, that—though they're the seemingly powerful one, the one who always takes care of the needy partner—that partner's needs are really controlling them.

Repetition, known to some as nagging, gets us our way by wearing our partner down. The following reconstructed conversation has been provided by a self-described Nobel Prize–winning nag:

Lynne informs her husband that she thinks their kitchen ought to be renovated.

Their kitchen, he replies, is fine as it is.

Lynne waits a couple of days before observing how nice it would be if they had space enough to eat in the kitchen. All of their friends, she adds, can eat in their kitchens.

A week or so later Lynne mentions that if they only owned one of those Viking stoves with the hood, the kitchen walls wouldn't turn this greasy yellow. She adds that, having turned this greasy yellow, the kitchen walls are in urgent need of a paint job.

A week after that, Lynne notes that their kitchen floor tiles are so hard that whatever is dropped is smashed into smithereens, which, she furthermore notes, everyone tells her doesn't happen with *wood* floors. She adds that everyone's switching to a wood floor, which, she furthermore adds, would pay for itself in the money that they're currently forced to spend replacing smashed crockery.

Two weeks down the road, Lynne notes that the refrigerator is probably on its last legs, that the counter by the sink has developed a crack, that there's not enough light in the kitchen, and that furthermore the walls have gotten greasier. She adds that, since they need a new stove, a new floor, a new fridge, a new counter, and a paint job, what does he think about renovating the kitchen?

Subversion allows us to look compliant, to seem to be saying, "Whatever *you* want, darling," while actually arranging to have things our way. Subversion lets us control without seeming controlling. Instead, we simply "forget" to make a reservation we promised we would make. We "lose track of the time" and arrive too late for the movie. We "make mistakes." We "miscalculate." We "misunderstand." We procrastinate. We mess up. While sweetly agreeing to go along with whatever our darling wants, we manage to subvert his—or her—intentions.

We also use subversive control when we say, "You handle it, darling," and then—when our darling has brought home a carpet or planned our trip to L.A.—we second-guess, sniping from the sidelines. "Don't you think that rug is a little garish?" Or, "I hate the idea of changing planes in Houston." While sweetly insisting that our darling handle it, we manage to subvert her—or his—decisions, and to reassert control.

• • •

Secrecy allows us to do what our husband or wife might well object to our doing. It gives us complete control over certain decisions, major and minor, because only *we* know the decision is being made. Our secret may be that our office closes at one on summer Fridays, that we've got some extra money in the bank, that this couple we abhor (but our spouse adores) has phoned to invite us over to dinner. And though our spouse might have wanted to accept that invitation, or to say how that time or money ought to be spent, we can operate unilaterally because . . . we've kept the information a secret.

Secrets are also maintained out of fear that any admission of weakness could alter the balance of power in the marriage. A man who had lost his job used to leave his house every day in a business suit, unwilling to tell his wife that he had been fired, keeping it a secret so that his authority wouldn't be undermined while he (safe from her anxiety and sympathy) tried to figure out what to do next.

Tannen notes that many men "are keenly aware of the imbalance in power that can result from telling secrets. For one thing, those who show weakness can feel they have put themselves in a one-down position. For another, they are giving away information that could be used against them," used to put them in somebody else's control.

Fait accompli is unsecretly doing what we want to do. We present our partner with an accomplished fact. George's version of *fait accompli* is to say to his wife, "I'm going to Vegas this weekend," making it clear that Vegas is a done deal. Angela's version of *fait accompli* is to go out and make some hugely extravagant purchase, then adorably say to her husband, "Guess what you bought me!" Considerably less adorable is the wife who says, "All right, so maybe once in a while I did buy myself something. So what? I'm not entitled to it? Fuck you if I'm not entitled to it." And in a similar spirit of don't-mess-with-me *fait*

139

accompli, Vic treats himself to a vest and a shirt and some pants and then declares to his furious wife, "I work for the money . . . and I'm gonna spend it the way I want to."

Fait accompli is taking control by taking what we want without explanation, apology, or permission.

Coercion involves intimidation through various forms of psychic and physical bullying. Coercion is control with an ungloved hand. Coercive behavior includes assorted forms of private and public verbal trashing: interruption, criticism, contradiction, denigration, ridicule. Coercive behavior is also barking out orders and yelling when they're not obeyed. ("Do not underestimate," one therapist said to me, "the power of the raised voice.") Coercive control can be threats—both very specific ("If you take that job, I'll leave you") and ominously vague ("I'll make you pay"). And in its extreme and ultimate form, perfected by battering husbands like O. J. Simpson, coercive control involves acts of physical violence.

It's been said that those "who are insecure and lacking in self-confidence will be more likely to use coercive power." I don't think this is necessarily true. For coercion is also a tactic of those who've been used to having everything given to them and who see their mate as just another "thing," a thing without rights, a thing that they can do with as they please. A chilling example of this view is presented in the testimony of Nicole Brown Simpson's sister Denise Brown, offered during Simpson's trial for the murder of Nicole and her friend Ron Goldman.

> And then at one point O. J. grabbed Nicole's crotch and said, "This is where babies come from. And this belongs to me." . . . He wasn't angry when he said it. He just made it a point. He wanted it to be known that that was his.

"The individual who uses violence against his intimate partner, or even threatens to," writes Michael Vincent Miller, "strikes at the heart of the other person's separateness, eliminating her freedom of will by attacking it directly through her body. He treats his victim as an extension of himself, something that exists solely to meet his needs." He physically attacks because he believes that he is entitled to attack.

In the interest of fairness, I have to point out that women can also control through physical, as well as psychic, coercion—hitting, kicking, smashing, slashing, squeezing sensitive body parts, and worse. A husband writes to Ann Landers that every three months or so his wife—they've been married six years—will "bounce some glassware off my head" or "kick my shins black and blue" or "hit me in the mouth and cut my lip." He says that the reason "she goes off half-nuts is because I like to read or watch TV" and "she thinks I should be talking to her instead."

Reward as a tool of control can be a crass (though tacit) payoff: Do what I want and I'll buy you expensive presents. Let me have what I want and I'll give you great sex. "The better the blow job, the bigger the stone" is how one wife explains it, delicately. But another wife observes that rewards can be oral without being sexual: "I make him feel real good when he's good to me by saying stuff like, 'It's wonderful!' '*You're* wonderful!' 'I adore you!' 'You've made me so happy!' " She says that she gets what she wants because her husband feels well repaid by her almost puppy-doggish expressions of gratitude. She gets what she wants because "I give great thank-you."

In relationships where one of the partners defers to the moral authority of the other, reward can come in the form of moral approval, which grants enormous power to the person authorized to do the approving. "I am my husband's rabbi and his mirror and his judge," explains Elizabeth, who can often control what he does because, despite his great worldly success and public self-confidence, "he constantly needs to know that I think well of him."

Autocracy involves an I-know-better-than-you-do assertion of authority, a claim of a special position or expertise. We can claim control on the grounds that we're smarter, we're shrewder, we're stronger, we're older, we're a professional. We can claim more understanding of money or politics or human nature or food. We cite statistics and facts. We cite experience—"I've been doing this a long time." We cite our degrees and academic awards. We insist on having the final word on the grounds that "You don't understand the kids the way I do," or "You don't understand investments the way I do," though we may not state it quite so blatantly. We say, "Don't worry about it. I'll take care of it." We say, "It's too hard to explain—trust me on this."

Some autocrats restrict their control to certain areas of expertise, areas which their spouse will gratefully cede them. Others, however, may claim the last word on anything and everything, from where they are going to dinner that night to where they are going to live for the rest of their days. But even a total autocracy can offer gratification to both of the partners, as long as they are both agreed on the terms, as long as—for instance—one wants to be the protector and one the protected, one wants to be the leader and one the follower, one wants to be the grown-up and one the child. There won't be any control wars unless or until the protection, the leadership, the parenting begins to feel more suffocating than safe, until the submissive partner becomes dissatisfied, or deeply resentful—like Marilyn.

Marilyn was initially very pleased to be taken care of by Larry, her husband. He made her feel lovingly sheltered and secure. But over the years her perception has changed—what she once used to view as protectiveness has begun to feel a lot like domination. Larry is quite bewildered; he can't for the life of him understand what his wife is complaining about. Hasn't he always been generous and kind? But whenever he tries to remind her that he "lets her have and do whatever she wants," Marilyn screams, "You *let* me? . . . What do you mean, you *let* me?"

Superiority is based on the view, a view subscribed to by us and our spouse, that—socially or morally or in some other way —we are the finer partner in the couple. Education, cultivation, pedigree, or probity may be the basis of this "superior" status, giving us control because our spouse feels so lucky and grateful to have been chosen by us.

In such marital arrangements the attribution of "superior" is often attached to a psychic designer label, while the "lucky" partner, in contrast, is (by mutual agreement) less well credentialed: Her family arrived on the *Mayflower*; his came in steerage. She's German Jewish and he's a Polish Jew. He went to Harvard and she to a junior college. He is known approvingly as "a pillar of the community" and she has what could be called a "checkered past." There's the congressman and the woman who used to do manicures. There's the woman who stands by her man and the man who does drugs. There's Richard Gere's multimillionaire and Julia Roberts' paid-by-the-night Pretty Woman. There's the husband whose tastes run to Shakespeare, the Impressionists, and Chopin, and the wife who likes Geraldo and *Days of Our Lives.*

Is the person labeled "superior" necessarily superior? Of course not. But a shared perception may be all that's required. For as long as both partners agree that he (or she) is "inferior goods" because Harvard or the *Mayflower* or election to Congress certifies superior, the "superior" mate will have the greater control.

143

• • •

Disengagement tactics punish our partner for failing to give us what we want by withdrawing our love or approval or our presence. We sulk. We mutely shake our head in disgust. We leave the room or the house. We refuse to converse. We sit staring bleakly into the middle distance, replying, when he or she asks, "What's bothering you?" with "Nothing. What makes you think that something's bothering me?" Or maybe we break the silence to say, "If you really and truly loved me, you wouldn't ask what's bothering me. You'd know."

In his research on marriage, professor of psychology John Gottman examines a disengagement tactic called "stonewalling," noting—by the way—that some 85 percent of the stonewallers are men. He describes stonewalling as often happening "while a couple is talking. The stonewaller just removes himself by turning into a stone wall," greeting his spouse's efforts to engage him or confront him with a crushingly unresponsive "stony silence." Gottman says it is very hard to be the victim of stonewalling, especially for wives, whose heart rates soar when they are stonewalled by their husbands. Stonewalling is a powerful act that conveys "disapproval, icy distance, and smugness." In delivering the message "I am withdrawing . . . from any meaningful interaction with you," stonewalling serves as a powerful act of control.

The withholding of sex delivers another disengagement message: "Well, if I don't get what I want, then neither will you." Sex can be outright refused—"I've got a headache" or "I've got too much on my mind." Sex can be evaded by arranging to go to bed at a different time. It can also be withheld when a husband prematurely ejaculates or a wife lies unresponsively under her mate, making it frigidly, unmistakably, punitively clear that— try as he might—the earth isn't moving at all.

Our disengagement tactics control by punishing present crimes and discouraging future ones. They leave our partner feeling guilty, condemned, abandoned, humiliated, or deprived, feelings that can be either relieved or avoided by simply letting us have our way.

Negotiation—the art of the deal—lets us get our way by bargaining and compromising and horse-trading. Negotiation means giving in order to get. When only one of us wants a fourth child or wants to move from Manhattan to Seattle, we may try to get what we want by making our partner an offer he or she can't refuse. Indeed, in the best of all worlds, a wife might give up Central Park West for the Pacific Northwest if her husband will agree to that fourth child.

In addition to the major negotiations of married life, we engage in many small negotiations, cutting deals on everything from opera versus basketball to how often we have to spend time with his (or her) sister. These may seem like minor matters but to the extent that the devil (or God) is in the details, the survival of couples' relationships may depend on how well these matters can be resolved. If we're reasonably well matched we will agree on many issues—at least we'd better! Constant negotiation is a fatiguing and joyless way to live a life. But we won't agree on everything and it's also not much fun to be dancing, day after day, to another's tune. Negotiation gives some control to each partner.

Most of us, all other things being equal, would prefer to simply take—or receive—what we want, or, if we have to ask for it, to say nothing more than "This is important to me." But when, for whatever reason, unvarnished directness doesn't suffice, all of us (except for those who decide that they'll just give up) are going to resort to power tactics, tactics that can give us control of some (though not all) situations, tactics that give us some (though imperfect) control.

One particular tactic (manipulation, for example) may turn

out to be the power ploy of choice. Many of us, however, will rely on different techniques for different circumstances. There's a theory that holds that those who are perceived by themselves or others to be dominant will use a wider range of power tactics. But some of us may try one power tactic after another, after another, not out of strength but out of desperation:

Even if I had a Ph.D. in psychology,
Even if I were a diplomatic whiz,
Even if I were Queen of the Charmers and more
    irresistibly sexual
Than whoever the current reigning sexpot is,
And even if I had a fortune to squander on payoffs,
And even if I had Mafia connections,
It still would be impossible to persuade my husband,
    when lost,
To stop—please stop—the car, and ask for directions.

Even if I were collapsing from thirst and from
    hunger,
Even if I were reduced to darkest gloom,
Even if I observed, between sobs, that we should
    have arrived three hours ago
And the inn was going to give away our room,
And even if I revived all my marital grievances:
Old hurts and humiliations and rejections,
It still would be impossible to persuade my husband,
    when lost,
To stop—just stop—the car, and ask for directions.

Even if I were to throw a full-scale temper tantrum,
Even if I were to call him an uncouth name,
Even if I were to not-so-gently note that should we
    wind up getting divorced,
He would have nobody else but himself to blame,

And even if I, in a tone I concede is called screaming,
Enumerated his countless imperfections,
It still would be impossible to persuade my husband,
   when lost,
To stop the goddamn car, and ask for directions.

When even our strongest power tactics fail, it is difficult to have a sense of control.

On the other hand, psychologist David Kipnis, who has done several studies of power, observes that when strong power tactics *succeed,* this success "increases the powerholder's sense of control." In examining how the successful use of power can transform our view of the world—the "metamorphic effects of power"—Kipnis and his colleagues found that husbands or wives "who believed that they controlled the decision-making power in the marriage . . . devalued the worth of their spouses." Kipnis also found that, along with this lowered view of their spouses, husbands' or wives' "unilateral control of decision-making power was associated with less affection, [and] less satisfaction with sexual relations."

Some studies of the relationship between power arrangements and marital satisfaction conclude that the happiest marriages are those in which the decision making is shared. Some studies also show that the unhappiest of marriages are those in which the wife controls the decisions. In contrast to Kipnis's findings, however, other studies have found rather high levels of satisfaction in marriages in which the husband dominates, perhaps—it has been suggested—because this man-on-top power arrangement meshes with conventional expectations. To all the above, add this: A group of studies suggests that happiness in marriage may depend primarily not on whether he or she has more control but rather on whether, in exercising control, the controller relies on the carrot or the stick.

• • •

Sometimes it's clear that the husband or the wife controls the couple, having—in most matters—the last word. Sometimes it's hard to figure out who controls whom. Sometimes we're certain we've figured it out, and then we discover we've erred—that, unlikely as it seems, the marital partner who is constantly, boundlessly giving has far more power than the partner who takes, the taker having been reduced to a state of abject I-can't-live-without-you dependency.

Sometimes the balance of power shifts back and forth, and back and forth, between the partners.

Take, for instance, Harriet and Roger, whose favored styles of control are supplication (hers) and coercion (his). He verbally attacks her and she "makes herself into nothing," apologizing and begging for forgiveness, so devastated (so it seems) by his yelling and criticizing that her suffering makes him feel extremely guilty. And so, out of guilt and a wish to atone, Roger gives in to Harriet's demands, and she becomes the one with the greater power, a state of affairs that lasts until Roger, in his one-down position, begins to feel submissive and humiliated. After which he resumes his attacks by verbally abusing her, criticizing and hollering while she grovels and apologizes until . . .

Harriet and Roger keep reversing their power positions. Sometimes, however, there is a permanent switch.

Look at the doll-wife Nora, in act 1 of Ibsen's *A Doll's House*, "twittering" and "scampering" and playing the adorable "little featherbrain" as she begs her husband, Torvald, to give her money: "Oh, *do*, Torvald . . . please, please do!" And contrast her with the newly self-aware, now-powerful Nora of act 3, commanding that same husband, "Sit down here, Torvald—you and I have a lot to talk over. . . . No, you mustn't interrupt—just listen to what I have to say. Torvald, this is a reckoning."

It is indeed.

She tells him, "I've lived here like a pauper. . . . I've lived by performing tricks for you, Torvald. That's how you wanted it."

She tells him, "It's no good your forbidding me anything any longer."

She tells him, "I believe that before everything else I'm a human being—just as much as you are. . . ."

She tells him, "I can't stay here with you any longer."

Torvald at first responds to Nora in his usual patronizing, autocratic way, with "You're out of your mind." And, "But this is disgraceful." And, "Oh, you're talking and thinking like a stupid child." But soon he comes to recognize the truth of her assertion that "I've never seen things so clearly and certainly." As Nora, slamming the door behind her, goes bravely forth to stand on her own two feet, and as Torvald is forced to face how much he needs her, the balance of power shifts—this time forever.

Whatever the balance of power, says Phyllis Rose in *Parallel Lives*, "every marriage is based upon some understanding, articulated or not, about the relative importance, the priority of desires, between its two partners. Marriages go bad," she concludes, "not when love fades . . . but when this understanding about the balance of power breaks down."

But even the best of relationships may be characterized by a shifting balance of power, as dependencies and competencies and the losses and gains of life diminish or increase our realm of control. And even in relationships where the partners share the power, they will not possess equal power over everything. Sharing the power means that both of the partners agree on how it should be divided, and that both intend the division to be fair. It means that they can relinquish control and defer to each other's wishes, confident that their turn will come, that they're not being taken advantage of, that their quid will be answered by an equivalent quo.

Power is sometimes equally shared even in traditional forms of marriage, where the wife runs the home and the husband makes the money. A wife's emotional power can often balance and even outweigh (as with Zach and Sylvia) the power derived from her husband's provider role. But for a commitment to power sharing, for conscious out-in-the-open egalitarianism, there is probably nothing (in theory, at least) like the companionate marriage, where, as defined by Wallerstein and Blakeslee in *The Good Marriage,* every issue is "settled by negotiation and compromise," and fairness is "far more important than exactly how the chores were allocated."

The companionate marriage is based on the "shared belief that men and women are equal partners in all spheres of life and that their roles . . . are completely interchangeable. . . . Whose career will be given priority? How will we take turns? Who will make the financial decisions? Will we have a joint bank account or separate accounts? Will she keep her maiden name, and if so, what will be the children's last name? All of the questions of contemporary married life are . . . examined closely and resolved in the light of principles—sometimes very abstract principles—of equality and fairness."

Now this all sounds very nice, but has it eliminated marital control wars? No, it has not. For many spouses, says Arlie Hochschild in *The Second Shift,* give earnest lip service to egalitarianism while remaining deeply resistant underneath.

"My mother was wonderful, a real aristocrat," says Nancy, a social worker married to Evan, a salesman. "My dad treated her like a doormat. . . . I grew up bound and determined not to be like her and not to marry a man like my father."

But Evan, although committed in theory to sharing the household chores, feared that Nancy would dominate him if he did. He also refused to agree to a specific clear-cut division of the duties (the "I'll cook Mondays . . . you cook Tuesdays" routine), on the grounds that he found such schedules too rigid. And so, in this pressured household of two full-time workers and one little boy, he promised to carry his load of the cooking and laundry—and then, to Nancy's annoyance and disappointment and resentment and outright rage, he messed up and "forgot." Eventually, all of her other tactics having failed to change the situation, Nancy tried to control his behavior through sex.

She says: "When I was a teenager, I vowed I would *never* use sex to get my way with a man. It is not self-respecting; it's demeaning. But when Evan refused to carry his load at home, I did, I used sex. I said, 'Look, Evan, I would not be this exhausted and asexual every night if I didn't have so much to face every morning.' "

Evan, however, continued not to shape up.

The ensuing marital tensions threatened to end in separation. Nancy surrendered. She wanted the marriage more than she wanted her way. "Why wreck a marriage," she asked herself, "over a dirty frying pan?" And besides, "Women always adjust more, don't they?"

The answer to that is usually—but not invariably.

Indeed, when Adrienne felt that her husband, Michael—by failing to help her with the housework—was failing to support her career ambitions, she refused to adjust. Instead, she "exploded in a burst of fury and tears. Why did *his* day entitle him to rest? Didn't *her* day count too?" She told him that if he "couldn't bring himself to value her career ambitions as he valued his own, if he couldn't symbolically express this by sharing housework, she . . . would leave." And when Michael turned her down she followed through on that major power ploy: she left.

Michael, who loved his wife and wanted her back, was forced to reconsider his views. The marriage, with Michael now doing his share, resumed.

But despite the social transformations that have produced what Miller calls "a tougher, more explicitly independent breed of women," marital power arrangements display odd inequities. Hochschild, for instance, finds that "the more severely a man's identity is financially threatened—by his wife's higher salary, for example—the less he can threaten it further by doing 'women's work' at home." Thus some husbands will decline to help with the housework as "a way of balancing the scales with their wives" when they feel that their wives, professionally or otherwise, have gained "too much" power.

Wives engage in the same kind of power balancing, says Hochschild, pointing to Nina, a beautiful and successful business executive, who "*made up* for outearning [her husband] Peter and inadvertently injuring his male pride" by doing most of the second shift herself. Another woman, an M.D. who was earning far more money than her musician husband—and who was a staunch feminist in every other matter—handled all of the house care and child care because she felt "that her status was 'too great' for their joint notion of the 'right' balance." What should we make of this? Hochschild concludes that "more crucial than cultural beliefs about men's and women's *spheres,* were couples' beliefs about the right degree of men's and women's *power.* Women who 'balanced' felt 'too powerful.' Sensing when their husbands got 'touchy,' sensing the fragility of their husbands' 'male ego,' not wanting them to get discouraged or depressed, such women restored their men's lost power by waiting on them at home."

It seems then that even though more and more couples aspire to egalitarian marriages, "entanglements of love and power" persist in these—as in all other—couples arrangements.

Why?

Because of our early experiences with authority and powerlessness.

And because of our ongoing struggle between the conflicting pulls of autonomy and intimacy.

And because of the collision between our romantic expectations and the flesh-and-blood facts of daily married life.

And because of the many differences that exist between even the most well-matched of partners.

And because of the differences between women and men.

And because—like everyone else—we want to have, and think we ought to have, our way.

All of the above are entangled with love in every marriage, including those based on beliefs in equality. And no matter what form our marriage takes, they are bound to set us asking (though with differing degrees of frequency), "Am I getting what I want? Am I getting what I deserve? Am I getting enough?"

Such questions arise more urgently when we enter into a relationship with the fear that "If I drop my guard, I'll be hurt." Or the fear that "Give her an inch and she'll take a mile." Or a devalued sense of self that pumps itself up by putting other people down. Or a commitment (usually futile) to making major alterations in our partner. Or an absolute conviction that we possess *the* right perception of reality, a perception we insist that our partner share. Or a family background where Father always knew best or Mother always ruled the roost, a model of patriarchal or matriarchal power arrangements that we are driven to repeat or avoid.

But even without undue psychological burdens, intimate partners will struggle over control, spending much time and effort trying to get each other to act as they desire. These struggles, though sometimes center stage, are often off in the wings, discreet and subtle. These struggles need not be acknowledged or ever discussed. Nor will we necessarily, when employing some power ploy, actually admit to ourselves what we're doing. Nevertheless, says psychologist Althea Horner, the fact that "the marital relationship is in large part a self-contained system" is bound to make it "a hothouse for the flowering of power politics." Or as a psychoanalyst friend of mine once wryly observed, "Marriage is war carried out by other means."

153

The more committed we are to this bigger-than-both-of-us marital structure we are creating, the more carefully we'll conduct our marriage control wars. The more conscious we are of the power tactics we're using, the more wisely we'll select our weapon of choice. Two of us trying to share a life cannot escape the fact that we're two different people, with different histories, dreams, fears, interests, needs. Nor can we escape the fact that when these differences clash, we will not always succeed in getting our way. Even the strongest sometimes have to surrender. Even the weakest have a few power ploys. And even the happiest couples are going to learn that the simple joys of married life are not that easy to come by (or that simple), that the joys of married life are often intermeshed with struggles for control.

6

Permanent Parenthood

At this very moment, some . . . sons are probably on
the phone to their mothers . . . , calling from their
medical clinics, law offices, their banks. Plenty of
these are respected men who can often be heard
yelling into the receiver, "Ma, would you stop it
already!"

—*The Wall Street Journal*

Parenthood as a psychobiologic process ends only
with the death of the parent.

—Therese Benedek

As part of a married couple or (through death, divorce, or
choice) as a single parent, we invest many years of our life in
raising our children, giving them more and more freedom to
make their own decisions and their own mistakes, giving up
more and more parental control. We salute their independence,
show respect for their autonomy, and actively encourage their
separation, telling ourselves, as they fashion their futures in
ways we don't necessarily adore, "This is *their* life, not ours."

That, anyway, is how the scenario is supposed to play out as we move from young to not-so-young mothers and fathers and as our children acquire mustaches, breasts, degrees, and families of their own. We know it would be unseemly to ask them to follow our agendas, or tell them what they should and shouldn't do, or proffer unsolicited advice, or expect them to abide by that advice. We know it would be unseemly to try to control our adult children.

We may try anyhow.

At one point in the meddlesome life of a fictional busybody named Brenda Kovner, she becomes convinced she is dying of a brain tumor. Unable to bear the vision of her children, their mother gone, trying to manage without her helpful suggestions, she writes a series of letters to be opened and read by them—after her death—on birthdays well into the twenty-first century.

"Full of warmth and wisdom"—this is Brenda talking now—"these letters provided motherly guidance as my boys passed through their teens, twenties, thirties, and forties: Don't slouch. Don't mumble. Help the needy. To thine own self be true. Marry for character rather than for breasts. Never give up on poetry. Floss now or be sorry later. And do not forget that your mother, though dead, still loves you."

Reaching beyond the grave to try to run the lives of our children may, even to control freaks, seem overreaching. On the other hand, it's quite appealing, too. For our children, in their growing-up years, were very much in need of our caretaking skills. We knew what was best for them then. We think we still do. And although, as they have grown older and up, they are done (or so they insist) with being children, we mothers and fathers don't feel that our job is through. They may be children no longer—but we remain in a state of permanent parenthood.

We continue to feel responsible for their happiness.

We continue to ache and bleed when they feel pain.

We want to protect them from major, and minor, disasters.

We feel compelled to remind them to water their plants and to never wash light and dark laundry together and to leave themselves enough time so they won't miss their train.

And if anything should go wrong, in either their laundry or their life, we yearn to fix it and kiss it and make it better.

We want to guide them and shield them, to exert some degree of what might be called control.

Note: This year I received a Mother's Day card that pictured a mother driving a car, her son in the passenger seat and her outstretched arm protectively flung across his chest. I've heard a great deal from my sons about my overprotective tendencies but I think that this card's message said it best. The message said, "To Mom, the original seat belt."

Why can't we always be our children's seat belts?

As the parents of adult children, we may look back fondly on our first decade of child-raising when, despite the battles over toilet training and bedtime and wearing their mittens, we basically felt that *we* were in control. (We were, after all, essential to their survival, plus undeniably stronger and, usually, smarter.)

Even in our second decade of parenthood, despite the battles over cars and curfews, we felt that we were still—though not all the time, and often quite shakily—in control. (We did, after all, possess more money and power, plus legal authority and the keys to the car.)

But in our third decade of parenthood, despite their lack of experience and their imperfect grasp of the pitfalls and perils of the world, our daughters and sons officially become grown-ups and we are supposed to let *them* take control.

We may find it hard to believe that they are ready for this.

Do they grasp the urgency of health insurance? Are they sufficiently terrified of AIDS? Will they eat fruits and vegetables and always wear their seat belts and remember never to open their door to strangers? We shudder as they announce their plans to move to a high-risk neighborhood, to quit their job without another lined up, to marry a person whom anyone but a lovesick fool would recognize as BIG TROUBLE. We shudder at some of their choices, and we don't simply shudder, of course —we are frequently impelled to express our views, incapable of choosing, in what we regard as highly threatening situations, to back off, butt out, shut up, give up control.

We confess to a broad definition of "highly threatening."

Psychologist Angela Barron McBride has written about parental "savior tendencies" and about our fears that our kids will make "big-time mistakes." She has written about our distress at being displaced from "decision-maker" to (at the very best) "valued consultant." She has written about our feeling unappreciated, irrelevant, and ignored. And she has written about how hard it is to acknowledge our children's separateness and maturity.

Though Dr. McBride's observations were intended for the parents of teenage children, the issues that she raises have no time limits. The mothers quoted below, for instance, most of them over seventy-five years old, remind us of how permanently invested we can be in the lives of our "kids."

"We want things for our children," says Rose Fichtelberg, "that they don't even know they want."

"That's our problem," says Rita Kingsley, "we're too devoted, too concerned, we never let go."

"My son," says Evelyn Noloboff, "says, 'Ma, don't worry about me.' I tell him, 'Listen, my pleasure is worrying.' "

She also says, "Everyone needs someone to watch over them."

Small wonder then that many respected, competent, grown-up *middle-aged* men (and women) are still yelling into the receiver, "Ma, would you stop it already!"

"Respecting your adult children as adults, as separate individual human beings who are entitled to make decisions on how they will live their lives, is the single most important task to master if you are to move out of old parent-child interactions," write therapists Jean Davies Okimoto and Phyllis Jackson Stegall in their book *Boomerang Kids.* "It's a job so difficult," they add, "that many parents never quite get there."

While Brenda, Rose, Rita, and Evelyn are, all of them, Jewish mothers, the wish to control our children is not restricted to one religion or one gender. And although we may want to control them in order to gratify important needs of our own, we are likely to persuade ourselves that we're doing what we're doing for their own good. And if, in fact, we can make an urgently helpful contribution to our children's health or happiness or well-being, is it so bad to be a little controlling?

Item: Kay and Jason can't stand the difficult woman their son is living with, a beautiful brittle journalist who, because of her own damaged background, views all families as "toxic" and keeps making him choose between his family and her. "We've always been really close," Jason says. "And we've always done things together—vacations, the holidays. But she insists they make separate plans of their own." Says Kay, "Forget about us. She resents the time he spends with his sister—and they adore each other. Or at least they did until this . . . bitch came along." Kay and Jason see their son's live-in love as a serpent in their familial paradise. They also see her as bad news for their son. "This woman is going to isolate him from all the people who love him, and I think that is a tragedy," says Kay. Before he does something permanent, like marry her, shouldn't they warn him?

Item: My middle son's living-room window opens directly onto a burglar-accessible fire escape. We know it is burglar-accessible because a burglar has already accessed it, stripping his apartment of every valuable from his TV to his suits and inflicting no bodily harm on him only because (as I was quick to point out) he wasn't at home. I have established, through research, that my son can purchase a window gate that bars entry into the room without barring exit, which means that he can keep burglars out while easily escaping in case of fire. He tells me he is not interested in purchasing this gate, nor will he accept it as a gift, although he expresses regret that his lack of a gate has been causing me many sleepless nights. But perhaps he will change his mind if I bring up the subject, and bring up the subject, and bring up the subject, every single time we talk on the phone. How, then, can I possibly stay silent?

Item: Alma's only daughter who, at the age of thirty-one, is still trying to find herself, asked Alma to have a joint session with her therapist. One hour with this woman left Alma appalled. "She's indulging my daughter's dependencies, she tells me I expect too much of 'this child,' she is calling my daughter 'this child'—can you believe it!" Alma, who says that the therapist is "infantilizing my daughter when she really ought to be helping her grow up," would like to tell her daughter—no, would like to *urge* her daughter—to get a new therapist. Mustn't she do it?

Along with wanting to guide our children on how they ought to live, we have many opinions on how they should raise our grandchildren, opinions that we hold with a great deal of certainty, opinions that we believe could be illuminating, opinions that (alas) our grandchildren's parents haven't invited us to share.

Like, a baby should not be picked up whenever he cries.

Like, a child needs her bottom smacked when she runs into the street.

160

Like, maybe if they gave their two-and-a-half-year-old more to eat, he would not be in the lowest percentile for weight.

We also have some thoughts about three-year-olds who sleep with their parents and almost-four-year-olds who are still in diapers. And one of us wants to ask the lawyer mother and lawyer father who are working so hard to make partner that they see their son about fifteen minutes a week, "Will you just remind me again why you had him?" She isn't going to say this, of course, nor does a grandpa I know intend to suggest to his daughter that she should think about weaning her son (ha, ha) before high school. But when we see what seems to be suffocation, outright neglect, insensitivity, or overindulgence, can't we say *something*?

There are those who would strongly argue that Kay and Jason and Alma and I, and all the grandparents, shouldn't say anything. But some of us did. For it's difficult keeping our mouths shut when we're convinced that speaking out could help our kids, even when our opinion has not been solicited. And although we're prepared to grant that adults (including our adult children) are entitled to eat and sleep and dress exactly as they wish, to choose their political party and their religion, to make their own decisions regarding their work and their friends and their lovers and their spouses, and to spend their money and raise *their* kids as they please, we still feel compelled to intrude when we are sure that they are risking or ruining their lives, or doing irreparable damage to our grandchildren.

We don't need anyone telling us why we shouldn't intervene. We know why we shouldn't.

We know they must be responsible for their lives. We know they must face the consequences of their actions. We know they need to learn from their mistakes. We know they won't learn if we don't let them make mistakes. We know all this but we can't stand by and let them go down the tube. So whether or not they want our help, and whether or not they want to call it control-

161

ling, we may—because it's good for them, not because we're intrusive—intrude on our children.

WARNING! DANGER! PROCEED AT YOUR OWN RISK, I sometimes write in letters to my sons. EVERYTHING THAT FOLLOWS WILL BE ADVICE. I figure that they can't resist reading what follows. I know I can't resist writing it, because I'm so certain it's all for their own good.

Yes, the control we attempt to exercise may be for that noblest of reasons—their own good. But we may be mistaken about what that "good" should be, pushing them in directions that we —not they—believe it's important for them to go in, pushing them because we're sure we know what's right for them, even if (at least in our view) *they* don't.

Another reason for wanting to control our adult children involves our competitiveness and vanity, because, as McBride notes, "the child is the parents' report card" and we aspire to an "A." In trying to get that "A," we may burden our children with perfectionist expectations, making it clear which career, which mate, which qualities of character—even which weight—would do us proud. We may burden them, as well, observes psychiatrist Norman Kiell, with our own stifled hopes and blunted aspirations, becoming one of those parents who wishes "to see his unfulfilled dreams realized through his seed."

A mid-thirties woman, who recently left her law career to become a grade-school teacher, tells me she hated lawyering right from the start. "But my father made it something I *had* to do. Challenging him was simply not in my repertoire," she explains, because she very well knew that if she followed her own inclinations, he would disown her.

She couldn't leave the law, she says, until she could live with the fact that he would disown her.

There are indeed parents who, when their children don't live as they want them to live, decide to cut them completely out of their hearts, not because these children are in any sense "bad" people but because, as one woman put it, "this is not the kind of child I had in mind." There are parents who turn their back on a child who marries "out of the faith." There are parents who repudiate a child who chooses an interracial partner. Same-sex orientation can also be a source of parental alienation, with one father actually saying, upon hearing that his daughter was a lesbian, "You're dead. You should be dead. I prefer you dead."

Brett, a concert pianist, says that since telling his parents that he was gay, "they've never invited me to their gatherings. They don't invite me for holidays. They don't call. It's hard to be the ideal son one day and an embarrassment the next. It's as if I'm not a person to my parents anymore." Brett concludes: "I guess my parents could love me only as long as they could . . . show off my musical awards, my trophies, and photos. . . . Maybe they only saw me as an appendage—as a way of making up for their own failures."

And maybe they, and all of these get-out-of-my-sight-forever rejecting parents, could not accept children whose lives they could not control.

Controlling our children may also serve to maintain our sense of importance, allowing us to cling to what some of us view, says psychotherapist Ruth Caplin, as "the most important position of our life."

Caplin speaks of our children's "flattering dependence, their respect for our superior wisdom and experience, the sense— theirs and ours—that they cannot live without our ministrations," noting that mothers who mother full-time may have the greatest difficulty in losing and letting go of such gratifications. Thus some may continue "ministering" to their often exasperated adult children, telling them when they need haircuts, reminding them that it's time for their dental check-up, urging a little more blusher upon their daughters, urging perkier ties upon their sons, arriving at their apartments with their rubber gloves and Easy-Off, determined to give that filthy stove a good cleaning, rearranging linen closets, rearranging furniture—seeking to retrieve what one woman called "that bliss of early parenthood, when they needed you so much and clung to you so much and thought that everything you did was perfect."

Even those of us who weren't mothering full-time sometimes still miss that bliss of early parenting, of being—as I was for a while—the One and Only Indispensable Mommy. The mommy who put on the Band-Aids. The mommy who buttered the bread. The mommy in "I want Mommy" and "Mommy's home." The mommy who was expected to instantly leap out of the shower and get off the phone when she heard her child call her. And while all of that need and dependence were often encroaching and sometimes oppressive, there were, in exchange, some exceedingly sweet payoffs. As a friend of mine once observed, "My son was the only one in my life who squealed with delight whenever I entered a room."

Why wouldn't we miss that!

Erik Erikson's seventh stage in his "Eight Ages of Man" is called generativity versus stagnation, with generativity seen as our "establishing and guiding the next generation" and stagnation as the "personal impoverishment" that results when we fail to invest in concerns beyond our own selves. Erikson observes that a mature person needs to be needed, and generativity fulfills that need. But the question that many parents, many *mothers*, have to answer, says Ruth Caplin, is, "When does something that was absolutely yours stop being a part of you—your responsibility, your glory, your pain, yours to control?"

There's another question—it's an old joke—that asks, "When does life begin?" the final answer to which is, "Life begins when the children leave home and the dog dies." But for many mothers this is no laughing matter. The departure of the children, writes psychoanalyst Paul Dewald, "is a particularly stressful period for the mother who has devoted a major portion of her activity and energy to childrearing. Unless suitably equipped to participate in other forms of activity and interest, she may feel useless and unneeded."

Psychoanalyst Therese Benedek talks about "the overinvolvement of mothers in their married children's lives" as a response to not being needed by them, "a defense against and overcompensation for such depressing feelings." Rather than trying to interfere *less* when their children strike out on their own, such mothers, Benedek says, "want to be involved in every detail of their new life." In their wish to remain indispensable, however, they may turn into domineering know-it-alls, intruding themselves into everything, expecting their opinions to be deferred to and becoming unwelcome guests in their children's homes.

I recently witnessed this scene at the Cleveland airport:

Grandma comes off the plane, eagerly rushes toward her grandchild, and sweeps the smiling six-year-old into her arms. "It's wonderful to see you. I love you to pieces. I love you so much. I—what in the name of God have they done to your hair!" Upon which, her son steps forward, glaring and saying with great irritation, "Mom, just keep your mouth shut. Don't start in."

I can't say whether that mom was feeling useless and unneeded and prompted by depression to interfere. I do know, however, that having a full-time career is no guarantee that parents will refrain from giving advice or trying to run the lives of their grown children, sometimes demanding from them the same kind of you're-the-boss obeisance they get in the workplace, and sometimes (if they are powerless in the workplace) trying to run their children precisely because they cannot run anything else. In addition, some parents regard their children, including their adult children, as their property, rather than separate people with rights of their own. As analyst Harold Blum points out, there is "no commandment to 'Honor Thy Son and Thy Daughter,' no commandment that parents should show their children respect. Without this respect for their separateness, they may feel entitled to script their children's lives—and may never acknowledge the need to relinquish control.

Some of these parents go to astounding extremes.

There's the multimillionaire who installed his oldest son as head of the family business, but insisted on being consulted at every turn, throwing him out of the business—and then suing him!—when he dared to make a decision on his own.

There's the mother who—without his permission—put an ad for her unmarried son in the Personals, describing his virtues as only a mother could, touting him (somewhat excessively) as handsome, successful, and charming—and good to his mother —and inviting marriage-minded maidens to contact him.

And then there's the father who asked his son's fiancée to come to his office, where he unabashedly told her to end the engagement. "Your family's too poor and your thighs are too fat," he informed her. "I think my son can do a whole lot better."

Most parental controllers have more polished, more tactful techniques for conveying their wishes. They suggest instead of demand, they hint at the costs of disobedience, the advantages of doing things their way. But although they may not be as brutal as that father who trashed his son's stunned fiancée, they're just as invested in their own agenda. And they can—in their own charming way—be just as controlling.

And, in some situations, so can we.

In some situations.

For no matter how sincerely we try to support our children's autonomy, we sometimes *know* that our way is better than theirs. And no matter how sincerely we try to treat them as full-fledged adults, they're still our kids. And no matter how sincerely we try to respect their freedom to decide for themselves, we may feel profoundly disturbed by their decisions.

Consider Joseph Brazzi, whose only son is the very first Brazzi to go to college and also the very first Brazzi to own his own home. But his son, alas, is also going to be the very *last* Brazzi, because he and his wife have decided they're not having children. Says Joseph: "I tell them, nicely, politely, that if they don't have kids, they could be sorry someday. But what I want to say, and not so nicely or politely, is, 'Get in that goddamn bed and make me a grandson.' "

Even when we and our children seem to be sharing the same set of premises, their choices may still be quite uncongenial to us, as Jane Adams confesses ruefully when she talks about her relationship with her daughter in her wise and funny book, *I'm Still Your Mother:*

"Our politics, values, and lifestyles are remarkably similar," she writes, but "she and I are not peers. . . . And when as an adult she makes decisions that will have major life consequences —about career, marriage, children, health—I am galled to discover that it's just as hard to let her make them herself, particularly if I think they're the wrong ones, as it must have been for my mother."

It's just as hard for *us* not to control.

Still, some of us manage not to control as long as our children are living outside our orbit. If we don't know what they're up to (driving in blizzards, snorting coke) how can we fret? But the minute they come for a visit, the minute they're staying under our roof (if just for a weekend), some of us may find ourselves getting bossy and overprotective and hyperparental. And, if an adult daughter or son should move back home for an extended stay, we may really regress.

Some sample conversations from the summer a son of mine

167

(I'm not saying which one) lived at home after being out on his own:

"Please take a sweater with you. I know it's ninety-seven outside. But inside that movie theater it will be freezing."

"No, Mom."

"Guacamole, chips, and a bowl of ice cream is an irresponsible lunch."

"Stop, Mom."

"I'm not being nosy—I just want to know if you're sleeping at home tonight. How else can I tell, when you're not back at four in the morning, whether or not I need to call the police?"

"Mom, I love you a lot, but I've got to get out of here."

But whether or not we're full-time controllers, or part-time controllers, or just-when-they're-home controllers, we are probably sometimes impelled to control our grown children. And many of the same tactics that spouses use to control each other will also work intergenerationally. Two control techniques that parents (including ourselves, perhaps) have found to be particularly effective are the giving and the withholding of money and the strategic application of guilt.

We may, for instance, try to exert what some call checkbook control. This old strategy is tried and true. It involves our using money to keep our children dependent upon us and to get them to do what it is we want them to do. We may even write our checks to them without exacting any quid pro quo, but our silent demands—unspoken and sometimes unconscious—will nonetheless succeed in coming through: Do what I say. Please continue to need me. Let me tell you how to live your life.

"I supported my daughter," says the father of a twenty-six-year-old, "until I cottoned to the fact that I was afraid that if she didn't need me anymore, she wouldn't have any reason to stay connected to me. I told her I would only pay for college if she went to the state university, a few miles away, instead of the school she wanted, at the other end of the country. Later I wouldn't let her live in the only apartment she could afford. I told her it wasn't safe and talked her into a more expensive place she could only manage with my help."

Another parent adds that when you're writing your grown child a check, "You have to ask yourself, 'Who am I doing this for?' And if it's for you, not them, you shouldn't be writing it."

We surely control through money when we give it or withhold it, lend it interest-free or at 7 percent, offer it to one child and deny it to another, on the basis of whether we like how our kids plan to use it. We might, for instance, say yes to a treadmill and no to liposuction, yes to a new computer and no to new ski boots, yes if they're going back to school to get an M.B.A. and no if they're going around the world to find themselves, yes if they're buying a house on our coast and no if they're buying a house on the other coast, yes if they do what we want and no if they don't.

My husband and I, for instance, would be happy to go into hock if any son of ours should want to give up his current career and become a doctor. No son would get a penny from us, however, if he got a sudden urge to acquire a motorcycle.

I guess that's a kind of control, but we think that we're nicer than Matty's father who, complained Matty, "called me a 'good for nothing' " because she decided to be an artist. Blaming her psychotherapist for her choice of a career, he then exerted his brand of checkbook control, announcing that he wouldn't pay for any further therapy unless she found "a different kind of therapist."

We can also, by how much money we leave and whether it's left free and clear or tied up in trusts, try—like letter-writing Brenda Kovner—to reach beyond the grave to control our children. Says one furious middle-aged child, "He doled out his money to me cent by cent while he was alive. And now that he's dead, I'm left with this spendthrift trust and these two damn trustees, doling out his money to me cent by cent."

Therapist Heidi Spencer, who has written a useful guide for the parents of children in therapy, is familiar with manifestations of checkbook control. She notes that "if a parent has an unconscious [or, I would add, conscious] need to control or manipulate the adult child, this tendency often becomes evident in relation to financial matters."

To control our children through money, we need to have money. But controlling through guilt is an option open to all. And while its more blatant, outrageous expressions are found less in life these days than they are in old jokes ("Marry whoever you want. It's up to you to decide. Now excuse me while I stick my head in the oven"), controlling our children through guilt remains for many, many of us the ultimate weapon.

"It's quite okay with me, but your dad will be heartsick."

"I'm not angry. I'm just . . . disappointed."

"You only should come if you want to come but remember, we may not have that many years left."

"I haven't had a good night's sleep ever since you moved into that apartment."

We're willing to grant that guilt control is unconscionable. But sometimes it is (or seems to be) unavoidable.

For how else do we make them show up for our anniversary?

How else do we persuade them to reconsider becoming a therapeutic masseuse?

How else do we get them to spend an entire week of their two-week vacation visiting us?

How else do I finally get him to put a safety gate on his window to keep out the burglars?

Making our children feel guilty because they are causing us such anxiety—can't sleep, can't eat, my blood pressure has gone through the roof—is surely a way of exerting guilt control. So is generating guilt, as some older parents do, by complaining, "My life is so empty," and leaving no doubt that their kids are supposed to fill it up with daily telephone calls and other attentions. There is also disapproval guilt, which sometimes is simply evoked by the flaring of the nostrils, or one raised eyebrow. And then there is heavy-duty guilt—the bring-out-the-big-guns guilt —which, it seems, is not entirely outmoded.

Alfred, a German refugee, wants his children and grandchildren with him at Passover and he always does his best to make sure they're there, responding to every excuse—"I've got a case in court the next day" or "It's my due date"—with a reproachful "For this I lived through Auschwitz?"

Eunice's Irish version of the heavy-duty guilt trip, whenever her daughter refuses to do things her way, is to sigh, lift her eyes to heaven, and solemnly say to some Unseen Listener, "Maybe it was for the best that her father died young—at least he was spared moments like this."

But while guilt is a burden we parents may lay on our children, it is also often a burden we lay on ourselves, a burden we claim as ours whenever our adult daughters and sons are having difficulties. Convinced that we had complete control of the outcome, we claim complete responsibility, holding ourselves accountable for their failings, insisting "you shouldn't blame my kid—blame me," flagellating ourselves for their current sufferings, and sifting, sifting, sifting through the past to figure out where we went wrong:

> Quality time and vitamin C and a book before
>   bedtime at night,
> I did everything right.
> Then why, when I reach out to touch him, does he
>   hold me at bay?
> Something inside of me dies
> When I look in my son's shuttered eyes,
> So far from here. So very far away.

Tricking and treating and soccer games and the
  second grade's Halloween show,
I was sure to go.
And yet he is stumbling through jungles of bitterest
  black.
Lost in the fog that he buys.
Wearing a rebel's disguise.
Unwilling, or unable, to come back.

  I never claimed to be the perfect mother.
  I made mistakes. Well, everybody did.
  But God, I was so glad to be his mother.
  And God, oh God, oh God, I loved this kid.

  I love this kid.

Patience and laughter and trips to the beach and
  tickles and song,
Did I do something wrong?
Am I kidding myself? Am I simply rewriting the
  poem?
Telling myself a few lies,
While somewhere a frightened child cries,
And I wait, and I hope, and I pray that he'll find his
  way home.

Did we do something wrong? Did we fail to follow the fool-
proof recipe that guarantees a happy, healthy child? We know
it's our fault—we just haven't figured out why. We may understand (in theory) that, important though we are, we parents
aren't our children's sole creators. We may understand (in theory) that the nature they were born with, and that tempting,
perilous world outside their door, have shaped them too. We
may understand this in theory but we often have trouble be-

lieving that it is true when something goes awry in the lives of our children. We may have trouble believing that, hard as we tried, we had only imperfect control.

"Deep in their hearts," writes Philip Slater in *The Pursuit of Loneliness*, "most middle-class . . . mothers believe that if they did their job well enough, all their children would be creative, intelligent, kind, generous, happy, brave, spontaneous, and good—each, of course, in his or her own special way."

And if they're not the perfect people we were supposed to produce, and if they're not merely imperfect but deeply damaged, it surely must be because we did something wrong.

We did something wrong, which is why he's schizophrenic.

We did something wrong, which is why she joined a cult.

We did something wrong, which is why he committed suicide at the age of twenty-four.

We did something wrong, which is why she is bingeing and purging.

We did something wrong, which is why he can't hold a job.

We did something wrong, which is why those little boys and little girls that we adored grew up to be adults in terrible trouble.

George McGovern, former U.S. senator and presidential candidate, writes about his beloved daughter Terry, whose valiant fight to stay sober came to an end at age forty-five when, in an alcoholic daze, she stumbled into a snowbank and froze to death. Despite his conviction that alcoholism has a genetic base, despite his knowledge that this disease runs in his family, McGovern says he still asks himself, "What could I have done differently? What if I had been a more concerned and actively involved parent when she was a little girl, or a fragile adolescent?" He also says, "When your child develops serious troubles and then dies, no amount of assurance from friends that you were not responsible for the outcome is entirely persuasive. You're going to suffer a thousand regrets and seizures of grief

173

no matter how many times you intellectually agree that it is not your fault."

Many mothers and fathers share this same torment.

"You know," says Lois Wagner, "you go back to the year one and say, 'What did I do?' "

"I always blame myself," says Bonnie Scott. "I always think it's my fault. I did something or I didn't do something."

"I ask myself," says Harold Ross, 'Did I ruin Rebecca?' "

"What was my sin?" sobs Jayne. "What was my sin?"

What was our sin? Was it getting divorced? Was it being an absentee father, a working mom? Was it being depressed, self-centered, too lenient, too stern? And if our kids are in trouble today because of our past sins, aren't we obliged to make it up to them?

Some parents make it up to them by bankrolling their lives, hoping to expiate their guilt through money. Some parents constantly cancel their plans and put their own lives on hold in order to be around to meet their kids' needs. And some parents, when their children break laws or commit atrocious crimes, take full responsibility for their deeds, though few go as far as Claudia Rolling, who offered to die for her son, a serial killer, after his conviction for five brutal murders. Explaining that her thirty-something child was the product of an abusive home, she implored the judge to "Take me. I'm the one who had to have failed him somewhere."

But don't all parents fail their children—somewhere?

"I struggled for a long time with guilt," writes Anne Roiphe, whose oldest daughter became addicted to alcohol and heroin and has tested positive for HIV. "I have just about wrestled it to the ground." Roiphe's former husband, this daughter's biological father, is also an alcoholic, Roiphe notes, and for a time she clung "to the image of genetic programming as if it were a life raft that would keep me afloat in a sea of guilt." She has concluded, however, that, "Genes provide an excuse, a kind of half-assed alibi, but they . . . aren't the whole story." She has also concluded, "I am not responsible. I am not alone responsible."

Perhaps we parents can recognize where we have, in fact, failed our children, and still understand the limits of our control, still understand the powers that we did—and didn't—possess to shape their lives. But what do we do when our adult children, more in anger than sorrow, blame all their current difficulties on us, insisting that we could have made them happy and whole human beings—and that we blew it?

Terry McGovern, says her father, found it "painful to accept responsibility for her own life . . . and she had to find some deeper explanation for the alcoholism that caused it all." He believes that in her search for that explanation "she tended to construct in her mind an exaggerated image of an unhappy childhood and an insensitive family."

Other children, perhaps including our own, may notify their parents that they are holding them fully responsible for their difficulties. Sometimes encouraged by therapists to confront us with the damage they feel we have done, they document our parenting failures one by one by one, telling us that yes, we did something wrong.

They tell us we put too much pressure on them. They tell us we put them down. They tell us we tied them to our apron strings. They tell us we laid too much guilt on them. They tell us we loved their younger sister more. They tell us we failed to shore up their self-esteem. They even tell us, as one daughter did, that we were perfect parents—and that it's much too hard to have perfect parents. This, I believe, is what is called You Can't Win.

Our children may also tell us that since we wouldn't give them dessert until they finished their mashed potatoes and beans, it's entirely our fault that now, at age twenty-seven, they are overweight, unemployed, lonely, and loveless.

175

Rosie begs to differ. Conceding that she used to stuff her daughter with too much food when she was a child, she says, "Still, it's not my fault that she's twenty pounds overweight today. I haven't been putting food in her mouth for years. But as long as I accept the blame, she never has to deny herself a chocolate éclair."

When our children confront us with their complaints about our past behavior, we must recognize that this is how they experienced it, that whether or not what they're talking about is objectively true, it is true for *them*. We can listen sympathetically, non-defensively. We can tell them that we're sorry they're in pain. We can try to explain what was going on in our lives at the time. And we certainly can apologize where it's appropriate. But what we certainly shouldn't do is allow our adult children to completely shift the blame from their shoulders to ours, allow them to make us responsible for the sorrows and the troubles they're going through now.

This isn't to deny that there aren't monstrous, unspeakable, children-destroying parents, but those parents aren't the kind I'm discussing here. I'm discussing us, the flawed but basically decent and trying-hard-to-do-our-best kind of parents, even if we're not Parent of the Year. For us the message is clear: Our adult children's lives, including their sorrows and troubles, belong to our children.

For whether or not we blame ourselves (or our children blame us) for the troubles they are in, they must begin to see these troubles as *theirs—their* divorce, *their* business disaster, *their* drug problem. They—and we—also need to know that we're being loving, caring, respectful parents when we allow them to solve these problems themselves, instead of—as a friend puts it —"always needing to rush right in with the mop and the bucket." But what if they don't solve their problems? And what if they can't solve their problems? And what if they ask for our help in solving their problems?

What if . . .

. . . a son lets his health insurance lapse and then winds up in the hospital. Do we help pay the bills?

. . . a daughter is downsized and can't afford the rent on her apartment. Do we help pay the rent?

. . . a son totals his car but without a car he can't get to work. Do we help buy a car?

. . . a daughter wants us to care for her child while she attends nursing school. Do we become nannies?

. . . a drug-using son is down and out and wants to move back home? Do we say welcome home?

. . . an alcoholic daughter falls off the wagon yet again. Do we still pick her up?

"I don't think Terry will ever get well," the McGoverns' daughter Susan told her father, "as long as you and Mom keep bailing her out." But what's best for one's child? The McGoverns, on a counselor's advice, had limited contact with Terry for a while, "hoping that our maintaining a certain distance might prompt her to confront her alcohol dependence." McGovern now agonizes over that decision, regretting "every phone call not made, every letter not written." He says, "There is no such thing as too much compassion, understanding, support, and love for the sick and dying." He says, "Alcoholics are sick unto death."

He is, however, clearly of two minds on this sore subject, because he also writes about setting limits. "In retrospect, we probably should have said: 'We'll finance this thirty-, or sixty-, or ninety-day treatment program, but only on the condition that you go directly from treatment into a halfway house for at least a year. During that halfway experience you must get a part-time job for a few weeks and then a full-time job."

McGovern is suggesting that he and his wife should have offered Terry only their *conditional* support. But what if she had refused to accept their conditions?

Says Shelly, who wants to keep giving help to her twenty-six-year-old son because she believes he's emotionally disturbed: "If your kid really can't make it, it's not a choice, it's a duty. It doesn't stop just because he's grown up."

When a child has a serious illness, either physical or mental, it's hard to say, "I'll help this far—but no farther." Each of us must figure out for ourselves how much we should, and are able to, do. As for the course we pursue in less cataclysmic situations, most of the experts urge us to let our children "own" their problems—and their lives—and to offer our support (and, if they ask for it, our guidance) without taking over.

I never want to take over—I just want my sons, of their own free will, to do what I say. But the experts say we're not supposed to say it.

Instead, we're urged to listen rather than sermonize, to ask them questions rather than give them answers, to help them explore alternatives, to refrain from reminding them of their past misjudgments, to accept and respect the decisions that they make. But watching a diabetic son "forgetting" to take his insulin, watching a love-blind daughter preparing to lend her bum of a boyfriend all her money, watching a just-divorced son neglecting his heartbroken little boy, watching them poised to fail or mess up, watching them in handcuffs or in pain, we may be compelled to vigorously—I mean very very *vigorously*—intervene. We may, indeed, try our damnedest to take control.

Could we reach a point where we do not?

In their book *Mother, I Have Something to Tell You*, Jo Brans and sociologist Margaret Taylor Smith examined the responses of "traditional" mothers to their adult children's "unexpected," "untraditional," and often "unacceptable" behavior. Impressed with these mothers' capacity to "maintain the important bonds of affection and concern while relinquishing the shackles of unreasonable responsibility," they identify six stages in their coping process:

Stage 1 is shock, where the mother "feels an overwhelming sense of responsibility and guilt."

Stage 2 is attention, where the mother learns to see "the real child who exists under the ideal child she had created in her mind."

Stage 3 is action, where the mother "looks for help for herself, . . . for her child and for the other members of the family" in order to understand and to cope.

Stage 4 is detachment, where the mother "recognizes the limits of her responsibility . . . and frees her child from her expectations of him."

Stage 5 is autonomy, where the mother "turns back to the only life for which she is completely responsible—her own."

Stage 6 is connection, where the mother forges "a new bond with the child and [or] with the world."

These mothers—faced with a wide range of "shocks," including eating disorders, mental illness, crime, cults, drugs, and threats of suicide—were forced to attend to the people their kids really were. Most of them took action, making extraordinary, repeated efforts to help. Even those mothers who failed—and a full half of them believe that they had failed—seem to have achieved some degree of detachment, learning (like Ann Rourke, who couldn't rescue her son from the Moonies) to give up the idea that "Everything depended on me. It was all up to me."

This achievement of detachment—emotional, physical, and financial—begins, say the authors, when a mother can recognize "that *her child is not herself*" and that "she can neither control nor make sense" of all that happens to him. Ideally, maternal detachment "frees her child from her definition of his life" and allows him both to define it and control it. But even when a child is so sick that he'll always need physical care and financial support, a mother can seek satisfactions that are independent of her concerns for her child.

Even when an adult child cannot, does not, or will never make it, a mother can seek emotional detachment.

"He still has lots of problems . . . ," says a mother whose thirty-two-year-old was only recently released from prison. "We've handled it by turning them over to him."

Or, as another mother says, talking about her alcoholic son, "I don't give up on him, ever! But I'm not going to let it destroy my life."

And from one more mother, whose son blew out his brains at age twenty-six: "Basically, you know, you're just a human being. You can only do so much. We can't be God."

We can't be God, we can't be in charge of our sons' and daughters' lives, but we can make an effort to be in charge of our own. We may be permanent parents, intensely and lovingly invested in our children, but we also "could turn from them to something else," says the luminous novelist Mary Gordon, "something they couldn't touch or be a part of." Being able to turn to work, to play, to outside concerns, and to fulfilling *non-motherhood* relationships is, say Brans and Smith, quoting Mary Gordon, "the 'tremendous mercy' of autonomy."

Brans and Smith also note that when a mother achieves autonomy she is better able to grant it to her children, though that's got to be much easier when we're talking about an uncongenial lifestyle rather than drugs and crimes and cults and other major threats to their bodies and minds. But having achieved autonomy, these mothers may be more inclined to accept this daughter's interracial marriage or that son's homosexuality or this daughter's plan to have a child without first having a husband or that son's plan to become a Buddhist monk. These mothers may find themselves ready to accept their children's "untraditional" choices and to form a "respectful connection between equals."

But even if we do achieve autonomy and connection, most of us will have trouble maintaining detachment. It comes, and it goes. As Ellen Galinksy puts it in *Between Generations*, "There are moments when the parent and grown child are together, when they talk or even share silence in the spirit of near-perfect communion. . . . But then the next time they see each other, one says something that sets the other off (a you-should-lose-weight or not-smoke or buy-some-new-clothes or move-to-a-smaller-place statement), and . . ."

And they tell us that we're trying to control them.

And we tell ourselves that we'll do better next time.

And we tell ourselves that we don't own their lives, that they're now adults, that it's time for us to let go of them.

And we tell ourselves that they must make their own mistakes and be responsible for their actions.

And we try to tell ourselves that they'll be okay.

We also try to tell ourselves that we alone didn't make them the people they are, that we can't accept full blame for their present distress, that we cannot always rescue them from that distress, and that sometimes it's better to let them rescue themselves.

"Mom, stop helping me so much," a son, age thirty-one, implores his mother. "Every time you help it makes me feel helpless."

We don't want to make them feel helpless. But we very much want, we desperately want, to help. Permanent parenthood is a double bind. It requires us, at the same time, to live with our fierce and undiminished love for our children, while making peace with the limits of what we can and can't and shouldn't try to do for them, while making peace with the limits of our control.

7

Bossing and Being Bossed

Working for and with other people necessarily entails getting others to do what you want and dealing with others' efforts to get you to do what they want. This introduces a constant potential source of tension and battles of will.
— Deborah Tannen, *Talking from 9 to 5*

Battles of will are frequently fought with our spouses and parents and children, within the privacy of family life. But of course they're fought in the public arena as well, particularly in that hotbed of ambition and hierarchy called the workplace. Whether it's our intention to claw our way to the top of the heap or simply to keep our head down and keep our job, we'll have to deal with issues of control. And whether we're bossing or being bossed, we are going to bring to our on-the-job relationships a legacy of conscious and unconscious needs and assorted anxieties that importantly determine how we function (and why we fail) in the world of work.

Many of these anxieties and needs will be expressed in our exercise of, our surrender of, or our refusal to submit to, control.

In one of my first jobs I left the cozy comforts of my suburban home to work as a waitress at a seaside hotel, where I put in twelve-hour days every day and seven-day weeks every week and was housed in a stifling room in the hotel attic. When, mid-season, I told my slave-driving boss that I was quitting, she set her hands on her ample hips and denounced me. "I treated you like a daughter," she screamed. "I treated you like my own daughter. I took you out of the gutter and made a waitress of you!"

The weird thing was that she truly felt she had taken me out of the gutter. The other weird thing was I felt like an ungrateful daughter.

Abraham Zaleznik, a psychoanalyst who has taught at Harvard Business School, thinks that it's useful to ask the questions "What do people want from authority figures?" and "What are people's conscious and unconscious fantasies about power?" The answers, he says, are relevant both to those who are just setting out in the world of work and to those who are in charge of the whole operation, for they "establish the conditions for the misuse and abuse of power and for disappointment." In the course of growing up, he notes, we learn a great deal about the nature of power, lessons that can propel us to achievement and lessons that also can do us substantial harm, burdening us in the workplace with displaced fears and highly inappropriate longings and sabotaging our dreams of success and mastery. Without necessarily being aware of what we are doing, or why, we may use or refuse control and power in our work relationships to repeat or repair, or avenge, events from our past.

What we often are repeating are the lessons we learned from our mothers and our fathers, lessons that—though modified by subsequent events—dwell in us still. These are, among others, lessons about our own competence and effectiveness, about the risks of responsibility, about the relief, or humiliation, of having to submit to another's authority, about guilt and rivalry and anger and love. Psychologist Horner notes that because the workplace "is a situation where there will be leaders and followers, bosses and the people who work under their direction," it "sets the stage for . . . parent-child power struggles."

So if, for instance, like Tom, we tend to see all employers as overbearing parents and we are determined to prove they can't push us around, we might repeatedly challenge their authority —and find ourselves repeatedly out of a job.

Or if, at the other extreme, like Mel, we've never challenged our parents, no matter how overbearing they were (or still are), we may unprotestingly let our bosses mistreat us—and find ourselves unhappy in every job.

Or maybe we strike back at our bosses by smiling oh-so-compliantly but doing the absolute minimum on the job.

"Your objective as an employee," advises cartoonist and writer Scott Adams, in his tongue-in-cheek guide for office workers, *The Dilbert Principle*, "is to bilk as much unearned money as possible out of the cold, oppressive entity that masquerades as an employer while it sucks the life-force out of your body."

Which, confesses Velma, is precisely what she does, evening up the score with her domineering mother—whoops, boss—by coming in late and leaving early and calling in sick "right up," she says, "to the max" and routinely taking two-and-a-half-hour lunches.

But responding to bosses as if they're oppressive parents is not the only way in which we bring our childhood issues into the workplace.

Malcolm, for instance, is able and smart but he never takes the initiative on the job, preferring that all decisions be made by

184

his boss, hoping that this boss will soon reward his devoted, unthreatening passivity by being the caring, supportive, loving, I'll-look-after-you father he never had.

And then there's Holly, who always works at jobs below her capacity because she is terrified of responsibility, having been convinced very early in life that she simply doesn't have what it takes to take charge.

And then there's Tyler, who's using his native talents and back-stabbing wiles to try to do in, and replace, his elderly boss.

Each has entered the workplace with needs and anxieties linked, in part, to unconscious issues of power and control. These compelling needs and anxieties can stand in the way of professional fulfillment and can lead to major problems on the job.

They can lead to major problems not just on the lower rungs of the ladder but all the way up to, and including, the top, where there will be bosses (some may be us) who are bad news in the workplace because they mishandle the powers at their command. Carlton, for instance, is rapidly running his company into the ground because he needs to be universally loved, which means he cannot fire, demote, critique, or even deprive of their full bonuses employees who are mediocre or worse. Stanley, who is also running his company into the ground, is doing so for quite another reason. Constantly feeling threatened (as he did with his brilliant kid brother) by the best and the brightest of his junior executives, he blocks their advancement, thus squelching their creativity or driving them into the arms of the competition.

I'm not suggesting that everyone with a need to be loved or with sibling-rivalry issues invariably brings those issues into the workplace. I'm not suggesting that everyone who is reluctant to take the initiative on the job is in search of a supportive father-figure. Our earlier experiences don't always explain our professional behavior. And sometimes we feel completely inadequate in a position of power because . . . we are. But sometimes our past experiences, operating completely beyond our awareness, follow us through the years and into the office. And until we become aware of how they affect what we are doing, they'll cast their long, long shadows on what we want and how we perform in the world of work.

Carlton is afraid to use his power. Stanley is afraid he'll lose his power. And Dana, whom we're about to meet, is driving herself and all her employees nuts, because she simply cannot delegate power.

Dana is down in the mailroom making certain that the mail is properly sorted. She is also in the washroom making certain that Central Supply has bought the right soap. She is also going from desk to desk, monitoring everybody's phone calls, shaking her head or writing a say-this note, or maybe suicidally drawing a finger across her throat if she decides that the phone call is going badly.

Dana doesn't really need a staff of competent men and competent women. All she really needs are a dozen cloned Danas, each and every one of them thinking like, talking like, writing like, being . . . her. Only with clones could Dana overcome her reluctance to delegate authority. Dana is one version of that familiar workplace nemesis—the control freak.

So is Alan, a capable and highly successful lawyer who is always pushing people to do their jobs faster, who relentlessly pounds his partners with the rightness of his positions, and who rages at his secretary whenever she slips and makes the slightest mistake. This is a man who overcontrols because he sees himself "as eminently qualified—and therefore obligated—to take charge of any situation and give other people the benefit of his knowledge and experience whether they wanted it or not." Life, in Alan's view, is for the purpose of making things happen, and he makes things happen by being in control.

186

George, another control freak, gives no apologies for being a full-time controller but sees it instead as something in which to take pride, certain that had he operated in a less pushy, take-charge, overbearing way, he would never have accomplished what he has accomplished. He may grant, "Well, maybe I shouldn't be so controlling—I'll try to lighten up. I guess I do come on a little strong sometimes." But then he is quick to add, "I get things done, don't I? And I don't take crap from anyone!"

Control freaks, as defined by business psychologist Gerald Piaget, are "people who control too much, too often or when control is not actually required." Piaget concedes that it is quite normal for you, him, and me to want control, and to exercise control "to make our lives as successful, interesting, and secure as possible, and to aid those around us when and as we can." But the major difference between us normal controllers and control freaks is that "Control freaks can't stop. They are, in essence, control addicts. They have *lost control of their urge to control.*"

While Dana, Alan, and George are, all of them, overconfident, I-know-best control freaks, Irene is more of a tormented, anxious, one-false-move-and-I-am-dead control freak. But anxiety doesn't seem to be any easier than arrogance on the poor people in a control freak's employ.

A director of public relations for a national chain of department stores, Irene—leaving nothing to chance—hovers over her staff, providing exhaustive instructions on how to handle jobs they have done countless times before, repeatedly checking up on them to see if they have forgotten any detail, and compelled to know what each of them is doing every minute of every day. She even asks her staffers to keep an eye on each other—to, in fact, spy on each other—and then report back on what they have seen and heard, establishing an environment that, as Irene's assistant observes, "didn't do much for our morale."

If we could get into her head, we might hear Irene continually warning herself, "One slip-up and I could lose everything I've gained," terrified that some foolish mistake will occur . . . and her clients will leave . . . and then she'll get fired . . . and then she'll fall apart. In her effort to make very sure that there will be no slip-ups, ever, Irene is compulsively driven to control.

Irene controls because she's afraid of failure. Others—"egomaniacs with inferiority complexes"—control because of a sense of inadequacy, hoping to build themselves up (or at least to protect themselves from ridicule or rejection) by taking over. Still others control because they enjoy the "heady rush of power" that simply feeling in control provides. And some control preemptively, as a way to stop other people from (so they fear) abusing them, exploiting them, controlling them.

We recognize that control freaks aren't restricted to the workplace—they are everywhere. And they want to control not only their lives, but ours too. They're the husband or wife who insists on having the final say, the tie-breaking vote, in the marriage. They're the parent or the in-law who aggressively imposes his point of view—a maddening, meddlesome " 'Father Knows Best' on a power trip." They're also the friend who informs us (unasked) that it's time to color our hair, and who badgers us to go on this, not that, cruise, and who, when she comes for a visit, rearranges our living-room furniture and pokes through our closet, throwing out all our scuffed shoes, and who, should we foolishly mention that we're having this little problem, calls us every day with twenty solutions. (And calls us every night to question us closely on whether we did what she told us to do.)

In contrast to these personal relationships, however, workplace control freaks can claim some right to control us, especially when they are bosses instead of the bossed, though certain essential employees (perfect nannies, super-secretaries, and file clerks who know the secrets of the filing system) sometimes achieve control-freak power too. And as long as a Dana or Alan or George is the boss of a job we urgently need to hold on to, or as long as we are dependent on having our office run by our fascist office manager, we will be at the mercy of workplace control freaks.

On the other hand, we may want to ask ourselves an unsettling question: Could it be that *we* are a Dana, an Alan, or a George, or maybe even a fascist office manager?

Still, whether we're world-class control freaks or occasional control freaks or merely normal everyday controllers, we'll sometimes resort to control techniques in the workplace, though some of us will use them far more often and more insistently than others. Some managers, asked to describe their techniques —their strong or weak or rational "tactics of influence"—for trying to get their way with their subordinates, superiors, or colleagues, gave these replies:

(a) "I simply order him or her to do what I ask."

(b) "I act very humble while making my request."

(c) "I explain the reasons for my request."

(d) "I offer an exchange (if you do this for me, I will do something for you)."

(e) "I obtain the informal support of higher-ups."

(f) "I threaten an unsatisfactory performance evaluation."

Note: It's likely that (a) and (f) are tactics most often used with subordinates; that (b) and (c) are most often used with superiors; and that (d) and (e) are most often used with colleagues, but several of these tactics will also be used at every level of the hierarchy.

I once worked with a colleague who had to provide me, from time to time, with information. She was excellent at obtaining this information, but her skills at conveying it were virtually nil, which meant that I had to ask her to repeat, rephrase, and clarify what she was telling me. In order to get what I needed—without offending her—I chose to use the God-I'm-stupid technique, persuading her to go over and over and over the same material

189

by saying, "Why can't I grasp this—what's the matter with me!" I concede that I always appeared to be the dummy of the duo, but I always, sooner or later, got what I needed. And I am prepared to argue that, though it certainly didn't look that way, I was always the person in control.

Many of the tactics effective in marital control can be readily adapted to the workplace: intimidation, subversion (withholding important information), repetition (wearing everyone down), flattery (known around the office as brown-nosing), and reward (the dispensing of raises, promotions, and bonuses). In addition, there is the "takeover" (unabashedly seizing control of the situation), and the "bandwagon" (telling each colleague that everyone else has agreed—though they haven't, as yet—to our plan). Sabotage is not unknown (making mistakes and taking very long coffee breaks); nor is "triangulation" (going over our supervisor's head right to the top man), though failing to show the proper respect for the office chain of command could get a person into a lot of trouble.

A friend of mine describes the resentment and anger she stirred up during the time she worked for a government agency, where, impatient "to get the job done and not wait months for everybody's approval," she'd skip the seven people through whom her proposals ought to have passed and talk directly to the project chief. Failing to defer to the power hierarchy, she learned, was not a good way to win friends or influence people. And because of the alienation and the lack of cooperation that her "power insensitivity" engendered, it was also not a good way to get the job done.

But sometimes triangulation works. And so does the generation of guilt or anxiety. And, for the major meanies among us, so does control through public humiliation, which can range from a screaming "You *really* screwed up on this one!" to a bone-chilling "*This* is the best that you could do?" to a shocked and appalled "I can't believe you just said that!" to a dismissive

"Thanks for your input. Next!" We might even resort to control techniques like those described in *Dogbert's Top Secret Management Handbook*, Scott Adams's satiric (but, come to think of it, maybe not all *that* satiric) guide for managers.

Noting that serious threats can be effective in increasing productivity, he asks us to imagine dropping "two scuba divers in shark-infested waters at the same time. One diver is motivated by a desire to be the best shark avoider he can be. The other diver is motivated by the fear of being eaten. Which one will swim faster?"

Managers can also control their employees, Adams tells us, by inviting them to evaluate their own weaknesses and, when they've foolishly done so, to "zero in . . . like a dog digging for a soup bone":

> *You:* I see that your technical skills are inadequate.
>
> *Employee:* Uh, actually I'm a recognized expert in my field. But I like to keep up with emerging trends by taking classes.
>
> *You:* Then you admit there are things you need to know that you don't know.
>
> *Employee:* Well . . . yes. I mean NO! I wouldn't put it that way.
>
> *You:* It sounds like you have a communication problem too.
>
> *Employee:* What the hell is going on here?
>
> *You:* Have you ever considered counseling? The company has a program . . .

In the world according to Adams, other tactics for wielding managerial power include "shifting blame from yourself to the employees"—and taking credit for their good ideas. As for the manager's ultimate weapon, he notes, "It's never fun to fire someone. . . . But it can be very entertaining to torment employees until they quit on their own."

Although most studies of workplace control focus on how the bosses control the bossed, a study of intraorganizational tactics for getting one's way finds that "everyone is influencing everyone else in organizations, regardless of job title," and that, regardless of title, those on the bottom and in the middle are doing it as often as those on the top. In other words, the bossed are trying as hard to control the bosses as vice versa, and though they may use very different strategies, they want (along with raises and promotions) to control the environment in which they work: They want to set their own deadlines—"I can do this either by March twenty-seventh, or right." They want to limit their workload—"I really don't think that I can handle any more pressure." They want to resist new procedures—"I'll be happy to file it your way, but I can't guarantee that I'll ever find it again." And they want to discourage criticism (by sulking, sighing, crying, hyperventilating, storming out of the room, or counterattacking).

Despite their lower position in the power hierarchy, employees try to exert control in the workplace. And so, of course, do colleagues—those folks who, in power terms, are on an equal footing and who, in defense of their turf or because they want to be a star or for some other (to them) compelling reason, will engage in an assortment of workplace control ploys.

Vaughn, an account executive, is making a presentation at a meeting. He wants everyone to get behind his idea. And then he looks over at Ned, who is very quietly shaking his head but who, when asked to speak, replies, "No comment." Vaughn continues speaking and Ned continues shaking his head, this time refusing to comment with a collegial, "I don't like raining on Vaughn's parade." On the third go-round, however, Ned is (reluctantly) persuaded to totally annihilate Vaughn's presentation, something it would be easier to believe that he hated to do if he hadn't been shaking his head throughout the meeting.

Ned sabotages Vaughn under cover of friendship. At another office meeting Charley zaps coworker Deirdre mercilessly, ostentatiously checking his watch while she speaks and, in a kid's whine, asking, "Are we there yet?" and tossing out snide remarks like, "Where did you get those amazing numbers from, your astrologer?" and making it clear that Deirdre is a fool and her proposal a waste of time.

Both Ned and Charley are using public put-downs to engage in workplace control ploys, trying to look good at their colleague's expense. Lucy puts down her colleagues privately, oh-so-sweetly persuading them that their facts are wrong, that their projects are pie in the sky, that they haven't really grasped the situation, and that the only person who has a viable project to bring to the boss is (guess who?) Lucy.

Lucy wants to stand out. She wants to be the first among equals. She wants to be the star of the Fourteenth Floor. She triumphs over her colleagues through expertise ("I've already studied this matter exhaustively") and negation ("They already tried that plan—and it failed") and sometimes shading the truth ("There are twelve different surveys"—there's actually one— "that support me on this") and sometimes even concealing information that most definitely does *not* support her on this.

Lucy, Charley, and Ned want to beat out their colleagues. Justin just wants to keep them off his turf, but he does so by responding to the slightest comment, suggestion, or incursion as if it were a nuclear attack. His explosions of rage—"Dolts! Idiots! Incompetents!"—are notorious at the magazine where he works, and devastating enough to keep all but the massively foolish or fearless from challenging him. Abusive and aggressive and at-the-top-of-his-voice confrontational—and doing what he's doing quite consciously—Justin uses his bomb-going-off explosions to control his colleagues by intimidation.

Other colleague-versus-colleague hardball power ploys include passing on (or inventing) hostile rumors, hogging all of the credit on a joint project, and failing to provide the authorization or list or figures that a coworker needs to finish up a job. In a famous killer-colleague move, a man who was striving for salesman of the year disabled his closest competitor's computer, wiping out his database long enough for the killer to come in first.

But collegial power ploys are not restricted to hardball players, to killers, to Justins and Lucys and Charleys and Neds. The weak in the workplace have ways of controlling too. Camille, for example, is always enlisting others to do her work for her by the shrewd use of desperation and flattery, moaning, "My back is against the wall. I'll never be done on time. And you"—my incredibly competent and brilliant and compassionate coworker —"are the only one I can count on to help me." There's always a family emergency in the life of poor Camille, or yet another mystery ailment or injury, which is why she has fallen behind and is crying, "Help! Help!"—and why some softie always does. Disorganized on the job, chaotic in her life, and persuasively insistent that her colleague can write this release ten times faster and better, she uses her weakness to exercise workplace control.

Though colleague control may be prompted by feelings of rivalry or inadequacy, it can sometimes be prompted by positive motives too: To encourage a teammate to do his best work. To try to alleviate tensions during a meeting. To win someone over to a new point of view. In ways both nasty and nice, in horizontal as well as vertical relationships, most women and men (and that includes me and you) will attempt to exercise workplace control.

• • •

Some studies say that women and men at the same level of power tend to use similar tactics of control. Deborah Tannen would surely disagree. In *Talking from 9 to 5* she argues, most convincingly, that women and men have strikingly different conversational styles and that these styles strongly "affect who gets heard, who gets credit, and what gets done at work."

Tannen finds that women's styles are less effective than men's in winning recognition and promotions. And she says that women speak as they do because they fear the possible negative consequences of "being assertive, sounding sure of themselves, talking up what they have done to make sure they get credit for it." In a world where nonaggressive men are known as "losers" or "wimps" and nonaggressive women are known as "feminine," where aggressive men are "go-getters" or "winners" and aggressive women are "ball-breakers" or "arrogant," women are more inclined to play down their certainties, while men are more inclined to play down their doubts. Women are also more willing, it seems, to ask questions (as well as ask for directions) and reveal what they don't know when they don't know it and, when they've made a mistake, to accept the blame.

In addition, women are more reluctant to trumpet their accomplishments, which makes it more difficult to advance their careers, for it isn't enough to do good work if your boss is unaware that you are doing it. While a man will often say "I" when he is talking about a project done as a group, a woman will often say "we" when she is talking about a project she did on her own. By trying not to toot their own horn, to sound show-offy or arrogant, women run the risk of masking their competence.

There are other ways in which women's speaking styles, in contrast to men's, result in camouflaging their abilities. Take, for instance, Carol and Ron, coworkers at a radio station, both of whom—at different times—would speak to the other in a lowered voice. But while Ron spoke loudly to Carol when he was providing her with suggestions and information, and only spoke softly when he needed assistance, Carol spoke softly when she was helping Ron. "By lowering her voice," Tannen says, "Carol downplayed her suggestions, so as not to threaten Ron's competence," while Ron "not only spoke loudly but also frequently said . . . 'you follow?' and 'you see this?' "—patronizing expressions that suggest that maybe the listener isn't too sharp.

If women's styles of speaking tend to be less assertive than men's in dealing with their bosses and their coworkers, they're also less assertive when they're dealing with the people who work under them. A study found that when men had to criticize someone in the workplace, they showed a lot more concern for his or her feelings if that person was their *superior*. Women, however, were much more concerned with feelings when they criticized a *subordinate*. And so, for instance, when Marge informed her secretary that she'd made a mistake, she laughed and made light of the seriousness of the error—"You know, it's *hard* to do things around here"—thereby getting her message across while also letting her secretary save face. Like Marge, the other women in this study were "keenly aware of the power inherent in their authority and expended effort to avoid wielding it carelessly." By speaking in ways that showed concern for the feelings of their subordinates, they chose to avoid an authoritarian stand.

Many women exercise their authority in the workplace by playing it down and refusing to pull rank, preferring to treat their subordinates as equals. The wish to be liked will frequently prompt women in high positions to avoid the impression of throwing their weight around. It may also prompt them to make it loudly and repeatedly clear that, despite their high status, they don't have it all. Or, as one female head of a nonprofit charity explained, "I'm well respected by my superiors and peers at the other nonprofits, I'm well paid, I have power and influence, and

I have an intact marriage to boot. If I were thin too, I wouldn't last a minute."

Tannen observes that the efforts of high-status women to tout their flaws and be nicer than nice may let them both have power and be liked. But the downside, she says, is that if they keep acting and speaking in ways that denigrate that power, others may doubt that they have it, or treat them with disrespect, or try to steal that power for themselves.

On the other hand, women whose speaking styles resemble those of men may run into trouble in the world of work. A woman internist, for instance, recently claimed that discrimination was the cause of her losing privileges at a hospital, that she was being punished for being abrasive and demanding, for raising her voice and for sometimes using "the f word." She argued that other physicians at the same hospital could, with impunity, be just as abrasive, demanding, and profane, noting that the difference between these other physicians and her was that they were men.

So here's the problem, "the damned-if-you-do-damned-if-you-don't double bind that women in authority confront." If they talk like women, they'll be more liked than respected. If they talk like men, they'll be more respected than liked. Men, who are far less likely to face this double-bind dilemma, have fewer conflicts with power in the workplace.

Now we doubtless all know women whose style is less like Carol's and Marge's and more like the doctor's. We all know highly successful women who function in the workplace "just like men." We also all know men, including some highly successful men, who don't toot their horns and are willing to ask questions. We all know some exceptions but the fact that there are exceptions doesn't discredit the patterns that Tannen describes.

It's clear that our talking styles can sometimes bolster, sometimes undercut, our position and our authority in the workplace.

Our talking styles can get us, or can lose us, influence and promotions and control. If power is the "ability to influence others, to be listened to, to get your way rather than having to do what others want," then we have to conclude that "how you talk creates power."

But maybe the workplace is modifying its attitudes toward power to incorporate a more "feminine" style of wielding it, a style that is more democratic, more empathic, more cooperative, more people-oriented. According to Shoshona Zuboff, a Harvard Business School psychologist, "There was a long period of managerial domination of the corporate hierarchy when the manipulative, jungle-fighter boss was rewarded. But that rigid hierarchy started breaking down in the 1980s. . . . The jungle fighter symbolizes where the corporation has been; the virtuoso in interpersonal skills is the corporate future."

One indication of this new direction is the emergence of the executive coach, hired by corporations to train valuable executives with weak or nonexistent people skills. Some of these bosses are older white males accustomed to a "command-and-control" style of management and unaccustomed to working with a rainbow of employees who are sexually and racially diverse. But there also are younger executives—including women executives—who need the guidance of an executive coach because, as comptroller Carolyn Piecherowski said of herself, "You had a dictator rather than a mentor for a boss," and because, as another midlevel female executive bluntly admitted, "People found me to be a pain in the neck."

While some of the coaching recipients have said that the line between coaching and therapy blurs, most of the coaches sharply distinguish the two, noting that psychotherapy tends to link current behavior to earlier issues, while coaching is focused on figuring out what is currently going wrong—and fixing it now. Zaleznik and Horner remind us that people in power may bring childhood conflicts into the workplace, with sometimes quite unfortunate results. But while some of these people need therapy and some coaches will, at times, recommend that they get it, the aims of executive coaches are highly practical: to encourage a boss to become a better team player and better listener, to not belittle employees and to allow them to have "ownership of their job," and also to discourage a boss from bossily issuing orders with an autocratic "Don't worry about the whys."

"Years ago, if you were good," says executive coach Judith Blanton, "you could get away with being abrasive. Nowadays people don't want to work with you." Coaches can help here, she says, but it's important that they're aware of corporate realities. "A clinical psychologist who tells someone to share their feelings," she warns, "can end up getting that person fired."

The movie *Jerry Maguire* entertainingly makes that same point when it shows a high-octane sports agent, played by Tom Cruise, finding himself unemployed soon after urging his organization to be more people-oriented. Though his colleagues applaud him in public, they all agree in private that he is a schmuck, demonstrating the disconnection between rhetoric and corporate reality.

Zaleznik, commenting on the kinder, gentler trends in the workplace, expresses some reservations about their effectiveness. He also notes that the "nice guy" image can mask a manager's sneakier intents, diverting people's attention "from reality toward a collective myth" while forwarding the aims of his secret agenda. In other words, the "new" manager could "be a nice guy, make people feel good about themselves, get them to like you"—and be every bit as controlling as the old one.

So are we fools to want to be, and to encourage others to be, more sensitive bosses? Are there any real benefits in striving for more democracy, less control? A true and chilling and often cited cautionary tale tells us, "No, we're not!" and "Yes, there are!"

In 1978, a pilot was flying his airplane into Portland, Oregon, when he noticed that there was a problem with the landing gear. Going into a holding pattern, he circled the field and tried to fix the gear mechanism, unaware that the gauges that measured his fuel were moving relentlessly toward empty. His copilots watched the fuel levels drop but said nothing because, as they knew, their boss was a domineering and hot-tempered man, and though they surely feared the consequences of their silence they were even more afraid of drawing his wrath. And so the airplane crashed and ten people died because an autocratic boss had thoroughly intimidated his subordinates, because power was used in a way that stifled constructive communication and the freedom for people to frankly speak their mind.

Says Daniel Goleman, who retells this story, "The cockpit is a microcosm of any working organization. But lacking the dramatic reality check of an airplane crash, the destructive effects of miserable morale, intimidated workers, or arrogant bosses . . . can go largely unnoticed."

There are, however, consequences—and risks.

Consider, for instance, the intern who needs to give a medication to a patient but can't remember exactly what dosage to give. She does remember, however, that the attending physician, the man who could tell her the answer, thinks poorly of interns who ask too many questions. Fearful that her questioning could earn her a black mark and that a few black marks could injure her career, she guesses at the dosage instead of asking.

Her guess is probably right, or right enough. But what if it's wrong?

Those who advocate "managing with heart" cite studies that conclude that using power humanely is cost-effective, increasing productivity and decreasing errors and accidents and missed deadlines. By taking the trouble, for instance, to be tactful and constructive when offering criticism on the job, employers can often avoid stirring up defensiveness and resentment and can motivate their employees to do better. Employees will also do better when their bosses succeed in reducing stress in the workplace, for stress (along with not asking questions) interferes with learning and "makes people stupid." And other studies show that when people work together as a team or a group, harmony yields far better results than competitiveness, a finding that should prompt bosses to rethink old power tactics and promote cooperation in the workplace.

Authoritarian leadership, Horner observes, "is conducive to apathy or resistance on the part of others, while in a situation of democratic leadership, one finds more originality, less aggression, and more productivity."

Psychologist David McClelland, in his exhaustive study of power, supports her point. "Slaves," he writes, "are the most inefficient form of labor ever devised by man. If a leader wants to have a far-reaching influence, he must make his followers feel powerful and able to accomplish things on their own."

A friend of mine, the hugely successful owner of several companies, talks about how he runs his organization. "You can insist on having control over *everything*," he tells me, "but the people who'll stand for that will be second-rate. To keep the best people, you have to give them the freedom to make decisions and run their own show. To be the top dog of a first-rate organization, you need to be willing to give up some of your power."

You need to accept having only imperfect control.

But even in work situations where the boss claims total control and feels only scorn for this humane-management stuff, he most likely will find himself having to bow to one new constraint on his power: no longer can he, invulnerably, make sexual moves on the women working under him. Though he

201

technically has the power to promote those who please him and to hold back those who don't, it's risky these days equating "please" with "have sex with." For though sexual harassment is still alive and well in the workplace, it's not nearly as respectable as it used to be.

So bosses better beware this advice from Scott Adams:

"It will no longer be necessary to be witty or attractive in order for people to pay attention to you . . . ," he writes in his retrograde guidebook for managers. "In fact, you can be physically repulsive and still have a good chance of bedding one of your attractive employees through the use of subtle intimidation." He grants that this is against the law, but then goes on to observe that "you didn't become a manager so you could get the best parking space. You did it so you could talk dirty to attractive people who couldn't complain."

My own experience with dirty talking in a work situation involved not a manager but a famous literary figure I was trying to interview. At our meeting he assured me he'd be glad to tell me all, but first, he said softly, why didn't we have sex? Actually, he phrased it a lot more crudely, but in my role as an intrepid young reporter, it didn't seem appropriate to be shocked. Instead, I moved on to my questions, which he listened to in silence before countering with some of his own: How about sex? And, by the way, did I enjoy being spanked? I'd enjoy getting this interview, I told him, but I left without my story, unable to move the man off his favorite subject. He talked very very dirty, but this was the late 1960s and I didn't feel entitled to complain. Not to him. And not to the people he worked for.

But in 1991, professor of law Anita Hill complained that her former boss, Supreme Court nominee Clarence Thomas, had talked dirty to her.

And in 1993, Gena Hutton, who'd worked in Bob Packwood's 1980 campaign, complained that the Oregon senator "just reeled me around and grabbed me and pulled me close to him," after which he delivered a tongue-in-mouth kiss.

And in 1996, some 15,000 complaints about sexual harassment were received by the Equal Employment Opportunity Commission, proving that though harassment is not as respectable as it used to be, it still causes plenty of misery in the workplace.

While many women, dependent on their boss for their job and their livelihood, put up with dirty talk and unwanted attentions, many are now objecting—and filing complaints. Some men, in response, are protesting that they are the victims of vengeful or supersensitive women whose outright lies or overreactions to innocent gestures or words can destroy their careers. In David Mamet's disturbing play *Oleanna*, for example, a college professor is driven to violent rage, provoked by a woman student who has falsely charged him with sexual harassment. And in real life, in 1992, Professor Richard Dinsmore, who taught history at the University of Maine, lost his tenured position after a woman student accused him of harassing her "by touching her shoulder during a viewing of a film, by helping her put on her coat, and by acting overly friendly while taking her out for coffee."

Dinsmore later sued, and he won damages, attorneys' fees, and his job back; but such stories chill the blood of many males. As one executive told me, "I don't do pats on the back and I don't do personal compliments. I don't take any chances with what I say. Because, if I tell my secretary she's looking good today, she could feel flattered or she could report me for hitting on her."

We need to remember that women are far more likely to be harassed than they are to lie about it, and that they have been penalized—including being fired—for filing complaints. We also need to remember that most men don't intend to sexually harass, that they don't set out to hurt, offend, or threaten women sexually by the power they exercise at work. But because there are many men, including some very decent men, who—as that well-worn saying goes—"just don't get it," some sensitivity training could help set them straight. And appropriate sanctions applied to those who force themselves on the women in their employ can redress the misuse of power in the workplace.

All of us in the workplace—the women and men, the bossed and the bosses—are dealing with issues of power and control. We'll deal with them better if we know what we're doing, if we recognize our abuses of power, our fear of claiming and using power, and the many constraints on our power imposed by the law, by our own early conflicts, by those we work with. In the workplace—as everywhere else—we will have to learn which powers are ours and which ones aren't, and when we should claim them and when we should let them go. In the workplace —as everywhere else—we'll flourish only if we know both how to take and how to surrender control.

8

Victims and Survivors

A knife at someone's throat forces the victim to
acknowledge the power of the attacker and his
control.

— P. G. Zimbardo

I will walk all night. I will not die of cancer.
Nothing will make me dance in that dark.
— Reynolds Price, "The Dream of Refusal"

As we mate and marry, raise our children, go about our
work, we're bound to have our share of bad breaks and bad
news, which may include, along with the more expectable
losses, some exceptional assaults on our bodies or psyches.
Whether we suffer a "minor" blow, like being robbed at knife-
point, or a major one, like becoming crippled for life, we may
find ourselves precipitated into the unhappy role of victim. Becoming a victim—defined here as someone whose life has been
deeply affected by some negative, often out-of-the-blue experience—is a part we tend to think others, not we, will play. But
although we may believe that we are the authors of our own

lives and insist upon the primacy of our control, we sooner or later learn that no one is granted full immunity from crime or violence or accidents, from natural disasters or grave diseases. We sooner or later learn that no one is guaranteed immunity from victimhood.

Victimhood is a quick and brutal reminder of how limited, how imperfect is our control.

Studies of victimization have found that most of us, until we have been victimized, share three basic, often unconscious, assumptions:

We assume that we are personally invulnerable.

We assume that the world we live in is comprehensible.

We assume that we are essentially worthwhile.

In other words, though we're well aware of cancer rates, crime statistics, and car fatalities, we don't live with the fear that we ourselves will be mugged or raped, or will plunge headfirst through the windshield, or flunk our physical. And though we're quick to agree that life is often unfair and often unpredict-able, we tend to behave as if we believe that people deserve what they get—and vice versa. Victimhood smashes our sense of it-can't-happen-to-me safety. It leaches order and meaning from our world. And it batters our positive sense of self with undermining images of powerlessness, weakness, unworthi-ness, even deviance. Leaving us with the fear:

That there will be a recurrence—another mugging, another earthquake, another malignancy.

That life makes no sense, that it follows no known rules.

That we are fate's fools, singled out for this misfortune by forces that are far beyond our control.

But although becoming a victim is often out of our control, we have some control over whether we stay a victim. Our abso-lute abject helplessness in the face of some shattering blow need not be matched by our helplessness after the fact. There are, of

206

course, situations where the last two statements simply don't apply, where the blow sustained by the body or brain, the psyche or the soul, makes an absurdity of the word "control." But short of such total catastrophes we all have some capacity to rebound. And although there will be great differences in the resources each of us brings to victimization, there are ways of thinking and acting that may help us to "de-victimize" ourselves.

I've learned, to my surprise, that most of us want to.

I'm surprised because I keep hearing that people are willing and eager to wear the victim label. The popular wisdom claims that we are living in a culture of victimhood. But psychological studies of responses to tragic events have put together quite a different story. They say that, for the most part, people dislike being seen as—or feeling like—a victim.

For along with the damaged self-regard that victimization brings, there are changes in how the victim is treated by others, treatment that can make him feel weak and pathetic and undeserving and basically flawed, treatment that can include contempt and rejection and sometimes even outright hostility. It's unfortunately a fact that nonvictims get scared when disasters happen to folks just like them, and one way to stop being scared is to convince themselves that the victim is *not* just like them, and one of the ways to convince themselves of that is to believe that the victim is—maybe always has been—a loser. People who become victims wish to escape being seen, and from seeing themselves, in this painfully marginalized and stigmatized way. Thus people who become victims will try mightily to de-victimize themselves.

Nobody is saying that this is easy.

For there are, for some of the victims, physical consequences to deal with, and the disabilities and injuries, or the loss of material goods, can be almost unimaginably daunting. There may also be a host of emotional consequences to deal with:

anxiety and depression, shock and confusion, phobias, guilt, and the repeated reliving of the traumatic event. In addition, there is the struggle to restore their shattered confidence in safety and order and their own self-worth. Victims succeed in this struggle by finding coherent and positive ways to think about their victimizing experience. Indeed, some accounts of victimhood are so positive and upbeat that they "can lead to the conclusion," as some researchers wryly put it, "that there are no victims."

These victims, for instance, tell themselves that it could have been much worse. They were robbed but—lucky them!—they weren't beaten. Or they were robbed and beaten but they weren't raped. Or as a friend of mine told me after two men, high on drugs, had robbed, pistol-whipped, and raped her, at least—lucky, lucky her!—she was still alive.

Psychologist Shelley Taylor and her colleagues, in a study called *It Could Be Worse,* report the de-victimizing remarks of women who had undergone treatment for breast cancer:

From a woman who had a lumpectomy: "I had a comparatively small amount of surgery. How awful it must be for women who have had a mastectomy."

From a woman who had a mastectomy: "It was not tragic. . . . Now if the thing had spread all over, I would have had a whole different story for you."

From a woman in her seventies: "The people I really feel sorry for are those young gals. To lose a breast when you're so young must be awful. I'm seventy-three, what do I need a breast for?"

From a young married woman: "If I hadn't been married, I think this thing would have really gotten to me. I can't imagine dating or whatever knowing you have this thing and not knowing how to tell the man about it."

The Taylor study notes that a significant number of women made what the authors call "self-enhancing" comparisons, choosing to compare themselves with those who were *worse* rather than *better* off. "Even some who were dying," the authors observe, "focused on the fact that they had achieved spiritual peace whereas other people might never reach that state." And when breast cancer victims compared the loss of a breast to other kinds of bodily losses, they also managed to come up with advantages:

"There are worse things," said one woman, "that can happen to you, that are more disfiguring. You could lose an arm, you could lose a leg, you could lose an ear, you could lose an eye, you know. That's a hell of a lot worse."

I think of some of my relatives, who engaged in an ongoing game of competitive suffering, and who never would have conceded it could have been worse. Among the masters and mistresses of this medical one-upsmanship, the pseudonymed Ida particularly stands out:

> Whatever happens to me
> Has already happened to Ida, the one who suffers.
> Only worse,
> And with complications,
> And her surgeon said it's a miracle she survived,
> And her team of lawyers is suing for half a million,
> And her druggist gave a gasp when he read the
>   prescription,
> And her husband swore he never saw such courage,
> Because (though it may sound like bragging) she's
>   not a complainer,
> Which is why the nurse was delighted to carry her
>   bedpan,
> And her daughter flew home from the sit-in in order
>   to visit,
> And absolute strangers were begging to give blood
>   donations,
> And the man from Prudential even had tears in his
>   eyes,

Because (though it may sound like bragging)
  everyone loves her,
Which is why both her sisters were phoning on day
  rates from Dayton,
And her specialist practically forced her to let him
  make house calls,
And the lady who cleans kept insisting on coming in
  Sundays,
And the cousins have canceled the Cousins Club
  annual meeting,
And she's almost embarrassed to mention how many
  presents
Keep arriving from girlfriends who love her all over
  the country,
All of them eating their hearts out with worry for Ida,
The one who suffers
The way other people
Enjoy.

In contrast to my family back in New Jersey, the victims of
the Taylor study didn't seek pleasure by proving they suffered
the worst. Instead, they preferred to believe that they were not
only better off than most other victims, but that they were also
coping a whole lot better.

"Some of these women just seemed to be devastated. And
with really less problems than I encountered."

"I really don't think they cope with it that well. I don't understand it, because it doesn't bother me at all."

"I think I did extremely well under the circumstances. I know
that there are just some women who aren't strong enough."

Taylor and her colleagues were intrigued to find that some of
these coping comparisons were not between good copers and
actual women. For in their wish to believe that they were doing
extremely well, some of these women "manufactured" a person

—a hypothetical *bad* coper—"so as to make [their] own response appear exceptional."

By such self-enhancing "selective evaluations," by seeing themselves as lucky (it could be worse) or well-adjusted (I'm doing great), victims minimize their victimization.

They can also de-victimize themselves by telling themselves that their suffering is serving some larger and beneficial purpose, a purpose they may—or may not—be able to see. Indeed, many victims, seeking to answer the anguished question, "Why me?" have concluded that the earthquake or violent criminal attack or disease or diving accident they have endured has somehow transformed them into better people.

"I feel as if I were for the first time really conscious."

"The ability to understand myself more fully is one of the greatest changes I have experienced."

"I was happy to find out that I am a very strong person. . . . And I have become more introspective."

"I have much more enjoyment of each day, each moment."

A forty-nine-year-old woman, in the final stages of AIDS, said to me, "Since I've had the virus, I've been taking time to look at the beauties of nature. These trees, these tulips, they've been here all along, but now I am looking at them."

A woman who had endured twenty-three years of multiple sclerosis wrote to the advice columnist Dear Abby: "MS has brought our family closer together. We tend to do things *now* rather than postponing them. . . . MS is no fun, but there are worse things. I consider myself very lucky."

And a man who suffered from polio said, "I know my awareness of people has deepened and increased, that those who are close to me can want me to turn all my mind and heart and attention to their problems. I could not have learned *that* dashing all over the tennis court."

A flood victim found that the flood produced not only per-

211

sonal but communal advantages. "I never knew my neighbors before. It was never really what you could call a neighborhood. But in the last two days, I've gotten to know everyone. We're all pulling together and taking care of each other. It's a nice feeling."

Even victims of incest—some 20 percent of the incest victims in one study—came up with a positive spin as they looked back on their horrendous childhood experiences. Said one: "I learned over the years that nothing as bad as what I had been through was going to happen again. Now I know there is virtually nothing I cannot overcome."

It's constructive, I agree, to put a positive spin on negative experiences. It's admirable and noble—and mature. But before we pick ourselves up off the floor to surmount the devastation and find benefits in suffering and disease, I think we first get to curse, to cry, to shake our fist at the heavens, to want our old lives back. And I don't think we have to be *grateful* for the wonderful opportunities that floods or AIDS or MS or cancer afford us.

Some of us don't think that we need them at all.

"I get so sick of these people who talk about how cancer made them better people," says the poet Nikki Giovanni, who was diagnosed in 1995 with lung cancer. "I don't think I'm any nicer or kinder. If it takes a near-death experience for you to appreciate your life, you're wasting somebody's time."

She goes on: "I'm glad I'm not dead, but I don't think any cosmic being sent cancer to change my life. If it did, there are easier ways to get my attention. It could have whispered in my ear. I'm a quick study."

Ms. Giovanni notwithstanding, many victims respond to victimhood by minimizing its impact and giving it meaning. Some of them may also, like David Gelernter, a Yale computer-science professor, ferociously reject the status of victim.

"Any morally healthy person would rather bash in his head with a cinder block than choose to call himself a victim," says Gelernter, who speaks from deeply personal experience. Back in June of 1993 he opened a package containing a pipe bomb, sent to him by the notorious Unabomber, and the ensuing explosion blew two fingers off his right hand and left him with damaged hearing, damaged eyesight, and scars all over his body. But rather than "step forward and take my rightful share of victimhood," as reporters and TV producers urged him to do, Gelernter has not permitted the bomb or the bomber to define the terms of his life. Declining to be one of those people who "assume disgraceful and pathetic spiritual stances," he will not, he says, be a part of the "victim culture." Instead he takes the position that "to be a victim is a choice you make." He has chosen not to.

Gelernter also fights victimhood by the way he characterizes the bombing episode, refusing to see this attack on him as anything singular or out of the ordinary. "In the physical sense," he says, "everybody takes his lumps in one way or another. I got injured in a particularly dramatic way, but innocent people are injured in auto accidents by the thousands every day."

Gelernter has even managed to put a positive spin on the whole Unabomber experience, emphasizing "the extraordinary kindness of our various communities . . . and even strangers all over the world." And although he isn't claiming that the bombing was all for the best, he does say this:

"Getting seriously hurt and pulling through has a salutary effect on the clarity with which a person looks at his own life. In my case, I've shaken the tendency to assume I'd eventually get around to the important stuff. As the Talmud asks, what if there never *is* an 'eventually'?"

In trying to make some sense of victimization, some victims find comfort and relief in blaming themselves for this or that awful event: "I wasn't wearing my seat belt." "I had too much to drink." "I shouldn't have been on that street so late at night." "I should have noticed much earlier that that guy was acting peculiar." "The way I worried, no wonder I got cancer." In other words, my misfortune wasn't random and it wasn't unavoidable. It happened because I brought it on myself.

Even in situations where the actions of others clearly caused the misfortune, victims may insist on taking the blame, like the fellow who became paralyzed when the driver of the car in which he was riding fell asleep at the wheel. Why was this his, not the driver's, fault? Because, the man explained, the driver had wanted to stay out late, and even though he, the victim, wanted to leave, "I didn't press it. . . . If I would have pressed it and he refused, [then] it would have been his fault."

The research on self-blaming has presented us with two unexpected findings. The first is that, far from trying to pin the blame on someone, or on something, else, many victims *overrate* their responsibility. The second is that, rather than feeling rotten when they blame themselves, the victims who do so (even those who are paralyzed for life) tend to feel better than the victims who don't. There's an important qualification. It seems that self-blame is only helpful when the blaming is for a specific hapless act—some momentary lapse, some dumb or careless *but controllable* piece of behavior. If, however, it is ascribed to some basic (and immutable) flaw in their character, self-blame will not do much for the victims' morale. In other words, self-blame is a plus when we're able to say a specific "I made a mistake," and a minus when we globally say, "I'm a fool."

It's hard to think of self-blame as a plus, for like most of the people I know, I find it painful to say, "I made a mistake." I would find it ten times harder to admit that my mistake had brought this or that misfortune upon myself. (And I'd find it almost impossible to live with the guilt I would feel if my mistake had visited serious harm on another.) So why would many victims *prefer* to blame themselves for their victimhood? The researchers give a reply that makes sense to me: They say that, for many people, feeling incompetent and guilty is considerably more tolerable, considerably less frightening, than feeling that they are helpless and out of control.

It's been found, for instance, that women who react most extremely to rape—women with a "total fear reaction"—are those whose attacks took place in a situation where they had reason to think they were safe, where they can't in any way hold their conduct responsible, where—in their view—"the attack simply should not have happened."

"Going to a doctor's at seven-thirty in the evening to have him try to help you with your back, it never occurred to me . . ."

"Who expects to be raped at ten o'clock in the morning?"

"I always thought two [walking on the street together] was safe."

"They always say, 'Drive, don't walk. You're safer when you drive.' And I got attacked in this vehicle, in a car which I was driving, which I should have been safe in."

Because these women regarded their conduct as absolutely "blameless" (in the sense of not having put themselves in harm's way), they may feel that there's little they can do to prevent such dire events from happening in the future. In contrast, when victims of rape or other disasters can blame their behavior for their fate, they are able "to maintain the belief that they are in control of their lives" and "that the world is a 'just' and orderly place where bad things do not happen by chance. . . ." In addition, self-blame helps victims believe that by changing their ways, by improving their behavior, by taking action, they can avoid the risk of future misfortune.

This, anyway, is what some studies tell us and, as I said, the logic makes sense to me. But only up to a point, for I can surely also see how blame can increase a victim's victimization.

215

Keirsten Rain (called Rain), who at the age of seventeen was sexually assaulted and grievously injured, disputes this it's-better-to-blame-yourself point of view, and provides an important corrective to all the positive tales of triumphant post-victimization. Twenty years after a man attacked her one morning at a Philadelphia train station, dragging her from the empty platform down a flight of stairs, smashing her head against the floor, and raping her, she says that she believes she might have had a less anguished recovery if others—including herself—hadn't blamed the victim.

Comatose for two weeks, Rain awoke to fractures, paralysis, constant pain, and brain injuries, and today she walks with a brace, can't use her right hand, and sometimes loses her train of thought. But the emotional fallout was harder. She became, for a while, a bulimic—"I had really lost myself. But I could control how much food I put into me"—and tolerated a long abusive relationship because, she explains, "I didn't know I deserved a real relationship."

Rain is now dating a colleague at a school for the deaf where she works as a speech therapist, but despite these signs of recovery she continues to struggle with recurrent depression. She believes that the girl she used to be was murdered twenty years ago and that her life "will never be the same." She also says, "For fifteen years, my father would say every time I would leave his sight, 'Don't let it happen again.' " She says, "I was always wondering, what could I do to stop it happening again?"

Rain could not answer her question. But other victims, whether or not they engage in self-blame, may respond to victimization by engaging in various actions intended to "stop it happening again." The victim of a robbery may install a security system in his house. The victim of a rape may learn self-defense. And the victim of an earthquake may (as my friend Vera did) sell her Los Angeles house and move to New York.

"Direct action," write psychologists Ronnie Janoff-Bulman and Irene Hanson Frieze, "can provide the victim with a sense of environmental control and can thereby minimize their new-found perception of vulnerability."

Direct action can also mean learning—by reading studies and books and, now, by using the Internet—everything that is known about the subject. And it often means an intense involvement in every part of the rehabilitation process, joining a victim's support group for psychological repair, lining up nutritionists and every other "ist" who has something to offer, and/or engaging in arduous physical therapy.

Take actor Christopher Reeve, who once played Superman in the movies and who now is playing Superman in real life as he strives to "take a proactive role" in the recovery he has pursued since a fall from a horse turned him into a quadriplegic. Reeve keeps driving himself to extend the length of time he can breathe without a respirator—"I'm not going to be chained to this respirator for the rest of my life"—and he keeps exercising his legs to keep them in shape because, he explains, "I totally believe that within a decade, I'm going to be up and walking again." Faced with a crushing catastrophe, Reeve has refused to be crushed, or to sit there with, as he puts it, his "motor in neutral." He says, "You have to push," you have "to move up," you have to do "something that's forward progress." And he says that he is enlisting his competitive spirit in the recovery process as if it were simply "a different kind of sport."

Victims may also take action that is designed to prove to *others* that they shouldn't be regarded as a victim. This can include concealing (as President Franklin Roosevelt did) their disability. It can also include rejecting offers of help—"Help? who needs help? I'm doing just fine." Some may make wise-guy comments or jokes about their situation to suggest that their impairment is "no big deal." And others may insist upon participating in so-called "normal" activities, or refuse—after overcoming what seem like insurmountable obstacles—to be treated as having accomplished something exceptional.

Take, for example, John Craven, who, one August day in 1971, was smashed by an ocean wave while body-surfing, an accident that snapped his neck between the third and fourth vertebrae and left him paralyzed—from the neck down—for life. Craven, who at the time was a young physicist employed by the CIA, spent the following decade or so in a nursing home, though he now has his own apartment—and a full-time caregiver. Faced with the question of "whether it's all worth it to go on," he decided to "make the best of a bad situation."

And so, in the ensuing years, Craven continued to work for the CIA, tapping on a typewriter, then a computer, by pressing the keys with a pointer held in his mouth, and moving steadily up—to the Senior Intelligence Service. In 1996, because of the "breakthroughs" he had accomplished in his field, Craven, at age fifty-seven, was honored as CIA's scientist of the year.

Keep in mind that while he works with his fax, computer, and voice-activated phone, he is mostly working from a hospital bed. Keep in mind that he taps out no more than fifteen words a minute—it's hard on the jaws to work with a mouth-held pointer. Keep in mind, as he told the reporter who wrote a story about him, that if a fly should land on his nose, somebody else must be asked to brush it away. And keep in mind that he is a quadriplegic.

But here's what Craven says about that: "You read these maudlin stories about 'So-and-so triumphs under trying conditions.' I don't want to contribute to that kind of story because I don't want to make myself out as either a poor, pathetic person or as somebody who's a hero or remarkable in some ways. I think a lot of people in the same circumstances would do just as well. I think people are very resilient and a lot tougher than they even think they are, till their time comes."

Some people are, and some aren't.

Some can surmount their victimhood, and some can't.

Perhaps, on occasion, you've asked yourself, if you have thus far been spared life's harsher blows, how you would deal with them. I sometimes ask myself that question too, knowing that every time I get a mammogram or a blood test or check out those dizzy spells or this mole or that pain, the findings could transform my existence forever. I once watched a middle-aged woman skipping out of my doctor's office and down the long, long hallway to the elevator, happily chanting, "I'm fine! I'm fine! I'm fine!" But we walk a very thin line—*"la vie est fragile,"* is how a French friend of mine once put it—and next year maybe we won't be fine, and maybe we'll be victims. And we may—or may not—surmount our victimhood.

What makes some of us feel so utterly hopeless and helpless in the face of adversity? And what makes some of us feel that we have the power to de-victimize ourselves? To a certain extent, of course, the answer depends on the dimensions of the adversity. It depends as well on whether we have the financial and the human supports we need. It may, in some situations, depend on how old we are. But it also depends, enormously, on whether or not we see ourselves as effective, competent people whose actions and choices can determine the shape of our life.

A belief that we have control will serve us well as we encounter the challenges and setbacks of everyday life, allowing us to tell ourselves—when we fail a test, lose a job, or get dumped by a lover—that next time we'll study harder, that we'll go get another job, that we'll find true love. It can also serve us well in the wake of a shattering, uncontrollable life event, prompting us —even against all odds—to resist victimhood.

The intention of those who resist victimhood is to make the tough journey from "victim" to "survivor," though both of these words, I confess, make me squirm in my chair. But while Gelernter and Craven weren't inclined to offer survival tips to the public, editor Norman Cousins, struck with an incurable disease, wrote a best-selling antidote to despair, arguing in his *Anatomy of an Illness* that we can increase the odds in favor of survival—as he did—by mobilizing our powers, by taking control.

In 1964 Cousins was diagnosed with ankylosing spondylitis, a bad-news disease which meant that the connective tissue of his spine was disintegrating. The prospects of recovery were poor. Cousins, clearly not your passive type, moved quickly to participate in his treatment, forming an equal partnership with his remarkably accommodating doctor and directing the full force of his formidable intellect to determining what might have caused his disease (heavy-metal poisoning in Moscow) and what might have made him susceptible (adrenal exhaustion, which lowered his resistance) and what he could do to combat it (restore his endocrine system, especially his adrenals, to their full functioning).

Cousins remembered reading that buried rage, frustration, or other emotional tensions had been implicated in adrenal exhaustion, that negative emotions could have a negative impact on body chemistry. He decided that he would explore the opposite side of this intriguing proposition: That "the positive emotions produce positive chemical changes." That "love, hope, faith, laughter, confidence and the will to live have therapeutic value." He then formulated a treatment plan in the hope that "even a reasonable degree of control over my emotions might have a salutary physiologic effect."

Cousins decided to take a lot of control.

His control included getting rid of certain medications, which, he suspected, were toxic to his system, and taking high doses of vitamin C, having read that ascorbic acid might help control inflammation and "feed" the adrenal glands. He also arranged to remove himself from the hospital, on the indisputable grounds that the atmosphere of a hospital was not conducive to an upbeat attitude. But the most unconventional aspect of his unusual treatment plan was a systematic regimen of funny laugh-out-loud films and books of humor.

Cousins believed that laughter would be of significant benefit to his body chemistry. And so it was, or surely seemed to be, for he discovered that "ten minutes of genuine belly laughter had an anesthetic effect and would give me at least two hours of pain-free sleep." He also found that the blood test he took right after a laughing episode always looked better than the test taken before, that technicians could actually measure—by something called a "sedimentation rate"—the medical advantages of laughter.

Norman Cousins credited his astonishing recovery to a combination of laughter and vitamin C. But he also subscribed to the view that his treatment succeeded because he was certain that it would succeed. Indeed, he was quite comfortable contemplating the notion that his cure was due to the so-called placebo effect.

The placebo, which in Latin means "I shall please," is a useless procedure or fake medication that a patient receives from his doctor and thinks is real. The placebo effect occurs when the placebo, despite its lack of objectively curative attributes, affects the patient as if it *were*, in fact, real, sometimes producing measurable biochemical changes and in documented cases relieving a wide array of symptoms and diseases. "The placebo," according to Cousins, "is proof that there is no real separation between mind and body."

A placebo will not help if a patient doubts its authenticity and effectiveness. Or if he distrusts his doctor. Or if he lacks a "robust will to live." But he doesn't really need the placebo itself, a tangible treatment, in order to benefit from the placebo effect, for "the mind," Cousins argued, "can carry out its ultimate func-

221

tions and powers over the body without the illusion of material intervention."

In other words, we don't need a phony medicine or medical procedure to trick our body into healing itself. Our mind can transform our "will to live from a poetical conception to a physical reality and a governing force."

Cousins was not suggesting that the mobilization of positive emotions will always cure diseases or relieve symptoms. Nor was he suggesting that we should stop using medical treatments that are widely known to be effective and safe. No, Cousins was simply arguing that we, and our doctors, must recognize and encourage the power of "the doctor who resides within," the "natural drive of the human mind and body toward perfectability and regeneration." He concluded: "Protecting and cherishing that natural drive may well represent the finest exercise of human freedom."

The central point of the Cousins book is that when victims of illness accept responsibility for their recovery, they have a far better chance of becoming survivors. Surgeon Bernie Siegel, who is the author of *Love, Medicine & Miracles*, emphatically and flamboyantly agrees, adding (this makes me uneasy) that if patients feel somewhat responsible for *getting* their disease, they will feel they have more control of the healing process. He also says that patients shouldn't be seeking to cure themselves but should, instead, be seeking peace of mind, which he believes is achievable and will help them to get well by creating "a healing environment in the body." Relaxation, meditation, hypnosis, and visualization (the summoning up of positive mental images) can contribute, he says, to creating that healing environment and can foster the development of a "survivor personality" that enables patients to become "exceptional."

Exceptional patients, Siegel writes, possess—among a host of positive qualities—a capacity for unconditional love, a full love

222

of self and others that, or so he is convinced, "is the most powerful known stimulant of the immune system." Exceptional patients refuse to be helpless and hopeless, refuse to be victims or statistics. They participate, very actively, in their treatment, informing themselves, asking questions, prepared to change. By insisting upon maintaining their "dignity, personhood, and control, no matter what the course of the disease," exceptional patients, according to Siegel, take charge of their lives, improve their lives, prolong their lives—and sometimes even effect "miraculous" cures.

Siegel has his exceptional patients. What endocrinologist Deepak Chopra has are "geniuses of the mind-body connection," patients whose minds, by leaping to a whole new level of consciousness, are capable of what he calls "quantum healing." Such a patient, writes Chopra with, I suspect, a good deal more optimism than evidence, can control diabetes, cancer, heart disease, *any* disease, because he

> experiences a dramatic shift in awareness. He knows that he will be healed, and he feels that the force responsible is inside himself but not limited to him—it extends beyond his personal boundaries, throughout all of nature. Suddenly he feels, "I am not limited to my body. All that exists around me is part of myself."

Chopra says that this quantum leap into a higher consciousness is greatly facilitated by Ayurveda, an Eastern system of medicine that emphasizes three powerful healing techniques. There's meditation, which takes the mind "out of its boundaries" into a "free zone" untouched by disease. There's the "bliss technique," which involves an active paying of attention, producing an awareness so effective, according to Chopra, that "there is no innate reason why [it] cannot heal any disease." But

223

just to play it safe there is, in addition, the "primordial sound" technique, where patients focus all of their attention with great specificity on the organ or tumor or joint they wish to heal.

Both Chopra and Siegel offer tale after tale of miraculous cures and remissions. Of patients remaining alive and well years after their disease was supposed to have killed them. Of pain abating, of tumors melting away. Of healing that occurred because she told herself, "I would never be sick another day in my life"; or because "he had just decided that he was not going to let himself die of cancer"; or because "she had taken the path of her own choosing"; or because "she jettisoned her anger and depression, her spirit, like a balloon freed of useless weight, soared—and her tumors started to shrink. She was cured." We are told of the forty-something man who, thanks to meditation and the bliss technique, was living—four years after his diagnosis—"as if the AIDS were not there." And we are told of the eighty-eight-year-old woman who no longer suffered from angina attacks after practicing the primordial sound technique.

Deepak Chopra and Bernie Siegel strike many, including me, as over the top—the late Anatole Broyard once called Siegel "a sort of Donald Trump of critical illness." But although I read them both with a host of "yes, buts" and "wait a minutes," I am by no means dismissing the body-mind connection. For there are, along with the many thrilling but inconclusive anecdotes, a variety of more-or-less rigorous studies, done by well-credentialed scientists, whose purpose is to document the effects of our mental state on our physical health.

Item: In the late 1970s, Stanford University psychiatrist David Spiegel and his colleague Irving Yalom ran a support group for women with metastasized breast cancer, finding in a follow-up study that those who participated in weekly group-therapy sessions lived twice as long as those who did not—that's an average of 36.6 months for the women who participated as compared to 18 months for the control group.

Item: In the 1980s, psychiatrist Redford Williams of Duke University found, in several studies, a high correlation between chronic hostility and heart disease. For instance, in a study involving almost 2,000 men, those displaying the highest hostility levels were 1.5 times more likely to die of heart disease than those whose hostility levels were in the low range. His conclusion: "Hostility predicts mortality better than any other specific cause."

Item: In 1986, Blue Cross–Blue Shield studied 2,000 meditators in Iowa and found that, compared to nonmeditators, they were hospitalized 87 percent less frequently for heart disease and 50 percent less frequently for tumors.

Item: In 1988, internist Dean Ornish put twenty-two patients with advanced heart disease on a program that included a low-fat diet and daily exercise, along with meditation, twice-weekly group therapy, and other techniques "designed to help people identify and transcend their sense of isolation." His program was based on the theory that alienation (from one's own feelings, from other people) can lead to stress and, often, to heart disease, while "anything that leads to real intimacy and feelings of connection can be healing." Two years later, Ornish reported unprecedented improvements in eighteen of his twenty-two heart-disease patients, while the majority of the control-group patients got worse. In a later interview with Bill Moyers, Ornish called his work with his patients "emotional open-heart surgery."

There are other studies suggesting that isolation may be hazardous, and connection beneficial, to our health. There are other, sometimes contradictory, studies that have claimed to match up personality traits and diseases. There are also various theories about the ways in which emotions are translated into physical

225

manifestations. But all we know for sure is that by a process we don't really understand, the mind seems to have a say in the body's health.

The mind can tell the body to produce symptoms. Researchers report that patients possessed of multiple personalities may have symptoms that change as their personalities change, with one persona displaying the insulin deficiency of diabetics, or allergic reactions to orange juice or cats, while another persona —when it becomes ascendant—exhibits (this is in the very same body!) no symptoms of diabetes or of allergies.

The mind can tell the immune system to shut down. Psychologist Robert Ader and immunologist Nicholas Cohen gave a group of animals an immunosuppressant—a drug that impairs the immune response by suppressing the production of antibodies. Along with this drug they were also given saccharin. When the immunosuppressant was taken away and the animals were given only the saccharin, they continued the shutting down of their immune system, just as if they were still receiving the drug.

The mind can produce physiological damage. Patients given a drug called Mephenesin responded, in some instances, with nausea, dizziness, palpitations, and various other negative reactions—and showed *the same reactions* when a placebo was substituted for the drug. In one dramatic response a woman, ten minutes after she had received the placebo, experienced abdominal pain and a build-up of fluid in her hips.

The mind can tell the body not to feel pain. Pediatrics professor Karen Olness went under the knife—had forty-five minutes of surgery on her finger—using self-hypnosis as her anesthesia. Drawing on a favorite memory of the farm where she grew up, she says, "I simply focused on my image of the farm during the entire procedure, and I was extremely comfortable."

These stories and studies tell us that it's obviously a fiction to treat the mind and body as two separate entities. They tell us that the mind and body "talk" with each other, though these conversations are often outside our awareness. They also suggest, however, that there are actions—conscious actions—we might take to expand the healing powers of our mind, allowing us, in matters of sickness and health and the relief of symptoms and pain, to gain greater control of what happens to our body.

Can we thus conclude that we can learn to use our mind to think ourselves—to will ourselves—into health? Can we defeat disease by *consciously* exercising control of our immune system? Can we—isn't this what all of us really want to know?—use positive emotions to beat back cancer? There are some serious researchers who are willing to say this is hypothetically possible, but most of them hasten to add that at this point we have no proof that it can be done.

"Documented, spontaneous remissions from cancer are reported in the medical literature . . . ,"says Dr. Michael Lerner, cofounder of the Commonweal Cancer Help Program, "but . . . the likelihood that someone with a metastatic breast cancer or a lung cancer or a pancreatic cancer will, by his or her own inner resources, be able to reverse this cancer and have it go away forever—well, that's a very steep slope."

Dr. Margaret Kemeny, a psychologist with training in immunology and psychoneuroimmunology, adds that there has been no research data to support the notion that we can kill a tumor cell by, for instance, summoning up the image of a natural killer cell that would go and zap it. She says that "nothing that we understand about physiology leads us . . . even to speculate on how a particular thought about a particular physiological process . . . could get to the cell and alter it."

And then there are all of those people—like my sister, who valiantly fought against her cancer, thinking positive thoughts, refusing to be a statistic, absolutely determined not to die—who battle against their disease with every single thing they've got, and lose the battle. Their deaths are a mute rebuttal to Bernie Siegel's distressing claim that "there are no incurable diseases, only incurable people."

A not-so-mute rebuttal to various superheated the-mind-runs-the-body premises is offered by social critic Susan Sontag, who, in *Illness as Metaphor,* offers a fiercely opposing point of view. Sontag argues that it is outrageous to blame patients for their diseases, to suggest to patients that they have an unconscious wish to be sick, and to tell them that their failure to cure themselves is essentially a failure of will. Disdainful of the claims of a "scientific link between cancer and painful feelings," she dismisses the assertion that cancer victims have actually victimized themselves because of their depression, dissatisfaction, self-pity, unexpressed hostility, hopelessness, or emotional isolation.

Sontag notes that various commentators have attributed the cancers of Napoleon, Ulysses S. Grant, Robert A. Taft, and Hubert Humphrey to their "reaction to political defeat and the curtailing of their ambitions." She reports psychoanalyst Wilhelm Reich's claim that Sigmund Freud's cancer began when this "very unhappily married" and "very much dissatisfied genitally" man resigned himself to giving up "his personal pleasures, his personal delights." She tells us of Norman Mailer's conviction that if he had not acted out "a murderous nest of feeling" by stabbing his (then) wife, he would have contracted cancer and "been dead in a few years himself." And she quotes W. H. Auden, whose poem about repressed, cancer-ridden Miss Gee offers this "Cancer's a funny thing" diagnosis:

> Childless women get it,
>> And men when they retire;
> It's as if there had to be some outlet
>> For their foiled creative fire.

228

Sontag hates these theories a lot. She believes that making "the luckless ill" responsible both for getting their disease and getting rid of it is not only a burden but a cruel delusion. It deludes them into thinking that they have the power to control "experiences and events (like grave illnesses) over which people have in fact little or no control."

Somewhere between Siegel and Sontag there is surely a middle ground on these mind-body issues. Surely we can say that our mental states can have an impact on our health without, if we should fall ill, blaming ourselves. For even if our emotions play a role in the emergence of a cancer, other factors—powerful and multiple—also make contributions to the disease. We cannot control all those factors even if we could—which we can't— direct our emotions and thoughts to attack our diseases.

Two mavens of mind-body healing offer these answers to people who ask, "Did I give myself cancer?" and "Isn't it my fault if I don't get better?"

Says clinical and research psychologist Lawrence LeShan, whose decades of pioneering work with cancer patients has focused on their powers of self-healing: *Thoughts and feelings do not cause cancer and cannot cure cancer. . . .* Anyone who even hints that the person with cancer is responsible for getting it and/or for not getting better . . . should be completely ignored."

And says Andrew Weil, a Harvard-trained physician who has made the cover of *Time* as one of the leading gurus of alternative medicine: "I reject the idea that people give themselves cancer by failing to express anger and other emotions. And I emphatically reject the notion that failure to heal represents any kind of judgment about a person's state of mind or spirituality." Noting that so many saints have died of cancer "that cancer seems almost to be an occupational hazard of sainthood," he advises, "Keep this in mind if you are tempted to believe that healing depends on enlightenment and transcendence of negative emotions."

So it isn't our fault—we're not guilty—if we get cancer. And it isn't our fault if our cancer doesn't get cured. Nor did we give ourselves, or fail to heal ourselves of, heart disease, arthritis, or other ailments. Though our psychological states—along with our genes, our environment, and our personal habits—can undoubtedly affect the state of our body, there are limits to the power that we can mentally exercise over our physical health. Still, it's possible to give up misplaced self-blame and absurd self-healing expectations, and to nonetheless find ways to be responsible for, to take some control of, our health.

We know, for instance, that outside of our awareness, beyond the involvement of our conscious mind, our body can be conditioned to respond in certain ways to certain stimuli, can be conditioned—as Robert Ader's research showed—to respond to "useless" saccharin as if it were an immunosuppressant drug. The next step, says Karen Olness (she's the physician who had surgery without anesthesia) is "to take charge and to say, okay, if I'm going to be conditioned, then I'm going to be in control of that." Olness also says that we can begin to take control—of our symptoms, of our pain, of our anxiety—by learning various self-regulation techniques. And she says that these techniques —biofeedback, self-hypnosis, visualization, meditation, and so forth—are available not just to a select few but to ordinary people like you and me.

"I think the average person, properly motivated, could certainly learn self-regulation," says Dr. Olness, noting that it can be particularly helpful to young people suffering from chronic diseases. "They can't control when they're going to get sick or come into the hospital—but if they learn these strategies, then they can have something they control, and they can contribute to their own healing."

Are these self-regulation techniques really useful?

Yes, concludes a technology assessment conference cosponsored by the National Institutes of Health's Office of Alternative

Medicine (OAM) in October 1995 to examine that very question. An independent twelve-person panel reported that relaxation techniques (the repetitive focus on a word, sound, or phrase; the blocking out of negative thoughts; and the assuming of a comfortable position in a quiet environment) can lower blood pressure, heart rate, and breathing rate and "are effective in treating a variety of chronic pain conditions such as low back pain, arthritis, and headache." The panelists also found hypnosis effective in relieving a variety of conditions, including irritable bowel syndrome, nausea brought on by chemotherapy, and chronic cancer pain. And they found that biofeedback and relaxation techniques were effective in alleviating insomnia.

The more dramatic examples of "self-induced" cures, remissions, and symptom relief are not evaluated in this report. But perhaps they will be examined another day, for a major mission of OAM is to appraise the research produced by the alternative medicine community. Such appraisal is very important because a surprising *one out of every three* Americans is using alternative, unconventional therapies. We need more information on which of these therapies are effective, and which are not. And we need more information on how these therapies—when they work—actually work.

What seems to be clear, however, is that the use of various self-regulation techniques makes "patients feel empowered or less helpless and better able to deal with pain sensations." Feeling in charge can be beneficial to health. And these benefits derive not only from unconventional medical techniques but from other take-charge tactics like exercising, eating sensibly, giving up smoking, or making important decisions (not necessarily health decisions) about one's own life. Many studies have found that most patients—and, in fact, most people—feel a lot better physically simply by feeling that they have some control.

Item: In studies comparing terminal cancer patients who receive morphine injections from a doctor or nurse with those who

231

are allowed to inject themselves, those in control of their own pain management have better pain relief even though they use less of the morphine.

Item: At the University of Wisconsin Medical School, children with severe burns were divided into two groups. One group was fully cared for by the nurses while the children in the other group were taught how to change their own dressings. The second group, the kids with the greater control, developed fewer complications and needed less medication than those in the first group.

Item: Researchers investigating the effects of control and loss of control on the health of nursing-home residents gave one group great freedom in making choices about a variety of matters (arranging their rooms, setting up social engagements, venting complaints) and told another group that the staff would be fully responsible for, fully in control of, their well-being. In addition, everyone received a small plant, but while the members of the first group were invited to tend their plants themselves, the staff took care of the plants of the second group. Within three weeks, 71 percent of those in the staff-controlled group had deteriorated, while 93 percent of those with enhanced personal control had become more active, felt happier, and showed improvement in mental alertness. A follow-up study eighteen months later found that while 30 percent of the first group had died, the deaths in the second group were only *half* of that amount—15 percent.

Item: Forty college students were given a series of six-seconds-long electric shocks and asked to press a reaction switch immediately upon feeling each shock. After the first series, half of the students were told that if they reacted quickly enough they could decrease the duration of each shock to three seconds. In reality, however, they had no control—the shock time was cut down to three seconds whether their reactions were fast or slow. Nevertheless, their mistaken belief that they could control the duration of each shock made the shocks less stressful to them than they were to the other half of the college students, who were given shocks of exactly the same duration but who hadn't been tricked into thinking that they could control them.

This last study makes another important point about health and control: that believing we have control—*whether or not we actually have it*—helps us feel better.

Elaborating on that point, a number of researchers have noted that a belief in control can produce a placebo effect, that—as psychologist Herbert Lefcourt has put it—"the sense of control, the illusion that one can exercise personal choice, has a definite and a positive role in sustaining life." Or as the authors of the electric-shock study wryly observed: "Perhaps the next best thing to being master of one's fate is being deluded into thinking he is."

As that nursing-home study showed, having some personal control could literally mean the difference between life and death. On the other hand, total loss of control could be fatal. Psychologist Bruno Bettelheim writes of the "Muselmänner," those inmates of the Nazi concentration camps who "came to believe the repeated statements of the guards—that there was no hope for them, that they would never leave the camp except as a corpse" and who, having concluded "that their environment was one over which they could exercise no influence whatsoever," turned into walking corpses and swiftly died.

There are other descriptions of human deaths, including "sudden death syndrome," attributed to hopelessness and help-lessness, to being without either real or imagined control. There are also some famous animal experiments that connect sudden death with uncontrollability. But even when the issues involve something less than life and death, it appears that being in control is for the most part better than being helpless. Many studies testify to the benefits of believing that we have control:

233

People who believe that they possess a good deal of control are less troubled by stressful events than people who don't.

People who believe that they possess a good deal of control are happier than people who feel that they don't.

People who believe that they possess a good deal of control take better care of themselves than people who don't.

People who believe that they possess a good deal of control are less likely to feel that they are—and are less likely to become —and are certainly less likely to remain—victims.

Consider this intriguing study, which compared residents of Illinois with residents of Alabama and found that those from Illinois were considerably more inclined than the Alabamians to believe that they themselves—rather than luck or God—controlled their destiny. Thus, when tornadoes threatened these states, the folks from Illinois were some five times more likely to take tornado precautions. Not surprisingly, the tornado deaths were higher in fatalistic Alabama than they were in masters-of-our-fate Illinois.

This is not to suggest that believing in God has to be incompatible with believing that we have—and can take—control. The distinguished writer Reynolds Price, sustained through the drawn-out horrors of spinal cancer by a religious vision of great intensity, nonetheless offers this advice to those beset by grave illnesses or other catastrophes:

"You're in your present calamity alone, as far as this life goes. If you want a way out, then dig it yourself, if there turns out to be any trace of a way.... *Come back to life.... Only you can do it.*"

He continues: "To be sure, either God or the laws of nature will eventually force you to fall and die. But that event can tend to itself, with slim help from you. Meanwhile ... your known orders are simply to *Live*. Never give death a serious hearing. ... And keep control of the air around you."

• • •

When disaster strikes—attacking our bodies or psyches, piercing our hearts, destroying what we love, smashing our dreams—we will bleed and tremble and weep, and we will curse and bemoan our fate, but sooner or later some of us will start to pick up the pieces and move on. As victims of serious damage or loss, of life's mindless and random atrocities, we'll be bowed by the power of uncontrollable forces. As survivors, however, we'll do what we can to arrange that we, not fate, have the final word, repairing what is reparable, figuring out how to live with what is not, and trying to keep control—as much control as we can keep—of the air around us.

9

Varieties of Surrender

An assumption shared by many theories in social
psychology is that control over one's behavioral
outcomes is desirable, and that individuals strive for
mastery over their environment. . . . However, there
are many life situations in which there is no
possibility of exerting control.

—Wortman and Brehm, "Responses to
Uncontrollable Outcomes"

In good times and bad times, we who value control expect to
control the central circumstances of our life. We establish goals
and actively strive to achieve them. We acknowledge—when we
mess up—responsibility. We try again when things don't go as
planned. Some people, however, don't want to possess, or don't
believe that they *can* possess, control. Destiny rules them with a
mysterious hand. This lack of control may be an abdication or
moral failing, but not all the time and not necessarily. For even
we lovers of control can see (or certainly ought to be able to see)
that sometimes we need to back off, back down, let go, give up,
give in, submit, surrender.

There are many ways of giving up control.

Surrendering control is sometimes good sense and sometimes bad news. It sometimes enriches and sometimes constricts and destroys. It may be unconscious or conscious, eagerly chosen or reluctantly accepted. It may be imposed.

There are many reasons for giving up control.

We insist, "It isn't my fault" or "They made me do it."

We insist, "I did it because I was scared not to do it."

We insist, "I'm helpless, I'm powerless, I can't do it."

We insist we can't do it because, "I'd be out of line."

We say to ourselves, "It's impossible to do it."

We say to ourselves, "I'll fail if I try to do it."

We say to ourselves, "I shouldn't have to do it."

We say to ourselves, "This is their problem, not mine."

Or we say to ourselves, "For peace of mind, resign as general manager of the universe."

We also may say a pragmatic "It's out of my hands," a reverential "Thy will be done," a defeated "You win; I lose," or a defensive "I was only following orders."

We also may say, as my young friend Emmet told his Courtney on their wedding day, "I give my heart in sweet surrender."

There are many different varieties of surrender.

There are many different ways to surrender control.

Social psychologists talk about our sense of having (or not having) control in terms of a concept called "locus of control," distinguishing those who believe in an *internal* locus of control from those who possess *external* control beliefs. Comparing the two, psychologist Herbert Lefcourt says that internals (sometimes called "Origins") "perceive events as being largely contingent upon their personal efforts," while externals (sometimes called "Pawns") tend to "feel more fatalistic about the manner in which outcomes occur." But we're also told to keep in mind that control beliefs can be variable and reversible.

For people who act like internals in some situations will sometimes act like externals in others—like the powerful CEO who always reverts to the obedient child when he visits his mother. And people's control perspectives can change in response to other changes in their life. That CEO, for instance, maybe after some help from a therapist, might feel in greater command of himself with his mother, able to tell her (with more or less finesse) that she really must quit telling him what to do. On the other hand, in the wake of a hostile takeover of his company, he might feel a loss of professional control, might fear that he'll never again be running a company, or even that he is permanently through. But despite these shifts and changes it is useful, in discussing control beliefs, to think of people as tending toward one perspective, as commonly having one of these two points of view. It's useful, in considering their behavior and responses and expectations, to think in terms of their having an internal or external locus of control.

As someone who feels, within limits, that my efforts have shaped my life, as someone who surely would qualify as an internal, I can't imagine living a life perceived as essentially out of my control. But, then, I grew up enjoying the freedoms of middle-class, twentieth-century America, where I had no preordained place or preordained role, where neither my personal nor my social history crushed me with crippling, no-you-can't-be-that constraints. So before I start patting myself on the back for being the person I am—active, take-charge, and (let's face it) rather controlling—I need to consider why some people aren't.

There are good reasons.

A personal family history devoid of opportunities to explore, make choices, solve problems, initiate action may foster an external view of control, where credit or blame for what happens is ascribed to fate, luck, God, or some powerful other. An external view of control may also result from a social history devoid of opportunities for status and work and a place in the larger society, producing the kind of fatalism described by "tamale eater" Manuel Sanchez:

> To me, one's destiny is controlled by a mysterious hand that moves all things. Only for the select, do things turn out as planned; to those of us who are born to be tamale eaters, heaven sends only tamales. . . . I firmly believe that some of us are born to be poor and remain that way no matter how hard we struggle and pull this way and that. God gives us just enough to go on vegetating, no?

Those who belong to groups that have been chronically impoverished, shut out, and denigrated may conclude from daily experience that their lives are shaped by unyielding external forces. But even among those people whom Manuel Sanchez would surely characterize as the "select," there are some who, through their early rearing or later encounters with the wider world, learn lessons of ineffectiveness, of powerlessness. In the way they look at life they too, despite their seemingly privileged lives, are externals who, given these sets of paired statements and asked to pick the one with which they more strongly agree, would probably choose (A), (B), (A), (A), (B), (B):

> (A) Many of the unhappy things in people's lives are partly due to bad luck.
> (B) People's misfortunes result from the mistakes they make.

> (A) In the long run people get the respect they deserve in this world.
> (B) Unfortunately, an individual's worth often passes unrecognized no matter how hard he tries.

(A) Without the right breaks one cannot be an effective leader.
(B) Capable people who fail to become leaders have not taken advantage of their opportunities.

(A) I have often found that what is going to happen will happen.
(B) Trusting to fate has never turned out as well for me as making a decision to take a definite course of action.

(A) When I make plans, I am almost certain that I can make them work.
(B) It is not always wise to plan too far ahead because many things turn out to be a matter of good or bad fortune anyhow.

(A) What happens to me is of my own doing.
(B) Sometimes I feel that I don't have enough control over the direction my life is taking.

Externals, seeing themselves as pawns on a board where somebody else is moving the pieces, find it hard to believe that their actions count. They are less inclined to persist, for they see no relation between persistence and success. Some of them, having taken to heart the lessons of learned helplessness, will expect to be defeated even when, if they would just try, they could prevail. Externals run the risk of far too often, and far too readily, surrendering.

My friend Lenny, for instance, has never done well in his marketing career. This has never, according to Lenny, been his fault. His first boss took a dislike to him. His second boss took advantage of him. His third boss passed him over for promotion. And all of his other bosses, in the way they've treated Lenny—

according to Lenny—have been "SOBs" or "out to get me" or "dumb." There is nothing that Lenny can do because, in his view, his professional life is completely controlled by unjust and irrational forces. There is nothing Lenny can do because, in his view, his bosses are movers and he is their pawn.

John Marcher is also convinced that there is nothing he can do about the special fate for which he is destined, a "rare and strange" and "possibly prodigious and terrible" fate that will one day spring "like a crouching beast in the jungle." While awaiting the arrival of his unknown, inescapable destiny, he detachedly goes through the motions of existence, as his voided days become decades and he becomes old. It is only at the end of his passive, passionless, empty life that Marcher understands the fate he was marked for: that he has been destined to live his entire life as a man to whom nothing whatever has happened.

John Marcher is the fictional creation of Henry James, who wouldn't use terms like "locus of control." But his story of this man who watched and waited, and never loved, and never lived, offers a fearsome image of the risks of failing to choose and to change our experiences, of the risks of leaving our fate "in the lap of the gods."

In contrast to the "apathy and withdrawal" of those with external control beliefs, internals display what Lefcourt calls "vitality." Their belief in their freedom to act, and in the efficacy of their actions, promotes "an active grappling with . . . events." Though Lefcourt says he's uncomfortable with the suggestion that internals are the "good guys," he doesn't argue his point convincingly, for the research that he offers concludes that, compared to externals, internals tend to be:

More "open to experience," more "self-actualizing."

More concentrated and curious and alert.

More sensitive, ready to learn, persistent, achieving.

More capable of resisting moral corruption.

More willing to blame themselves for their failures and failings.

And more adept at coping with adversity.

In view of all the advantages of being an internal, small wonder that Lefcourt wants us to be one too, urging man "to perceive himself as the determiner of his fate" and to avoid "surrender to indomitable forces."

But how do we *not* surrender to indomitable forces? How do we fight them? How do we even try? The fictional Brenda Kovner, who offers advice in a column she calls "IN CONTROL OF OUR LIVES," is happy to provide a constructive reply, noting that "when confronted with a stone wall that is blocking your path, you need to recognize its stone-walledness and not go banging your head against it." But, she goes on to point out, "you could dig a tunnel under it, walk around it, climb over it, dismantle it, or find another road to where you want to go."

In refusing to surrender, Brenda is drawing on what she calls her " 'can-do' attitude," which "has equipped me to help hundreds of thousands of readers (and two dozen or so of my closest friends) with troubled marriages, difficult children, midlife crises, aging parents, and blasted dreams." Brenda's "can-do" attitude might be called an extremist's version of Lefcourt's internal locus of control.

Parental supportiveness, love, warmth, and encouragement help foster an internal locus of control. So does parental protectiveness, which insulates us from life's more brutal blows. It's also important, however, for this "warm, supportive maternal-child relationship" to be followed by a maternal "push out of the nest," allowing us to develop skills and experience our effectiveness and competence.

We looked, in chapter 2, at how we are helped—or not helped—to develop that sense of competence:

242

As a teeny tiny baby evoking resonant responses from our mother, we learn to control our emotional environment. Or we learn that our coos and cues, no matter how clear and how importunate, are likely to be unanswered or misunderstood.

As a toddler exploring the world with our parents protecting us while also letting us go, we learn to master some part of our physical universe. Or we learn that our eager strivings toward autonomy will be viewed either as desertion or mortal danger.

As a three-, a four-, a five-year-old pursuing our tasks with purpose and direction, we learn to move effectively toward our goals, encouraged by parents who help us balance delay and gratification, restraint and initiative. Or we learn that we shouldn't do it, and that we really don't have to do it—they'll do it for us. Or we learn that it can only be done their way. Or we learn that if we resist and rebel, they'll cast us out—"You're on your own," they'll say—leaving us to struggle under-equipped and all alone, with overwhelming events and run-away feelings.

Failing to respond to us or to validate us, giving us too little freedom or too much, our parents can leave us feeling uncon-firmed and ineffective and out of control. But encouraged to take action and make decisions, while provided with a structure, with standards, with guidance, protection, limits, and restraints, we acquire the conviction that we are basically the author of our own life.

That this is our very own life—and we're in control.

But if those with external control beliefs minimize their pow-ers of control, and are thus less persistent in trying to solve problems, internals sometimes err in the other direction. They sometimes fail to recognize that further efforts don't always lead to success and may instead be futile and even destructive. Assuming they have control in all situations, internals may be blind to the uncontrollable, persisting long after—sometimes

243

long, long after—it's time to give up. As Ronnie Janoff-Bulman and Philip Brickman observe in their study of this subject, "the ability to quit is every bit as vital as the ability to persist," and, in fact, persistence in trying to solve what is essentially unsolvable is sometimes more "maladaptive," more "pathological," than giving up when persistence would have succeeded.

Or, as Lefcourt puts it, "man must accommodate to many circumstances where a realization of helplessness would be the wiser choice and where belief in one's ability to control the situation could prove to be detrimental."

Or, as psychologists Camille Wortman and Jack Brehm point out in their "Responses to Uncontrollable Outcomes," "When an organism is confronted by outcomes that are truly uncontrollable, the most adaptive response may be to give up."

Okay, we internals get the message—or do we?

For internals—as well as externals—will sooner or later learn they are helpless in situations they really can't control, but because we internals *expect* control we are going to learn that lesson much more slowly. And so, instead of giving up, we insist on hanging in there. We persist—and we persist—and we persist. And some of us, Louisa, for example, show an enormous—excessive—amount of persistence.

Louisa married Ed, a man who had entered marriage with extreme reluctance. Shortly after the honeymoon, he started his first extramarital affair, explaining—when shocked Louisa found out—that this was nothing of consequence but just an expression of his fear of commitment. Louisa hung in there, figuring that as soon as they had a child he'd settle down.

But as soon as they had a child, Ed embarked on a second and third and then a fourth affair, explaining to tearful Louisa that he had been driven to other beds by the oppressive responsibilities of fatherhood. Louisa hung in there, certain that when they'd moved—as planned—to a sleepy New England town, far from the frisky ladies of the Big City, and when they'd estab-

244

lished warm and close relationships with a group of stable married-with-children couples, Ed would feel less oppressed by responsibility.

Instead, Ed had sequential affairs with two of the wives of the married-with-children couples, with whom he'd established quite warm and close relationships. But as he explained to a hurt and humiliated Louisa, how else does a man get through a midlife crisis? Louisa hung in there, waiting for Ed to get too old to be having a midlife crisis.

When Ed reached fifty-one, their only child was severely hurt in an auto accident. She moved back home for a long stretch of family care. Louisa was sure that this sad situation would bring her and Ed together. Instead he initiated another affair, explaining to heartsick Louisa that he needed it to relieve the depression he suffered because of this sad situation.

Louisa hung in there, confident that Ed's depression would eventually pass.

Approaching sixty-five, Ed made plans to retire. With his more-than-comfortable pension, and with their daughter finally healed and out of the house, Louisa and Ed could travel everywhere. Except—you know the end of this story—Ed entered into yet another affair, finding true love, or so he explained to the disbelieving Louisa on the day that he told her he wanted a divorce.

Louisa, left with the ruins of a life she had tried so hard to preserve, wonders when she should have stopped hanging in there.

If some of us find it difficult to give up when we ought to give up, it's because giving up has a terrible reputation, associated with weakness and failure and disappointing others and breaking our word. For obvious reasons, for excellent reasons, we're taught that hanging in there is far more estimable than dropping out, that "winners never quit and quitters never win"

245

is always more noble than "enough already." The psychological research also emphasizes the benefits of believing we have, and can exercise, control, making us healthier, happier, better able to tolerate stress and more productive, even when our control is sheer illusion. On every level, say Janoff-Bulman and Brickman, little attention has been paid to the risks of mindless persistence, to the risks of mistaken assumptions of control.

"We are in favor," the authors hasten to add, "of dreaming impossible dreams, being willing to make a fool of oneself, letting one's reach exceed one's grasp." But, they note, "this works only if a person knows how to fail, how to recognize when control has been lost."

This works only if a person isn't caught up in pathological persistence.

Pathological persistence keeps us trapped in dead-end jobs and sick relationships.

It keeps us fighting unwinnable wars and trying to fix what cannot be repaired.

It keeps us rejecting the good or the pretty-damn-good or the good-enough while we stubbornly pursue the perfect mate, the perfect career, the perfect . . . whatever, a pursuit that can leave us as empty-handed as the passive John Marcher after consuming the best years of our life.

It keeps us mindlessly striving to master what never has been, and never will be, mastered, leaving us depleted, despairing, or dead.

"The weak may drift irresolutely from goal to goal," write Janoff-Bulman and Brickman, "but only the strong can destroy themselves in the manner of Captain Ahab."

In order not to destroy ourselves, we need to stop hunting white whales and banging our heads against unyielding stone walls. We need to "know when to hold them, know when to fold them." We need to learn when we ought to say, "I can't solve this," "I can't fix this," "I can't win this." We need to learn when we ought to say, "I surrender."

Sometimes, however, surrender goes hand in hand, or alternates, with not surrendering. Sometimes we choose neither one nor the other, but both. The "victims" we met in chapter 8 survived by their insistence upon control. Cornelia "Neil" Biddle, age fifty, offers a different model of survival.

Neil became a "handicapped person"—she can't quite accept this image of herself—when she was left profoundly deaf after the removal of a brain tumor. Good-looking, funny, bright, insightful, vital, and outspoken, she is the remarried mother of two (and the stepmother of seven, and also the step-grandmother of nine), whose job description has always been a combination of housewife and civic activist. She suffers from a genetic condition called neurofibromatosis (NF2), which grows benign tumors in her nervous system, tumors which can press on nerves and cause big problems—like deafness, blindness, paralysis—at any time, and any place, in her body. The first of these tumors was found in her shoulder during her late teens; others were found in her brain after each childbirth. It was one of these tumors, grown huge, which eventually led to the longest of her many surgeries and which left her, at age forty-two, with her permanent hearing loss.

"Stupidly," she says, "I thought that deafness was the worst and most traumatic thing that this condition would have to offer, that after adjusting to that, there would be no more major changes to adjust to." She was wrong. A recent surgery caused some facial paralysis—"I am fretting about that terribly"—and her balance, her ability to walk without flopping or falling, "has been sorely challenged by NF2." In addition, it has turned out that her daughter also carries the gene and, at the age of twenty-one, she too had to have a tumor removed from her brain.

Neil has dealt, and still deals, with bad depressions and self-pity and major frustrations having to do with all of the above, and with losing her role "as the one who stirs the pot of talk" at all the family gatherings, and with misperceived and thwarted communications, and with sometimes (not always, but sometimes) feeling somewhat "like less of a person because I am deaf," and with the absence of music and the sound of her husband's famously sexy voice, and with being "an old dog trying to learn new tricks." Sometimes, she says, she allows herself to depend far too much on her husband and family members. Other times, she resents it when they take charge. She is trying, with great difficulty, to live the way she used to, to travel and entertain and run a household, to do "pretty much the same things as before." She says, "I change my mind many times a day about whether surrendering or control is called for."

Neil's concept of control has to do with trying to do for herself, which gives her a "sense of power and accomplishment," and with trying to stay on top of the latest NF2 research, and with paying attention to exercise and nutrition and other kinds of preventive health care that, she believes, help the body stave off illness. But control is a difficult concept when you're living with the threat of unpredictable, devastating tumors, and Neil understands this very well indeed. "I have become an expert," she says, "at dealing with what is in front of me with regard to my health and not worrying what might be in the future. Every time I develop 'something,' I view it as a reminder that I am mortal and had best get back to the business of living a full life."

In getting back to this business of living, she is sustained by a deep but "not very churchy" faith, which allows her (when she's at her best) to do what she needs to do while also "letting go and letting God." She struggles to make the " 'right' decisions, one second at a time." She feels that, on her "good days," she possesses sufficient courage, sufficient tenacity, to "overcome life's obstacles. . . . that's on good days." But she also has learned "the hard way" that control—"controlling *results*"—is an illusion. She has learned, she says, to surrender a lot of control.

In matters of health, Neil tells us, and in matters of love and marriage, Louisa has learned, we sometimes fare better surrendering control. This is also true when we deal with authority. For compliance—doing what we are asked or told or expected to do—is constantly demanded of you and of me. Compliance with authority is a very important variety of surrender.

Like quitting instead of persisting, "like letting go and letting God," compliant surrender can sometimes be a positive, and sometimes a negative, act.

In our everyday life we all must practice a certain amount of compliance, deferring—like it or not—to the rules of the game, to the laws and regulations, obligations and expectations, of our world. We stop when the traffic signal is red, even if we're the only car on the road. We don't push ahead of the line, though we're in a mad rush. If our boss wants to hold the meeting at the ridiculous hour of 6:15 A.M., that's when we arrive. We take courses we don't want to take to earn Ph.D.s we don't think we need to do what they won't let us do unless we're credentialed. We thank people to whom we're not grateful and wear a suit when the temperature soars to a hundred degrees, all of this to pacify, accommodate, or please assorted constituencies. Out of fear or respect or courtesy or decency or pragmatism, we willingly or resentfully, barely or extensively, comply.

There are, of course, rules we agree with or find tolerable. There are others we object to or hold in disdain. And as psychoanalyst Joseph Braun informs us in "The Healthy Side of Compliance," our feelings about the rules not only determine if we comply but whether, when we do, we comply internally or externally—or both.

249

We're harmoniously compliant when our visible behavior matches our convictions and ideals, when we stand up and salute because we want to salute the person we are saluting.

We're internally compliant (but not externally compliant) when we honor the spirit rather than the letter, when we live a profoundly spiritual life but don't attend church or engage in religious rituals.

And we're externally compliant (but not internally compliant) when we go through all the required, expected motions—bowing, scraping, saluting, and attending church every Sunday—while despising what we do or whom we're doing it for.

Refusing external compliance can make us feel radiant with integrity, but sometimes it's really dumb to refuse to salute. Fighting those petty battles can distract us from more serious pursuits. Agreeing to do it *their* way instead of insisting on doing it *our* way needn't always be framed as "selling out." We can save ourselves a good deal of wasted time and wasted energy by allowing ourselves to engage in external compliance.

Complying with authority, Dolly takes that dreary course in statistics, because she needs it in order to get her degree.

Complying with authority, Caleb fills out twenty forms in quadruplicate, because that's what it takes to get his building permit.

Complying with authority, Sophie runs errands for her boss's wife to keep what (errands aside) is "the best job there is."

Complying with authority, I agree with the traffic policeman, despite the fact that he's wrong and I'm totally right, because (though I swear on my children's heads I didn't run that light) I'd much much rather grovel than get a ticket.

"Paradoxically, then," Braun concludes, "external compliance may be a necessary substructure for genuine creativity, attention to priorities, and inner autonomy. Similarly, true internal freedom is often being exercised under the cloak of compliance and submissiveness."

• • •

While making the case for the healthy side of compliance, Braun observes that it has its darker side too, and that among its negative meanings are "obsequiousness, spinelessness, unworthy subservience, . . . and reprehensible collusion." These darker meanings include not only the doing of harm by active sins of commission but passive do-nothing sins of omission as well.

For sometimes external compliance can be morally reprehensible because of actions we consciously choose not to take, allowing our inaction to betray our dearly held principles and beliefs. Of course we'd never sit silently while somebody used the word "nigger" or "kike" or "dyke." We'd probably never hang out in that kind of company. But what if these very same sentiments were ever-so-slightly lacquered or disguised? What about those times when someone at work or in a social situation made a denigrating remark about blacks, or told a vicious joke about Jews or lesbians, or tossed off a sexist slur that left us feeling angry, disgusted, and appalled? And we didn't object because (says Ann) "everyone else was laughing, and I didn't want to come off like Little Miss Prim." Or we didn't protest because (says Dale) "I was worried I'd sound obnoxiously self-righteous." Or we didn't speak up because (says Elaine) "it would have embarrassed the person telling the story." Or we didn't say a word because (says Lisa) "you have to pick your fights."

We didn't say a word—but an awful feeling in our gut matched the shameful knowledge in our head: that by sitting there in silence while someone spoke in a way we found morally unacceptable, we had failed—by our own standards—to do the right thing.

It's true that none of us wants to turn into the quick-to-be-offended thought police, leaping up from chairs to swiftly denounce any hint of political incorrectness. But sometimes denunciation is appropriate, and sometimes we can protest in a lower key, and sometimes we can be self-restrained and civilized and courteous and still display the courage of our convictions. But if we keep silent out of the wish to get along by going along, we give up our moral control of the situation. If we fail to take a stand when it is morally imperative to do so, we're complying with and colluding with the bad guys—or, at the very least, supporting a moral climate that supports the bad guys.

"Whenever you don't speak out against a gay-bashing crack," a young gay man once told me, "you ally yourself with those guys who literally bash us. Of course *you* wouldn't beat us up, but you make it easier for the people who do."

Sometimes we become the people who do.

Sometimes, when our moral beliefs collide with what an external authority asks of us, we behave in ways we would otherwise view as unthinkable. Surrendering moral control to that authority, we allow ourselves to commit immoral acts. We may commit such acts because we fear for our lives, because we are forced or coerced. But we may behave immorally without any fear of harm, willingly giving up our moral control, our responsibility for our actions, in obedience to an authority we perceive to be legitimate or unchallengeable.

Back in the 1960s, Yale University psychologist Stanley Milgram conducted a series of deeply troubling experiments, recruiting people to participate in what they were told was a study of the impact of punishment on the learning process. Assigning the recruits to the role of "teachers," the experimenter strapped a "learner" into a chair, telling the teacher to give the learner a test and, every time his answer was wrong, to administer an electrical shock—intensifying the voltage with each mistake. The shocks, which ranged from 15 volts (SLIGHT SHOCK) to 450 volts (DANGER—SEVERE SHOCK), evoked grunts, then pleas to stop ("Experimenter, get me out of here . . . I can't stand the pain"), then agonized screams, sometimes followed by ominous silence. But whenever the teacher hesitated, expressed concern, insisted he wanted to stop, said, "The guy is suffering in there" or "I'm sorry, I can't do that to a man," the person in authority —the experimenter—urged him to go on and complete the experiment. And so, in spite of the learner's ever-escalating suffering, and in spite of the teacher's unease with the learner's distress, almost two-thirds of the teachers kept on shocking him up to the full 450 volts.

As you may already know—this brilliant study is frequently cited—the learner (unbeknownst to the teachers) was acting; his screams of agony were simulated; he suffered no jolts of electricity. But the teachers, convinced they were causing great pain and convinced—at least in some cases—that this was wrong, were nonetheless unable to challenge authority, choosing, instead, to comply with this "cruel" experiment.

Why?

Bruno Batta, a thirty-seven-year-old welder, said: "I was paid for doing this. I had to follow orders."

Jack Washington, a thirty-five-year-old drill-press operator, said: "Because I was following orders. . . . I was told to go on. And I did not get a cue to stop."

Elinor Rosenblum, a housewife, said: "It is an experiment. I'm here for a reason. So I had to do it. You said so. I didn't want to. . . . I was tempted so much to stop and to say, 'Look, I'm not going to do it anymore.' . . . But . . . I went on with it, *much* against my will."

And Pasqual Gino, a forty-three-year-old water inspector, said: "I figured . . . Yale knows what's going on, and if they think it's all right, well . . . I'll go through with anything they tell me to do." Mr. Gino, who had not considered disobeying the instructions even when he believed that the shocks were fatal, also said: "I faithfully believed the man was dead until we opened the door. When I saw him, I said, 'Great, this is great.' But it didn't bother me even to find that he was dead. I did a job."

Probing beyond these replies to the whys of surrendering moral control, Milgram offers the view that a willing submission to authority "is a powerful and prepotent condition in man." Indeed, he maintains that, like having an inborn potential to learn a language, we are born with the potential to obey, a potential which (like language) will develop only within a human social context. He makes the interesting argument that obedience is the prerequisite for a stable, efficient social organization, which—evolutionarily—has great survival value and which is characterized by a hierarchy, a division of labor—and a significant loss of personal control. For as members of society, we will find ourselves in countless situations where we're deferring to the authority of others, beginning with our parents and moving on to our teachers and bosses, and usually being rewarded (by loving approval or A-pluses or a promotion) only if we are willing to obey. When people, Milgram continues, have been "civilized" in this way, they internalize the concept of compliance.

This tendency toward compliance is what, says Milgram, his subjects brought into the lab. He sees the process then unfolding like this:

They willingly signed on for the experiment.

They viewed the experimenter as a legitimate authority.

They wished to do a good job for this authority.

They accepted his definition of a "good job."

And they felt—this is very important—that they were responsible *to* the authority, but not *for* the content of the job they were doing.

Those who, sooner or later, wished to stop shocking the learners, says Milgram, were often unable to act upon their wishes, even when they insisted, "He can't stand it. I'm not going to kill that man in there." They continued because they didn't want to renounce the commitment they'd made to the authority or because they were concerned with hurting his feelings. They also continued because they were filled with anxiety, an anxiety that was produced by their daring to think of breaching a fundamental social rule, by their daring to think of disobeying authority.

Perhaps all this helps explain why, with what Milgram calls a "numbing regularity," the decent, responsible people who engaged in his experiment were able to act so callously, so harshly, "unhindered by the limitations of individual morality, free of humane inhibition, mindful only of the sanctions of authority." He concludes that his experiments "raise the possibility that human nature . . . cannot be counted on to insulate its citizens from brutality and inhumane treatment at the direction of malevolent authority. A substantial proportion of people do what they are told to do."

Outside the lab, there's abundant and quite terrifying evidence that a substantial proportion of people do what they're told. And though you and I are convinced that we'd be incapable of engaging in such atrocities, we mustn't forget that those who did were, for the most part, ordinary people.

Like Adolf Eichmann, convicted and hanged for his role in the Final Solution, the Nazi plan to exterminate the Jews, a man who "left no doubt," writes Hannah Arendt in her famous book on Eichmann's trial, "that he would have killed his own father if he had received an order to that effect." Indeed, she continues, since dutiful Eichmann was following orders *and* the law of the land, "he would have had a bad conscience only if he had not done what he had been ordered to do—to ship millions of men, women, and children to their death with great zeal and the most meticulous care."

Explaining his increasing ease with mass murder as the answer to the Jewish question, Eichmann recalls attending the

255

meeting—the notorious Wannsee Conference outside Berlin—at which the Final Solution was discussed. Seeing with his own eyes the eager and widespread support for this plan, Eichmann spoke of sensing "a kind of Pontius Pilate feeling, for I felt free of all guilt." In other words, writes Arendt, *"Who was he to judge? Who was he 'to have [his] own thoughts in this matter?' "*

Arendt, and Milgram, argue that Eichmann was not a special case, an exception to the rule, a "sadistic monster." Others continue to fiercely dispute their view. But the Milgram experiments demonstrate what the ordinary citizen will do, and how very few of such citizens have what it takes to resist "legitimate authority."

Few in Nazi Germany resisted Hitler's "legitimate authority."

Indeed, Eichmann's conscience was eased, he explained, because "he could see no one, no one at all, who actually was against the Final Solution." Nonetheless, at the end of World War II, a number of Germans claimed that yes, they were. Among them were people who, despite their holding important positions in the Third Reich, insisted that they had been "inwardly opposed" to it, their resistance expressed not by any defiant actions that they took but by a so-called "inner emigration." Among those making these claims was a man who presided over the killing of a minimum of 15,000 people. Another man, who was hanged for his crimes in 1946, went so far as to argue that although his "official soul" had committed those crimes, his "private soul" had always been against them. There were also those who maintained that they remained in their positions only because they wanted to "mitigate matters," only because they wanted to prevent the "real Nazis" from moving into their jobs. They were even at times compelled (in order, they said, not to blow their cover) to behave more like the Nazis than the real Nazis. But despite their external compliance they never swerved, they said, from their "inward opposition." Despite their external compliance with every crime of the Hitler regime, their hearts—or so this fairy tale goes—remained pure.

The Holocaust offers testament to the capacity of humans to comply with the most monstrous of demands. So does the Serbian "ethnic cleansing" in Bosnia. And so does the Lieutenant Calley–led massacre of helpless civilians at My Lai. Though each is of a differerent order of magnitude, the common theme is moral abdication, a willingness to tolerate, facilitate, or actively participate in what one knows or used to know—and is obligated to know—is reprehensible.

The mass suicide-murders at the Reverend Jim Jones's Jonestown in Guyana and at David Koresh's Ranch Apocalypse in Waco, Texas, were also expressions of moral abdication, the climax of the surrender of individual judgment to malignant leaders. In both of these dances of death, cult members, at their leaders' behest, sacrificed not only themselves but their children, with Jones urging, "Mothers, you must keep your children under control. They must die with dignity," and mothers—flying in the face of all we know about mother-love—complying.

"We need to remember," writes psychoanalyst Peter Olsson, "that 260 children were the first to die in Jonestown. Children also died in Waco's Ranch Apocalypse. . . . These children's parents not only did not protect them, they led them into the complex group dynamics of death that permeate an apocalyptic cult family and its father-God."

In trying to understand the moral submission to a leader like Jim Jones, therapist Max Rosenbaum, the editor of a book called *Compliant Behavior,* focuses on the "promise of transcendence that they offered their disciples," generating the feeling that they —the followers, the disciples—belonged to something larger than themselves. Echoing this point, Peter Olsson writes that the "lesson to be learned [from Jonestown and Waco] is the insatiable human longing to submit," a longing dramatized yet again in San Diego, in 1997, when members of the Heaven's Gate cult joined their leader in a mass suicide, shedding the human "containers" they called their bodies to reach a higher plane of existence.

This longing to submit can sometimes be understood, says psychoanalyst Braun, in terms of serious failures in early development, resulting in the lack of a sense of self and in pervasive feelings of emptiness. Seeking relief from this emptiness, people may find it through a "shared identity," through fusion with a someone or a something they see as "greater" than themselves. In other cases surrender may be spurred, suggests psychiatrist E. Mansell Pattison, by a need for "an alternative family structure" or, says therapist Rosenbaum, by feeling powerless and "left out of the mainstream of life." Becoming the disciples or the pawns of fanatic leaders who meet their needs but insist upon total compliance—including dying on demand—these empty, alienated, fanatic followers may, like this member of Jones's cult, say:

"I made up my mind to follow you wherever you go. I'll be with you until the end. If I can't go with you . . . I'll lay down my life to die."

Though surrendering to a power that is larger than ourselves can sometimes lead to apocalyptic endings, there's another, more positive, side to such surrender. Indeed it has been argued that our willingness to do so can express the highest level of human maturity. In his book about what he calls "the inner experience" of power, David McClelland offers a psychological analysis of how we progress to this state of mature surrender. Defining power as "the need primarily to *feel strong*, and secondarily to act powerfully," he describes four different stages in the developing expression of power needs.

Stage I begins with our infant self taking strength from an

outside source—our mother. If we could speak, says McClelland, we would describe our feelings as, " 'It' strengthens me." We feel stronger inside because we have incorporated her milk and the other kinds of physical and emotional provisions she supplies. Our power is obtained through our dependency.

This way of feeling powerful may persist into later life, with our adult self seeking strength from our friends or our spouses. Or perhaps we'll go to work for a U.S. senator or a billionaire tycoon. One danger for Stage I people is that, when they can't draw the power they seek—either from private relationships or as the employee of some powerful boss—they may turn to drugs or alcohol for the outside supplies they need to "strengthen me."

In Stage II, as we learn both self-restraint and self-assertiveness, we move from external control to internal control. We're able to say, *"I strengthen myself,"* seeking our strength not outside of ourselves but within. Knowing how to say "No" and taking charge of our body and mind and getting what we want through our own efforts, we meet our needs to feel strong by exerting our will and exercising our autonomy.

One of the dangers for Stage II people is obsessive-compulsiveness, a need to control all their actions and all their thoughts. Some of them may engage in compulsive don't-step-on-the-cracks-in-the-pavement rituals. It has also been observed that while Stage I people are "more distressed by events involving loss of external support," Stage II people are "more distressed by events involving loss of control over one's destiny."

In Stage III we might say, *"I have an impact on others,"* for now we begin to feel powerful by exerting control over those outside ourselves, influencing and persuading them, outwitting and outmaneuvering them, competing with and succeeding in defeating them. Sometimes we even offer help as a tactic of domination, for when they accept they acknowledge they're weaker than we. But helpful though we may be, we will probably have to reach Stage IV before we can help in a nonmanipulative way,

259

before we can offer help without the conscious or unconscious aim of exerting control.

Pathology at Stage III can produce parents who smother their children, who try to control their lives in the name of love. It can sometimes produce Don Juans, who seek to feel strong by defeating their rivals and establishing sexual power over women. It can also, I would add, produce people like a woman I know—let's call her The Vulture—whose friends are her friends only when they are down, only when they are suffering, helpless, rejected, sick, in trouble, or otherwise in need of the assistance of healthy, competent, powerful her.

Arriving at Stage IV, "the most advanced stage of expressing the power drive," we might—surrendering private goals to some greater goal or authority—say something like, "*It moves me to do my duty.*" It is here that we can find strength through acts of self-subordination, by serving as the instrument of some higher power or purpose, by acting on behalf of some organization, political cause, or religious faith. We can willingly choose to lay down our life for our country, regretting that we have only one life to give. Or we can gratefully say, in the words of Psalm 18, "The Lord is my rock, and my fortress, and my deliverer; my God, my strength, . . ."

Some of the strongest people I know are women and men who believe that their strength comes from God.

McClelland understands that the pathology of Stage IV can lead to all of the horrors already described—"What he would not dare do on his own behalf, he will do . . . as his duty to the higher authority." He understands that power plays in the name of collective authority carry more legitimacy and therefore are potentially far more dangerous than those that are based on personal authority. Nevertheless he would surely agree that we can serve God without becoming Inquisitors, and the French Revolution without becoming Robespierres, and the Women's Movement without becoming members of the Society to Cut Up

Men. Giving up our self-concerns in the name of some greater ideal doesn't require our losing ourselves in the process. Mature surrender to something that is beyond ourselves doesn't require surrendering moral control.

If we give up moral control, we might blame our government or our God for whatever immoral actions we engage in. But there are other ways to argue that we're not responsible for the evil we do. We can claim (and believe that it's true) that we weren't able to control ourselves because self-control was beyond our capability, because our control was impaired by bad parents, bad genes, bad medication—bad things that were done to us.

We were abused, unloved, adopted, misunderstood. We were messed up biochemically by pernicious prescription drugs or an excess of junk food. We were driven to do what we did by the person we married or by the nature we were born with, or maybe by the distress induced by menopause or a hostile work environment.

Read all about it in the daily newspapers.

Read about the man who fought to stay out of prison after pleading guilty to stealing $1.6 million from the government agency at which he was employed. He claimed that he had done so under the influence of the antidepressant Prozac which, taken along with an anti-anxiety drug, had significantly diminished his mental capacity to control his behavior.

Read about the officer of a national organization who was accused of embezzling over two million dollars. While she made no explicit admission of doing wrong and claimed no memory of any misdeeds, she offered to make restitution and said she was receiving psychiatric help to deal with a breakdown caused by factors outside herself and connected to the workplace, where she had felt abused and powerless.

Read about the government employee who pleaded guilty to tampering with and destroying government documents and

261

who was sentenced to fifteen months im prison. While, at the judge's prompting, she said that she fully accepted responsibility for what had happened, her witnesses and court records suggest that she was putting the blame for her personality disorder on: her husband (for physical abuse), her supervisor at work (for sexual harassment), and her parents, particularly her domineering father (for forcing her to become a lawyer when she really wanted to be a veterinarian.)

Read about the man, unemployed and depressed, who was charged with attempted murder in two subway bombings. He too used the Prozac defense, claiming that he was unhinged by a toxic combination of that antidepressant and other drugs.

Then there's Dan White, who, in 1979, killed fellow San Francisco Supervisor Harvey Milk and Mayor George Moscone, and whose defense argued "that Mr. White's huge intake of sugar-laden junk food, like Hostess Twinkies, heightened his emotional distress to a point where he came unglued."

And then there's Richard Davis, who, in 1993, murdered twelve-year-old Polly Klaas after kidnapping her from a slumber party in her own bedroom, and who sought to escape the death penalty on the grounds that "his mother was distant, once held his hand over a flame, and all but abandoned him after a bitter divorce from his father," while his father was "neglectful and abusive, once punching the boy's jaw so hard he broke or dislocated it." In other words, "Davis was so damaged by his environment he could not help but make damaged choices in life."

And then there are poor-little-rich-boys Erik and Lyle—the Menendez brothers—who, in 1989, gunned down their father and mother in their home, later blaming the murders on the terrors engendered by parental abuse. Like others who use the excuse of a rotten childhood, these two young men defended themselves by saying that, though they did it, it wasn't their fault, that forces outside themselves were responsible for their criminal lack of control.

Let's grant, for argument's sake, that those who confessed to their crimes were pressed by circumstances outside their control. Let's grant that these circumstances impaired their judgment or caused severe emotional damage. Nevertheless, I see nothing in their stories to suggest that there were no alternatives to the actions they took, that they did what they did because they could not do otherwise. And as long as there were—and it's clear that there were—other choices, they're accountable for the choices that they made.

There are indeed people who, having victimized others, insist that they themselves are really the victims. There are indeed people who, when they hurt themselves, hurt those they love, fall short, flunk out, shrug off all blame. There are indeed people who, when their life is totally screwed up, refuse to be responsible for any of its defects and disappointments. There are indeed people who are inclined to hold everyone except themselves responsible.

But having deplored such irresponsibility, we must also consider another point of view: that refusing responsibility, *under certain conditions,* may be not only permissible but essential.

Refusing responsibility can show respect for other people's boundaries.

Refusing responsibility concedes that some things are truly out of our hands.

Refusing responsibility releases us from unnecessary guilt.

And refusing responsibility permits us to allow ourselves what psychologist Shelley Taylor has wittily termed "acknowledged pockets of incompetence."

These pockets of incompetence are areas of functioning where we have expressly chosen to throw up our hands, declaring: "I can't do that," "I don't know that," "I don't want to know that," and even a shameless "I don't want to try." Pockets of incompetence give us permission to turn to other people for help. They

263

protect us from making public fools of ourselves. They allow us, while granting that something is certainly doable, and even while granting that it needs to be done, to declare that we do not intend to do it. They permit a controlling person to—in certain selective matters—surrender control.

My pockets of incompetence include, among other incompetencies, reading a road map, filing a tax return, understanding electricity, speaking French, not to mention playing tennis, grasping the metric system, and making coffee. I am prepared, in all these matters, to abdicate and/or delegate, earnestly explaining, for instance, that I suffer from geographical dyslexia or piously observing that if God had wanted me to be dealing with tax returns He wouldn't have created tax accountants. Though I think of myself as competent (and controlling) in many aspects of my life, I'm prepared, in selected areas, to opt out—to brazenly and comfortably and unhesitatingly surrender control.

People who basically feel in control may feel freer to designate pockets of incompetence. They'll let others run this or that show —my husband speaks French for both of us when we're in France—without being scared that these others, having been given an inch, will completely take over their lives. On the other hand, there are people like Vicky, whose fears about losing control, and being controlled, have transformed her into a vigilant control freak, rigidly insisting that the beds must be made just so, that the family must dine precisely at seven o'clock, that all bills must be paid by the twelfth of the month, that these lights must be turned on and those lights turned off, that no invitations be issued without her permission—insisting that her husband and her children live by her timetable and her rules.

Not every control freak, however—as we learned from those we met in chapter 7—is propelled by fear-of-losing-control anxieties. Some of us are control freaks because we feel we're doing good when we're in control. Convinced that our ways are the best and that our intrusions aren't intrusions but actually "constructive interventions," we find great value and pleasure in our role as general manger of the universe. And so, while some surrenderers may need more get-up-and-go, we control freaks could use a lot more sit-down-and-shut-up. While some surrenderers surely should learn to persist and to accept responsibility, those of us who seem to be excessively fond of control need to be reminded of the many positive aspects of surrender.

Yielding to sexual passion (under something I'll simply call the "right" conditions) is surely an act of positive surrender.

Accommodating our needs to the greater good of a love relationship is often an act of positive surrender.

Allowing our adult children to live their own lives, and even to make their own mistakes, is mostly an act of positive surrender.

Delegating authority and (within moral limits) complying with authority are other acts of positive surrender.

Quitting when it's sounder to surrender than persist is clearly an act of positive surrender.

Serving as the instrument of a higher purpose or power is sometimes an act of positive surrender.

And accepting the fact that we have, at best, only imperfect control is—yes—an act of positive surrender.

It's important to keep in mind that surrendering control isn't necessarily a weakness. It's important to keep in mind that insisting upon control isn't necessarily a strength. But it's also important to keep pursuing our possible (and a few impossible) dreams, to refuse to comply with malevolent authority, to restrain ourselves from acting upon the more barbaric impulses of our own hearts, to be actors not pawns. In this world of multiple choice, we need to know both how to hold them and how to fold them. We need to know when we're free to, when we're compelled to, when it's wrong to, and when we really ought to surrender control.

10

In Control of Our Death

This morning it occurred to me for the first time that
my body, my faithful companion and friend, truer
and better known to me than my own soul, may be
after all only a sly beast who will end by devouring
his master.

—*Memoirs of Hadrian*

Oh Lord, grant each his own, his death indeed,
the dying which out of that same life evolves
in which he once had meaning, love, and need.

—Rainer Maria Rilke

We can give up steak and cigarettes. We can keep our cholesterol low. We can go for daily runs, tread treadmills, pump iron. We can pop whatever pills are currently touted as the secret of longevity. We nonetheless must surrender to the inevitable. We nonetheless must die.

We must die, and, short of suicide, we cannot select the moment our life will end. Nor do we have the power to choose what will end it. But we ought to be able to have some significant say in the circumstances of our dying. We should—if we can work with (or around) our doctors and family, and our own confusions, ambivalences, and fears—be able to achieve some hard-won control, some imperfect control, over our death.

But if we're to take some control of our death we will need to think about dying before we are dead. We will need to be conscious of the fact of our finitude. We will need to attend not only to the mechanics of our dying but to the decisions we make about how we live.

Back in the fifteenth century, a monk called Thomas à Kempis eloquently and urgently spoke to this point:

> Your time here is short, very short; take another look at the way in which you spend it. . . . Perhaps, before now, you've seen a man die? Remember, then, that you have got the same road to travel. . . . If you hope to live well and wisely, try to be, here and now, the man you would want to be on your deathbed. . . . My friend, my very dear friend, only think what dangers you can avoid, what anxieties you can escape, if you will be anxious now, sensitive now to the thought of death!

Five centuries later John Rau, a business school dean who had formerly been a bank CEO, offered his secular version of this same advice. His words were addressed to successful senior executives, but they obviously have far broader application:

> *Write your obituary.* Make it long. . . . Think about when you are gone and what you would like it to say, not what it would say today. . . . If you are like most

people, you will tear up the first draft because it will be about accomplishments, successes, and positions in organizations. You'll realize you want it to be about character, doing useful things, being a good partner, an exceptional friend. Put a copy in your locked desk drawer. . . . Read it every morning.

By writing our own obituary, so Rau's advice suggests, we learn who we want to be, what really matters to us, how we hope to be remembered. We learn if we're heading where we in fact wish to go. We also are reminded that, within limits, we still can make changes, we still can make choices, that we can—this day—begin to create a life that more closely resembles the life of that wonderful person in our obituary.

But facing the fact of our finitude means more than projecting ourselves into the future. It also means seizing the day, the moment, now. It means living our life with a heightened awareness of what it is we're experiencing, accompanied by the knowledge that this day, this moment, will not come again. We can't always live this intensely, of course. It would make our existence ponderous and exhausting. A little memento mori goes a long way. But consciousness of our finitude helps us to live more fully before we die, helps us to live more fully precisely because we understand that we will die. Edna St. Vincent Millay put it like this:

Yet not as one who never sojourned there
I view the lovely segments of a past
I lived with all my senses, well aware
That this was perfect, and it would not last. . . .

David Morowitz, an internist with an earthier sense of finitude, echoes these thoughts in an essay called "Bagels on Sunday":

One pleasant ritual of my relatively uncomplicated life is the Sunday morning purchase of freshly baked bagels, a happy task repeated with undiminished delight. And why not? The bagels are wonderful, and the bakery is filled with an animated friendly crowd in lines growing out the door onto the sidewalk. . . .

But like a slowly expanding dark spot in the shaving mirror I face each morning is the sense, occurring more frequently with age, of how fragile are the good fortunes of all of us in that particular time and place. Waiting in turn, I find myself wondering which of us will be the first absentee on some future Sunday, sensing also the miracle of our weekend reunions. . . . For all of us here at the bakery have managed to avoid or survive life's historical, medical, or psychiatric catastrophes and, in doing so, seem blissfully forgetful of how closely we approach them every day. While not part of the turbulence in a happy shop on Sunday, the tragic possibilities may be just offstage. . . .

Life, companionship, health, solvency: these are gifts none of us fully understands. But shouldn't we at least sense the wondrousness of the luck involved? . . . The short trip for our bagels ought to be seasoned with gratitude: for each future errand, for the life and health they represent, and for our nonchalance in forgetting temporarily that this cannot last, not even an act so small and perfect as going for bagels on Sunday.

In Thornton Wilder's play *Our Town*, the dead Emily revisits a happy, "unimportant" day in her past, watching her younger self and her family going about their business, unaware that it's perfect and will not last. Their failure to know what they have

while they have it overwhelms her with sorrow and she turns
back to her grave, with this final farewell:

> Good-by, Good-by, world. Good-by, Grover's Corners.
> . . . Mama and Papa. Good-by to clocks ticking. . . .
> and Mama's sunflowers. And food and coffee. And
> new-ironed dresses and hot baths . . . and sleeping and
> waking up. Oh, earth, you're too wonderful for any-
> body to realize you.

"Do any human beings," she asks through her tears, "ever
realize life while they live it?"

The poet Jane Kenyon, who died of leukemia at the age of
forty-eight, did:

> I got out of bed
> on two strong legs.
> It might have been
> otherwise. I ate
> cereal, sweet
> milk, ripe, flawless
> peach. It might
> have been otherwise.
> I took the dog uphill
> to the birch wood.
> All morning I did
> the work I love.
>
> At noon I lay down
> with my mate. It might
> have been otherwise.
> We ate dinner together
> at a table with silver
> candlesticks. It might

have been otherwise.
I slept in a bed
in a room with paintings
on the walls, and
planned another day
just like this day.
But one day, I know,
it will be otherwise.

As we face the end of our life, we are—all of us—vulnerable to feelings of regret. We wish we'd done this, not done that, acted, abstained. We cannot always control the circumstances that give rise to our aching "if only's." But we may have fewer regrets if we endeavor to control what we can control—becoming more mindful of life's fine fleeting moments; striving to become the person who, at the end of life, we hope to be. We may have fewer regrets if we choose to live with a clear consciousness of finitude.

The poetry of life can be found in ordinary things—in bagels and new-ironed dresses and ticking clocks. But it's difficult to find poetry in a hospital. And it's difficult to find a way to take control of our death in a medical environment where the prolongation of life is more highly valued than the reduction of suffering.

"Every time a patient dies," writes physician Sherwin Nuland in his thoughtful, compassionate book *How We Die*, "his doctor is reminded that his own and mankind's control over natural forces is limited." This is a reality that earlier generations of doctors accepted. This is a reality that many doctors today resent and resist. Indeed, Dr. Nuland observes that with the enormous advances in medical science to draw on, doctors have been afflicted with a serious case of what he calls "medical hubris," determined to try almost anything to keep us (on whatever terms) alive—even when it's time to let us go.

271

And even when we want them to let us go.

A troubling study, known as SUPPORT, which looked at end-of-life care at five major medical centers, found that many doctors were unaware of, and that some doctors chose to ignore, their dying patients' wish to be spared "heroic" medical measures to keep them alive. Almost 40 percent of these patients spent a minimum of ten days in intensive care, while 50 percent of those conscious were in pain, the suffering of their final days the consequence of aggressive interventions. Furthermore, and more shocking, when systematic efforts were made to improve physician-patient communication, these efforts produced *no* improvement in end-of-life care.

"Many Americans today," write the SUPPORT investigators, "fear they will lose control over their lives if they become critically ill, and their dying will be prolonged and impersonal." This report, with its descriptions of doctors subjecting dying patients to procedures these patients would never choose for themselves, makes it clear that such fears are justified.

My aunt Florence, for instance, who watched a good friend preserve the life of her dog long after that poor animal needed to die, said to her one day, "I've just signed papers that are going to make it impossible for doctors to do to me what you did to your dog." But in fact, when she was comatose and I—her next-of-kin—asked that all care but painkillers be withdrawn, the doctor in charge of her case refused, telling me, "For that, you'll need Dr. Kevorkian."

It was not until the doctor had been replaced (by a hospital staffer—not by the suicide doctor, Jack Kevorkian) that Florence was allowed the death she had chosen. I was technically able to fight for her choice because I could produce her signed directive, and emotionally able to fight because her friend had told me the story about the dog.

I was not, however, prepared for how fearfully difficult it is to let someone die—even when her body and mind are destroyed, even when there's no possible hope of improvement, even when allowing her to keep living in such a state would be a betrayal. I wasn't prepared for the anguished reluctance I felt to make decisions that I intellectually knew were the right ones to make, the strangled voice with which I asked to have my aunt removed from the ventilator, the you're-playing-God uneasiness with which—when she continued to breathe on her own—I answered the final questions in a grim catechism:

Do you give your permission to stop her antibiotics?

Yes, I do.

Do you give your permission to stop her nutriments?

Yes, I do.

Do you give your permission to stop . . .

I gave permission.

And whenever I doubt my decision, I think of the man in the ICU with tubes running in and out of his dying body, a man whose unhappy final words were: "They are cheating me out of my own death!"

That "they" might have been, like me, a family member who —in the case of this poor man—couldn't make the tough call that had to be made. "They" surely thought they were doing the right thing. It's perfectly human for spouses or siblings or children to worriedly wonder, "Maybe we're giving up on him too soon," to soul-searchingly ask, "Are we sparing him—or ourselves?" and to therefore be tempted to hope that "just one more treatment, just one more procedure, might do the trick." The most devoted families, out of love or guilt or uncertainty, or misplaced optimism, or misinformation, may wind up cheating us out of our own death.

Not all of us, however, want our plugs pulled.

The SUPPORT study seemed to assume that patients would not choose further treatment if they understood how miserable the quality of their remaining life would be. But this isn't, it turns

273

out, necessarily so. Among those whom doctors characterize as terminally ill are many who are determined not to let go. And among the currently healthy are many who, when their time comes, don't intend to go gently. Violinist Nathan Milstein, for instance, when asked in an interview how long he would like to live, replied, "As long as possible, and that goes for whatever condition I am in. I would choose to survive," he declared, "under all circumstances. . . . I love life."

If Milstein were a patient he might be expected to reject any argument for withholding treatment. But even patients who do, in advance, subscribe to an informed no-treatment view may change their minds when faced with a medical crisis. The reason for this shift, says Dr. Russell Phillips of Boston's Beth Israel Hospital, may be that "what we think of as poor quality of life doesn't seem so bad if that's all you have left." In their eager clinging to life, in their grasping after essentially futile treatment, such patients resemble the wretched man who kept calling and calling for death to come his way but, when it finally arrived, cried out, "Come no nearer, O death! O death, leave me alone."

Only those who have chosen to stay alive "under all circumstances" can evaluate the wisdom of their choice.

Other terminal patients may want to have everything possible done for them because they seek not a reprieve but a cure, because—in their secret heart of hearts—they do not really believe that they must die. Indeed, whether sick or well, there are those who can't seem to comprehend that we all, each and every one, are terminal cases.

"In normal times," says therapist Hattie Rosenthal, "we move about actually without ever believing in our own death, as if we fully believe in our own corporeal immortality. We are intent on mastering death . . . we marshal all forces which still the voice reminding us that our end must come some day, and we are suffused with the awareness that our lives will go on forever."

"Granting that death is inevitable . . . ," I once began a discussion with a friend, who quickly interrupted with, "Who's granting?" And I've read about the Frenchman who, in writing his last will and testament, introduced his bequests with, "*If* I should die . . . " It's true that most of us recognize that the word is "when" not "if," that death isn't waiting for us to grant it or greet it, that no matter how low our cholesterol count and no matter how far we run, death will lay us low, death will always outrun us. But even those who understand that everybody dies may think of themselves as exceptions to the rule, may think, with Vladimir Nabokov: "A syllogism: *other men die; but I / Am not another; therefore I'll not die.*"

There are also those few who believe that, while it is true—thus far—that everybody dies, this isn't the way it always has to be. They argue that advances in science could, eventually, allow us to be physically immortal:

> Soon it will be possible to extend human life indefi-
> nitely. After thousands of years of desperate struggle
> against death and deepest anguish at its inevitability
> there is at last hope of winning that struggle. In re-
> search centers around the world efforts are now accel-
> erating to overcome aging and, in time, death itself.

Those with such faith in science dismiss the view that every species has a natural, finite, genetically programmed life span. They dismiss the fact that, although there has been an enormous increase in average life expectancy, *maximum* life expectancy hasn't budged. (It's around 100 to 110 years.) Some of them make the argument that nobody dies of old age. We die (except for suicide, murder, and accidents) only because diseases do us in. Eventually, so this argument goes, our medical knowledge will conquer all diseases. In conquering disease, it will conquer death.

Until this final victory, patients with a boundless faith in medicine will turn to aggressive treatment to keep them alive. For, as the old saying goes, where there's life there's hope. Every day they read about astonishing new scientific breakthroughs. So if they can just hang in there—for maybe a week, or a month, or a year—there might be a cure for this currently fatal condition.

Thus patients may submit to drastic and futile interventions because, out of fear or hope, they cannot give up. And sometimes they are subjected to drastic and futile interventions because their nearest and dearest cannot give up. But often, far too often, they will undergo drastic and futile interventions because the doctors who treat them, particularly the specialists, cannot give up.

Dr. Timothy Quill, addressing the subject of overzealous medical intervention, offers the following terrifying parable:

> Three sailors are shipwrecked on a remote island, and captured by a primitive tribe. They are tied up by the tribesmen and brought before a tribunal of elders. The elders gave the first sailor a choice: "What would you rather have, death or Chi-Chi?" The sailor hesitated only a moment. "I know what death is, and I surely don't want it. I will take Chi-Chi." The sailor was then slowly skinned alive by the tribesmen, and had his heart cut out while he was still conscious, after which he died.
>
> After watching this horrible ritual, the second sailor was brought before the tribunal. He was much more circumspect, and thought very carefully before giving his answer. "I certainly don't want to die, but I also don't want to be tortured and die anyway. But maybe Chi-Chi changes. Maybe it's a relative phenomenon. Maybe it won't happen to me. Given these limited choices, I guess I will take Chi-Chi." The second sailor

was then subjected to the same ordeal, skinned alive, after which his heart was cut out while it was still beating.

The third sailor was then offered the same choice. His perspective was radically altered by the disturbing ritual he had witnessed. "Maybe death isn't all that bad. I certainly don't want Chi-Chi. I guess I will take death." The elders looked a bit surprised and said, "Okay, but first Chi-Chi."

Dr. Quill explains that the sailors are patients, the tribesmen are hands-on medical practitioners, and the elders represent the attending physicians, whose treatment decisions may "unintentionally prolong and dehumanize the dying process." Quill grants that there are times when patients are snatched from the brink of death and restored to long and productive lives by treatments almost as agonizing as Chi-Chi. But before we opt for Chi-Chi, he says, we should know what Chi-Chi means, and what kind of odds we're up against, and what kind of life we'll have left should we survive. And before our doctors err, as they usually do, on the side of aggressive medical treatment, they should be clear on the consequences and costs. Without such clarity we run the risk of ending our life as "the victim of a brutal medical death ritual"—suffering and diminished and completely stripped of all hope of having what has been called a "beautiful" death, a "good" death," our "own" death, a "death with dignity."

The decision to try every possible life-prolonging intervention can make it harder to die a death with dignity. And once we're subjected to breathing tubes and feeding tubes and surgeries and CPR and all of the other Chi-Chi, it's just about impossible to approach our death with any sense of control. If we're to have control, we will need to give thought to these matters well in advance of our death day. If we're to have a prayer of thwarting

277

unwanted medical efforts to keep us alive, we must be prepared to contemplate some gritty end-of-life considerations.

Specifically, we'll need to sign a medical directive, popularly known as a living will, which is going to confront us with discomfiting intimations of mortality.

The Medical Directive that is offered by the *Harvard Health Letter,* for instance, attempts to be quite graphically inclusive, covering four different heavy-duty crisis situations and asking us to check boxes that will request or reject different medical interventions. For instance, "If I have brain damage or some brain disease that . . . cannot be reversed . . . *and I also have a terminal illness . . . ,"* do we or don't we want the following treatments: Cardiopulmonary resuscitation? Artificial nutrition and hydration? Mechanical breathing? Dialysis? Major surgery? Antibiotics? And so forth. And will our answers be different, "If I have brain damage or some brain disease . . . that cannot be reversed and that makes me unable to recognize people, to speak meaningfully to them, or to live independently, *but I have no terminal illness . . ."?*

Are we having fun yet?

Having signed a medical directive, we nonetheless should also sign a health-care proxy, which sometimes also goes by the name of durable power of attorney for health care. This authorizes a person, if our wishes on medical matters are in dispute and if we cannot clarify our wishes, to make all health-care decisions on our behalf. We ought to name someone, of course, who understands under what conditions we most surely would not want our life prolonged. In addition, it should be someone who—should we be in no shape to fight for our right to die—can do it for us.

We've learned that signing such papers gives us no absolute guarantee that our stop-the-treatment wishes will be honored. The disturbing SUPPORT study showed that our wishes are, in fact, too frequently ignored. But every state now recognizes living wills and similar medical documents. And recently some doctors and some hospitals have been sued for overriding right-to-die directives. Advance directives *potentially* can do what the Harvard directive claims it can do: "permit the greatest possible control over one's final days."

Even if we can arrange to escape from misguided medical efforts to preserve us, we are warned by Dr. Nuland that "the quest to achieve true dignity fails when our bodies fail." But many of us will continue to aspire to some sort of dignity in our death. And some of us will argue that we can best achieve this dignity by coming to death before it comes to us, by controlling the when and the where and the how of our dying.

Several years ago a friend and I arranged a lunch date with a distinguished elderly man who had just moved to town, a man who seemed quite unhappy with his new home and the new conditions of his life. My friend didn't know him well and I had met him only once, but in asking him out we were not simply being kind. For the man was Bruno Bettelheim, the brilliant and controversial child psychologist, and we anticipated an interesting afternoon. It never happened.

The morning of our date, when we put in a call to arrange for a time to pick him up, we were informed that he was unavailable. We called again and received the same reply. Later that day we learned that Dr. Bettelheim would be permanently unavailable. He had killed himself.

Not knowing the state of his mental or physical health, I have no opinion on why Bruno Bettelheim chose to end his life. But an arrogant fantasy lingered long in my head: If only he'd waited for lunch . . . If only we three had shared a nice afternoon . . . If only we'd then made plans for another date, and then for another date after that. . . . If only, then maybe . . .

Lacking information, our quite human response to suicide is to feel that there are better ways to fix "it," to feel that something could have been done to make that terminated life worth living. But in fact I agree with those who believe in the concept of rational suicide. I agree with those who believe that there are times when it makes sense to do ourselves in. I also believe, however, that we are entitled to make that choice (or to ask for assistance in carrying out that choice) only under certain stringent conditions:

We must be in the terminal phase of a devastating illness, or unmanageably, insupportably disabled.

The decision to die must originate from us, and we must be competent to make it.

We obviously will be sad, but our decision should not be distorted by a depression that may be transient and reversible.

All efforts must be exhausted to control our intractable pain, to make our daily living conditions tolerable, and to rectify whatever careless, callous, or demeaning health-care practices are breaking our spirit and grinding down our soul.

Before we choose to kill ourselves we must understand that death is the end—forever—of living in this world of music and lilacs, sunrise and sunset, the taste of fresh bagels, the touch of someone we love. Before we choose to kill ourselves we must understand that we're dead a very long time. We must know with absolute clarity exactly what—and why—it is we're leaving. We must know that there is no other way to fix it.

I'll grant that all the above is almost unreasonably rational. But it seems to me it ideally should be the only kind of suicide we should support.

In a process a German psychiatrist, Alfred Hoche, has characterized as "balance-sheet suicide," we can weigh the pros and cons of living and dying. But even the strongest advocates of such balance sheets would preclude the option of suicide for the young, recognizing their tendency to see their sorrows and setbacks as unendurable, recognizing their readiness to seek an ultimate remedy in death.

A thirty-three-year-old woman, clearly contented with every aspect of her life now, wrote a letter responding to a newspaper article on "self-deliverance." It said: "Ten years ago . . . I attempted suicide several times, sincerely believing that death was the 'only satisfactory release.' I thank God that I did not have access then to any guides to supposed self-deliverance. . . . Please . . . give other people a chance to have a new life in *this* world."

Her point was echoed in a letter sent to the *Journal of the American Medical Association* by two child psychiatrists and a clinical social worker who voiced strong objections to a book on suicide, maintaining that its "lurid examples, explicit instructions and vigorous advocacy . . . may have an especially pernicious effect on adolescents." Considering that a 1991 survey of 11,631 high-school students found that in the previous year *one out of twelve* had attempted suicide, we must, in any justification of suicide, remember the vulnerability of the young.

It takes a lot of years, a lot of experience, and a lot of common sense to be the kind of bookkeeper who can weigh the pros and cons of living and dying. But although it seems clear that balance-sheet suicide isn't meant for kids, it also seems clear that for certain adults, under certain conditions, suicide may be a legitimate choice.

"The thought of suicide," writes philosopher Friedrich Nietzsche, "is a great consolation: by means of it one gets successfully through many a bad night." But when the future holds nothing but a succession of bad nights, it may be time to move from the thought to the deed. "When even despair ceases to serve any creative purpose," writes the English critic Cyril Connolly, "then surely we are justified in suicide."

There is surely nothing like suicide for asserting control, for taking control, of our death.

Charlotte Perkins Gilman, a distinguished writer and feminist, ended her life at the age of seventy-five, explaining in her suicide note that "I have preferred chloroform to cancer." She also left a manuscript defending suicide as a release from "the suffering and waste we now calmly endure," noting that "the record of a previously noble life is precisely what makes it sheer insult to allow death in pitiful degradation."

Sixty years later, in 1995, Earl Blaisdell of Falls Church, Virginia, chose not to *live* in pitiful degradation. Eleven years of multiple sclerosis had left him almost a hundred pounds thinner. He could move only his face and neck and left hand. He was bedeviled by chronic bedsores. He was starting to go blind. He no longer had control of his bladder and bowels. Earl wanted out.

But Carmi, his wife, had already refused to help him with an overdose. His doctor had refused to help with an overdose. And his efforts to locate the famous suicide doctor, Jack Kevorkian, had failed. And so, one day, having finished a buttered slice of seven-grain bread, he announced to his disbelieving wife, "I want you to know that I've just eaten my last meal." Forty days later, surrounded by his family, Earl—age fifty-seven—died of starvation, having killed himself in the only way he still retained the power to do.

In a tape he made in secret, to be given to his family after he died, Earl forcefully defends his desperate decision:

> I know you folks are trying to convince me that I should stay alive. But if you were layin' in this bed like this, you wouldn't do it either. . . . If I can find a way to get out of here, I'm going to try to find it. . . . I don't want to exist anymore . . . I'm going through hell. . . . Don't feel bad about me being gone. I'm plain better off.

One year later Earl's wife and Elaine and Michael, his two grown stepchildren, were still struggling to make peace with the way he died. But Elaine said that she understood why Earl chose suicide. She said that "he was finally in control."

Michael was willing to grant that Earl showed "strength and a lot of will," but he nonetheless felt that "he took the coward's way out." He said that he "respected his choice" but added, "I don't respect the way he died."

Some—I among them—would say that the only thing wrong with Earl Blaisdell's suicide was that he hadn't been able to do it more easily.

There are many passionate arguments against suicide—philosophical, psychological, and religious. Suicide is cowardly. Suicide is sick. Suicide is a major mortal sin. Or, as the great philosopher Immanuel Kant pronounced, "Suicide is not abominable because God forbids it. God forbids it because it is abominable."

But Earl Blaisdell and others might argue that what truly is abominable is a protracted and degrading death. And having resolved to die, their only remaining urgent question may be "How?"

That answer, as Blaisdell's death made clear and as Dorothy Parker's poem sardonically tells us, is considerably more difficult than we might think:

> Razors pain you;
> Rivers are damp;
> Acids stain you;
> And drugs cause cramp.
> Guns aren't lawful;
> Nooses give;
> Gas smells awful;
> You might as well live.

If we choose not to live, however, we will want to kill ourselves painlessly and nonviolently, which usually means with enough and the right kind of pills. And indeed there are publications that provide precise information on how this is done. Nevertheless, it's quite possible to botch the job of suicide and to have to go through the whole damn thing again. We may want someone on the scene not only to be with us in our hour of death but also to lend us a hand should our efforts fail.

For help at the time of suicide, or for help in obtaining the means of suicide, we may turn to our family or friends or to our doctor, though assisted suicide is still illegal in most states and those who lend a hand risk prosecution. The United States Supreme Court has ruled that the Constitution gives us no right to obtain a physician's help in killing ourselves, though this ruling doesn't prevent individual states from legalizing assisted suicide. Thoughtful people have made, and will continue to make, strong arguments on both sides of this agonizing issue. Among the seminal writings in support of assisted dying, Timothy Quill's brave discussion in the *New England Journal of Medicine* stands out.

Quill modestly describes how he came to provide a dying woman—a longtime patient of his—with a prescription for a fatal dose of barbiturates. Diane, as he called his patient, had chosen not to seek treatment for her acute leukemia—a treatment involving devastating assaults upon the body and a failure rate of 75 percent. Although abstaining from treatment meant certain death within a few months, or perhaps even weeks, Diane convinced both Dr. Quill and her family of the rightness of her decision. She also expressed the wish to make something good of whatever time she had remaining to her, a wish that was being thwarted by her persistent terrors of a lingering death. In order to live well she needed to know that she would be able to die when she wanted to die. She asked for pills.

"I wrote the prescription with an uneasy feeling about the boundaries I was exploring—spiritual, legal, professional, and personal," Dr. Quill explains. "Yet I also felt strongly that I was setting her free to get the most out of the time she had left, and to maintain dignity and control on her own terms until her death."

Diane had some time of "relative calm and well-being," some time well spent with her son and husband and friends. And when it was clear that the good times were done and the future held only bad choices, Diane used the barbiturates to kill herself.

Dr. Quill concludes: "Diane took charge and made active decisions that helped to control her fate in a way that had meaning and purpose for her. . . . At the end, Diane was less afraid of death than she was of dependency and progressive debility. Though she did not wish for death, for her it became the lesser of two unfortunate evils. Diane did not ask to become ill or to face these difficult choices, but she did ask to be allowed to control her destiny."

While many of us may strongly support physician-assisted suicide, we doubtless agree with Quill, who has said that we don't want to make such aid-in-dying too easy. We may also prefer to see it occur—as it did with Quill and Diane—in the context of a long and close relationship. Indeed, this absence of intimacy, this lack of a genuine patient-doctor relationship, contributes to our uneasiness with Kevorkian, whose zeal in helping folks die gives a new definition to the concept "the kindness of strangers."

The notorious Jack Kevorkian, a.k.a. Doctor Death, is a crusader for physician-assisted suicide, responding to calls for help from women and men who want to kill themselves, either because they have a terminal illness or because (like Blaisdell) they suffer from an incurable, insupportable condition. Kevorkian hooks them up to a device that they themselves will be able to activate—he has used both a lethal-injection machine of his own invention and a face mask attached to a carbon-monoxide canister. And far from helping them quietly, he is unabashedly public about his involvement. "I assisted Thomas Hyde [a thirty-year-old man with Lou Gehrig's disease] in a merciful suicide," he announced to the press in 1993. "There's no doubt about that. I state it emphatically."

Frequently risking a prison term, Kevorkian—with his eccentric, insistent crusading—has earned the support of some and the outrage of others. His detractors include Derek Humphry, who is the founder of the pro-euthanasia Hemlock Society, an organization which favors the decriminalization of assisted suicide. Explaining his quarrel with Kevorkian's "open-ended euthanasia," which he described as "full of risks" and "a slippery slope," Humphry said, "No conditions, no waiting periods. Any doctor can help any incurably sick person anytime at any place. The thinking people in our movement are appalled by it."

Still, how many doctors have privately done what Kevorkian does publicly? How many terminal patients, seeking release from a rotten end, depend on the kindness of their family physician? And how many men and women, determined to take control of their death, have been assisted by people who know them and love them, by spouses or children or siblings or friends who can help (and can live with the fact that they've helped) them die?

In a touching article about his mother's death, Andrew Solomon writes about the lost innocence of assisting in a suicide, describing the experience as the loss of "a fragile virginity." He offers a defense of euthanasia, telling us that it "is a legitimate way to die, and, at its best, . . . full of dignity. But," he adds, "it is still suicide, and suicide is the saddest thing in the world."

Solomon's mother, in the late stages of a terminal illness, had worked out all the details of her suicide, though her husband and sons were aware of what she was planning. Over the course of months she acquired the pills she needed to die, she resolved old family disputes, she spent time with each friend, she reupholstered the furniture so the house would be left looking good, she chose the design she wanted for her tombstone. On the day she had picked to kill herself, she put on a robe and a nightgown with pink roses. With her husband and sons at her side, she took antiemetics, ate a light snack, then swallowed the pills. And during the less than an hour after she'd taken the pills, Andrew Solomon recalls, she told them, and they told her, all of the final things that they needed to tell each other.

Then, writes Solomon, his mother's voice grew slow and drowsy. She said, "I'm sad today. I'm sad to be going." And yet, despite this sad dying, she said, she wouldn't trade her life for anyone else's. "I have loved completely, and I have been completely loved, and I've had such a good time."

Her eyes, reports Solomon, closed and then opened again, resting, in turn, on each family member and settling at last on her husband. "I've looked for so many things in this life, . . ." she said in her slowed-down voice. "And all the time Paradise was in this room with the three of you."

After that she thanked her son David for giving her a backrub. And after that she closed her eyes forever.

My mother died her "natural" death after several days of agony. The father of a dear friend of mine kept begging, till his voice was gone, for release. An almost ninety-three-year-old woman, whose mind stayed cruelly clear as her body wasted and wasted and wasted away, died—her cousin reports—"a horrified, captive, lucid witness to her own decay." Setting these bleak endings against Carolyn Solomon's graceful, easeful death, this "good" death of fable, this death with dignity, I cannot find it in my heart to agree that "suicide is the saddest thing in the world."

But sad though he found it to be, Solomon says that it's his intention to someday die the way his mother died. He says this is true of his father and brother as well. He writes that if they are not cut down by cars or random bullets, or by fatal heart attacks or strokes, "then, in keeping with our last inheritance from my mother, we will certainly all kill ourselves." He says that he is amazed that people die any other way, having witnessed the "logic of euthanasia in action." He says that it would surprise him if he died any other way, having "witnessed the comfort of that control."

Control. Control. Suicide lets us die in complete control. Solomon calls it "the comfort of that control." Quill speaks of "a patient's right to die with as much control and dignity as possible." And a social worker, talking of Blaisdell's death by self-starvation, says, "Clearly, it was the last thing that he could control.

Daniel Callahan, an expert on medical ethics, is troubled by this insistence on control and troubled too by the movement to legalize both assisted suicide and "active euthanasia"—the right, if we're suffering, to have somebody kill us. He points to the collision between, on the one hand, our society's fierce individualism, "which asserts our right to autonomy, to be the master of our own fate, to be in control of our bodies" and, on the other hand, a medical tradition whose determination to save human life too frequently results in what he calls "an uncontrollable momentum toward relentless, aggressive, unthinking treatment." How do we individualists manage to gain control over this uncontrollable medical juggernaut? For many, says Daniel Callahan, the answer is perfectly clear—we gain control by legalizing assisted suicide and "mercy killing."

Callahan believes that we should be spared physicians' dragging out our life "past any point of benefit or common sense." But he strongly opposes our right to ask to be killed. He says that it's bad for society to sanction "private killings between its members." He says that it "gives to the value of control over self and nature too high a place at too high a social cost."

There is also, of course, the argument that allowing private killings is a slippery slope that leads to deadly abuse, pressuring people to die by making them feel that they are a burden, doing away with the elderly or the powerless or the infirm for economic or other personal gain. Some activists for the disabled

288

fear that the blind or the deaf or the wheelchair-bound might one day be viewed by physicians as not worth saving. Some critics of managed care are afraid that HMOs, determined to keep down costs, will press for assisted suicide over expensive life-preserving treatments. Others are concerned that as family members watch their inheritance depleted by a parent's round-the-clock nurses, they might discourage that parent from clinging to life. And others are concerned that the stress of caring for a disabled husband or wife might prompt a weary caretaker to suggest—or even insist—that he or she has an obligation to die.

The slippery slope is composed of ambiguities.

Consider George Delury, who kept a diary recording his all-too-human thoughts in the months before he helped his wife, Myrna Lebov, a victim of MS, to commit suicide. "Just taking care of the physical shell of a loved one for years," he wrote, "is not a life I want to live." In another entry, addressing his wife, he said, "You are sucking the life out of me like a vampire." He also told his diary that he saw himself as having four different choices: Abandoning his wife. Continuing to take care of her, which, he said, would make him die or go crazy. Killing himself. Or . . . killing her, "which remains an option, though far more difficult without her cooperation." After the death of Myrna Lebov, her sister expressed some doubts about whether she had been all that eager to die and these doubts, when coupled with George Delury's brutally honest diary, raised some troubling legal and moral questions: Did Delury help his wife die to release her from her misery, or did he help her die to release himself? And what do we do with him if the answer is both?

Psychiatrist Herbert Hendin, who is the head of the American Suicide Foundation, an organization concerned with preventing suicide, sees a precipitous slippery slope in the Netherlands, a country where physician-assisted suicide and euthanasia are common practice. This "slippery slope," he warns, "descends inexorably from assisted suicide to euthanasia, from those who are terminally ill to those who are chronically ill, from those who are physically ill to those who are mentally ill, and from those who request euthanasia to those whose lives are ended at the doctor's discretion." He says that the Dutch experience teaches us that euthanasia can be "a seemingly simple solution for a myriad of problems."

But slippery slope aside, the idea of helping others die evokes a host of powerful objections. One of the chief arguments, made by Daniel Callahan, among others, is that there's an important difference between actually killing a person—active euthanasia —and withholding or removing certain life-sustaining treatments, allowing that dying patient to die "naturally." In blurring that distinction, he says, "the euthanasia movement has embodied the assumption, the conceit actually, that man is now wholly in control of everything, responsible for all life and all death."

Callahan acknowledges that our wish to control our death by arranging to do ourselves in, or be done away with, has been powered, in part, by our fear of a drawn-out death in the too-helpful hands of modern medicine. But he argues that we might be more willing to die a "natural" death, to die unassisted by ourselves or by others, if we weren't in danger of overzealous medical treatment—and if we could depend on the unstinting use of effective drugs to relieve our pain.

Under such conditions, he says, we might be less afraid of the dying process. Under such conditions we might not insist on taking complete control of our death.

Callahan's argument surely wouldn't satisfy Earl Blaisdell, or any of those who are contemplating not a terminal illness but an unbearable life that is dragging on and on. Nor would it satisfy those who fear that, if they don't act *before* life becomes unbearable, they'll no longer have the capacity to kill themselves. Suicide, assisted or solo, and active euthanasia can free desperate people from a living hell. But those in the terminal stage of an illness, those who are soon to die, may—like Daniel Callahan—prefer a humane alternative to suicide. For a growing number of people that humane alternative is hospice care.

The philosophy of hospice is that, without resorting to suicide, we can have some real (though imperfect) control of our death. We can die not in search of a cure, not hooked to machines, not assaulted by yet another procedure, but (for the most part) in dignity, comfort, and peace. Under hospice care we can't choose the hour and the day of our death, but we *can* choose the where and, to some extent, the how. Hospice makes us some promises that it keeps a vast proportion of the time: That we won't die in pain. That we won't die alone. And that we'll be helped to live as fully as possible "during the part of [our] living which is called dying."

Hospice offers palliative care and special services to people who (typically) have six or fewer months to live, allowing them to control—as much as possible—all of the daily details of their life. Hospice care, in most instances, is given in the home, but it's also offered in inpatient hospice facilities, where (at least at Hospice of Washington, where I volunteer) visitors, including pets, are welcome twenty-four hours of every day. Physicians, nurses, social workers, home health aides, spiritual counselors, and volunteers are available both to the patient and the patient's family, who are invited to participate in any of the decisions that need to be made. One of the most important decisions has to do with pain and symptom control, an area where hospitals frequently fail us. But if, when we are dying, we choose hospice, we get to decide how much pain relief we need.

"If you're hurting and you ask for more medication," a hospice nurse told me, "there's no such thing as you can't have any more."

(I think about my dying mother, weeping with pain in the hospital and the nurse withholding her shot because "it's not

291

time yet," while I frantically and futilely try to explain that my mother is a stoic woman, a woman who never never never cries, and that if my mother is weeping with pain, she really must be in pain, AND THEY HAVE TO GIVE HER THAT GODDAMN SHOT RIGHT NOW.)

Hospice provides whatever it takes to free the dying from pain, while allowing them to be as alert as possible. But the care that it offers goes well beyond medication. For an important part of hospice is the efforts of its workers to promote their patients' emotional well-being: Sitting with them as they recollect the past. Sitting with them as they go through old photograph albums. Listening as they wrestle with unfinished business. Listening as they voice their thoughts about death. Helping them write farewell letters to their children. Helping them to plan their funeral service. Or simply hanging out, to talk about trivia, laugh, watch Oprah on TV, or share a wordless companionable silence.

Hospice, a writer once explained, is "a movement, not a place," and in helping people live while they are dying, it "bathes their wasting bodies, combs their thinning hair, loves them unreservedly, diminishes their pain, sees to their joy, and improves their ending lives as if to do so were an honor rather than a chore." He got it right.

Spiritual counseling is given if requested. But it's never pressed, nor is it necessarily always surrounded with solemnity. "I'm the chaplain," a longtime hospice-care worker tells a patient, during the course of a visit that she makes to him. "I'm the chaplain," she says, "so we've got to do something holy before I get out of here."

Whether or not it's doing something holy, hospice can sweeten the final stage of life.

When a woman dying of cancer wanted to look her best at her final birthday party, a hospice worker searched every shop in the city until she found the perfect dress.

When a home-care patient expressed his fondness—indeed, his passion—for oysters, a hospice worker acquired a number of recipes for oysters, then regularly purchased and prepared them so that the man could eat oysters once a week till his death.

When a dying woman yearned for a visit from her retarded child, a member of the hospice staff drove for two hours to bring that child to his mother.

And when a couple was troubled because they had not been married in the Catholic church, a hospice nurse arranged for a priest to come to the dying man's bedside and perform a proper Catholic marriage ceremony. (She even found them a tape of "Ave Maria.")

One hospice worker recalls the rare request she couldn't grant. It came from a born-again Christian, with whom she'd established a very warm and close relationship. She had asked him, she said, to tell her if there was anything in particular that he wanted. He said that yes, there was something he wanted— a lot. And then, to her surprise, he said that what he wanted was . . . a deathbed conversion. However, there was a problem: The conversion that he longed for wasn't *his* conversion—it was *hers.* Because he liked her so much, she said, he wanted to save her soul "by getting me to take Jesus into my life. He wanted to convert me from Judaism to Christianity on *his* deathbed!"

Though she had to tell him no, she likes to feel that she's willing to go the extra mile. So, it seems, does everyone at hospice.

Hospice workers think that the top sheets and bottom sheets should match, even if the patient can no longer see.

Hospice workers explain the purpose of every shot and suppository, even if the patient can no longer hear.

Hospice workers don't offer false hope to a patient, nor do they say, "Eat, you have to eat or you won't get better."

Hospice workers believe that respect for the patient, and respect for the dying process, can help contribute to a death with dignity.

Those who are facing death and "can see a meaning in this time," says Hospice of Washington home-care nurse Fran Dunphy, can be helped by hospice to take "an emotional journey." That this journey ends in death most certainly doesn't, she says, preclude the possibility of moments of sweetness, of insight, of reconciliation, of—even—extraordinary joy.

Hear this testimonial from a patient:

"I went to the hospital to be cured and I almost died. I went to the hospice to die and I lived."

And hear this from the sister of a hospice patient:

"Hospice gave my brother a way to live the life we had always seen him live, bold and courageous, with dignity, a touch of grace and mostly . . . choice."

Hospice is far from perfect. Home-care aides may not always show up when expected. Medication can't always handle the pain. The primary caregivers—family or significant others or friends—may, despite hospice support, become overwhelmed. And though twenty-four-hour nursing is available at inpatient hospice facilities, health-insurance restrictions make it increasingly difficult to obtain extended inpatient hospice care.

We also need to be wary of claims like those of Dr. Elisabeth Kübler-Ross, that pioneering figure of death and dying, who has stated that "many of my terminal patients have emphasized to me that the last six months of their life were the most valuable months of their entire existence." As the former head of the New York State Hospice Association more soberly observes, this "is not a realistic hope for most hospice patients."

Nor is hospice the place to go in hope of assisted suicide. The national organization is clear on this point, stating in its literature: "Hospice neither hastens nor postpones death." Thus, in submitting to hospice we're accepting something less than complete control, and running the very small (but, alas, not nonexistent) risk of dying in some physical pain or respiratory distress that can't, despite every effort, be alleviated. In addition we will most likely have to yield to certain conditions that we well may regard as very hard to take: Like becoming increasingly bedridden and helpless. Like seeing our body ravaged by our disease. Like dying (as many in hospice die) in diapers.

We who love hospice must find a definition of "death with dignity" that isn't dependent on an absence of diapers, that isn't dependent, in fact, on not being dependent. Morrie Schwartz, a retired sociology professor dying of ALS—Lou Gehrig's disease —offers us his up-close-and-personal view of the matter.

In a 1995 interview with ABC's Ted Koppel, Morrie (that's what he preferred to be called) spoke of maintaining his dignity at a time when he was no longer able to feed himself, to sit up or go to the bathroom unassisted or even, as he put it, to "wipe my ass." He explained: "I have no shame. . . . My dignity comes from my inner self and the fact that I can keep myself composed and. . . . fully human—fully human all the time."

Others—men and women who work with the dying—offer their own definitions of death with dignity.

Sister Barbara Marie, who for seventeen years has been Holy Cross Hospice's pastoral-care coordinator, says that for her, death with dignity is "peaceful, pain-free, at home, surrounded by loved ones, with your business—emotional and otherwise—completed."

Home-care nurse Fran Dunphy's definition of death with dignity is "dying with composure, dying free enough of pain to collect your thoughts, dying knowing you're dying—being an active participant in the dying process."

Dr. Timothy Quill, in his book about dying with dignity, stresses the importance of informed control and choice, of minimized suffering (physical and emotional), and of nonabandonment—not dying alone.

Rabbi Leonard Beerman, retired rabbi of Leo Baeck Temple in

Los Angeles and a member of a committee on end-of-life issues, believes that dying with dignity "is having the sort of care that allows one to die within a kind of embrace." He adds that, ideally, it also includes accepting, as our own, the life we have lived.

In his statement about accepting our life, Rabbi Beerman echoes Erik Erikson, whose eighth and final stage in his "Eight Ages of Man" is what he calls ego integrity versus despair. What he means by ego integrity "is the acceptance of one's one and only life cycle as something that"—for better and worse—"had to be," as something that has its own order, meaning, validity, as something that is "the ultimate of life." If we can come to such an acceptance, so Erikson asserts, "death loses its sting."

Despair, in contrast, is the belief that our time is now too short to begin a new life. And yet we cannot accept—we cannot love and find meaning in—the life we have lived. Without this acceptance, says Erikson, we'll suffer from "a thousand little disgusts." Without this ego integrity, we will fear death.

But fear of dying and fear of death may torment even those whose egos are magnificently well integrated. Most of us are scared to death of death, which threatens us with abandonment, helplessness, loneliness, Hell, or eternal obliteration, and which is for many of us the nightmare "far field" of Theodore Roethke's powerful poem:

> I dream of journeys repeatedly:
> Of flying like a bat deep into a narrowing tunnel,
> Of driving alone, without luggage, out a long
>   peninsula . . .
> Ending at last in a hopeless sand-rut,
> Where the car stalls,
> Churning in a snowdrift
> Until the headlights darken.

At the field's end, in the corner missed by the mower,
Where the turf drops off into a grass-hidden culvert,
Haunt of the cat-bird, nesting-place of the
    field-mouse,
Not too far away from the ever-changing
    flower-dump,
Among the tin cans, tires, rusted pipes, broken
    machinery,—
One learned of the eternal;
And in the shrunken face of a dead rat, eaten by rain
    and ground-beetles
(I found it lying among the rubble of an old coal bin)
And the tom-cat, caught near the pheasant-run,
Its entrails strewn over the half-grown flowers,
Blasted to death by the night watchman.

How can death not sting with such fearsome images of eternity, of mortality? How can we be reconciled to death?

In reviewing Jessica Mitford's *The American Way of Death*, Evelyn Waugh was troubled by the fact "that she has no stated attitude towards death." Ms. Mitford sent a rebuttal to him through her sister, a friend of Waugh's. "Tell Evelyn," she said, "that I *do* have an attitude towards death. I'm against it."

Most of us are.

Against it we may be, but death will come get us. Death, writes psychoanalyst Mary Chadwick, is "the power over which we have no control." All we can hope to control is how, when death appears at our doorstep, we receive it. And if it doesn't take us unaware, and if it isn't soul-destroyingly cruel, we perhaps can transform "that ultimate moment when we surrender to death" into what Rabbi Beerman calls "a willed decision, an active choosing to let go."

A willed decision. An active choosing to let go. It may be

that the only control that remains at the end of life is an act of acquiescence—to our own death.

Some of us, of course, will not acquiesce. We will rage against the fading of the light, fighting our death to the death, doing till dying. Or perhaps we will succumb to death in bitterness or helpless resignation, the victim of what we perceive to be a "brute biological fact, permeated with pain, horror, and despair." Or perhaps we will die so early or late, so cheated or depleted, that we cannot wish or will or choose our death. Or perhaps we will die refusing, until our last breath, to recognize that we are dying.

Some of us, however, will die what Nietzsche has called a "free death"—which he defines, somewhat excessively, as a "death which comes to me because *I* want it." Death, in this sense, is collaborative—something we do together rather than something that is merely done to us. We acquiesce.

It's said that Woodrow Wilson's last words were "I am a broken machine. I am ready to go." I suppose that this is a sort of acquiescence. A World War II kamikaze pilot, writing to his parents before his suicide mission, anticipated his death with an eager "Please congratulate me. I have been given a splendid opportunity to die . . . I shall fall like a blossom from a radiant cherry tree." Those who look forward with confidence to a spiritual or secular immortality will sometimes embrace their death in glad expectation of entering paradise or history. And we're often told that those who feel they have lived fulfilling lives are content to greet their death with "Be welcome then, . . . more is not needed."

The critic Anatole Broyard, who kept a journal during the months of his dying, wrote: "At the end, you're posing for eternity. It's your last picture. Don't be carried into death. Leap into it."

Roethke's poem about death, "The Far Field," which begins so frighteningly, moves to an exquisite vision of acquiescence, inviting us to consider how we might "be renewed by death, thought of my death," by connecting our frightened finite self to something larger than self, benign and enduring:

A man faced with his own immensity
Wakes all the waves, all their loose wandering fire.
The murmur of the absolute, the why
Of being born fails on his naked ears.
His spirit moves like monumental wind
That gentles on a sunny blue plateau.
He is the end of things, the final man.

All finite things reveal infinitude:
The mountain with its singular bright shade
Like the blue shine on freshly frozen snow,
The after-light upon ice-burdened pines;
Odor of basswood on a mountain-slope,
A scent beloved of bees;
Silence of water above a sunken tree:
The pure serene of memory in one man,—
A ripple widening from a single stone
Winding around the waters of the world.

The dying Morrie Schwartz also draws upon images of water to tell a story that makes a similar point:

There's this little wave, this he-wave, who's bobbing up and down, off the shore, bobbing up and down on the ocean, having a great time, and all of a sudden he recognizes he's going to crash into the shore . . . and he'll get annihilated. And he gets so despairing, "My God, what's going to happen to me?" and he's got this sour, despairing look on his face. Along comes a female wave, bobbing up and down, having a great

299

time. And the female wave says to the male wave, "Why are you so depressed?" The male says, "You don't understand. You're going to crash into the shore and you'll be nothing." She says, "You don't understand. You're not a wave, you're part of the ocean."

In his last interview with Koppel, Morrie Schwartz quoted an aphorism—one of his own—that seems to address the issue of acquiescence: "Don't let go too soon, but don't hang on too long. Find the balance."

> Ted Koppel: "The very notion, Morrie, of letting go implies a degree of control."
> Morrie Schwartz: "Yep."
> Ted Koppel: "Do you think you have that degree of control?
> Morrie Schwartz: "I don't know. I'm going to try."

I put in a call to Ted Koppel to ask him how Morrie actually died, but halfway through the dialing I hung up the phone. He had faced a difficult dying and I wanted to believe that he had indeed been granted a death of his own. I wanted to believe that, at the end, Morrie Schwartz had possessed comfort and companionship, humanity and dignity, sufficient—even though imperfect—control.

Last Words

Maybe everything would be all right after all, and if
you worked almost till you dropped . . . and if you
kept your fires burning and picked your friends with
care—maybe if you made sure that everything was
just so, life would not spin out of control.

—Laurie Colwin

We can work till we drop. We can keep our fires burning. We
can pick our friends, and everything else, with care. We can be
competent, prudent, persistent, resilient, resourceful, and
strong, and thoroughly prepared for every contingency. We can
be watchful and wise, but we can't always stop life from spinning out of control.

We can work with and around our personal history. We can
surmount the limits of our biology. We can rebound from even
the cruelest blows. We can develop strategies to impose, with an
iron fist, our iron will, or, with a velvet glove, to persuade and
manipulate. We often can get what we want as long as we aren't
trying to get complete control.

We need to understand the possibilities and the limits of our control. We need to balance power and surrender.

From our very earliest years to our final days, control is an aspect of most of our experiences: Control as self-control, as constraint on our freedom. Control as increasing mastery of our universe. Control as self-possession. Control as influence over the people in our life. Control as the actions we take in the wake of adversity, after the lump in the breast, the mugger's knife. Control as acceptance of moral responsibility for our failures and our cruelties and our crimes. Control as memento mori, because—although we can't choose the cause or the time of our dying—we can make choices in life that will help determine the meaning and manner of our death.

We also can choose when we want to let go, when we'd love to let go, when we need to let go, when the best thing we can do is to relinquish control. We can engage in positive surrender: Giving ourselves to God, or to sexual passion. Quitting when it's futile to persist. Acknowledging when we've lost and they've won. Deciding that it's none of our damn business. And, within reason, complying with—rather than stubbornly trying to resist—the strictures and the rules of our society.

We also, whether we choose to or not, will have to surrender control because some of the things we encounter will be unfixable, non-negotiable, uncontrollable.

We need to recognize what's uncontrollable.

We need to recognize when surrender makes sense.

But we also need to remember that the events of our fragile lives can be shaped, importantly shaped, by our actions and choices, by the exercise of our physical, mental, emotional, moral—though always imperfect—control.

Notes and Elaborations

Chapter One—How Free to Be?

page 13

"Humanity cannot be cut adrift":
Lewontin, Rose, and Kamin, *Not in Our Genes,* p. 10.

page 15

a "happiness" gene:
Scientist Dean Hamer, writing in *Nature Genetics,* reviews studies that suggest that our happiness level is, in large measure, a matter of heredity, though it's likely that many more than one "happiness" gene is involved. Several scientists writing in *Science* report on the discovery of a gene that is significantly associated with neuroticism, tension, and pessimism. A group of scientists, writing in *Nature Genetics,* reports finding a link between a gene and the trait of novelty seeking. And an Associated Press story appearing in *The Washington Post,* July 27, 1996, p. A2, reports: "Scientists have discovered a good mother gene, an inborn trigger that prompts female mice to care for their young. When this gene is missing, mice show no interest in their babies."

page 16

DNA:
This is deoxyribonucleic acid, the basic stuff of heredity, the substance of which our genes are made.

page 16

"I am the master of my fate":
William Henley, "Invictus," in *The Best-Loved Poems of the American People,* selected by Felleman, p. 73.

page 16

"Every man is the son of his own works":
Cervantes, *Don Quixote,* cited in Tripp, *The International Thesaurus of Quotations,* entry 860.

page 16

"The fault, dear Brutus":

Shakespeare, *Julius Caesar,* act 1, scene 2.

page 16

"And you and me are free to be":

Stephen Lawrence and Bruce Hart, "Free to Be . . . You and Me," in *Free to Be . . . You and Me,* ed. Hart, et al., p. 16.

page 16

extensive research on identical twins:

The most famous studies of twins have been produced by the Minnesota Center for Twin and Adoption Research in Minneapolis, headed by Thomas Bouchard. Since 1979, Bouchard and his colleagues have examined almost 1,000 pairs of identical and fraternal twins, of which 128 pairs were reared apart.

pages 16–17

"Genes and glands":

Tellegen, Lykken, Bouchard, Wilcox, Segal, and Rich, "Personality Similarity in Twins Reared Apart and Together," *Journal of Personality and Social Psychology,* Vol. 54, No. 8, June 1988, p. 1037.

page 17

For substantial studies have shown:

For a review of ten research designs and findings from a selection of twin studies, see Segal, "The Importance of Twin Studies for Individual Differences Research," *Journal of Counseling & Development,* Vol. 68, July/August 1990, pp. 612–22. She concludes: "The majority of twin studies of personality and temperament converge on the common themes that (1) genetic factors substantially influence these behaviors, and that (2) the important environmental effects are those that are nonshared" (p. 616). See also Bouchard et al., "Sources of Human Psychological Differences: The Minnesota Study of Twins Reared Apart," *Science,* Vol. 250, October 12, 1990, pp. 223–28.

page 17

traditionalism and job satisfaction:

See Bouchard et al., "Sources of Human Psychological Differ-

304

ences: The Minnesota Study of Twins Reared Apart," *Science*, Vol. 250, October 12, 1990, pp. 223–28.

page 17

As for personal quirks:
These and other such stories can be found in Zanden, *Human Development*, p. 81, describing work done by the Minnesota researchers; Hamer and Copeland, *The Science of Desire*, p. 198; and Lykken, McGue, Tellegen, and Bouchard, "Emergenesis: Genetic Traits That May Not Run in Families," *American Psychologist*, December 1992, pp. 1565–66. Obviously some shared twin traits are simply crazy coincidences; nor is anyone using these anecdotes to postulate the existence of "jewelry" genes or "coffee" genes.

page 17

the "nature of nurture":
Plomin, Owen, and McGuffin, "The Genetic Basis of Complex Human Behaviors," *Science*, Vol. 264, June 17, 1994. In explaining the meaning of this phrase, the authors state: "To some extent, individuals create their own experiences for genetic reasons" (p. 1735).

page 17

"elicit, select, seek out, or create":
Bouchard et al., "Sources of Human Psychological Differences: The Minnesota Study of Twins Reared Apart," *Science*, Vol. 250, October 12, 1990, p. 227.

page 18

"nonshared environment":
See Plomin, Owen, McGuffin, two references above, where they write: "Environmental influences on most behavioral disorders and dimensions serve to make children growing up in the same family different, not similar. This effect [is] called nonshared environment" (p. 1735).

page 18

Some 20 percent of us:
See Kagan's book *Galen's Prophecy*, where he states that some "one in five healthy Caucasian infants reacts to stimulation with vigorous motor activity and distress, and about two-thirds of these highly reactive four-month-olds become inhib-

ited children. About two of every five infants inherit a bias that favors a relaxed, minimally distressed reaction to stimulation, and two-thirds of these become uninhibited in the second year." But, he adds, the "initial temperamental biases are not deterministic" (p. xix). Kagan also notes that "many shy, quiet adolescents did not inherit that disposition; they acquired it. Only a proportion of very shy adolescents began life with an initial temperamental bias" (p. 168).

For further information, see Kagan's discussion of the biological origins of temperament, pp. 50–56. See also chapter 5, "The Physiology of Inhibited and Uninhibited Children," and chapter 6, "Early Predictors of the Two Types." Kagan says that the heart of his book "summarizes our attempts over the last fifteen years to persuade ourselves and others that inhibited and uninhibited children inherit unique neurochemistries that affect their thresholds of reactivity to novelty" (p. xviii).

page 19

may color our moods and behavior:
Ibid. In discussing the later activities of "inhibited" or "introverted" and "uninhibited" or "extroverted" types, Kagan notes "that a large number of eminent writers, composers, computer programmers, mathematicians, and scientists were introverts, and that more incarcerated criminals were extroverts" (p. 41). He notes that "introverts are less frequently represented in the United States Senate" (p. 17) and that "inhibited adolescents are unlikely to become test pilots, salespeople, investment bankers, CEOs, or trial lawyers" (p. 252). Kagan also found that the four most fearful three-year-old boys he had studied "had chosen careers that permitted them to avoid interaction with large groups and to control unpredictability in their daily lives: one had become a music teacher, two had become science professors, and one was a psychiatrist. By contrast, the four least fearful boys had chosen competitive or entrepreneurial professions: one was a high school athletic coach, one was a salesman, and two were self-employed engineers" (p. 114).

page 19

as many temperaments as there are Baskin-Robbins flavors:
Kagan writes in Galen's Prophecy: "Progress in neurobiology

will aid the discovery of new temperaments." He predicts that while most temperamental types will be associated with neurochemistry, some will be the product of anatomy and some of prenatal events affecting the brain's growth. "There will be neurochemical temperaments, anatomical temperaments, and prenatal temperaments" (pp. 284–85).

page 20

My youngest son, Alexander:
An almost identical version of this description of Alexander appeared in Viorst, "Is Your Child's Personality Set at Birth?" *Redbook*, November 1995, pp. 174, 178.

page 20

Current studies of alcoholism, manic-depression:
See Plomin et al., "The Genetic Basis of Complex Human Behaviors," *Science*, Vol. 264, June 17, 1994. See also, same issue, Holden, "A Cautionary Genetic Tale: The Sobering Story of D2."

page 20

a substantial genetic basis for schizophrenia:
In Plomin et al., "The Genetic Basis of Complex Human Behaviors," *Science*, Vol. 264, June 17, 1994, p. 1733, the authors cite adoption and twin studies that support this conclusion.

page 21

obesity gene:
Researchers have discovered an ob (for obese) gene in mice— and its likely counterpart in humans—that helps control the body's appetite by causing fat cells to produce a hormone called leptin. It is believed that leptin travels through the bloodstream to the brain, which then tells the body to turn appetite and metabolism up or down. Defects in this mechanism may prevent the brain from delivering a you've-had-enough-to-eat message to the body, resulting in obesity. (Two other brain hormones have also been identified as appetite suppressors.)

A different kind of study suggests that our overweight may be the result of another sort of flawed mechanism. According to *The New York Times*, November 10, 1994, p. A30, the November *Pediatrics* reports a study of three-to-five-year-olds that found that the children who had the most body fat had the most "controlling" mothers too, controlling in the sense that they closely regulated their children's eating habits. The researchers believe that children can figure out how much to eat, but may lose this natural instinct if their freedom to use their internal cues is impeded. Without these internal cues, they no longer know when it's time to stop eating—and therefore run the risk of becoming overweight.

page 21

links between genes and crime:
There is considerable concern that studies linking genes and crime will be used to stereotype and control minorities, or as an excuse to refuse to fund crucial programs that can alleviate the social conditions that help to foster crime. But, as some researchers note, the hope is that such research will yield useful information on who needs support and what that support should be.

page 21

22 percent of the biological sons of criminal fathers:
See Hutchings and Mednick, "Criminality in Adoptees and Their Adoptive and Biological Parents: A Pilot Study," in *Biosocial Bases of Criminal Behavior*, ed. Mednick and Christiansen, pp. 127–41. This study looks at nonfamilial adoptions in the city and county of Copenhagen, Denmark, focusing on male adoptees who had criminal records and whose biological and adoptive fathers were identifiable. It's important to note, however, that when both the adoptive and biological fathers were criminals, the statistic for criminal sons soared to a striking 36.2 percent.

page 21

low levels of serotonin:
See discussion of serotonin and aggression in Margaret M. McCarthy's "The Neurobiology of Affective Behaviors: From Animals to Man," pp. 16–17, prepared for a conference on The Meaning and Significance of Research on Genetics and Criminal Behavior, sponsored by the Institute for Philosophy and Public Policy, a part of the School of Public Affairs at the University of Maryland, and held September 22–24, 1995. See also Peter Kramer, *Listening to Prozac*, pp. 301–304. Kramer distinguishes between dominance (high status), which corre-

lates with high serotonin, and aggression and impulsivity, which correlate with low serotonin, noting that research with monkeys shows that dominant, high-serotonin monkeys are "well integrated socially" while aggressive, low-serotonin monkeys "tend to be socially deviant and ostracized" (p. 302).

page 21

Dutch-American research team:
See Mann's "Behavioral Genetics in Transition," *Science*, Vol. 264, June 17, 1994, p. 1689, for a discussion of the Dutch-American study.

page 21

"monster mice":
The phrase is from a story in *Time*, December 4, 1995, p. 76, reporting on the findings of Nelson et al., "Behavioral abnormalities in male mice lacking neuronal nitric oxide synthase," *Nature*, Vol. 378, November 23, 1995. For "substantial vocal protestations" and "excessive and inappropriate," see p. 383 of *Nature*.

page 21

"What we might have here":
Researcher Solomon Snyder's comments are quoted in *Newsweek*, December 4, 1995, p. 76, in a story on the violent mice (see note above).

page 22

"can push genetic constitution around":
Gallagher, "How We Become What We Are," *The Atlantic Monthly*, September 1994, p. 52. She is quoting research psychologist Stephen Suomi.

page 22

They interpenetrate:
The point here is that the contributions of nature and nurture are not merely added together to produce a certain behavior. They are intertwined and interacting.

page 22

"Just as there is no organism":
Lewontin, Rose, Kamin, *Not in Our Genes*, p. 273.

page 22

OGOD:
Huntington's disease, for instance, is caused by a single gene.

page 22

As for behavioral traits:

In "The Importance of Twin Studies for Individual Differences Research," in *Journal of Counseling & Development*, Vol. 68, July/August 1990, Nancy Segal, assistant director of the Minnesota Center for Twin and Adoption Research, says, "The majority of twin studies of personality suggest that 50 percent of the variance is associated with genetic influences, while the remaining 50 percent is associated with environmental effects" (p. 615).

page 23

less guilty and anxious about breaking rules:

In *Galen's Prophecy*, Kagan discusses the impact of environment on temperament, particularly in regard to conscience, on p. 167 and pp. 238–41.

page 23

"The psychopath and the hero":

Gallagher, "How We Become What We Are," *The Atlantic Monthly*, September 1994, p. 40. She is quoting psychologist David Lykken.

page 23

"a natural urge":

Kagan, *Galen's Prophecy*, p. xxii.

page 23

"learn to be kind to themselves":

Gallagher, "How We Become What We Are," *The Atlantic Monthly*, September 1994, p. 54. She is quoting psychologist Megan Gunnar.

page 24

the story of Amy and Beth:

Lykken et al., "Emergenesis: Genetic Traits That May Not Run in Families," *American Psychologist*, December 1992, p. 1568.

page 25

"the power of genes":

Kagan, *Galen's Prophecy*, p. 37.

page 25

"What I mean is":

Dew, *The Family Heart*, pp. 32–33.

page 25

"God. Something I've *chosen!*":
Ibid.

page 25

"sexual orientation":
Psychiatrist Richard Pillard's "directional marker" definition of this is: "Sexual orientation is, when you pass people on the sidewalk at lunch hour, which sex do your eyes flick on involuntarily: men or women?" Burr, *A Separate Creation,* p. 244.

page 25

male sexual orientation:
Some research findings indicate that women's sexual orientation is not as stable as men's. A small portion of women may move from straight at, say, age sixteen, to lesbian at twenty-four, bisexual at thirty-eight, and back to straight at age fifty-five. With men, says Dean Hamer, "This sort of movement is very very rare. It's pretty much a phenomenon we see exclusively in women." Furthermore, gay and straight men virtually never question their sexual orientation, while a number of straight and lesbian women do. Hamer's colleague Angela Pattatucci adds, "With women, we ask the question: Is this person a lesbian for political reasons? This is a question we *never* ask men" about their sexual orientation. See Burr, *A Separate Creation,* pp. 169–81, for a discussion of the question "If a homosexual is homosexual, just how homosexual is that homosexual?" (p. 169). Hamer's statement appears on p. 169, Pattatucci's on p. 174.

page 25

One study:
See Bailey and Pillard, "A Genetic Study of Male Sexual Orientation," *Archives of General Psychiatry,* Vol. 48, No. 12, December 1991, pp. 1089–96. Pillard and psychologist Michael Bailey studied 56 pairs of male identical twins, 54 pairs of male fraternal twins, and 57 adopted nonrelated brothers. A subsequent study of homosexual women, reported in Bailey et al., "Heritable Factors Influence Sexual Orientation in Women," *Archives of General Psychiatry,* Vol. 50, No. 3, March 11, 1993, pp. 217–

23, came up with the same first-, second-, and third-place ratings. Out of 71 pairs of identical twins, 48 percent were both gay. Out of 37 pairs of non-identical twins, 16 percent were both gay. And out of 35 adopted nonrelated sisters, only 6 percent were both gay.

page 26

Another important study:

This study, conducted by neuroscientist Simon LeVay, is reported in *Science*, Vol. 253, August 30, 1991, pp. 1034–37. For a discussion of his research, see Barinaga, "Is Homosexuality Biological?" in the same issue, pp. 956–57. See also The Hypothalamic Hypothesis in Hamer and Copeland's *The Science of Desire*, pp. 160–63. A caution: Another hypothesis is that sexual orientation affects the size of the hypothalamus instead of vice versa. There is, for instance, an NIH study which found that in people who became blind and read Braille, the part of the brain controlling the finger used in reading Braille grew larger.

page 26

a "gay" gene:

To understand this discovery, let's start with the fact that we all possess two sex chromosomes—XX if we're female, XY if we're male. One chromosome comes from our mother and one from our father, who must contribute a Y to make sons, which means that a son always get his X from his mother. On each of these sex chromosomes (and on all of our other chromosomes) are genes, which carry the blueprints for all we inherit encoded in molecules of DNA. What Hamer found was that a small section of Xq28, a strip of DNA on the X chromosome, matched up in thirty-three out of forty tested pairs of gay brothers. Brothers would ordinarily share some 50 percent of the same chromosomal terrain. Thirty-three out of forty is a significantly higher percentage of sharing. Hamer also discovered, when he investigated these gay men's family trees, a high rate of homosexual male relatives on the *mother's* side of the family. His search for the "gay" gene is described in Hamer and Copeland, *The Science of Desire*.

page 26

it is *polygenic:*

See Mann, "Behavioral Genetics in Transition," *Science*, Vol.

264, June 17, 1994, p. 1688, where he talks about multiple-gene effects—either "polygenic (caused by many genes) or oligogenic (caused by a small group of genes)." See also Plomin, "The Role of Inheritance in Behavior," *Science,* Vol. 248, April 13, 1990, pp. 183–84, where he states that "most behavioral traits appear to be influenced by many genes, each with small effects."

page 26

nurture can influence gayness:
See Burr's "Homosexuality and Biology," *The Atlantic Monthly,* March 1993, where he quotes Pillard as saying, "With individual cases, there are doubtless some that are mostly or all genes, and others that might be all environment. Our analysis [of twins] doesn't say anything about the individual" (p. 64).

page 27

may have just as little choice:
It is argued by many researchers that sexual orientation, whatever its source, is not a matter of choice; that environmental factors can sometimes change the brain in permanent ways; that biology versus choice is a false dichotomy; and that a trait can be immutable without being innate. See Burr, reference in previous note, pp. 82 and 91.

page 27

rewire the circuitry of our brain:
See Kramer, *Listening to Prozac,* where he talks about trauma altering biology and says that "the neural chemistry with which we arrive in the world is inevitably modified by development, environment, life events, and now by discrete medicine" (p. 149). See also p. 107, where he talks about psychic trauma becoming a "biologically encoded personality trait," and p. 298, where he says, "By the time they reach adulthood, people also differ biologically according to their good or bad fortune in periods of critical development."

page 29

"basic fault":
There is a brief discussion of Balint's concept in Grotstein, "The Psychology of Powerlessness: Disorders of Self-Regulation and Interactional Regulation as a Newer Paradigm for Psychopathology," *Psychoanalytic Inquiry,* Vol. 6, No. 1, 1986, p. 95.

313

page 29

"a blank sheet on which experience can write":
Rapaport, "The Theory of Ego Autonomy: A Generalization,"
in *The Collected Papers of David Rapaport*, ed. Merton Gill,
p. 726. Rapaport is describing, but not subscribing to, what
he calls the "Cartesian-Humian world view" (p. 726).

page 29

"virtually a slave of it":
Ibid.

page 29

"one doubts":
Darwin is quoted in Wright's *The Moral Animal*, p. 349.

page 29

Two tenets of psychoanalysis:
Discussed in Lewy, "Responsibility, Free Will, and Ego Psychology," *The International Journal of Psycho-Analysis*, Vol. 42,
1961, p. 262.

page 30

"pressures":
Waelder, "Psychic Determinism and the Possibility of Predictions," *The Psychoanalytic Quarterly*, Vol. 32, No. 1, 1963, p. 22.

page 30

"the acceptance of the restraints":
Rapaport, "The Theory of Ego Autonomy: A Generalization,"
in *The Collected Papers of David Rapaport*, ed. Merton Gill,
p. 741.

page 30

and valuable:
In Wilson, *Moral Judgment*, he argues that an insistence on
personal accountability "sends a message to people who are
learning how to behave that they ought to acquire those habits
and beliefs that will facilitate their conformity to the essential
rules of civilized conduct" and reminds those "choosing between alternative courses of action that there are important
consequences that are likely to flow from making a bad
choice" (p. 41).

page 30

"Doctrine of Necessity":
See Neely, "Freedom and Desire," *Philosophical Review*, Vol. 83,

1974, pp. 32–54. The quoted material from Mill appears on p. 52 and p. 53.

page 31

"The self is not a thing":
See Shields's Pulitzer Prize–winning novel, *The Stone Diaries*, pp. 231–34, for Alice's story and the quoted material.

page 32

"necessary illusion":
Berlin is quoted by Waelder, "Psychic Determinism and the Possibility of Predictions," *The Psychoanalytic Quarterly*, Vol. 32, No. 1, 1963, p. 25.

page 32

"If free will and responsibility did not exist":
Lewy, "Responsibility, Free Will, and Ego Psychology," *The International Journal of Psycho-Analysis*, Vol. 42, 1961, p. 268.

Chapter Two—The Taste of Control

page 33

"There is hardly":
Mill is quoted by Wright in *The Moral Animal*, p. 361.

page 33

"All those qualities":
Fraiberg, *The Magic Years*, p. 118.

page 33

Jan, age two and a half:
Ibid. Fraiberg relates Jan's story on pp. 139–40.

page 35

"from the very beginning":
Alice Miller, *For Your Own Good*, p. 11. Miller is quoting from "An Essay on the Education and Instruction of Children" by J. Sulzer, written in 1748.

page 35

"see something they want":
Ibid., pp. 10–11.

page 35

"a strict obedience":
Ibid., p. 12.

page 35

"it is quite natural":

Ibid, p. 13.

page 35

"It is essential to demonstrate":

Ibid.

page 36

"We satisfy, as far as possible":

Fraiberg, *The Magic Years,* p. 75.

page 36

"guilt":

See Emde, Johnson, and Easterbrooks, "The Do's and Don'ts of Early Moral Development: Psychoanalytic Tradition and Current Research," in *The Emergence of Morality in Young Children,* ed. Kagan and Lamb, for a discussion of pride, shame, and hurt feelings as a "possible forerunner of guilt" (p. 261).

page 36

Classic psychoanalysis says:

Freud's discussion of the superego can be found in a number of his writings, all in the *Standard Edition,* including "The Ego and the Id" (Vol. 19), "Civilization and Its Discontents (Vol. 21), and "New Introductory Lectures on Psychoanalysis" (Vol. 22). In classic theory the superego is described as a mental structure that comes into existence at a certain developmental stage and as a result of the dissolution of the Oedipus complex. Out of fear of injury and loss of our parents' love, we repudiate our unconscious wishes to murder the same-sex parent and possess the other parent sexually, internalize their moral standards and prohibitions, and feel guilty if we fail to live up to those standards or breach those prohibitions.

page 37

And current studies suggest:

See the discussion of early internalization "under the watchful eye of the care-giver," in Emde et al., "The Do's and Don'ts of Early Moral Development: Psychoanalytic Tradition and Current Research," in *The Emergence of Morality in Young Children,* ed. Kagan and Lamb, pp. 245–76. This paper also discusses the nonconflictual "positive" emotions—empathy, for instance —that contribute to the internalization of moral standards and prohibitions. For further examination of early moral development, see—from the same volume—Dunn, "The Beginnings of Moral Understanding: Development in the Second Year," pp. 91–112, and Snow, "Language and the Beginnings of Moral Understanding," pp. 112–22; the chapter called "Establishing a Morality," in Kagan, *The Nature of the Child*, pp. 112–53; and Wilson, *The Moral Sense*.

page 37

An eighteen-month-old girl:
The first two girls in this paragraph are described in Emde et al., see citation above, p. 267. The third girl, Julia, is described in Fraiberg, *The Magic Years*, p. 135.

page 38

"I love love love":
Viorst, "I Love Love Love My Brand-New Baby Sister," in *Sad Underwear and Other Complications*, p. 66.

page 38

"immoderate pursuit of immediate pleasures":
Wilson, *The Moral Sense*, p. 87.

page 38

Some notes from New York:
These examples come from *New York*, January 9, 1995, p. 13.

page 39

Some notes from elsewhere:
The Boston story comes from *The Washington Post*, August 1, 1995, p. A19. The Chicago story and the Stockholm story are also from the *Post*, November 29, 1995, p. A21, and January 1, 1996, p. C3. The *Post* also ran the Honolulu story, on October 14, 1995, in its Around the Nation section.

page 40

From the moment we arrive in this world:
See Brazelton, "Neonatal Assessment," pp. 203–33, and Murphy, "Psychoanalytic Views of Infancy," pp. 313–63, both in *The Course of Life*, Vol. 1, ed. Greenspan and Pollock. Murphy writes: "We see the baby not only as an organism which fits into the environment, but as an active, self-propelling creature being able to stimulate others, especially mother, to initiate changes in the environment from the time he arrives in the world" (p. 324). There is also a richly detailed description of

the newborn's capacities and of mother-infant interactions in Brazelton and Cramer, *The Earliest Relationship,* where "the accent is on activity rather than helplessness; on eliciting behaviors, not passivity. In this light, the infant came to be seen as an active participant in forming the parent-infant relationship" (pp. 89–90).

page 40

"Sometimes I want to be jiggled":
From Amy Schwartz, *A Teeny Tiny Baby,* unpaged.

page 41

"I hadn't expected":
Viorst, "First Baby." This is a song, with some small alterations, from *Love and Shrimp,* a musical with words by Viorst, music by Shelly Markham.

page 42

"eliciting competent":
Cath, "Fathering from Infancy to Old Age: A Selective Overview of Recent Psychoanalytic Contributions," *The Psychoanalytic Review,* Vol. 73, No. 4, pp. 65/469–75/479. The quoted material appears on p. 68/472.

page 42

we develop a burgeoning sense of personal effectiveness:
In Murphy's "Psychoanalytic Views of Infancy," in *The Course of Life,* Vol. 1, ed. Greenspan and Pollock, she says that the infant's success in "conquering the difficulties involved in these early experiences of nursing provides his first experiences of mastery" (p. 327). She notes that "wiggling to a comfortable spot, straining to see as much as possible, . . . getting mother . . . to come and lift him out of the crib . . . are ways of experiencing his effectiveness," and that as he struggles, at four or five months, to turn over, to reach things, to imitate his parents' sounds and as he evokes their smiles, "he continues to sense himself as successfully making things happen" (p. 336).

page 42

"I'm a teeny tiny baby":
Amy Schwartz, *A Teeny Tiny Baby.*

page 42

"Human infants":
Seligman, *Helplessness,* p. 137.

page 43

maternal deprivation:

Ibid., pp. 141–46. Seligman uses the work of Spitz (with mother-deprived institutionalized children) and Harlow (with motherless monkeys) to make his argument that "maternal deprivation results in a particularly crucial lack of control" (p. 146). See also p. 143, where he quotes Murphy on the consequences of severe asynchrony: "The discouraged, apathetic mother just sits, passively holding the baby, without face-to-face communication, much less active, playful mutual responses to the baby. The deprived baby does not have the experience which . . . leads him to the realistic expectation that reaching out, exploring the outside, trying out new impacts upon it would bring pleasant results."

page 43

"ghosts in the nursery":

Fraiberg is quoted in Brazelton and Cramer, *The Earliest Relationship*, p. 139. See also "The Infant as Ghost," pp. 139–49.

page 43

"a terrible little girl":

Ibid., p. 178. See the case of "Lisa: 'Angry Already,' " pp. 175–84.

page 44

"couldn't forge the connection":

See Gallagher, *I.D.*, p. 124, for this and the other quoted material. Monica's fascinating story appears throughout the book.

page 44

"basic trust":

Erikson, *Childhood and Society*, p. 247. In his chapter "Eight Ages of Man," Erikson talks about ego development in terms of a series of phase-specific conflicts. His discussion of the first age or stage, "Basic Trust vs. Basic Mistrust," appears on pp. 247–51; "that one may trust oneself. . . ." appears on p. 248; and "faith in the goodness of one's strivings and in the kindness of the powers of the universe" appears on p. 251.

page 44

In an experiment with three groups:

Seligman, *Helplessness*, pp. 139–40. He is describing J. S. Watson's experiment.

page 45

Just look, if you please, at this baby:
These valiant efforts are described in Murphy, "Psychoanalytic Views on Infancy," in *The Course of Life,* Vol. 1, ed. Greenspan and Pollock, p. 353.

page 45

"exploration drive":
White, "Motivation Reconsidered: The Concept of Competence," *Psychological Review,* Vol. 66, No. 5, 1959, p. 299. White discusses Butler and others who favor this concept.

page 45

"need for activity":
Ibid., p. 302. White discusses Kagan and others who favor this concept.

page 45

"manipulative drive":
Ibid., p. 302. White discusses Harlow and others who favor this concept.

page 45

"instinct to master":
Ibid., p. 307. White discusses Hendrick's mastery concept.

page 45

"will to conquer":
Adler, "Individual Psychology," *Psychologies of 1930,* ed. Murchison, p. 399.

page 45

"striving for superiority":
Ibid., p. 398.

page 45

"Funktionslust:
White, "Motivation Reconsidered: The Concept of Competence," *Psychological Review,* Vol. 66, No. 5, 1959, p. 312. White discusses Buhler and others who make a case for "pleasure in activity for its own sake."

page 45

"urge toward competence":
Ibid., p. 323.

page 46

"is directed, selective":
Ibid., p. 318.

page 46

"a feeling of efficacy":
Ibid., p. 322.

page 46

"a theme of mastery, power, or control":
Ibid., p. 320.

page 46

"instinct to master":
Ibid., p. 307. White is quoting Hendrick.

page 46

"a process of self-expansion":
Ibid., p. 324. White is quoting Angyal.

page 46

"hustling things about":
Ibid., p. 316. White is quoting Groos.

page 46

"joy in being a cause":
Ibid.

page 46

"Helpless as [an infant] may seem":
Ibid., p. 326.

page 47

sometimes almost as urgent to us as hunger:
White (see above reference) notes, however, that the urge toward competence is not as powerful and overriding as hunger,
sex, or fear. He says that although there "are plenty of instances in which children refuse to leave their absorbed play
in order to eat or to visit the toilet" (p. 321), the motivation
here is more often "moderate but persistent" (p. 330).

page 47

For the next several months:
In a landmark study of the separation-individuation process
by Mahler, Pine, and Bergman, *The Psychological Birth of the
Human Infant*, Mahler discusses four overlapping subphases of
separation-individuation. The first subphase, "differentiation"
(see pp. 52–64), begins at four or five months and ends at nine

or so months of age, during which time the infant achieves a "hatched" alertness. This is followed by the "practicing" subphase (see pp. 65–75), ending at around sixteen months.

page 47

the rapprochement crisis:
Mahler (see above citation) terms the third subphase of separation-individuation, which ends at around twenty-four months, "rapprochement" (see pp. 76–108). She says that the "optimal distance" established through the resolution of the rapprochement crisis allows the toddler "to go and come, to find mother available, but not intruding" (p. 291).

page 48

a "sense of loss of self-control":
Erikson, *Childhood and Society*, p. 254. His discussion of the second age of man, "Autonomy vs. Shame and Doubt," appears on pp. 251–54.

page 48

Fraiberg also speaks:
See Fraiberg's *The Magic Years*, pp. 112–19, for a lovely discussion of language acquisition. Fraiberg writes of her young soliloquizer: "In the darkness she re-creates her lost world, brings back the absent people and objects by uttering their names" (p. 114).

page 49

"Goodnight room":
From Margaret Wise Brown, *Goodnight Moon*, unpaged.

page 50

"Lord, You may not recognize me":
Glück, "The Gift," in *The First Four Books of Poems*, p. 144.

page 50

The use of language gives us:
See Katan's "Some Thoughts About the Role of Verbalization in Early Childhood," *The Psychoanalytic Study of the Child*, Vol. 16, pp. 184–88. She states: "It now becomes clear that verbalization of feelings leads to an increase of mastery by the ego. The young ego shows its strength by not acting upon its feelings immediately, but by delaying such action and expressing its feelings in words instead" (p. 186). See also Furman, *Helping Young Children Grow*, pp. 155–72, for her discussion of language.

page 51

We see ourselves as actors:
In Kagan's *The Nature of the Child,* he notes: "The two-year-old's insight is that she has become aware of her ability to act, to influence others, and to meet her own standards" (p. 137).

page 51

our sense of self:
The development of a cohesive sense of self occurs in the fourth subphase, which occurs from about twenty-four months to thirty-six months and is called "consolidation of individuality and the beginnings of emotional object constancy." See Mahler et al., *The Psychological Birth of the Human Infant,* pp. 109–20. Incidentally, Wilson points out in *The Moral Sense,* pp. 129–30, that this emerging sense of self is related to the defiance and rebellion that characterize the "terrible twos." He writes: "Rebellion and character formation occur simultaneously because having a moral sense first requires having a sense of self.... The tug-of-war between making claims for self and acknowledging the claims of others is exactly what makes this stage of life so tumultuous" (p. 130).

page 51

a stable inner image of our mother:
The establishment of this inner image, called object constancy, also begins in the fourth subphase (see above citation). In McDevitt and Mahler, "Object Constancy, Individuality, and Internalization," in *The Course of Life,* Vol. 1, ed. Greenspan and Pollock, object constancy is characterized by a primarily positive attachment to the internal image of mother, by a uniting of the "good" and "bad" mother into a single image, and by the psychic availability of the maternal image "in the same way that the actual mother had been libidinally available—for sustenance, comfort, and love" (p. 408).

page 51

another Eriksonian crisis:
Erikson's discussion of the third age of man, "Initiative vs. Guilt," appears on pp. 255–58 of *Childhood and Society.* He says that the concept of "initiative adds to autonomy the quality of undertaking, planning, and 'attacking' a task for the sake of being active and on the move..." (p. 255). His statement

about the danger of our "primitive, cruel, and uncompromising" conscience constricting us "to the point of self-obliteration" appears on p. 257. It is important to note, however, that this cruel and excessively punitive conscience, which employs stern countermeasures to control our "wicked" impulses and imagines the most hideous punishments should we fail to be "good," does not necessarily mean that our parents were especially harsh in their treatment of us. Instead, the harshness of our superego (especially in the early stages of conscience formation) may simply be a measure of how intense our forbidden impulses are and how much effort it takes to fight against them.

page 52

the "marshmallow test":
See Goleman, *Emotional Intelligence,* pp. 80–83, for his discussion of this test, started in the 1960s by psychologist Walter Mischel. Goleman's "a microcosm of" appears on p. 81.

page 53

many small and major control wars:
Parens discusses battles of will in "Psychic Development During the Second and Third Years of Life," in *The Course of Life,* Vol. 1, ed. Greenspan and Pollock, pp. 459–500.

page 54

"my mommy got so mad":
This story appeared in Viorst, "What's a Good Mommy?" *Redbook,* October 1974, pp. 38, 40.

page 55

to "think he is the master":
See Alice Miller, *For Your Own Good,* p. 97. She is quoting from Rousseau's *Emile.*

page 55

"the mother who always knows best":
Horner, *The Wish for Power and the Fear of Having It,* p. 96. For "Succeed for me . . . ," see p. 97.

page 56

tamp ourselves down:
In Erna Furman, *Helping Young Children Grow,* she writes about "the damaging effects of excessively inhibited aggression, of the ways in which it deprives children of zest and initiative,

contributes to helplessness and hopelessness in the face of life's daily tasks and challenges, and interferes with feeling good and having fun" (p. 343).

page 56

when our buried feelings erupt:

In Alice Miller, *For Your Own Good*, she writes: "Those who were permitted to react appropriately throughout their childhood—i.e., with anger—to the pain, wrongs, and denial inflicted upon them either consciously or unconsciously will retain this ability to react appropriately in later life too. When someone wounds them as adults, they will be able to recognize and express this verbally. But they will not feel the need to lash out in response. This need arises only for people who must always be on their guard to keep the dam that restrains their feelings from breaking. For if this dam breaks, everything becomes unpredictable." Thus, some people, "fearing unpredictable consequences, will shrink from any spontaneous reactions; the others will experience occasional outbursts of inexplicable rage . . . or resort repeatedly to violent behavior such as murder or acts of terrorism" (p. 65).

page 57

overzealous toilet training:

Neubauer, "Phase-Specific Disorders of the Second and Third Years of Life," in *The Course of Life*, Vol. 1, ed. Greenspan and Pollock, says this about toilet-training conflicts: "We can find . . . either overorderliness and insistence on cleanliness, or a continuous messiness which includes the wish to be unclean and disorderly. If these struggles continue . . . , they can lead either to an obsessive-compulsive behavior disorder or . . . a submissive tendency to please and avoid conflict, or . . . a negative stance of opposition, obstinacy, and isolation. We may find [that] . . . either the controlling position is given to others, or only self-control is tolerated" (p. 543).

page 58

"I hate being needy":

Horner, *The Wish for Power and the Fear of Having It*, p. 147.

page 59

"In her righteous reaction":

Erikson, quoting Shaw in "The Problem of Ego Identity," *Jour-*

nal of the American Psychoanalytic Association, Vol. 4, Nos. 1–4, p. 61.

page 59

And in interviews I once held:

Viorst, "What's a Good Mommy?" *Redbook*, October 1974, pp. 38, 40. The quoted material appears on p. 40.

page 61

"but a child whose intellectual development":

Fraiberg, *The Magic Years*. The quoted material appears on p. 157.

page 61

"to wait for what will come in good time":

Murphy, "Psychoanalytic Views of Infancy," in *The Course of Life*, Vol. 1, ed. Greenspan and Pollock, p. 341.

page 61

love should have no strings attached:

In Fraiberg, *The Magic Years*, she states that "a child who can claim love without meeting any of the obligations of love will be a self-centered child," and that many such children grow up "to become petulant lovers and sullen marriage partners" who say, in effect, "I know I am selfish and I have a vile temper and I'm moody and a spendthrift, but you should love me in spite of my faults" (p. 282).

page 61

"Parents tend to underestimate":

Erna Furman, *Helping Young Children Grow*, p. 231.

page 62

A study of child-rearing practices:

In Wilson, *The Moral Sense*, he states that "there is abundant support for the view that a warm and affectionate bond combined with consistent and judicious discipline is found among families with few, if any, delinquent children" (p. 150). The study he cites in relation to this view, by Diana Baumrind of the University of California at Berkeley, is described on pp. 149–50. See also Yahraes's report on Baumrind's work in "Parents as Leaders: The Role of Control and Discipline," *Families Today*, Vol. I, ed. Corfman, pp. 289–97.

Chapter Three—
Taking Possession of Ourselves

page 64

Teenager to parent:
Bell and Wildflower, *Talking with Your Teenager*, p. 21.

page 65

"your children are not your children":
Gibran, *The Prophet*, p. 17. The full thought is: "Your children are not your children. They are the sons and daughters of Life's longing for itself."

page 65

latency:
Freud's first discussion of latency can be found in the *Standard Edition*, Vol. 7, "Three Essays on the Theory of Sexuality." See also Benson and Harrison, "The Eye of the Hurricane: From Seven to Ten," in *The Course of Life*, Vol. 2, ed. Greenspan and Pollock; and Shapiro and Perry, "Latency Revisited: The Age 7 Plus or Minus 1," *The Psychoanalytic Study of the Child*, Vol. 31.

page 65

Erik Erikson's fourth age of man:
Erikson's discussion of the fourth age of man, "Industry vs. Inferiority," appears on pp. 258–61 of *Childhood and Society*. This is the time, he writes, of the child's "entrance into life" (p. 258), when he "becomes ready to handle the utensils, the tools, and the weapons used by the big people" (p. 259).

page 66

the world beyond our family:
In Schecter and Combrinck-Graham, "The Normal Development of the Seven-to-Ten-Year-Old Child," in *The Course of Life*, Vol. 2, ed. Greenspan and Pollock, the authors, drawing on the work of Sullivan, note that the child, "now entering into a broader interpersonal context, becomes subject to a variety of new experiences which he must learn to handle. Primarily these are related to the exposure to a group of peers who are not his siblings and therefore bring with them customs different from his family . . ." To adapt he must learn "to evaluate his own behavior . . . to 'differentiate authority figures' . . . to

327

reflect critically about his own parents and . . . to focus more on the reality of his existence in society" (pp. 94–95).

page 66

During the Middle Ages:
These facts about seven-year-old pages, apprentices, and so forth come from Shapiro and Perry, "Latency Revisited: The Age 7 Plus or Minus 1," *The Psychoanalytic Study of the Child,* Vol. 31, pp. 80–81.

page 66

Our brain:
The information in this and the following paragraph comes largely from Schecter and Combrinck-Graham, "The Normal Development of the Seven-to-Ten-Year-Old Child," in *The Course of Life,* Vol. 2, ed. Greenspan and Pollock, pp. 90–91, 98–99. A more detailed discussion of what Shapiro and Perry call the "biological and/or cognitive substrate for the preservation of latency" (p. 86) can be found in their paper (see note above). Elkind, *The Hurried Child,* discusses latency games and rules, and uses the phrase "the culture of childhood" (p. 106).

page 67

sibling rivalry:
See Sulloway, *Born to Rebel,* for his discussion of family niches, pp. 83–118. In his book Sulloway argues that competition over family resources, especially parental affection, creates rivalries between siblings, that each sibling develops strategies to increase the amount of attention he gets from his parents, that these strategies work best if they're not in direct competition with the strategies of other siblings, and that birth order is a powerful determinant of what these strategies are. His book mobilizes evidence from a vast array of sources that firstborns "identify more strongly with power and authority," that they are "more assertive, socially dominant, ambitious, jealous of their status, and defensive" (p. xiv), while laterborns are more likely to question the status quo and develop revolutionary personalities.

page 68

"I'm getting a higher bunk bed":
Viorst, "Good-bye, Six—Hello, Seven," in *If I Were in Charge of the World and Other Worries,* p. 51.

page 68

we do not measure up:

In Erikson, *Childhood and Society*, he writes that when a child "despairs of his tools and skills or of his status among his tool partners," he may consider himself "doomed to mediocrity or inadequacy" (p. 260).

page 68

"learned helplessness":

The concept is coined and discussed in Seligman, *Helplessness*.

page 68

In experiments with animals and humans:

Ibid. See Seligman's chapter on "Experimental Studies," pp. 21–44.

page 69

"Men and animals":

Ibid., p. 36. Seligman does note, however, that we do have some capacity to distinguish situations of helplessness from those that are not. If we couldn't, he points out, if we "went to pieces every time we flew on an airplane, life would be a madhouse" (p. 36).

page 69

Children who are convinced that they are helpless:

Seligman notes in *Helplessness* that "if a child believes he is helpless, he will perform stupidly, regardless of his I.Q. . . . On the other hand, if a child believes that he has control and mastery, he may outperform more talented peers who lack such a belief" (p. 137).

page 69

"Victor was a slow starter":

Ibid., p. 4.

page 69

Getting the lowest grades in the class:

In Selma Kramer and Rudolph, "The Latency Stage," in *The Course of Life*, Vol. 2, ed. Greenspan and Pollock, they note: "Mastery of the basic skills produces in the child a sense of accomplishment . . . resulting in a constancy of behavior and elevated self-esteem. Failure to master the needed skills results in lowered self-esteem and behavioral difficulties" (p. 112).

page 69

"intrinsic power":

Horner, *The Wish for Power and the Fear of Having It*, p. 68.

page 70

With a conscience:

Over time, experiences with our peers and nonparental adults help to modify our conscience, our superego. Indeed, many writings on latency divide it into two major phases, with our conscience strict and harsh in the first phase, kinder and gentler in the second phase.

page 70

a five-year-old girl:

These definitions of control appear in Weisz, "Understanding the Developing Understanding of Control," *The Minnesota Symposia on Child Psychiatry*, Vol. 18, ed. Perlmutter, p. 223.

page 71

Defining control:

Ibid. Weisz says, "Control means causing an intended event" (p. 221), adding that his definition excludes the occurrence of desired events that we have not brought about or undesired events that we have brought about.

page 71

contingency and competence:

Ibid. Weisz writes: "Contingency defines the relevance of attributes and behavior to an intended event, and competence defines the degree to which the individual can manifest the relevant attributes and behavior. Control is thus construed as a joint function of contingency and competence. . . . An accurate judgment about an individual's capacity to control an event is thus thought to depend on accurate assessments of (a) the contingency of that event, and (b) the competence of the individual" (p. 227).

page 71

The younger we are the greater:

Ibid. Citing experiments with children, Weisz "found little evidence that pre-elementary-school children could distinguish between contingent and chance outcomes in any way. The elementary-age children seemed to be aware of the chance-contingent distinction at a gross qualitative level. . . . Young adolescents and college students showed a definite ability to distinguish between contingent and chance events" (p. 245). For instance, kindergartners and fourth-graders played and were questioned about a game of chance (picking blue-spotted or yellow-spotted cards from a deck). Although there was nothing these children could do to affect the outcome of what was a pure guessing game, the kindergartners believed strongly that older, more practiced, and smarter children would win more often than those who were younger and less practiced and intelligent. Though fourth-graders could identify these games as noncontingent—as games of chance—they nevertheless thought that age, practice, and intelligence could have *some* impact on outcome, and they seemed to believe as strongly as kindergartners that effort made a difference in results. "These data suggest," says Weisz, "that most preadolescents are unable to identify chance outcomes as completely noncontingent" (p. 247).

page 71

The younger we are the higher:
Ibid. Weisz writes that "cross-sectional evidence from the period of early through late childhood certainly suggests that levels of perceived competence grow increasingly modest with development" (p. 249). For instance, in a study with first-, third-, and fifth-graders in which all grades received the same score in a game, the children's ratings of their own competence drastically declined from first, to third, to fifth grade.

page 71

combine information on competence and contingency:
Ibid. Weisz found that twelve-to-sixteen-year-olds and eighteen-to-twenty-five-year-olds (but not six-to-ten-year-olds) perceived control as a function of "contingency and competence *in combination,* over and above the influence of either factor considered in isolation" (p. 261).

page 71

We relinquish such beliefs, but not completely:
Ibid. Talking to children at a state fair about why they had or hadn't won a prize in a purely chance-determined game (like an electronic horse race), Weisz found: "Like many adults . . . , our mostly adolescent older group proved susceptible to

331

a subtle form of illusory contingency: the belief that factors . . . such as grade level, practice, etc. . . . will be associated with at least *slight* outcome differences. Attribution theorists should take note of the fact that even those youngsters explicitly attributing their outcomes to luck tended to make such contingency judgments" (pp. 240–41).

page 72

studies of gambling:

These studies, conducted by sociologist Erving Goffman and psychologist Ellen Langer, are described in Taylor, *Positive Illusions*, pp. 29–30.

page 72

"Any situation in which":

Ibid., p. 30.

page 72

Still, latency is when we begin to grasp:

In "Understanding the Developing Understanding of Control," in *The Minnesota Symposia on Child Psychiatry*, Vol. 18, ed. Perlmutter, Weisz writes: "The evidence reviewed thus far suggests that the consolidation of at least certain kinds of contingency and competence judgment may be taking place from middle childhood through early adolescence" (p. 258).

page 73

"I can get through most anything":

Taylor, *Positive Illusions*, p. 78. She is citing the research of learning theorist Albert Bandura.

page 73

"As soon as I get in the dentist's chair":

Ibid., p. 79. She is citing the research of Albert Bandura.

page 74

Then puberty strikes:

Discussions of the physical and psychological changes that bring latency to an end can be found in Kestenberg, "Eleven, Twelve, Thirteen: Years of Transition from the Barrenness of Childhood to the Fertility of Adolescence"; Sklansky, "The Pubescent Years: Eleven to Fourteen"; and Beiser, "Ages Eleven to Fourteen"; all in *The Course of Life*, Vol. 2, ed. Greenspan and Pollock. Kestenberg calls this period "prepuberty" and uses it as a synonym for "pubescence"; Beiser calls it "prepuberty"

and equates it with "preadolescence"; and Sklansky calls it—
as I shall—"puberty" and equates it with "pubescence."

page 74

"an outlaw or pariah even":
Clampitt, "Gooseberry Fool," in *What the Light Was Like*, p. 13.

page 75

Erikson calls an identity crisis:
In *Identity: Youth and Crisis*, Erikson states that at adolescence
we "develop the prerequisites . . . to experience and pass
through the crisis of identity" (p. 91). His discussion of the
fifth age of man, "Identity vs. Role Confusion," appears on pp.
261–63 of *Childhood and Society*.

page 75

struggle to affirm and assert our autonomy:
In Sklansky, "The Pubescent Years: Eleven to Fourteen," in *The
Course of Life*, Vol. 2, ed. Greenspan and Pollock, he writes:
"The adolescent experiences the longing for autonomy intensely and equates it with becoming adult—being *his own
man or her own woman*. (In our culture, it is felt as being only
fair and right that an individual be allowed to be himself—a
feeling of entitlement, a constitutionally guaranteed right to
equality with the adult)" (pp. 280–81).

page 76

"There's no way to compare":
Norman and Harris, *The Private Life of the American Teenager*, p.
26. The Norman-Harris report, which surveyed 160,000 American teenagers, provided this chapter with many of the comments made by teens about their parents.

page 76

"I can understand":
Ibid., p. 22.

page 76

"At least while they're having sex":
From Jane Shapiro, "Poltergeists," in *Mothers*, ed. Kenison and
Hirsch, p. 238.

page 76

"the acquisition of a mature body":
Noshpitz, "Disturbances in Early Adolescent Development,"
in *The Course of Life*, Vol. 2, ed. Greenspan and Pollock, p. 329.

page 76

"My parents try to prevent":
Norman and Harris, *The Private Life of the American Teenager*, pp. 22–23.

page 77

from early to middle to late adolescence:
Eugene Kaplan, "Adolescents, Age Fifteen to Eighteen: A Psychoanalytic Developmental View," in *The Course of Life*, Vol. 2, ed. Greenspan and Pollock, distinguishes among three different stages of adolescence and concludes: "The early adolescent must redefine himself and his relationships to his parents in the wake of his momentous physical transformation. The middle adolescent must venture from the protective scaffolding of the peer group into dyadic heterosexual love relationships. The late adolescent must define his spiritual and worldly standards and goals of achievement, while initiating their implementation. These developmental redefinitions involve: first, his body and his family; second, sexual identity and intimacy; third, standards, goals, and the relationship to society" (p. 393).

page 77

the developmental tasks of adolescence:
Staples and Smarr, "Bridge to Adulthood: Years from Eighteen to Twenty-Three," in *The Course of Life*, Vol. 2, ed. Greenspan and Pollock, quote a list of the tasks of adolescence on p. 479.

page 77

our sexual identity:
In "Mid-Adolescence—Foundations for Later Psychopathology," in *The Course of Life*, Vol. 2, ed. Greenspan and Pollock, Esman distinguishes between gender and sexual identity, noting that although gender identity as male or female "appears to be laid down in the pre-oedipal years," adolescence is when we establish our sexual identity, which he defines as "a clear sense of self as masculine or feminine and one's mode of function in one's sexual life" (p. 423).

page 77

our still-harsh superego:
Esman, "Mid-Adolescence—Foundations for Later Psychopathology," in *The Course of Life*, Vol. 2, ed. Greenspan and Pol-

lock, points out that "adolescence affords an opportunity for the reshaping of the ego ideal" and for a modification of the superego's harsh, "categorical, all-or-none quality" (p. 427).

page 77

"In the process":
Loewald, "The Waning of the Oedipus Complex," *Journal of the American Psychoanalytic Association*, Vol. 27, No. 4, p. 756.

page 77

"In an important sense":
Ibid., p. 758.

page 77

"more than symbolic":
Ibid., p. 764.

page 78

"There was an issue of loyalty":
Horner, *The Wish for Power and the Fear of Having It*, p. 75.

page 78

"without the guilty deed of parricide":
Loewald, "The Waning of the Oedipus Complex," *Journal of the American Psychoanalytic Association*, Vol. 27, No. 4, p. 762.

page 78

"What do we know about mothers and daughters?":
Anne Roiphe, *Lovingkindness*, p. 120.

page 79

"My daughter is so beautiful":
Bell and Wildflower, *Talking with Your Teenager*, p. 10.

page 79

"My son uses my car":
Ibid., p. 14.

page 79

our parents may envy our juiciness and potency:
Anthony writes in "The Reactions of Adults to Adolescents and Their Behavior," *Adolescence: Psychosocial Perspectives*, ed. Caplan and Lebovici: "It is clear that . . . the adolescent is on his way up when the caretaking adults are on their way down. This . . . distinction understandably provokes in the adult envy for the adolescent's youthful vigor with all its freedom, freshness, and joyful foolishness" (p. 68).

page 79

"I'm my father's only girl":
Norman and Harris, *The Private Life of the American Teenager*, p. 20.

pages 79–80

a study of parent-child strife concludes:
See Csikszentmihalyi and Larson, *Being Adolescent*, pp. 131–32, where they discuss Davis's analysis of factors leading to parent-youth strife.

page 80

"My father never gives me a chance":
Norman and Harris, *The Private Life of the American Teenager*, p. 10.

page 80

"frequently leads him to take stands":
Noshpitz, "Disturbances in Early Adolescent Development," in *The Course of Life*, Vol. 2, ed. Greenspan and Pollock, p. 318.

page 81

"My parents can never compromise":
Norman and Harris, *The Private Life of the American Teenager*, p. 8.

page 81

"If you're going to be sluts":
Melinda's story appeared in *The New York Times*, December 6, 1994, p. B6.

page 81

"Our adolescents":
Anthony provides this quote from Socrates in "The Reactions of Adults to Adolescents and Their Behavior," in *Adolescence: Psychosocial Perspectives*, ed. Caplan and Lebovici, p. 77.

page 82

"causing parents to respond":
Ibid., p. 54.

page 82

"keep things to myself":
Norman and Harris, *The Private Life of the American Teenager*, p. 11.

page 82
"want to know who, what, where, why":
Ibid., p. 11.
page 82
"My father gives me":
Ibid., p. 10.
page 82
"they get furious":
Ibid., p. 14.
page 82
"There's no way":
Ibid., p. 106.
page 82
"would look down on me":
Ibid., p. 106.
page 83
one former "very wild teenager" recalls:
Bell and Wildflower, *Talking with Your Teenager*, p. 28.
page 83
"I did this for you, Mom":
Ibid., p. 21.
page 83

various forms of rebellion:
Noshpitz describes forms of rebellion in "Disturbances in Early Adolescent Development," in *The Course of Life*, Vol. 2, ed. Greenspan and Pollock: "There can be a series of fantasied denunciations and devastating attacks on parents and teachers that are never verbalized by a youngster who is outwardly accepting and compliant. There can be alternating episodes of stubborn opposition and cheerful acceptance of rules. There can be a chronic nasty, negative attitude with sullenness and surliness within an overall context of basic good behavior. And there can also be overt hostile refusal to comply with the most elementary requirements of age-appropriate adjustment coupled with destructive outbursts, school failure, runaways and all manner of personal challenges to authority figures" (p. 318). Blos, in *On Adolescence*, discusses the very different rebellions of two adolescent boys, one who "accepts the value system and the class standards of his family" and rebels by

"usurping as quickly as possible the pleasure privileges of adults" and another who finds everything "alien to his milieu . . . worth doing, thinking, and feeling" (p. 208).

page 83

"spite and revenge attachments":
Isay, "Late Adolescence: The Second Separation Stage of Adolescence," in *The Course of Life*, Vol. 2, ed. Greenspan and Pollock, p. 514.

page 84

"illusory power":
Horner, *The Wish for Power and the Fear of Having It*, p. 88. Sklansky, in "The Pubescent Years: Eleven to Fourteen" in Greenspan and Pollock, *The Course of Life*, Vol. 2, talks about the shifting of dependency from parents to leaders and groups on p. 282. Coppolillo's "The Tides of Change in Adolescence" (same volume) adds that the adolescent's declarations of independence as he turns from parents to peer group also provide him with a sense of autonomy and freedom that "is in part illusory. The group prescribes dress, behaviors, and standards that are sometimes more intransigent than the parents ever dreamed of being" (p. 405).

page 84

anorexia nervosa:
Horner (see above reference) describes eating disorders as "an attempt to gain omnipotent control over the body, its form and its impulses" in order to counteract "the terror of helplessness against forces over which one has no control. The new helplessness re-evokes earlier terrors of helplessness against controlling and intrusive parents" (p. 85). Valuable discussions of anorexia include Bruch, "The Sleeping Beauty: Escape from Change," in *The Course of Life*, Vol. 2, ed. Greenspan and Pollock; Louise Kaplan's chapter on anorexia in *Adolescence: The Farewell to Childhood*; and Casper, "Treatment Principles in Anorexia Nervosa," in *Adolescent Psychiatry*, Vol. 10, ed. Feinstein, Looney, Schwartzberg, and Sorosky. While over-controlling parents have often been cited as playing a major role in anorexia, some studies—see Goleman, *Emotional Intelligence*, pp. 246–49—do not find parental control a prime factor. Note: Another common female adolescent eating disorder, bulimia,

is characterized by the following binge-purge cycle: The bulimic compulsively consumes enormous quantities of food (perhaps several thousand calories) within a brief period, after which she purges by self-induced vomiting, diuretics, or laxatives, or by fasting or compulsive exercising. Bulimia is often seen as another attempt by teenagers—at least in the purge portion of the cycle—to exert control and assert independence.

page 84

"Being thin is the most important thing":
Johnson and Connors, in *The Etiology and Treatment of Bulimia Nervosa*, offer an excerpt from Marcia Millman, *Such a Pretty Face*, to demonstrate one woman's lifelong obsession with food and weight. "Being thin" appears on p. 223, "I enjoy living" on p. 224, and "Well, I've stayed thin" on p. 225.

page 84

"believes her thinness to be":
Casper, "Treatment Principles in Anorexia Nervosa," in *Adolescent Psychiatary*, Vol. 10, ed. Feinstein et al., p. 433.

page 85

"formal operations":
See Jean Piaget's "The Intellectual Development of the Adolescent," in *Adolescence: Psychosocial Perspectives*, ed. Caplan and Lebovici, for his discussion of "formal operations"—the phrase appears on p. 24. Kaplan, "Adolescents, Age Fifteen to Eighteen: A Psychoanalytic Developmental View," in *The Course of Life*, Vol. 2, ed. Greenspan and Pollock, notes that the advance from "the more concrete, present-oriented, simplistic right-good vs. wrong-bad to the general, formal, logical, and abstract" leads, in middle-adolescence, to "the capacity to think about thinking, work with ideas not immediately tied to concrete examples, leads to a greater appreciation of cause and effect, and antecedent causes . . . , a sense of the causal signficance of the past in viewing the present" (p. 378). Noshpitz, "Disturbance in Early Adolescent Development," same volume, says that thanks to this "capacity to think abstractly, to draw ever finer distinctions, to see essential consistencies despite superficial differences, to hold a chain of cause-and-effect sequences firmly in mind, and to use concepts as manip-

ulable entities," the adolescent "reasons more effectively in academic pursuits and argues ever more trenchantly in his altercations with parents, teachers, and other authorities" (p. 311).

page 85

to invidiously compare our actual parents:
Sklansky, "The Pubescent Years: Eleven to Fourteen," in *The Course of Life,* Vol. 2, ed. Greenspan and Pollock, says that "in early adolescence, cognitive maturation, increase of experience with other adults, and the internal repellent force against the infantile and oedipal objects combine to make it possible for the adolescent to react to the limitations and faults of the parents with annoyed disappointment. The reaction is to the incongruity between the real parent and the internal idealized parent imago" (p. 277).

page 86

"There are few situations in life":
Anna Freud, "Adolescence," in *The Psychoanalytic Study of the Child,* Vol. 13, p. 276.

page 87

want—often desperately want—their love and approval:
Horner, in *The Wish for Power and the Fear of Having It,* notes that "no degree of intrinsic power will be likely to make the continuation of [our parents'] love and concern irrelevant to the grown son or daughter" (p. 88).

page 87

"Mother, Mother!":
From Robert Lowell, "During Fever," reprinted in *MotherSongs,* ed. Gilbert, Gubar, and O'Hehir, pp. 114–15.

page 87

aching ambivalence:
Kaplan, in *Adolescence: The Farewell to Childhood,* puts it like this: "Every vigorous thrust away, every rejection of them, is countered by passionate longings to go back, to become reabsorbed into the passions of infancy" (pp. 116–17).

page 88

"Until I asked her to please stop doing it and was":
From C. K. Williams, "My Mother's Lips," reprinted in *MotherSongs,* ed. Gilbert, Gubar, and O'Hehir, pp. 118–20.

page 88

perpetual adolescence:

In *On Adolescence*, Blos discusses what he calls *prolonged adolescence* on p. 12 and pp. 220–22, characterizing such adolescents as "living in the twilight of an arrested transition" (p. 220).

page 89

an unconscious rescue fantasy:

Blos, *On Adolescence*, discusses the rescue fantasy on pp. 153–55.

page 89

our own identity:

In *Childhood and Society*, Erikson says that ego identity is "more than the sum of the childhood identifications. It is the accrued experience of the ego's ability to integrate all identifications with the vicissitudes of the libido, with the aptitudes developed out of endowment, and with the opportunities offered in social roles. The sense of ego identity, then, is the accrued confidence that the inner sameness and continuity prepared in the past are matched by the sameness and continuity of one's meaning for others" (p. 261). See also Blos, *On Adolescence*, p. 175, and Staples and Smarr, "Bridge to Adulthood: Years from Eighteen to Twenty-three," pp. 484–87, in *The Course of Life*, Vol. 2, ed. Greenspan and Pollock. In GAP, *Psychotherapy with College Students*, identity consolidation is defined as the development of "a solid, cohesive identity, which will be felt to be one's own and not imposed by some outside force or person, and which will continue over time" (p. 55). And in Lidz, "The Adolescent and His Family," in *Adolescence: Psychosocial Perspectives*, ed. Caplan and Lebovici, he notes that parent-child troubles often subside in late adolescence and that as the adolescent "settles down to be responsible for himself and to himself," he "unwittingly [and, I would add, also wittingly] takes on the ways of his parents that he has so recently been repudiating" (p. 110).

page 90

"soulfree and fancyfree":

Joyce, *A Portrait of the Artist as a Young Man*, p. 270.

page 90

"I do not fear to be alone":

Ibid., p. 296.

page 90

"Welcome, O life!":
Ibid. Joyce gives these classic coming-of-age words to his alter-ego Stephen Dedalus: "Mother is putting my new secondhand clothes in order. She prays now, she says, that I may learn in my own life and away from home and friends what the heart is and what it feels. Amen. So be it. Welcome, O life! I go to encounter for the millionth time the reality of experience and to forge in the smithy of my soul the uncreated conscience of my race" (pp. 275–76).

page 90

"You have brains in your head":
Seuss, *Oh, the Places You'll Go!*, unpaged.

Chapter Four—The Power of Sex

page 91

"Every step along the way":
Michael et al., *Sex in America*, p. 220.

page 91

"Men rule the world":
Nicky Silver, *The Food Chain*, heard at the theater.

page 92

"I had been thinking about everything":
Katie Roiphe, *The Morning After*, p. 168.

page 93

"to keep our fantasies":
This and all the other quoted material from Meghan Daum appears in her article "Safe-Sex Lies," *The New York Times Magazine*, January 21, 1996, pp. 32–33.

page 94

"Zipless Fuck":
Jong, *Fear of Flying*, p. 11.

page 94

"the three of us being together":
Lobell, *John & Mimi*, p. 71.

page 94
> "Mimi and Ava":
> Ibid., p. 79.

page 94
> "with other couples":
> Ibid., p. 119.

page 94
> "free marriage":
> Ibid., from the subtitle of the book.

page 94
> "there will be nothing unusual":
> Ibid., p. 8.

page 95
> "Mrs. Coolidge":
> This story is recounted in Burr, *A Separate Creation*, p. 175.

page 95
> For boys, as they develop:
> See discussion of this in Viorst, *Necessary Losses*, pp. 121–22.

page 96
> *"Attached, dependent, reengulfed"*:
> Ross, *The Male Paradox*, p. 253.

page 96
> "unconnected lust":
> Levant, *Masculinity Reconstructed*; see chapter 9, subtitle and discussion.

page 96
> "I wish I knew a woman":
> Lawrence, "I Wish I Knew a Woman," in *Selected Poems*, p. 111.

page 96
> "I not only lost him":
> Jean Baker Miller writes in *Toward a New Psychology of Women* that "women's sense of self becomes very much organized around being able to make and then to maintain affiliations and relationships. Eventually, for many women the threat of disruption of connections is perceived not as just a loss of a relationship but as something closer to a total loss of self" (p. 83).

page 96
> 33 percent of the men:
> Michael et al. provide these figures in *Sex in America*, p. 236.

page 97

> that they *give* something to a man:
> Miller discusses this idea in *Toward a New Psychology of Women*,
> pp. 50–51.

page 97

> a very high number of women—22 percent:
> Michael et al., *Sex in America*, p. 223. The 3 percent figure for
> men appears on p. 227.

page 97

> "most men who forced sex":
> Ibid., p. 229.

page 97

> "Do you mean":
> Weinberg and Biernbaum, "Conversations of Consent: Sexual
> Intimacy without Sexual Assault," in *Transforming a Rape Culture*, ed. Buchwald et al., p. 92.

page 97

> "Well, I had consent":
> Ibid.

page 97

> "As far as I'm concerned":
> Katie Roiphe, *The Morning After*, quoting novelist Martin Amis,
> p. 80.

page 97

> "With this new definition of rape":
> Weinberg and Biernbaum, "Conversations of Consent: Sexual
> Intimacy without Sexual Assault," in *Transforming a Rape Culture*, ed. Buchwald et al., p. 91.

page 97

> "She got herself raped":
> Ibid., p. 92.

page 99

> "I like to dominate a woman":
> This survey is reported in Wolf, *The Beauty Myth*, p. 165.

page 99

> Another survey:
> This survey, called The Fantasy Project, is discussed in Person,
> "Male Sexuality and Power," *Psychoanalytic Inquiry*, Vol. 6, No.
> 1, p. 10. The Project also found that 11 percent of the males

reported fantasies of torturing their sexual partner and 20 percent reported fantasies of beating or whipping their partner. The figures for females were zero for torture, 1 percent for beating or whipping.

page 99

"the popular cultural notion":

Ibid., p. 6.

page 100

"this literal sense of genital inadequacy":

Ibid., p. 18. Dr. Person acknowledges the importance of castration anxiety in male development and fantasy life, but says that "what is missing in traditional formulations is the impact of the mother-son relationship at different developmental stages, and the nature of the male's sexual realities at different points in the life cycle" (p. 18).

page 100

"I never felt comfortable":

See Lisa Bannon, "How a Risky Surgery Became a Profit Center for Some L.A. Doctors," *The Wall Street Journal*, June 6, 1996, pp. 1, 8. Whitehead's statement appears on p. 1.

page 100

"having a gun and ammunition":

Person, "Male Sexuality and Power," *Psychoanalytic Inquiry*, Vol. 6, No. 1, p. 21.

page 101

"According to my experience":

Ibid., p. 19.

page 101

"overabundance of women":

Ibid., p. 11.

page 101

"compensatory mechanisms":

Ibid., p. 7.

page 102

a universal "fault" line:

Ibid.

page 102

"a large, powerful, untiring phallus":

Ibid., p. 3.

page 102

"I've got you under my skin":
Porter, "I've Got You Under My Skin," in *The Complete Lyrics of Cole Porter*, ed. Kimball, p. 142. "I'd sacrifice anything," same reference.

page 102

"So taunt me and hurt me":
Porter, "So in Love," in *The Complete Lyrics of Cole Porter*, ed. Kimball, p. 274.

page 103

so "heavily invested":
May is quoted by Person in "Male Sexuality and Power," *Psychoanalytic Inquiry*, Vol. 6, No. 1, p. 5.

page 103

date rape:
The case for a less inclusive definition of date rape is made in Roiphe's book *The Morning After*.

page 104

"rape culture":
See *Transforming a Rape Culture*, ed. Buchwald et al.

page 104

"conniving, coercing, pushing":
Kimmel, "Clarence, William, Iron Mike, Tailhook, Senator Packwood, Spur Posse, Magic . . . and Us," in *Transforming a Rape Culture*, ed. Buchwald et al., p. 125.

page 104

"Women have all the power here":
Danon is quoted in Sarah Crichton's article, "Sexual Correctness," *Newsweek*, October 25, 1993, p. 56.

page 104

97,464 female rapes in 1995:
The FBI's Uniform Crime Report provided these 1995 figures.

page 104

"*some* men rape":
Brownmiller, *Against Our Will*, p. 229.

page 104

"the deadly male myths of rape":
Ibid., p. 346.

page 104

That "a rape usually is . . .":
Ibid., p. 348. She is quoting from John Updike's novel *Rabbit Redux.*

page 105

"the act of a master":
Ibid., p. 349. She is quoting from Ayn Rand's novel *The Fountainhead.*

page 105

"I've been raped":
Ibid.

page 105

"Escalating a sexual encounter":
Kimmel, "Clarence, William, Iron Mike, Tailhook, Senator Packwood, Spur Posse, Magic . . . and Us," in *Transforming a Rape Culture*, ed. Buchwald et al., p. 128.

page 105

"Every woman adores a Fascist":
Brownmiller, *Against Our Will*, p. 364. She is quoting from Plath's poem "Daddy."

page 105

"secret erotic need":
Ibid., p. 363. She is quoting from *The Diary of Anaïs Nin.*

page 105

"primary, erotogenic masochism":
Blum, "Masochism, the Ego Ideal, and the Psychology of Women," *Journal of the American Psychoanalytic Association,* Vol. 24, No. 5, p. 158. He is quoting from Freud's "The Economic Problem of Masochism."

page 105

"a deeply feminine need to be overpowered":
Brownmiller, *Against Our Will*, p. 353. She is quoting from Deutsch's *The Psychology of Women.*

page 105

"immense masochistic beating fantasies":
Millett, *Sexual Politics*, p. 205. She is quoting from Bonaparte's *Female Sexuality.*

page 105

"anticipation of, as well as experience in":
Blum, "Masochism, the Ego Ideal, and the Psychology of Women," *Journal of the American Psychoanalytic Association*, Vol. 24, No. 5, p. 166.

page 106

"woman's anatomical destiny":
Barglow and Schaefer, "A New Female Psychology?" *Journal of the American Psychoanalytic Association*, Vol. 24, No. 5, p. 311.

page 106

caricatures femininity:
Blum, "Masochism, the Ego Ideal, and the Psychology of Women," *Journal of the American Psychoanalytic Association*, Vol. 24, No. 5, p. 180. Blum is referring to a comment by psychoanalyst Robert Waelder.

page 106

"What does a woman want?":
Ibid., p. 160. Freud's uncertainty about female psychosexual development is also expressed, notes Blum, in his statement that "our insight into these developmental processes in girls is unsatisfactory, incomplete, and vague" and his reference to adult female sexuality as a "dark continent" (pp. 159–60).

page 106

a weaker sexual instinct:
Ibid. Blum cites Freud's and Bonaparte's characterizations of the female libido as weaker, p. 163.

page 106

"asexual gatekeeper":
Kimmel, "Clarence, William, Iron Mike, Tailhook, Senator Packwood, Spur Posse, Magic . . . and Us," *Transforming a Rape Culture*, ed. Buchwald et al., pp. 123–24.

page 106

"the incessant humming of male desire":
Ibid.

page 107

some evidence suggests:
See Wolf, *Promiscuities*, for her discussion of cultures that view women as more sexual than men. Her sources are cited on p. 241.

page 107

"Do you know how to bargain?":
The quoted material appears in *The Piano*. The description of the scene is mine.

page 108

"Even the dumbest wife":
Landers, *Wake Up and Smell the Coffee*, p. 49.

page 108

"I mean it seems to me":
Loos, *Gentlemen Prefer Blondes*, pp. 18–19.

page 109

"like taking an advanced-placement course":
Sharon Thompson, *Going All the Way*, p. 235.

page 109

"I swear":
Ibid., p. 236.

page 109

"would make things better":
Ibid., p. 29.

page 109

"made herself available to him":
Ibid., pp. 29–30.

page 109

"generate caring and love":
Ibid., p. 24.

pages 109–110

"lasso that would give her control":
Ibid., p. 261.

page 110

almost 75 percent were still virgins:
Ibid., p. 7. Thompson's figures come from Hofferth, Kahn, and Baldwin, "Premarital Sexual Activity Among U.S. Teenage Women Over the Past Three Decades," *Family Planning Perspectives*, Vol. 19, No. 2, March/April 1987, p. 49.

page 110

"guys give girls" (and the lines that follow):
Landers, *Wake Up and Smell the Coffee*, pp. 92, 93.

page 110

more than half of the girls:

Thompson, *Going All the Way*, p. 7.

page 111

"See, the reason":

Ibid., p. 19.

page 111

"I tried to turn my thoughts":

Scott Spencer, *Endless Love*, p. 73. Although David is a fictional character, the emotions he expresses have surely been experienced by adolescent boys outside of the pages of novels.

page 112

"a weapon used by the self":

Horner, *The Wish for Power and the Fear of Having It*, p. 92.

page 113

A statistic:

Sex in America, ed. Michael et al., pp. 82, 85.

page 113

"You think that's unfair, right?":

Ibid., p. 84.

page 114

"Creative, Intelligent, Amusing":

New York, July 10, 1995, p. 132. See same reference for Attractive, Caring And Athletic Lady. For LI Lady, see same issue, p. 133. For Ravishing, Romantic Redhead, see *New York,* September 11, 1995, p. 197.

page 115

"When women bitterly complain":

Sex in America, ed. Michael et al., pp. 237–38.

page 115

"It's making you a whore":

This quoted material appears in *The Piano.* The description of the scene is mine.

page 115

"most physically pleased":

Sex in America, ed. Michael et al., p. 124.

page 117
> "My husband no longer":
> Landers, *Wake Up and Smell the Coffee*, pp. 52–53.

page 117
> "It was humiliating":
> Ibid., p. 46.

page 118
> "it is not normal":
> Ibid., p. 48.

page 118
> "Where do all the tired men":
> Ibid., p. 49.

page 118
> "can tell us the degree of power":
> Blumstein and Pepper Schwartz, *American Couples*, p. 206.

page 118
> "abdicating his maleness":
> Ibid., p. 225.

page 118
> "becoming the man":
> Ibid.

page 118
> "an elusive balancing act":
> Ibid.

page 119
> "When I'm going down on her":
> Ibid., p. 232.

page 119
> "Sometimes when I'm going down on him":
> Ibid., p. 236.

page 119
> "I think he likes it so much":
> Ibid., p. 232.

page 120
> "Just how kinky":
> Landers, *Wake Up and Smell the Coffee*, p. 41.

page 121
> "becoming a hostage":
> Scharff, *The Sexual Relationship*, p. 134.

page 121

intimacy versus isolation:
Erikson's discussion of the sixth age of man, "Intimacy vs. Isolation," appears on pp. 263–66 of *Childhood and Society.*

page 122

"the wild orgasms of love":
Lawrence, "Fidelity," in *The Complete Poems of D. H. Lawrence,* ed. de Sola Pinto and Roberts, pp. 476–77.

page 122

"with the desire to be wild":
Katie Roiphe, *Last Night in Paradise*, p. 193.

Chapter Five—Who Controls the Couple?

page 123

"It is almost impossible":
Michael Miller, *Intimate Terrorism*, p. 12.

page 124

"On the basis of family life":
Rose, *Parallel Lives*, p. 7.

page 125

"Marriage and other adult intimacies":
Michael Miller, *Intimate Terrorism*, p. 19.

page 126

"for the surrender of will":
In Rose, *Parallel Lives,* she discusses the marriage of John Stuart Mill and Harriet Taylor, noting: "The blueprint for loving was drawn, and drawn powerfully, by his father, who at one level was teaching his son to think for himself but at another was . . . drilling into him with every lesson the feel of domination, the surrender of will to a being stronger than himself. . . . It seems therefore inevitable that Mill would be drawn to a woman who made lavish use of rebuke and reproach, someone stronger than himself, someone controlling" (pp. 134–35).

page 126

"Love makes us anxious":
Michael Miller, *Intimate Terrorism*, p. 12.

page 126

"the anxiety of loving":
Ibid., pp. 12–13.

page 126

"to share intimately":
Toews, "Adolescent Developmental Issues in Marital Therapy," in *Adolescent Psychiatry*, Vol. 8, ed. Feinstein et al., p. 244.

page 127

"interminable arguments":
Ibid.

page 127

men (because of their history) tend to pursue autonomy:
See Carol Gilligan, *In a Different Voice*, for an excellent discussion of male-female differences in their feelings about autonomy and intimacy.

page 127

"principle of less interest":
Blumstein and Schwartz, *American Couples*, p. 283. The "principle of less interest" was formulated by sociologist Willard Waller.

page 128

" 'Mom,' she explained, 'with all the equality' ":
Wallerstein and Blakeslee, *The Good Marriage*, p. 154.

page 129

wives—as they grow older—want more time away:
See Blumstein and Schwartz, *American Couples*, for a discussion of men, women, and private time, pp. 176–77, 183–87.

page 130

"each wanting something from the other":
Michael Miller, *Intimate Terrorism*, p. 61.

page 130

"must decide what money":
Blumstein and Schwartz, *American Couples*, p. 51.

page 130

In married, cohabiting, and gay couples:
Ibid. For discussion, see pp. 53–56.

page 130

"notable exception" and "because women historically":
Ibid., p. 55. The authors add that because "lesbians are all too

aware of how money can function in a heterosexual relationship with the high earner receiving special privileges and the low earner being subservient," they "bend over backward to avoid letting money have that kind of control over their lives" (p. 75).

page 131

"likely to be in charge of most important decisions":

Ibid., p. 58.

page 131

"if she is employed full time:"

Ibid., p. 56. On *earns more money than he,* emphasis added.

page 131

"a sign of a more fundamental power":

Ibid., p. 63.

page 131

"property and assets are usually commingled":

Ibid., p. 79.

page 131

"evaluate her performance and find it wanting":

Ibid., p 81.

page 131

"and they are all related to power":

Ibid., p. 102.

page 132

"I had to explain why":

Ibid.

page 132

a study by psychiatrist Ann Ruth Turkel:

See Turkel, "Money as a Mirror of Marriage," *Journal of the American Academy of Psychoanalysis,* Vol. 16, No. 4, pp. 525–35.

page 133

"Nate," says one such wife:

Blumstein and Schwartz, *American Couples,* p. 103.

page 133

"If either partner is *too* dominating":

Ibid., p. 93. Emphasis added.

page 133

"He's so good to me":

Sylvia and Zach Newman are discussed in Klagsbrun, *Married People,* pp. 59–60.

page 134

26 percent of full-time working women:
This figure was provided in January 1997 by the Bureau of Labor Statistics.

page 134

"They do not want to dominate their men":
Blumstein and Schwartz, *American Couples,* p. 327.

page 134

"taxonomies of power":
See, for instance, Raven's "A Taxonomy of Power in Human Relations," *Psychiatric Annals,* Vol. 16, No. 11. The following categories and discussion of control techniques are derived from my synthesis of personal interviews, Raven's paper, and several other publications, including: Ostow, "The Control of Human Behavior"; Marwell and Schmitt, "Dimensions of Compliance-Gaining Behavior: An Empirical Analysis"; Falbo and Peplau, "Power Strategies in Intimate Relationships"; Falbo, "Multidimensional Scaling of Power Strategies"; Howard, Blumstein, and Schwartz, "Sex, Power, and Influence Tactics in Intimate Relationships"; Kipnis, "The Use of Power in Organizations and in Interpersonal Settings"; and Kipnis, Castell, Gergen, and Mauch, "Metamorphic Effects of Power." (See Bibliography for fuller reference information.)

page 135

"sneaky" and "underhanded":
Tannen, *You Just Don't Understand,* p. 225.

page 135

"If you get your way":
Ibid.

page 135

"leisure gap":
Hochschild, *The Second Shift,* p. 4. Hochschild used time studies done in the 1960s and 1970s to establish that working women put in a weekly fifteen hours more of child care and housework than men did, a figure adding up yearly to an extra month of twenty-four-hour days. In her book, published in 1989, she said that some later studies showed no increase in male participation. In contrast, in Barnett and Rivers's book *She Works/He Works,* the authors found that while "women still

do more of the housework and the child care than do men, the situation is changing substantially" (p. 177) with women now doing 55 percent and men 45 percent of the chores. However, their research also indicated the following shadows on this rosier picture: Low-control jobs like cooking, cleaning, and doing the laundry, jobs that can't be put off till another time, are more stressful than high-control jobs—and "women spend more time doing low-control tasks than do their husbands" (p. 179). Women working outside the home still feel so much guilt about it that "there's a temptation to try to be superwoman" (p. 183). The research also shows "that both women and men value the man's job most" (p. 199).

page 135
"Many men praised their wives":
Hochschild, *The Second Shift*, p. 202. Also on that page: "convenient" and "appreciating the way."

page 135
"I really need a few things":
Tannen, *You Just Don't Understand*, p. 225. She notes, "Indirectness itself does not reflect powerlessness. . . . For example, a wealthy couple who know that their servants will do their bidding need not give direct orders but can simply state . . . 'It's chilly in here,' and the servant sets about raising the temperature" (p. 226).

page 136
"that if she became excited":
Ford, *The Good Soldier*, p. 16.

page 137
"I think Nicole is less sick":
Fitzgerald, *Tender Is the Night*, p. 239.

page 137
"the plot of female power through weakness":
Rose, *Parallel Lives*, p. 9.

page 137
"As a mode of influencing human behavior":
Ostow, "The Control of Human Behavior," *The International Journal of Psychoanalysis*, Vol. 40, Parts 5–6, p. 276.

page 139

"are keenly aware":
Tannen, *You Just Don't Understand*, p. 109.

page 139

"All right, so maybe":
Blumstein and Schwartz, *American Couples*, p. 82.

page 140

"I work for the money":
Ibid., p. 58.

page 140

"who are insecure and lacking in self-confidence":
Raven, "A Taxonomy of Power in Human Relations," *Psychiatric Annals*, Vol. 16, No. 11, p. 636.

page 140

"And then at one point O. J.":
Denise Brown's testimony in the Simpson trial, February 3, 1995, The Associated Press, as provided by Westlaw, West Publishing Co.

page 141

"The individual who uses violence":
Michael Miller, *Intimate Terrorism*, pp. 48–49.

page 141

"bounce some glassware":
Landers, *Wake Up and Smell the Coffee*, pp. 294–95.

page 142

Marilyn was initially very pleased:
Marilyn and Larry are discussed in Horner, *The Wish for Power and the Fear of Having It*, pp. 112–13.

page 144

"stonewalling":
Gottman, *Why Marriages Succeed or Fail*, pp. 93–97, 145–49, discusses stonewalling. He notes that because during distressing marital discussions a husband's blood pressure and heart rate rise much higher than his wife's do, he avoids this physiological arousal—what Gottman calls "flooding"—by stonewalling. See pp. 94–95 for the quoted material.

page 146

There's a theory that holds:
This theory is offered by Kipnis, "The Use of Power in Organi-

zations and in Interpersonal Settings," in *Applied Social Psychology Annual,* Vol. 5, ed. S. Oskamp, p. 186.

page 146

"Even if I had a Ph.D. in psychology":
Viorst, "So My Husband and I Decided to Take a Car Trip Through New England," *The New York Times,* February 15, 1989, Op-Ed page.

page 147

"increases the powerholder's sense of control":
Kipnis, "The Use of Power in Organizations and in Interpersonal Settings," in *Applied Social Psychology Annual,* Vol. 5, ed. S. Oskamp, p. 200.

page 147

"metamorphic effects of power":
Kipnis, Castell, Gergen, and Mauch, "Metamorphic Effects of Power," *Journal of Applied Psychology,* Vol. 61, No. 2, p. 127.

page 147

"who believed that they controlled":
Ibid., p. 132.

page 147

"unilateral control of decision-making power":
Kipnis, "The Use of Power in Organizations and in Interpersonal Settings," in *Applied Social Psychology Annual,* Vol. 5, ed. S. Oskamp, p. 201.

page 147

power arrangements and marital satisfaction:
See Gray-Little and Burks, "Power and Satisfaction in Marriage: A Review and Critique," *Psychological Bulletin,* Vol. 93, No. 3, pp. 513–38.

page 148

"makes herself into nothing":
Horner, *The Wish for Power and the Fear of Having It,* p. 113. Harriet and Roger are discussed on pp. 113–14.

page 148

the doll-wife Nora:
The quoted material, from the Penguin edition of Ibsen's *A Doll's House and Other Plays,* can be found as follows: "twittering" and "scampering" and "little featherbrain," p. 148; "Oh, *do,*" p. 150; "Sit down," pp. 224–25; "I've lived," p. 226;

"It's no good," p. 227; "I believe," p. 228; "I can't stay" and "You're out" and "But this," p. 227; "Oh, you're talking," p. 230; and "I've never," p. 229.

page 149

"every marriage is based":
Rose, *Parallel Lives*, p. 7.

page 150

"settled by negotiation and compromise":
Wallerstein and Blakeslee, *The Good Marriage*, p. 167.

page 150

"far more important":
Ibid., p. 161.

page 150

"shared belief that men and women":
Ibid., p. 155.

page 150

"Whose career will be given priority?":
Ibid., p. 158.

page 150

"My mother was wonderful":
Hochschild, *The Second Shift*, p. 39. Nancy and Evan Holt are discussed on pp. 33–58. The other quoted material can be found as follows: "dominate him," p. 40; "I'll cook Mondays" and "rigid schedules," p. 38; "When I was a teenager," p. 42; "Why wreck a marriage" and "Women always," p. 43.

page 151

"exploded in a burst of fury":
Ibid., p. 175. Michael and Adrienne are discussed on pp. 173–87. The other quoted material, "couldn't bring himself," is on p. 175.

page 151

"a tougher, more explicitly independent breed":
Michael Miller, *Intimate Terrorism*, p. 68.

pages 151–152

"the more severely a man's identity":
Hochschild, *The Second Shift*, p. 221. The other quoted material in this paragraph can be found as follows: "a way of 'balancing' " and "too much," p. 200; *made up* for outearning," p. 88; "that her status," p. 224; "more crucial," p. 222.

page 152
"entanglements of love and power":
Michael Miller, *Intimate Terrorism*, p. 69.
page 153
"the marital relationship":
Horner, *The Wish for Power and the Fear of Having It*, p. 111.

Chapter Six—Permanent Parenthood

page 155
"At this very moment":
Ron Suskind, "An Aging Generation of Jewish Mothers Finds
a Place in Lore," *The Wall Street Journal*, May 6, 1994, p. A9.
The complete article appears on pp. A1, A9.
page 155
"Parenthood as a psychobiologic process":
Benedek, "Parenthood During the Life Cycle," in *Parenthood:
Its Psychology and Psychopathology*, ed. Anthony and Benedek,
p. 185.
page 156
"Full of warmth and wisdom":
Viorst, *Murdering Mr. Monti*, pp. 127–28.
page 158
"savior tendencies":
McBride, *The Secret of a Good Life with Your Teenager*, p. 84.
page 158
"big-time mistakes":
Ibid., p. 85.
page 158
"decision-maker":
Ibid., p. 91.
page 158
"valued consultant":
Ibid.
page 158
"We want things for our children":
Ron Suskind, "An Aging Generation of Jewish Mothers Finds
a Place in Lore," *The Wall Street Journal*, May 6, 1994, p. A1.

page 158

"That's our problem":

Ibid.

page 158

"My son":

Ibid., p. A9.

page 158

"Everyone needs someone":

Ibid.

page 159

"Respecting your adult children":

Okimoto and Stegall, *Boomerang Kids*, p. 91.

page 162

"the child is the parents' report card":

McBride, *The Secret of a Good Life with Your Teenager*, pp. 92–93.

page 162

"to see his unfulfilled dreams":

Kiell, *The Adolescent Through Fiction*, p. 234. He continues: "Too many sons and daughters, as adults, harbor deep resentments because they are unhappy in the vocational work that was forced upon them by their parents" (p. 234).

page 163

"they've never invited me":

Heidi Spencer, *"Did I Do Something Wrong?"* p. 86.

page 163

"I guess my parents":

Ibid., p. 88.

page 164

that bliss of early parenting:

Viorst, "The Messes, the Stresses, the Strains . . . the Joys . . . Kids," *Redbook*, June 1976, pp. 89, 141, 143, 144.

page 164

"establishing and guiding the next generation":

Erikson, *Childhood and Society*, p. 267. His discussion of Generativity vs. Stagnation appears on pp. 266–68.

page 165

"is a particularly stressful period":

Dewald, "Adult Phases of the Life Cycle," in *The Course of Life*, Vol. 3, ed. Greenspan and Pollock, p. 49.

page 165
> "the overinvolvement of mothers":
> Benedek, "Parenthood During the Life Cycle," in *Parenthood: Its Psychology and Psychopathology,* ed. Anthony and Benedek, p. 199.

page 165
> "want to be involved":
> Ibid., p. 197.

page 166
> "no commandment to 'Honor Thy Son and Thy Daughter' ":
> Blum, "The Maternal Ego Ideal and the Regulation of Maternal Qualities," in *The Course of Life,* Vol. 3, ed. Greenspan and Pollock, p. 105.

page 167
> "Our politics, values":
> Jane Adams, *I'm Still Your Mother,* pp. 62–63.

page 168
> "I supported my daughter":
> Ibid., p. 134.

page 169
> "You have to ask yourself":
> Ibid., p. 135.

page 169
> "called me a 'good for nothing' ":
> Heidi Spencer, *"Did I Do Something Wrong?"* p. 154.

page 170
> "if a parent":
> Ibid.

page 171
> "Quality time and vitamin C":
> Viorst, "Did I Do Something Wrong?" This is a song from *Love and Shrimp,* a musical with words by Viorst, music by Shelly Markham.

page 173
> "Deep in their hearts":
> Brans and Smith quote Slater in *Mother, I Have Something to Tell You,* p. 26.

page 173
   "What could I have done differently?":
   McGovern, *Terry*, p. 36.
page 173
   "When your child develops serious troubles":
   Ibid., pp. xii–xiii.
page 174
   "You know":
   Brans and Smith, *Mother, I Have Something to Tell You*, p. 84.
page 174
   "I always blame myself":
   Ibid.
page 174
   "I ask myself":
   Heidi Spencer, *"Did I Do Something Wrong?"* p. 5.
page 174
   "What was my sin?":
   Ibid., p. 10.
page 174
   "Take me. I'm the one":
   "Serial Killer Apologizes, Asks Judge for Mercy," *The Washington Post*, March 30, 1994, p. A4.
page 174
   "I struggled for a long time":
   Anne Roiphe, *Fruitful*, p. 228.
page 174
   "to the image of genetic programming":
   Ibid., p. 226.
page 174
   "Genes provide an excuse":
   Ibid.
page 175
   "I am not responsible":
   Ibid., p. 227.
page 175
   "painful to accept responsibility":
   McGovern, *Terry*, p. 21.

page 175
>"she tended to construct":
>Ibid.

page 176
>"Still, it's not my fault":
>Jane Adams, *I'm Still Your Mother,* p. 35.

page 177
>"I don't think Terry will ever":
>McGovern, *Terry,* p. 14.

page 177
>"hoping that our maintaining a certain distance":
>Ibid., p. 9.

page 177
>"every phone call not made":
>Ibid.

page 177
>"There is no such thing":
>Ibid., p. 19.

page 177
>"In retrospect":
>Ibid., p. 144.

page 178
>"If your kid really can't make it":
>Jane Adams, *I'm Still Your Mother,* p. 134.

page 178
>"traditional" mothers:
>Brans and Smith, *Mother, I Have Something to Tell You,* p. 2.

page 178
>"unexpected," "untraditional," "unacceptable":
>Ibid.

page 178
>"maintain the important bonds":
>Ibid., p. 5.

page 179
>"feels an overwhelming sense":
>Ibid., p. 6.

page 179
>"the real child who exists":
>Ibid.

page 179
> "looks for help":
> Ibid.

page 179
> "recognizes the limits":
> Ibid., pp. 6–7.

page 179
> "turns back to the only life":
> Ibid., p. 7.

page 179
> "a new bond with the child":
> Ibid., p. 283.

page 179
> "Everything depended on me":
> Ibid., p. 181.

page 179
> "that *her child*":
> Ibid., p. 188.

page 179
> "she can neither control nor make sense":
> Ibid.

page 179
> "frees her child from her definition":
> Ibid., p. 189.

page 180
> "He still has lots of problems":
> Ibid., p. 194.

page 180
> "I don't give up on him":
> Ibid., p. 196.

page 180
> "Basically, you know":
> Ibid., p. 197.

page 180
> "could turn from them":
> Ibid., p. 252. The authors are quoting from Gordon, *Men and Angels*.

page 180
> "the 'tremendous mercy' ":
> Ibid., p. 251.

page 181
> "respectful connection":
> Ibid., p. 286.

page 181
> "There are moments":
> Galinksy, *Between Generations*, p. 316.

Chapter Seven—Bossing and Being Bossed

page 182
> "Working for and with other people":
> Tannen, *Talking from 9 to 5*, p. 186.

page 183
> "What do people want":
> Zaleznik, *Learning Leadership*, p. 4. The rest of the quoted material in this paragraph also appears on p. 4.

page 184
> "is a situation where there will be":
> Horner, *The Wish for Power and the Fear of Having It*, p. 156.

page 184
> "Your objective as an employee":
> Scott Adams, *The Dilbert Principle*, p. 102.

page 186
> "as eminently qualified":
> Gerald Piaget, *Control Freaks*, p. 83. This is Piaget's description of Alan.

page 187
> "Well, maybe I shouldn't be":
> Ibid., p. x.

page 187
> "people who control too much":
> Ibid., p. 8.

page 187

"to make our lives":

Ibid., p. 12.

page 187

"Control freaks can't stop":

Ibid.

page 187

"didn't do much":

Ibid., p. 6.

page 187

"One slip-up and I could lose":

Ibid.

page 188

"egomaniacs with inferiority complexes":

Ibid., p. 81.

page 188

"heady rush of power":

Ibid., p. 87.

page 188

" 'Father Knows Best' ":

Ibid., p. 3.

page 189

"tactics of influence":

Kipnis, "The Use of Power in Organizations and in Interpersonal Settings," in *Applied Social Psychology Annual*, Vol. 5, ed. Oskamp, p. 185.

page 189

"I simply order him or her":

Ibid. The whole list appears on p. 186.

page 190

the "bandwagon":

Piaget, *Control Freaks*, p. 36.

page 190

"triangulation":

Ibid., pp. 41–42.

page 191

"two scuba divers":

Scott Adams, *Dogbert's Top Secret Management Handbook*, unpaged. This appears in "2.17: Increasing Productivity."

page 191

"zero in":

Ibid. This statement and the following dialogue appear in "7.7: One-on-One Review."

page 191

"shifting blame from yourself":

Ibid. This appears in "4.4: Empowerment." See also "4.1: Taking Credit for Your Employees' Ideas."

page 192

"It's never fun":

Ibid. This appears in "6.2: Encouraging People to Quit."

page 192

"everyone is influencing everyone":

Kipnis, Schmidt, and Wilkinson, "Intraorganizational Influence Tactics: Explorations in Getting One's Way," *Journal of Applied Psychology*, Vol. 65, No. 4, p. 451.

page 195

"affect who gets heard":

Tannen, *Talking from 9 to 5*, from the subtitle of the book.

page 195

"being assertive":

Ibid., p. 40.

page 196

"By lowering her voice":

Ibid., p. 182.

page 196

"not only spoke loudly":

Ibid., p. 183.

page 196

"You know, it's *hard*":

Ibid., p. 180.

page 196

"keenly aware of the power":

Ibid.

page 196

"I'm well respected":

Ibid., p. 191.

page 197

"the f word":

Other female doctors around the country have complained that they too have paid a price for sometimes being insistent or brusque, for raising their voices, for displaying the very same characteristics for which men are often praised as forceful. Says one, "What's strong in a guy in a woman is seen as hostile." And a female surgeon told me that "if they don't know we're around, we now and then catch male doctors attributing a testy tone of voice or a short temper to—depending on our age—PMS or menopause."

page 197

"the damned-if-you-do-":

Tannen, *Talking from 9 to 5*, p. 203.

page 198

"ability to influence others":

Ibid., p. 317.

page 198

"There was a long period":

Goleman, *Emotional Intelligence*, p. 149

page 198

"command-and-control":

See Trip Gabriel, "Personal Trainers to Buff the Boss's People Skills," *The New York Times*, April 28, 1996, Section 3, pp. 1, 10. The quoted material appears on p. 10.

page 198

"You had a dictator":

Ibid. The quoted material appears on p. 10.

page 198

"People found me to be":

Ibid.

page 199

"ownership of their job":

Ibid. The quoted material is from Ms. Piecherowski and appears on p. 10.

page 199

"Don't worry about the whys":

Ibid.

page 199

"Years ago":

Ibid. The quoted material is from Dr. Blanton and appears on p. 10.

page 199

"A clinical psychologist":

Ibid.

page 199

"be a nice guy":

Zaleznik, *Learning Leadership*. All the quoted material appears on p. 160.

page 200

"The cockpit is a microcosm":

Goleman, *Emotional Intelligence*, p. 148. Goleman also notes: "In 80 percent of airline crashes, pilots make mistakes that could have been prevented, particularly if the crew worked together more harmoniously" (p. 148).

page 200

"managing with heart":

Ibid. The phrase is the title of Goleman's chapter 10.

page 201

"makes people stupid":

Ibid., p. 149. Goleman is quoting a management consultant.

page 201

"is conducive to":

Horner, *The Wish for Power and the Fear of Having It*, p. 157.

page 201

"Slaves," he writes:

McClelland, *Power: The Inner Experience*, p. 263.

page 202

"It will no longer be":

Scott Adams, *Dogbert's Top Secret Management Handbook*. This appears in "1.5: Management Personality."

page 202

"just reeled me around":

See Tannen, *Talking from 9 to 5*, p. 247, where she is quoting from *The New York Times* account of the Hutton story.

page 203

some 15,000 complaints:

This figure comes from the EEOC. See also Frank Swoboda and Kirstin Downey Grimsley, "For Worker and Employer, Sexual Harassment Is a New Area of Law," *The Washington Post*, December 23, 1996, p. A6. This is a far higher figure than the 6,100 complaints of 1990, in part because women are more willing to go public with their complaints and because their complaints are now being taken more seriously. According to the *Post*, "the pervasive problem of sexual harassment now is the fastest-growing area of discrimination complaints in the workplace." And these complaints are arising all over, from mines, law firms, assembly lines, universities, the military.

page 203

"by touching her shoulder":

See Kirstin Downey Grimsley, "In Combatting Sexual Harassment, Companies Sometimes Overreact," *The Washington Post*, December 23, 1996, pp. A1, A6. The quoted material is on p. A6.

Chapter Eight—Victims and Survivors

page 205

"A knife at someone's throat":

P. G. Zimbardo, quoted in Wortman and Brehm, "Responses to Uncontrollable Outcomes: An Integration of Reactance Theory and the Learned Helplessness Model," in *Advances in Experimental Social Psychology*, Vol. 8, ed. Berkowitz, p. 278.

page 205

"I will walk all night":

Price quotes these lines from his poem "The Dream of Refusal" in *A Whole New Life*, p. 30.

page 206

three basic, often unconscious, assumptions:

These assumptions are described and discussed in Janoff-Bulman and Frieze, "A Theoretical Perspective for Understanding Reactions to Victimization," *Journal of Social Issues*, Vol. 39, No. 2, pp. 1–17.

page 207

"de-victimize":

The phrase is from Taylor, Wood, and Lichtman, "It Could Be Worse: Selective Evaluation as a Response to Victimization," *Journal of Social Issues*, Vol. 39, No. 2, p. 20.

page 207

studies of responses to tragic events:

Ibid. The authors state that the "scientific literature on coping with tragedy . . . suggests that relatively few people feel like victims for very long" and argue that this is because "perceiving oneself to be a victim and believing that others perceive one to be a victim are both aversive . . . over and above the tangible losses and suffering . . . experienced" (pp. 20–21). See pp. 21–26 for a discussion of Victimization as Aversive.

page 208

"can lead to the conclusion":

Ibid., p. 20.

page 208

"I had a comparatively":

Ibid., p. 29.

page 208

"It was not tragic":

Ibid.

page 208

"The people I really feel sorry for":

Ibid.

page 208

"If I hadn't been married":

Ibid.

page 208

"self-enhancing":

Ibid., p. 30.

page 208

"Even some who were dying":

Ibid.

page 209

"There are worse things":

Ibid.

page 209

"Whatever happens to me":
Viorst, "Ida, the One Who Suffers," in *People and Other Aggravations*, p. 24.

page 210

"Some of these women just seemed":
Ibid., p. 34. "I really don't think" and "I think I did" appear on the same page.

page 210

"manufactured":
Ibid.; "so as to make one's own response" also appears on p. 34.

page 211

"selective evaluations":
Ibid.

page 211

"I feel as if I were":
Ibid., p. 32.

page 211

"The ability to understand myself":
Ibid.

page 211

"I was happy to find out":
Ibid.

page 211

"I have much more enjoyment":
Ibid., p. 33.

page 211

"MS has brought our family":
Suzanne Thompson, "Will It Hurt Less If I Can Control It? A Complex Answer to a Simple Question," *Psychological Bulletin*, Vol. 90, No. 1, p. 98.

page 211

"I know my awareness of people":
Taylor, Wood, and Lichtman, "It Could Be Worse: Selective Evaluation as a Response to Victimization," *Journal of Social Issues*, Vol. 39, No. 2, p. 20.

page 212

"I never knew my neighbors":
Ibid.

page 212

some 20 percent:

The figure comes from a study conducted and described by Silver, Boon, and Stones in "Searching for Meaning in Misfortune: Making Sense of Incest," *Journal of Social Issues*, Vol. 39, No. 2, p. 90. The authors found that "those women who were able to make some sense out of their experience reported less psychological distress . . . , better social adjustment . . . , higher levels of self-esteem . . . , and greater resolution of the experience . . . than those women who were not able to find any meaning but were still searching" (p. 92). See "The Value in Finding Meaning," pp. 91–93, and "The Importance of Finding Meaning," pp. 93–94.

page 212

"I learned over the years":

Ibid., p. 90.

page 212

"I get so sick of these people":

See Felicia R. Lee's interview with Giovanni, "Defying Evil, and Mortality," *The New York Times*, August 1, 1996, p. C9.

page 213

"Any morally healthy person":

Jack Schwartz, "Hurt but Unbroken," *The Washington Post*, April 16, 1996, p. B1.

page 213

"step forward and take my rightful share":

Ibid., p. B6.

page 213

"assume disgraceful and pathetic":

Ibid., p. B1.

page 213

"victim culture":

Ibid., p. B6.

page 213

"to be a victim":

Ibid., p. B1.

page 213

"In the physical sense":
Ibid., p. B6.

page 213

"the extraordinary kindness":
Ibid.

page 213

"Getting seriously hurt":
Ibid., p. B6.

page 214

"I didn't press it":
Wortman, "Coping with Victimization: Conclusions and Implications for Future Research," *Journal of Social Issues*, Vol. 39, No. 2, p. 206.

page 214

two unexpected findings:
Dale Miller and Porter, in "Self-Blame in Victims of Violence" (*Journal of Social Issues*, Vol. 39, No. 2), state that "victims of negative events are often found to exaggerate the extent to which they are responsible for their fates" and that "the degree of self-blame evidenced by victims of negative events has been found to correlate positively with subsequent coping" (p. 139). The contradictory finding that some victims respond to self-blame by feeling depressed and helpless and unable to cope makes sense if this blame is understood to be "characterological blame, the identification of an enduring quality of oneself that led to the negative event" (p. 147).

page 215

"total fear reaction":
Scheppele and Bart, "Through Women's Eyes: Defining Danger in the Wake of Sexual Assault," *Journal of Social Issues*, Vol. 39, No. 2, p. 77.

page 215

"the attack simply should not":
Ibid.

page 215

"Going to a doctor's":
Ibid. The other three quotes from raped women appear on the same page.

page 215

"to maintain the belief":

Miller and Porter, "Self-Blame in Victims of Violence," *Journal of Social Issues,* Vol. 39, No. 2, p. 140.

page 216

Keirsten Rain:

Her story is told by Joyce Purnick in "A Victim Says Attack Injuries Never Heal," *The New York Times,* June 17, 1996, Metro Section, pp. B1, B3.

page 217

"Direct action":

Janoff-Bulman and Frieze, "A Theoretical Perspective for Understanding Reactions to Victimization," *Journal of Social Issues,* Vol. 39, No. 2, p. 10.

page 217

"take a proactive role":

Liz Smith, "We Draw Strength from Each Other," *Good Housekeeping,* June 1996, pp. 86–89, 172–73. All of the quoted material from Reeve appears on p. 89.

page 218

"whether it's all worth it":

Peter Maass, "From His Bed, CIA's Best Makes His Breakthroughs," *The Washington Post,* April 21, 1996, p. A20.

page 218

"breakthroughs":

Ibid., p. A1.

page 218

"You read these maudlin stories":

Ibid., p. A20.

page 220

"the positive emotions produce":

Cousins, *Anatomy of an Illness,* pp. 34–35.

page 220

"love, hope, faith":

Ibid., p. 35

page 220

"even a reasonable degree of control":

Ibid.

page 221

"ten minutes of genuine belly laughter":
Ibid., p. 39.

page 221

"sedimentation rate":
Ibid., p. 40. A "sed" rate, Cousins explains on p. 28, is "the speed with which red blood cells settle in a test tube." The faster the speed, the more severe the inflammation or infection. Cousins's sed rate dropped at least five points after a laughter episode, and the drops held and were cumulative.

page 221

placebo effect:
Ibid. Cousins discusses placebos on pp. 45–69. He cites a study testing the efficacy of ascorbic acid as a cold preventative, where those taking a placebo thought they were on ascorbic acid and those taking ascorbic acid thought they were on a placebo. The first group had fewer colds. He notes: "I was absolutely convinced, at the time I was deep in my illness, that intravenous doses of ascorbic acid could be beneficial—and they were. It is quite possible that this treatment—like everything else I did—was a demonstration of the placebo effect" (p. 47).

The placebo effect may be produced in some instances by promoting the release of endorphins, natural body chemicals that enhance positive moods and reduce physical pain.

page 221

"The placebo," according to Cousins, "is proof":
Ibid., p. 56.

page 221

"robust will to live":
Ibid., p. 66.

page 221

"the mind":
Ibid., p. 67.

page 222

"will to live":
Ibid., p. 66.

page 222

"the doctor who resides within":
Ibid., p. 69.

page 222
>"natural drive of the human mind and body":
>Ibid., p. 48.

page 222
>"Protecting and cherishing that natural drive":
>Ibid.

page 222
>"a healing environment":
>Siegel, *Love, Medicine & Miracles*, p. 112.

page 222
>Relaxation, meditation, hypnosis, and visualization:
>Ibid. Siegel discusses these techniques in chapter 6, "Focusing the Mind for Healing," and the appendix.

page 222
>"survivor personality":
>Ibid., p. 161.

page 222
>"exceptional":
>Ibid.; see chapter 8, "Becoming Exceptional." Siegel states that in any group of patients with a serious illness, some 15 to 20 percent wish to die, either consciously or unconsciously; 60 to 70 percent do what they're told but never actively work to get well; and 15 to 20 percent are "exceptional" (pp. 22–24).

page 223
>"is the most powerful known stimulant":
>Ibid., p. 181.

page 223
>"dignity, personhood, and control":
>Ibid., p. 24.

page 223
>"geniuses of the mind-body connection":
>Chopra, *Quantum Healing*, p. 17.

page 223
>"quantum healing":
>Ibid. Chopra says: "I would like to introduce the term *quantum healing*" and goes on to note that "many cures that share mysterious origins—faith healing, spontaneous remissions, and the effective use of placebos . . . point toward a quantum leap . . . in the healing mechanism" (p. 16).

page 223
>"experiences a dramatic shift":
>Ibid., p. 15.

page 223
>"out of its boundaries":
>Ibid., p. 223.

page 223
>"free zone":
>Ibid., p. 189.

page 223
>"bliss technique":
>Ibid., p. 223.

page 223
>"there is no innate reason":
>Ibid., p. 225.

page 224
>"primordial sound" technique:
>Ibid., p. 223.

page 224
>"I would never be sick":
>Ibid., p. 98.

page 224
>"he had just decided":
>Ibid., p. 21.

page 224
>"she had taken the path":
>Siegel, *Love, Medicine & Miracles*, p. 40.

page 224
>"she jettisoned her anger and depression":
>Ibid., p. 201.

page 224
>"as if the AIDS were not there":
>Chopra, *Quantum Healing*, p. 238.

page 224
>eighty-eight-year-old woman:
>Ibid., p. 124.

page 224
>"a sort of Donald Trump":
>Broyard, *Intoxicated by My Illness*, pp. 16–17.

page 224

David Spiegel and his colleague Irving Yalom:

The Spiegel study is discussed in Tony Schwartz, *What Really Matters*, pp. 211–15. Bill Moyers also discusses this study, and a second one that Spiegel has conducted, in *Healing and the Mind*, pp. 67–69. The Moyers book also contains an interview with Spiegel on his work, pp. 157–70. David Felton, Professor of Neurobiology and Anatomy at the University of Rochester Medical School, had this to say about the improvements produced by the first Spiegel cancer support group: "Now if someone had discovered a drug that did that, they would have had their face on every major newsmagazine in the world as the next Jonas Salk in medicine" (the Moyers book, p. 222).

page 225

"Hostility predicts mortality":

The Williams study is discussed in Tony Schwartz, *What Really Matters*, pp. 207–208. The quoted material appears on p. 207.

page 225

Blue Cross–Blue Shield studied 2,000 meditators:

This study is discussed in Chopra, *Quantum Healing*, p. 181.

page 225

"designed to help people identify":

The Dean Ornish study is discussed in Tony Schwartz, *What Really Matters*, pp. 226–30. The quoted material appears on p. 228.

page 225

"anything that leads to real intimacy":

Ibid., p. 229.

page 225

"emotional open-heart surgery":

Moyers, *Healing and the Mind*, p. 69. An interview with Ornish appears on pp. 87–113.

page 225

There are other studies:

These studies show, for instance, that patients with cancer survive longer if they are married than if they are not; that single people and widows who live alone are at greater risk for getting cancer; that loneliness predicts a diminished immune response. On the other hand, an investigation by Cassileth, Lusk,

Miller, Brown, and Miller, "Psychosocial Correlates of Survival in Advanced Malignant Disease?" *The New England Journal of Medicine*, Vol. 312, No. 24, concludes that there is "a need for caution in interpreting studies that claim a positive association between psychosocial factors"—social ties, hopelessness, helplessness, job satisfaction, etc.—"and survival in malignant disease"; that while "one may speculate that psychosocial factors have a role in causing or influencing the course of malignant disease under some circumstances and in some persons . . . , it is likely that such factors represent only one link in a very long causal chain"; and that in "patients with advanced, high-risk malignant diseases . . . the inherent biology of the disease alone determines the prognosis, overriding the potentially mitigating influence of psychosocial factors" (p. 1555).

page 225

personality traits and diseases:

For instance, "The cancer-prone person has been described as inhibited, conforming, oversocialized, compulsive, and depressive," with "trouble expressing tension, anxiety, or anger, instead presenting the self as pleasant, calm, compliant, and passive" (Taylor, *Positive Illusions*, p. 103).

pages 225–226

emotions are translated into physical manifestations:

A popular theory is that stress can produce changes in the functioning of the immune system, making us more vulnerable to certain diseases. See Rogers, Dubey, and Reich, "The Influence of the Psyche and the Brain on Immunity and Disease Susceptibility: A Critical Review," *Psychosomatic Medicine*, Vol. 41, No. 2. See also Siegel, who talks about the "surveillance" theory of cancer—the theory that our body is constantly producing cancer cells, that our white blood cells destroy them before they become dangerous, and that impairment of the immune system makes it unable to deal with this "routine threat" (*Love, Medicine & Miracles*, p. 68). The flip side of this theory is that a "happy and contented mood may create a biochemical state in the body that is conducive to healing, and it may have direct effects on immune functioning" by mechanisms not yet known (Taylor, *Positive Illusions*, p. 142).

page 226

tell the body to produce symptoms:

Psychologist and science writer Daniel Goleman cites a child with many separate personalities, one of which reacts to drinking orange juice by breaking out into hives, while the appearance of another personality will cause the hives to subside (Chopra, *Quantum Healing*, p. 116). Molecular biologist Candace Pert talks about people with multiple personalities who "sometimes have extremely clear physical symptoms that vary with each personality," citing allergies to cats and diabetic symptoms, with "one personality . . . making as much insulin as it needs" while "the next one, who shows up half an hour later, can't make insulin" (Moyers, *Healing and the Mind*, p. 182).

page 226

tell the immune system to shut down:

Ader discusses this study in an interview with Bill Moyers (Moyers, *Healing and the Mind*, pp. 239–48).

page 226

produce physiological damage:

Cousins describes this study in *Anatomy of an Illness*, p. 61.

page 226

"I simply focused":

Olness discusses this experience in her interview with Bill Moyers (Moyers, *Healing and the Mind*, p. 73).

page 227

"Documented, spontaneous remissions":

Dr. Lerner's statement appears in Moyers, *Healing and the Mind*, p. 325.

page 227

"nothing that we understand":

Dr. Kemeny's statement appears in Moyers, *Healing and the Mind*, p. 207.

page 228

"there are no incurable diseases":

Siegel, *Love, Medicine & Miracles*, p. 99.

page 228

"scientific link":

Sontag, *Illness as Metaphor and AIDS and Its Metaphors*, p. 50.

page 228

"reaction to political defeat":

Ibid., p. 49.

page 228

"very unhappily married":

Ibid., p. 23.

page 228

"a murderous nest of feeling":

Ibid., p. 22.

page 228

"Cancer's a funny thing":

Ibid., p. 49. The title of the Auden poem is "Miss Gee."

page 229

"the luckless ill":

Ibid., p. 57.

page 229

"experiences and events":

Ibid., p. 55.

page 229

"Thoughts and feelings":

LeShan, *Cancer as a Turning Point,* p. ix, p. x.

page 229

"I reject the idea":

Weil, *Spontaneous Healing,* pp. 112–13.

page 230

"to take charge and to say":

Olness's statement appears in her interview with Bill Moyers
(Moyers, *Healing and the Mind,* p. 85).

page 230

"I think the average person":

Ibid., p. 75.

page 231

"are effective in treating":

NIH Technology Assessment Conference press release, October 8, 1995, p. 1. A full description of the findings appears in
National Institutes of Health Technology Assessment Conference Statement, *Integration of Behavioral and Relaxation Approaches into the Treatment of Chronic Pain and Insomnia, October
16–18, 1995.*

page 231

one out of every three:
This figure comes from Eisenberg, Kessler, Foster et al., "Unconventional Medicine in the United States," *The New England Journal of Medicine*, Vol. 328, No. 4, p. 246.

page 231

"patients feel empowered or less helpless":
National Institutes of Health Technology Assessment Conference Statement, *Integration of Behavioral and Relaxation Approaches into the Treatment of Chronic Pain and Insomnia*, October 16–18, 1995, p. 15.

page 231

Many studies have found that most patients:
See, for instance, Suzanne Miller, "Controllability and Human Stress: Method, Evidence and Theory," *Behaviour Research and Therapy*, Vol. 17, pp. 287–304; Marks, Richardson, Graham, and Levine, "Role of Health Locus of Control Beliefs and Expectations of Treatment Efficacy in Adjustment to Cancer," *Journal of Personality and Social Psychology*, Vol. 51, No. 2, pp. 443–50; and Affleck, Tennen, Pfeiffer, and Fifield, "Appraisals of Control and Predictability in Adapting to a Chronic Disease," *Journal of Personality and Social Psychology*, Vol. 53, No. 2, pp. 273–79.

page 231

terminal cancer patients who receive morphine:
Felten discusses these patients in his interview with Bill Moyers (Moyers, *Healing and the Mind*, p. 223).

page 232

children with severe burns:
Siegel, *Love, Medicine & Miracles*, p. 52.

page 232

nursing-home residents:
The first study is discussed in Langer and Rodin, "The Effects of Choice and Enhanced Personal Responsibility for the Aged: A Field Experiment in an Institutional Setting," *Journal of Personality and Social Psychology*, Vol. 34, No. 2, pp. 191–98. The follow-up study is discussed in Rodin and Langer, "Long-Term Effects of a Control-Relevant Intervention with the Insti-

tutionalized Aged," *Journal of Personality and Social Psychology*, Vol. 35, No. 12, pp. 897–902.

page 232

Forty college students:

This experiment is described in Geer, Davison, and Gatchel, "Reduction of Stress in Humans Through Nonveridical Perceived Control of Aversive Stimulation," *Journal of Personality and Social Psychology*, Vol. 16, No. 4, pp. 731–38.

page 233

"the sense of control":

Lefcourt, "The Function of the Illusions of Control and Freedom," *American Psychologist*, May 1973, p. 424.

page 233

"Perhaps the next best thing":

Geer, Davison, and Gatchel, "Reduction of Stress in Humans Through Nonveridical Perceived Control of Aversive Stimulation," *Journal of Personality and Social Psychology*, Vol. 16, No. 4, p. 738.

page 233

"Muselmänner":

The Bettelheim material is quoted in Langer and Rodin, "The Effects of Choice and Enhanced Personal Responsibility for the Aged: A Field Experiment in an Institutional Setting," *Journal of Personality and Social Psychology*, Vol. 34, No. 2, p. 192.

page 233

"sudden death syndrome":

Documented by psychiatrist George Engel, sudden death syndrome results "from two main factors. The first is some preexisting bodily weakness.... The second is ... usually an unexpected, uncontrollable, and severe shock" which "produces a sense of total loss of control" (Taylor, *Positive Illusions*, p. 101).

page 233

famous animal experiments:

Seligman, in *Helplessness*, describes the following experiment: Wild rats placed in a vat of water with no escape possible will swim for about sixty hours before drowning of exhaustion. If trained in helplessness by being held in a researcher's hand until they have stopped struggling, the rats will swim for only a few minutes before sinking to the bottom of the tub and drowning (pp. 169–70).

page 234

are less troubled by stressful events:
From Taylor, *Positive Illusions*: "If control is introduced into stressful circumstances, is the stress of those experiences reduced? The answer appears to be yes" (p. 77).

page 234

are happier than people:
Ibid. "People who believe that they have a lot of control in their lives and who believe that the future will bring them even more happiness are happier by their own reports than people who lack these perceptions" (p. 49).

page 234

take better care of themselves:
Ibid. "A belief that one can control adverse events in one's life may lead one to practice good health habits and to cope effectively with the stresses of life, thereby minimizing or ameliorating adverse effects on health" (p. 91).

page 234

Consider this intriguing study:
This study is described in Lehman and Taylor, "Date with an Earthquake: Coping with a Probable, Unpredictable Disaster," *Personality and Social Psychology Bulletin*, Vol. 13, No. 4, p. 553.

page 234

"You're in your present calamity":
Price, *A Whole New Life*, p. 182. *"Come back to life"* appears on p. 184, "To be sure" appears on p. 186.

Chapter Nine—Varieties of Surrender

page 236

"An assumption shared by many theories":
Wortman and Brehm, "Responses to Uncontrollable Outcomes: An Integration of Reactance Theory and the Learned Helplessness Model," in *Advances in Experimental Social Psychology*, Vol. 8, ed. Berkowitz, pp. 279, 330.

page 237

"locus of control":

This concept is exhaustively discussed in Lefcourt's *Locus of Control: Current Trends in Theory and Research.*

page 237

"Origins":

In *Personal Causation,* de Charms writes that he uses "the terms 'Origin' and 'Pawn' as shorthand terms to connote the distinction between forced and free. An Origin is a person who perceives his behavior as determined by his own choosing; a Pawn is a person who perceives his behavior as determined by external forces beyond his control" (pp. 273–74).

page 237

"perceive events as being largely contingent":

Lefcourt, *Locus of Control,* p. 148. The formal term, "the generalized expectancy of internal control, refers to the perception of events, whether positive or negative, as being a consequence of one's own actions and thereby potentially under personal control" (p. 35).

page 237

"Pawns":

See "Origins" reference, two notes above.

page 237

"feel more fatalistic":

Lefcourt, *Locus of Control,* p. 148. The formal term, "the generalized expectancy of external control, . . . refers to the perception of positive or negative events as being unrelated to one's own behavior and therefore beyond personal control" (p. 35).

page 237

variable and reversible:

Ibid. See Lefcourt's chapter on "Changes in Locus of Control," pp. 148–67.

page 238

some help from a therapist:

Lefcourt (see above reference) quotes Hilde Bruch, who writes that "the task of therapy in general terms is to assist a patient in the development of a center of gravity so that he experiences himself as self-directed . . . free to assert himself and to pursue satisfaction in terms of his own goals of living" (p. 150).

page 239

"tamale eater" Manuel Sanchez:

Ibid., pp. 19–20. Lefcourt is quoting from Oscar Lewis, *Children of Sanchez.*

page 239

"Many of the unhappy things in people's lives":

Ibid., pp. 210–12. These items are taken from the Rotter Internal-External Locus of Control forced-choice questionnaire found in appendix 7 of Lefcourt's book.

page 240

They are less inclined to persist:

Lefcourt (see above reference) notes: "Individuals who develop with little expectation that life's satisfactions and misfortunes can be determined by personal efforts have been less apt to exert themselves or to persist over lengthy time intervals in the pursuit of distant goals" (p. 98).

page 240

learned helplessness:

See chapter 3 of this book.

page 241

"rare and strange":

James, "The Beast in the Jungle," in *The Turn of the Screw and Other Short Fiction*, p. 331: "You said you had had from your earliest time, as the deepest thing within you, the sense of being kept for something rare and strange, possibly prodigious and terrible, that was sooner or later to happen to you, that you had in your bones the foreboding and the conviction of, and that would perhaps overwhelm you."

page 241

"like a crouching beast":

Ibid., p. 336. "Something or other lay in wait for him, amid the twists and the turns of the months and the years, like a crouching beast in the jungle."

page 241

"in the lap of the gods":

Ibid., p. 340: "It isn't a matter as to which I can *choose.* . . . It isn't one as to which there *can* be a change. It's in the lap of the gods."

page 241

"apathy and withdrawal":

Lefcourt, *Locus of Control,* p. 184.

page 241

"vitality":

Ibid.

page 241

"an active grappling":

Ibid.

page 241

the "good guys":

Ibid., p. 182.

page 241

"open to experience":

Ibid., p. 61.

page 241

"self-actualizing":

Ibid.

page 242

"to perceive himself as the determiner":

Ibid., p. 3.

page 242

"surrender to indomitable forces":

Ibid.

page 242

"IN CONTROL OF OUR LIVES":

Viorst, *Murdering Mr. Monti,* p. 5.

page 242

"when confronted with a stone wall":

Ibid.

page 242

" 'can-do' attitude":

Ibid., p. 6.

page 242

"has equipped me":

Ibid., p. 5.

page 242

"warm, supportive maternal-child relationship":

Lefcourt, *Locus of Control,* p. 139. He is quoting Virginia Crandall, who presents data about the influence of maternal behavior on locus of control.

page 242

"push out of the nest":

Ibid. He is quoting Crandall, who says that "the internal adult has at some time during childhood experienced a greater push out of the nest than the external adult" (p. 139).

page 244

"the ability to quit":

Janoff-Bulman and Brickman, "Expectations and What People Learn from Failure," in *Expectations and Actions*, ed. Feather, p. 207.

page 244

more "maladaptive," more "pathological":

Ibid.

page 244

"man must accommodate":

Lefcourt, *Locus of Control*, p. 8. He is paraphrasing Averill.

page 244

"When an organism":

Wortman and Brehm, "Responses to Uncontrollable Outcomes: An Integration of Reactance Theory and the Learned Helplessness Model," in *Advances in Experimental Social Psychology*, Vol. 8, ed. Berkowitz, pp. 330–31.

page 245

"winners never quit":

Janoff-Bulman and Brickman, "Expectations and What People Learn from Failure," in *Expectations and Actions*, ed. Feather, p. 219. The authors observe that "messages reminding people that it is important to know when to quit are far less frequent than messages preaching the virtues of persistence. Winners never quit and quitters never win. Heroes defy the odds. Admiral Peary grew up with a sign pinned to his wall, 'I will find a way or make one.' People who persist are valued because they contribute to others' well-being, if not their own. People who quit are derogated not only because quitting is failing but because quitting is often refusing to continue with a line of action that other people wish to see pursued."

page 246

The psychological research:

In Wortman and Brehm, "Responses to Uncontrollable Outcomes: An Integration of Reactance Theory and the Learned Helplessness Model," in *Advances in Experimental Social Psychology*, Vol. 8, ed. Berkowitz, the authors note: "The theories and empirical work discussed so far, then, suggest that individuals are motivated to maintain control over their environment, and that perceived control is generally beneficial to the organism. One implication of the research is that, if people can be induced to believe that they have control over outcomes that are actually uncontrollable, they will respond more favorably to the outcomes" (p. 282).

page 246

little attention has been paid:

In Janof-Bulman and Brickman, "Expectations and What People Learn from Failure," in *Expectations and Actions*, ed. Feather, the authors write that surveys of "the psychological literature on perceived control" show a "general bias toward assuming that the belief that one has control is good. It is really quite remarkable that the literature has been so sensitive to the consequences of people's mistakenly assuming that they do not have control and so insensitive to the consequences of people's mistakenly assuming that they do have control" (p. 220).

page 246

"We are in favor":

Ibid., p. 227.

page 246

"The weak may drift":

Ibid., p. 212.

page 246

"know when to hold them":

Ibid., p. 218. The authors are quoting from "The Gambler," a country-western song sung by Kenny Rogers.

page 247

Cornelia "Neil" Biddle:

My interviews with her were conducted during the summer of 1996.

page 249

"The Healthy Side of Compliance":
See Braun's discussion of internal and external compliance in his chapter "The Healthy Side of Compliance," in *Compliant Behavior*, ed. Rosenbaum.

page 250

"Paradoxically, then":
Ibid., p. 146.

page 251

"obsequiousness, spinelessness":
Ibid., p. 137.

page 251

sins of omission:
This discussion, through "people who do," is based on Viorst's "Are You a Moral Wimp?" in *Redbook*, September 1993, pp. 72, 74. The quoted material from Ann, Dale, Elaine, Lisa, and the gay friend appears on p. 72.

page 252

deeply troubling experiments:
See Milgram, *Obedience to Authority*, for a discussion of these experiments.

page 253

"Experimenter, get me out of here":
Ibid., p. 23.

page 253

"The guy is suffering":
Ibid., p. 32.

page 253

Bruno Batta:
Ibid., p. 47.

page 253

Jack Washington:
Ibid., p. 50.

page 253

Elinor Rosenblum:
Ibid., p. 83.

page 253

Pasqual Gino:
Ibid., p. 88.

page 254

"is a powerful and prepotent":
Ibid., p. 123. See chapter 10, "Why Obedience?—An Analysis," and chapter 11, "The Processes of Obedience: Applying the Analysis to the Experiment."

page 254

"He can't stand it":
Ibid., p. 148.

page 255

"numbing regularity":
Ibid., p. 123.

page 255

"unhindered by the limitations":
Ibid., p. 188.

page 255

"raise the possibility":
Ibid., p. 189.

page 255

"left no doubt":
Arendt, *Eichmann in Jerusalem: A Report on the Banality of Evil*, p. 22.

page 255

"he would have had a bad conscience":
Ibid., p. 25.

page 256

"a kind of Pontius Pilate feeling":
Ibid., p. 114.

page 256

"sadistic monster":
Milgram, *Obedience to Authority*, p. 5.

page 256

"he could see no one":
Arendt, *Eichmann in Jerusalem: A Report on the Banality of Evil*, p. 116.

page 256

"inwardly opposed":
Ibid., p. 126.

page 256

"inner emigration":

Ibid., p. 126. Arendt notes that "the term itself has a definitely equivocal flavor, as it can mean either an emigration into the inward regions of one's soul or a way of conducting oneself as though he were an emigrant" (p. 127).

page 256

"official soul":

Ibid., p. 127. The phrase "private soul" appears on the same page.

page 256

"mitigate matters":

Ibid., p. 128.

page 256

"real Nazis":

Ibid.

page 256

"inward opposition":

Ibid., p. 127.

page 257

massacre of helpless civilians:

A participant in the My Lai massacre, which occurred during the Vietnam War, estimated that some 370 men, women, children, and babies were rounded up and shot. "They were begging and saying, 'No, no.' And the mothers was hugging their children, and . . . we kept right on firing" (Milgram, *Obedience to Authority*, p. 186). See pp. 183–86, where Milgram quotes this interview, reported in *The New York Times*, November 25, 1969.

page 257

"Mothers, you must keep your children":

Rosenbaum, "Compliance," in *Compliant Behavior*, ed. Rosenbaum, p. 26. He is quoting from tape-recordings made at Jonestown.

page 257

"We need to remember":

Olsson, "In Search of Their Fathers-Themselves: Jim Jones and David Koresh," *Mind and Human Reaction*, Vol. 5, No. 3, August 1994, p. 85.

page 257

"promise of transcendence":

Rosenbaum, "Compliance," in *Compliant Behavior*, ed. Rosenbaum, p. 26.

page 257

"lesson to be learned":

Olsson, "In Search of Their Fathers-Themselves: Jim Jones and David Koresh," *Mind and Human Reaction*, Vol. 5, No. 3, August 1994, p. 95.

page 258

Heaven's Gate cult:

These followers of cult leader Marshall Herff Applewhite, many of whom had been with the cult for two decades, committed mass suicide because they believed that they would go to a better place—that a spaceship hidden behind the Hale-Bopp comet would carry them, after their death, to God's Kingdom.

page 258

"shared identity":

Braun, "The Healthy Side of Compliance," in *Compliant Behavior*, ed. Rosenbaum, p. 143.

page 258

"an alternative family structure":

Pattison, "Religion and Compliance," in *Compliant Behavior*, ed. Rosenbaum, p. 122.

page 258

"left out of the mainstream of life":

Rosenbaum, "Compliance," in *Compliant Behavior*, ed. Rosenbaum, p. 27.

page 258

"I made up my mind":

Olsson, "In Search of Their Fathers-Themselves: Jim Jones and David Koresh," *Mind and Human Reaction*, Vol. 5, No. 3, August 1994, p. 87. He is quoting from Reston's book *Our Father Who Art in Hell.*

page 258

"the inner experience":

David McClelland's book *Power* is subtitled *The Inner Experience.*

page 258
"the need primarily to *feel strong*":
Ibid., p. 77.

page 258
four different stages:
McClelland (see note above) relates his power stages to stages first set forth by Sigmund Freud and later by Erikson. Stage I is Freud's oral stage, Stage II his anal stage, Stage III his phallic stage, Stage IV his Oedipal resolution. In Erikson's terms, Stage IV would be the generative stage of ego development.

page 259
" *'It'* strengthens me":
Ibid., p. 13.

page 259
through our dependency:
McClelland (see note above) argues that "there is no such thing as a need for dependency, a need to feel weak and dependent; what is sometimes described as a need for dependency is the act of being dependent or weak, which has as its goal feeling strong" (p. 15).

page 259
"*I strengthen myself*":
Ibid., p. 15.

page 259
"more distressed by events involving loss of external":
Ibid., p. 16. He is citing some of Stolorow's research.

page 259
"more distressed by events involving loss of control":
Ibid.

page 259
"*I have an impact on others*":
Ibid., p. 17.

page 260
"the most advanced stage":
Ibid., p. 20. McClelland notes, however, that "Maturity involves the ability to use whatever mode is appropriate to the situation," which sometimes means expressing power needs through Stage I dependencies or Stage II autonomy or Stage III influence and competitiveness; "Immaturity involves using

perhaps only one mode in all situations or using a mode inappropriate to a particular situation." He stresses that "the earlier modes should remain available to provide the opportunity for a richer, more varied life" and that "it is abnormal to reject any mode of power expression totally or to use one mode at the expense of all others" (p. 24).

page 260

"It moves me to do my duty":
Ibid., p. 20.

page 260

"What he would not dare do":
Ibid., p. 21.

page 261

abused, unloved, adopted:
Joel Rifkin, who confessed to murdering seventeen women, was at one point going to offer an adopted-child-syndrome defense, arguing that he killed because of an irreparable psychological impairment produced by the trauma of being adopted. See Dershowitz, *The Abuse Excuse,* for a discussion of it's-not-my-fault defenses.

page 261

distress induced by menopause:
A TV listing for *Picket Fences* summarizes the program's plot as follows: "The town must decide the fate of a woman who claims insanity induced by menopause caused her to run over her husband with a steamroller." (Not having seen the show, I don't know if this was serious or a spoof.)

page 262

Dan White:
Clyde Haberman, "Firebombing: Putting Blame on Prozac," *The New York Times,* February 6, 1996, p. B1.

page 262

Richard Davis:
"Jury Recommends Execution for Klaas's Killer," *The Washington Post,* August 6, 1996, p. A5.

page 262

Erik and Lyle—the Menendez brothers:
See Ron Rosenbaum, "Staring into the Heart of the Heart of Darkness," *The New York Times Magazine,* June 4, 1995, pp. 36–

72. The Menendez story is discussed briefly on p. 41, and was widely reported in the national press.

page 263

They're accountable for the choices:
On the other hand: "Some advocates for the mentally ill . . . contend that people . . . with serious disorders should be able to present insanity defenses but are precluded by traditional legal standards that have been outmoded by modern psychiatric insight. Under the 19th century standards of insanity used in Florida and many other states, defendants can be found insane only if they cannot distinguish between right and wrong.

" 'That is an archaic criterion made up by lawyers, not by psychiatrists,' said Dr. Dorothy Otnow-Lewis, a professor of psychiatry at New York University School of Medicine.

"Furthermore, the advocates say, judges are often unwilling or legally unable to appropriately consider psychiatric diagnoses while deciding on punishment." Fox Butterfield, "This Way Madness Lies: A Fall from Grace to Prison," *The New York Times*, April 21, 1996, p. 14.

page 263

"acknowledged pockets of incompetence":
Taylor, *Positive Illusions*, p. 152–54.

page 265

"constructive interventions":
The controlling heroine of Viorst's *Murdering Mr. Monti* likes to describe each of her often intrusive efforts to run the lives of her nearest and dearest as "a constructive intervention" (p. 16).

Chapter Ten—In Control of Our Death

page 266

"This morning it occurred to me":
Yourcenar, *Memoirs of Hadrian*, p. 4.

page 266

"Oh Lord":
Rilke is quoted in *The Oxford Book of Death*, ed. Enright, p. 46.

page 267

"Your time here is short":

Thomas à Kempis is quoted in *Endtime,* compiled and ed. William Griffin, pp. 17–18.

page 267

"Write your obituary":

Rau, "On Top of the World—and Afraid to Fall," *The Wall Street Journal,* January 8, 1996, p. A18.

page 268

"Yet not as one":

Millay, "Those hours when happy hours were my estate," in *Collected Poems,* p. 719.

page 269

"One pleasant ritual":

Morowitz, "Bagels on Sunday," *The American Scholar,* Vol. 65, No. 1, Winter 1996, pp. 121–22.

page 270

"Good-by, Good-by, world":

Wilder, *Our Town,* p. 100.

page 270

"I got out of bed":

Kenyon, "Otherwise," in *Otherwise,* p. 214.

page 271

"Every time a patient dies":

Nuland, *How We Die,* p. 259.

page 271

"medical hubris":

Ibid.

page 272

SUPPORT:

SUPPORT (The Study to Understand Prognoses and Preferences for Outcomes and Risks of Treatments) is described in "A Controlled Trial to Improve Care for Seriously Ill Hospitalized Patients," *Journal of the American Medical Association,* Vol. 274, No. 20, November 22–29, 1995, pp. 1591–98. The study had two phases. In the first phase, a study of 4,301 critically ill patients "documented shortcomings in communication, frequency of aggressive treatment, and the characteristics of hospital death" (p. 1591). In the second phase, which studied 4,804 patients who were critically ill, half were placed in an intervention program where doctors received "reliable prognostic information and timely reports of patient and surrogate perceptions, the two most important factors . . . when considering life-support decisions," and the "intervention nurse . . . undertook time-consuming discussions, arranged meetings, provided information, supplied forms, and did anything else to encourage the patient and family to engage in an informed and collaborative decision-making process with a well-informed physician" (p. 1596). Despite all this effort, the half in the special program fared no better than the other half, and were just as likely to have their wishes ignored, to wind up in the ICU, and to die in pain.

page 272

"Many Americans today":

Ibid., p. 1591.

page 273

"They are cheating me":

Aries, *The Hour of Our Death*, p. 567. Aries is quoting the last words of Père F. de Dainville to Père Ribes in 1973.

page 274

"As long as possible":

Milstein is quoted in Goodman's *Death and the Creative Life*, p. 39.

page 274

"what we think of as poor quality":

Phillips is quoted by Geoffrey Cowley and Mary Hager in "Terminal Care: Too Painful, Too Prolonged," *Newsweek*, December 4, 1995, p. 75.

page 274

"Come no nearer":

Aries, *The Hour of Our Death*, p. 15.

page 274

"In normal times":

Rosenthal, "Psychotherapy for the Dying," in *The Interpretation of Death*, ed. Ruitenbeek, p. 87.

page 275

"*If* I should die":

The Oxford Book of Death, ed. Enright, p. 26.

page 275
>"A syllogism":
>Nabokov, *Pale Fire,* p. 40.

page 275
>"Soon it will be possible":
>Goodman, *Death and the Creative Life,* p. 5. She is quoting from a 1974 *New York Times* article.

page 275
>life span:
>Nuland, *How We Die,* gives figures on life span and life expectancy on pp. 84–85.

page 276
>"Three sailors are shipwrecked":
>Quill, *Death and Dignity,* pp. 57–58.

page 277
>"unintentionally prolong and dehumanize":
>Ibid., p. 58.

page 277
>"the victim of a brutal medical death ritual":
>Ibid., p. 59.

page 278
>The Medical Directive:
>This directive was created by Dr. Linda Emanuel and Dr. Ezekiel Emanuel. It is described by Dr. Linda Emanuel as "a comprehensive worksheet that allows patient and doctor to discuss and record detailed options and goals for treatment, along with personal values, and is done in conjunction with a health-care proxy."

page 279
>some doctors and some hospitals have been sued:
>See Tamar Lewin, "Ignoring 'Right to Die' Directives, Medical Community Is Being Sued," *The New York Times,* June 2, 1996, pp. 1, 28.

page 279
>"permit the greatest possible control":
>From the order form of the Medical Directive described two entries above.

page 279

"the quest to achieve true dignity":

Nuland, *How We Die,* p. xvii.

page 280

"balance-sheet suicide":

Portwood, *Common Sense Suicide,* p. 33.

page 281

"Ten years ago":

This letter, sent in 1980 by Jean M. Haslam, is reprinted in *The Oxford Book of Death,* ed. Enright, p. 98.

page 281

"lurid examples":

Phillip Chappell, M.D., Robert King, M.D., and Michael Enson, C.I.S.W., "Final Exit and the Risk of Suicide," *Journal of the American Medical Association,* Vol. 267, No. 22, June 10, 1992, p. 3027.

Morgan, in *Dealing Creatively with Death,* is also concerned with adolescent suicide. He writes: "With time and experience, most of us learn that even profound grief is not permanent, that eventually light will return to our lives. Adolescents often lack this perspective and are likely to have extreme reactions to loss, particularly because adolescence by its very nature is a time of extremes. . . . When life seems meaningless or overflowing with pain and stress, death may appear a logical choice" (p. 38).

page 281

one out of twelve:

Nuland, *How We Die,* pp. 156–57. He obtained this information from the Centers for Disease Control.

page 281

"The thought of suicide":

The Oxford Book of Death, ed. Enright, p. 99.

page 281

"When even despair":

The International Thesaurus of Quotations, ed. Tripp, p. 940.

page 281

"I have preferred chloroform":

Gilman is quoted by Portwood, *Common Sense Suicide,* p. 29.

page 282

"the suffering and waste":

Ibid., p. 30.

page 282

"I want you to know":

Colburn, "Earl's Way," *The Washington Post,* January 9, 1996, Health Section, p. 12.

page 282

"I know you folks are trying":

Ibid., p. 13.

page 282

"he was finally in control":

Ibid., p. 16.

page 283

"strength and a lot of will":

Ibid.

page 283

"Suicide is not abominable":

Kant is quoted by Nuland in *How We Die,* p. 153.

page 283

"Razors pain you":

Parker, "Résumé," in *The Portable Dorothy Parker,* p. 154.

page 284

The United States Supreme Court:

Two federal courts ruled, in separate decisions, that laws in the state of Washington and the state of New York prohibiting physician-assisted suicide of the terminally ill were unconstitutional. In the New York case, the ruling was based on equal protection under the law, arguing that if it's legal (as it is) for people to speed death by refusing artificial life support, others should be allowed to speed death by obtaining a prescription for fatal drugs. In the Washington case, the court held that there was "a liberty interest in choosing the time and manner of one's own death." The Supreme Court agreed to listen to arguments on both sides of this issue. Those arguing against physician-assisted suicide included the state of Oregon, the state of New York, the Clinton administration, the American Medical Association, and the Catholic Health Association.

Those arguing for it included Timothy Quill (who brought the New York case), the American Medical Student Association, thirty-six religious groups, leaders and scholars, and a group of relatives of terminally ill people who had committed suicide. In June 1997 the Supreme Court ruled that physician-assisted suicide is not a constitutional right, upholding the laws in Washington and New York that make it a crime, but also allowing leeway for individual states to legalize assisted suicide.

page 284

"I wrote the prescription":

Quill, "Death and Dignity: A Case of Individualized Decision Making," *The New England Journal of Medicine*, Vol. 324, No. 10, March 7, 1991, p. 693.

page 285

"relative calm and well-being":

Ibid.

page 285

"Diane took charge":

Quill, *Death and Dignity*, p. 215.

page 285

"I assisted Thomas Hyde":

Current Biography Yearbook, 1994, ed. Judith Graham, pp. 299–300.

page 286

"open-ended euthanasia":

Ibid., p. 299.

page 286

"a fragile virginity":

Andrew Solomon, "A Death of One's Own," *The New Yorker*, May 22, 1995, p. 68.

page 287

"I'm sad today":

Ibid., p. 66.

page 287

"I've looked for so many things":

Ibid.

page 287

"a horrified, captive, lucid witness":
Dudley Clendinen writes of his cousin and others in "When Death Is a Blessing and Life Is Not," *The New York Times,* February 5, 1996, Op-Ed, p. A15.

page 287

"then, in keeping with our last inheritance":
Solomon, "A Death of One's Own," *The New Yorker,* May 22, 1995, p. 69. The other two quotations in this paragraph are also on p. 69.

page 288

"a patient's right to die":
Quill, "Death and Dignity: A Case of Individualized Decision Making," *The New England Journal of Medicine,* Vol. 324, No. 10, March 7, 1991, p. 692.

page 288

"Clearly, it was the last thing":
Don Colburn, "Earl's Way," *The Washington Post,* January 9, 1996, Health Section, p. 15.

page 288

"which asserts our right":
Callahan, *What Kind of Life,* p. 225.

page 288

"mercy killing":
Ibid., p. 222. It is defined here as "the killing of one person by another as an act of kindness, not as an act of malice or self-interest." A distinction, however, needs to be made between asking to be killed (voluntary euthanasia) and having someone decide without our explicitly requesting it that killing us would be a merciful act (involuntary euthanasia).

page 288

"past any point":
Ibid., p. 226.

page 288

"private killings":
Ibid., p. 231.

page 288

"gives to the value of control over self":
Ibid., p. 242.

page 289

"Just taking care of":
Editorial, *The New York Times*, December 20, 1995. See also the *Times* article by Pam Belluck, "Man Will Get Prison Term for Helping His Wife Kill Herself," March 16, 1996, Metro Section, pp. 23, 26.

page 289

the Netherlands:
Although physician-assisted suicide is not legal in the Netherlands, it is not prosecuted if the doctor abides by some understood guidelines: The patient must have an incurable disease and intolerable suffering. The patient must be fully informed of the diagnosis, prognosis, and treatment possibilities. The request for aid-in-dying must come, uncoerced, from the patient, not from family members, nor should it be suggested by the doctor. The request must be made several times, over a period of time, and it should be documented. The doctor must regard the patient as competent and the request as reasonable. The doctor must consult with another doctor. (See Morgan, *Dealing Creatively with Death*, pp. 37–38, and Quill, *Death and Dignity*, p. 147.) Hendin, *Seduced by Death*, an impassioned critique of what he calls "the Dutch cure," argues that "virtually every guideline established by the Dutch to regulate euthanasia has been modified or violated with impunity" (p. 23).

page 289

This "slippery slope," he warns:
Hendin, *Seduced by Death*, p. 48.

page 290

"a seemingly simple solution":
Ibid., p. 214.

page 290

withholding or removing certain life-sustaining treatments:
Dr. Quill calls this "passive" euthanasia. The Supreme Court, in its rejection of a constitutional right to assisted suicide, also rejected the equating of physician-assisted suicide with the patient's right to refuse treatment or to request having the plug pulled.

page 290

"the euthanasia movement has embodied":
Callahan, *What Kind of Life*, p. 242.

page 291

"during the part of [our] living":
This statement by Sandol Stoddard is quoted in a brochure called "What Is Hospice?" put out by the Hospice Council of Metropolitan Washington, Inc.

page 291

Hospice care, in most instances, is given in the home:
"Family members or friends [called primary caregivers] coordinate the care of the patient at home with the support and guidance of the hospice team. As required, a member of the team provides care directly. . . . Members of the team make regular home visits. . . . The nurse is trained to recognize and respond to emotional and psychological problems. Home-care team members can counsel on practical matters . . . and guide the family in caring for the patient. They will also arrange for necessary supplies or additional help when it is needed" (see above reference).

page 292

"a movement, not a place":
Paul Richard, "Capturing the Last Light," *The Washington Post*, March 10, 1996, pp. G1, G6.

page 294

"I went to the hospital to be cured":
From a Hospice of Washington brochure.

page 294

"Hospice gave my brother":
Ibid.

page 294

"many of my terminal patients":
Kübler-Ross is quoted by Carole Selinske, Executive Director, New York State Hospice Association (1984–1993) in a book review appearing in *The Hospice Journal*, Vol. 10, No. 3, p. 65.

page 294

"is not a realistic hope":
Selinske, p. 65.

page 294
> "Hospice neither hastens":
> From a National Hospice Organization brochure called "The Basics of Hospice."

page 295
> "wipe my ass":
> ABC News *Nightline* transcript, March 17, 1995, p. 4.

page 295
> "I have no shame":
> ABC News *Nightline* transcript, October 13, 1995, p. 2.

page 296
> "is the acceptance of one's one and only":
> Erikson, *Childhood and Society,* p. 268. Erikson's discussion of "Ego Integrity vs. Despair" appears in his chapter "Eight Ages of Man," pp. 268–69.

page 296
> "the ultimate of life":
> Ibid., p. 269.

page 296
> "death loses its sting":
> Ibid., p. 268.

page 296
> "a thousand little disgusts":
> Ibid., p. 269.

page 296
> "I dream of journeys repeatedly":
> Roethke, "The Far Field," in *The Norton Anthology of Poetry,* ed. Allison et al., pp. 1137–39.

page 297
> "that she has no stated attitude":
> Morgan, *Dealing Creatively with Death,* from the foreword by Ms. Mitford, p. ix.

page 297
> "the power over which we have no control":
> Chadwick, "Notes Upon the Fear of Death," in *The Interpretation of Death,* ed. Ruitenbeek, p. 74.

page 298
>"brute biological fact":
>Marcuse, "The Ideology of Death," in *The Meaning of Death,* ed. Feifel, p. 67.

page 298
>a "free death":
>Nietzsche, *Thus Spoke Zarathustra,* p. 72.

page 298
>"I am a broken machine":
>Gardner Murphy quotes Wilson in the "discussion" section of *The Meaning of Death,* ed. Feifel, p. 333.

page 298
>"Please congratulate me":
>Walter Kaufmann quotes Japanese flier Isao Matsuo in "Existentialism and Death," above reference, p. 50.

page 298
>"Be welcome then":
>Walter Kaufmann quotes the poet Holderlin, see reference above, p. 59.

page 298
>"At the end, you're posing for eternity":
>Broyard, *Intoxicated by My Illness,* p. 67.

page 299
>"be renewed by death":
>Roethke, "The Far Field," in *The Norton Anthology of Poetry,* ed. Allison et al., pp. 1137–39.

page 299
>"There's this little wave":
>ABC News *Nightline* transcript, March 17, 1995, p. 3.

page 300
>"Don't let go too soon":
>ABC News *Nightline* transcript, October 13, 1995, p. 2.

Bibliography

Adams, Jane. *I'm Still Your Mother.* New York: Delacorte Press, 1994.

Adams, Scott. *The Dilbert Principle.* New York: HarperBusiness, 1996.

———. *Dogbert's Top Secret Management Handbook.* New York: HarperBusiness, 1996.

Affleck, Glenn; Howard Tennen; Carol Pfeiffer; and Judith Fifield. "Appraisals of Control and Predictability in Adapting to a Chronic Disease." *Journal of Personality and Social Psychology* 53, no. 2 (1987): pp. 273–79.

Allison, Alexander; Herbert Barrows; Caesar Blake; Arthur Carr; Arthur Eastman; and Hubert English, eds. *The Norton Anthology of Poetry.* New York: W. W. Norton, 1975, 1970.

Angier, Natalie. "How Biology Affects Behavior and Vice Versa." *The New York Times,* May 30, 1995, pp. C1, C5.

Anthony, James. "The Reactions of Adults to Adolescents and Their Behavior." In *Adolescence: Psychosocial Perspectives,* edited by Gerald Caplan and Serge Lebovici. New York: Basic Books, 1969.

Antill, John K. "Sex Role Complementarity Versus Similarity in Married Couples." *Journal of Personality and Social Psychology* 45, no. 1 (1983): pp. 145–55.

Arendt, Hannah. *Eichmann in Jerusalem: A Report on the Banality of Evil.* New York: Penguin Books, 1963, 1964.

Aries, Philippe. *The Hour of Our Death.* New York: Alfred A. Knopf, 1981.

Bailey, J. Michael, and Richard C. Pillard. "A Genetic Study of Male Sexual Orientation." *Archives of General Psychiatry* 48, no. 12 (December 1991): pp. 1089–96.

Bailey, J. Michael; Richard C. Pillard; Michael C. Neale; and Yvonne Agyei. "Heritable Factors Influence Sexual Orientation in Women." *Archives of General Psychiatry* 50, no. 3 (March 11, 1993): pp. 217–23.

Barglow, Peter, and Margret Schaefer. "A New Female Psychology?"

Journal of the American Psychoanalytic Association 24, no. 5 (1976): pp. 305–50.

Barinaga, Marcia. "Is Homosexuality Biological?" *Science* 253 (August 30, 1991): pp. 956–57.

Barnett, Rosalind C., and Caryl Rivers. *She Works/He Works.* San Francisco: Harper San Francisco, 1996.

Beiser, Helen. "Ages Eleven to Fourteen." In *The Course of Life,* Vol. 2, edited by Greenspan and Pollock, 1980.

Bell, Ruth, and Leni Wildflower. *Talking with Your Teenager.* New York: Random House, 1983.

Benedek, Therese. "Parenthood During the Life Cycle." In *Parenthood: Its Psychology and Psychopathology,* edited by E. James Anthony and Therese Benedek. Boston: Little, Brown, 1970.

Benson, Ronald, and Saul Harrison. "The Eye of the Hurricane: From Seven to Ten." In *The Course of Life,* Vol. 2, edited by Greenspan and Pollock, 1980.

Blos, Peter. *On Adolescence.* New York: Free Press, 1962.

Blum, Harold. "Masochism, the Ego Ideal, and the Psychology of Women." *Journal of the American Psychoanalytic Association* 24, no. 5 (1976): pp. 157–91.

———. "The Maternal Ego Ideal and the Regulation of Maternal Qualities." In *The Course of Life,* Vol. 3, edited by Greenspan and Pollock, 1981.

Blumstein, Philip, and Pepper Schwartz. *American Couples.* New York: William Morrow, 1983.

Bouchard, Thomas J., Jr. "Genes, Environment, and Personality." *Science* 264 (June 17, 1994): pp. 1700–1701.

Bouchard, Thomas J., Jr.; David T. Lykken; Matthew McGue; Nancy L. Segal; and Auke Tellegen. "Sources of Human Psychological Differences: The Minnesota Study of Twins Reared Apart." *Science* 250 (October 12, 1990): pp. 223–28.

Brans, Jo, and Margaret Taylor Smith. *Mother, I Have Something to Tell You.* Garden City, N.Y.: Doubleday, 1987.

Braun, Joseph A. "The Healthy Side of Compliance." In *Compliant Behavior,* edited by Max Rosenbaum, pp. 137–47. New York: Human Sciences Press, 1983.

Brazelton, T. Berry. "Neonatal Assessment." In *The Course of Life,* Vol. 1, edited by Greenspan and Pollock, 1980.

Brazelton, T. Berry, and Bertrand G. Cramer. *The Earliest Relationship.* Reading, Mass.: Addison-Wesley Publishing, 1990.

Brown, Margaret Wise. *Goodnight Moon.* New York: Harper & Row, 1947.

Brownmiller, Susan. *Against Our Will*. New York: Bantam Books, 1975.

Broyard, Anatole. *Intoxicated by My Illness*. New York: Fawcett Columbine, 1992.

Bruch, Hilde. "The Sleeping Beauty: Escape from Change." In *The Course of Life*, Vol. 2, edited by Greenspan and Pollock, 1980.

Buchwald, Emilie; Pamela Fletcher; and Martha Roth. *Transforming a Rape Culture*. Minneapolis: Milkweed Editions, 1993.

Burr, Chandler. "Homosexuality and Biology." *The Atlantic Monthly*, March 1993, pp. 47–65.

———. *A Separate Creation*. New York: Hyperion, 1996.

Buxbaum, Edith. "Between the Oedipus Complex and Adolescence: The 'Quiet Time.' " In *The Course of Life*, Vol. 2, edited by Greenspan and Pollock, 1980.

Callahan, Daniel. *What Kind of Life*. New York: Simon & Schuster, 1990.

Casper, Regina. "Treatment Principles in Anorexia Nervosa." In *Adolescent Psychiatry*, Vol. 10, edited by Sherman Feinstein, John Looney, Allan Schwartzberg, and Arthur Sorosky. Chicago: University of Chicago Press, 1982.

Cassileth, Barrie R.; Edward J. Lusk; David S. Miller; Lorraine L. Brown; and Clifford Miller. "Psychosocial Correlates of Survival in Advanced Malignant Disease?" *The New England Journal of Medicine* 312, no. 24 (June 13, 1985): pp. 1551–55.

Cath, Stanley. "Fathering from Infancy to Old Age: A Selective Overview of Recent Psychoanalytic Contributions." *The Psychoanalytic Review* 73, no. 4 (Winter 1996): pp. 65/469–75/479.

Chopra, Deepak. *Quantum Healing*. New York: Bantam Books, 1990.

Clampitt, Amy. *What the Light Was Like*. New York: Alfred A. Knopf, 1985.

Colburn, Don. "Earl's Way." *The Washington Post*, January 9, 1996, Health Section, pp. 12–16.

Coppolillo, Henry. "The Tides of Change in Adolescence." In *The Course of Life*, Vol. 2, edited by Greenspan and Pollock, 1980.

Cousins, Norman. *Anatomy of an Illness as Perceived by the Patient*. New York: Bantam Books, 1979.

Csikszentmihalyi, Mihaly, and Reed Larson. *Being Adolescent*. New York: Basic Books, 1984.

de Charms, Richard. *Personal Causation*. New York: Academic Press, 1968.

Dershowitz, Alan M. *The Abuse Excuse*. Boston: Little, Brown, 1994.

Dew, Robb Forman. *The Family Heart*. Reading, Mass.: Addison-Wesley Publishing, 1994.

Dewald, Paul A. "Adult Phases of the Life Cycle." In *The Course of Life*, Vol. 3, edited by Greenspan and Pollock, 1981.

Dobyns, Stephen. *After Shocks/Near Escapes*. New York: Viking, 1991.

Dunn, Judy. "The Beginnings of Moral Understanding: Development in the Second Year." In *The Emergence of Morality in Young Children*, edited by Kagan and Lamb. Chicago: University of Chicago Press, 1990.

Eisenberg, David M.; Ronald C. Kessler; Cindy Foster; Frances E. Norlock; David R. Calkins; and Thomas L. Delbanco. "Unconventional Medicine in the United States." *The New England Journal of Medicine* 328, no. 4 (January 28, 1993): pp. 246–83.

Elkind, David. *The Hurried Child*. Reading, Mass.: Addison-Wesley Publishing, 1981, 1988.

Elmer-Dewitt, Philip. "Fat Times." *Time,* January 16, 1995, pp. 58–65.

Emde, Robert; William Johnson; and M. Ann Easterbrooks. "The Do's and Don'ts of Early Moral Development: Psychoanalytic Tradition and Current Research." In *The Emergence of Morality in Young Children,* edited by Kagan and Lamb. Chicago: University of Chicago Press, 1990.

Enright, D. J., ed. *The Oxford Book of Death*. Oxford and New York: Oxford University Press, 1983.

Erikson, Erik. *Childhood and Society*. New York: W. W. Norton, 1950, 1963.

———. *Identity: Youth and Crisis*. New York: W. W. Norton, 1968.

———. "The Problem of Ego Identity." *Journal of the American Psychoanalytic Association* 4, no. 1–4 (1956): pp. 56–121.

Esman, Aaron. "Mid-Adolescence—Foundations for Later Psychopathology." In *The Course of Life,* Vol. 2, edited by Greenspan and Pollock, 1980.

Falbo, Toni. "Multidimensional Scaling of Power Strategies." *Journal of Personality and Social Psychology* 35, no. 8 (1977): pp. 537–47.

Falbo, Toni, and Letitia Anne Peplau. "Power Strategies in Intimate Relationships." *Journal of Personality and Social Psychology* 38, no. 4 (1980): pp. 618–28.

Faludi, Susan. *Backlash*. New York: Crown Publishers, 1991.

Feifel, Herman. *The Meaning of Death*. New York: McGraw-Hill, 1959.

Felleman, Hazel. *The Best-Loved Poems of the American People*. New York: Doubleday, 1936.

Fisher, Susan, and Kathleen Scharf. "Teenage Pregnancy: An Anthropological, Sociological, and Psychological Overview." In *Adolescent Psychiatry,* Vol. 8, pp. 393–403. Chicago: University of Chicago Press, 1980.

413

Fitzgerald, F. Scott. *Tender Is the Night*. New York: Charles Scribner's Sons, 1933.

Ford, Ford Madox. *The Good Soldier*. New York: Vintage Books, 1983.

Fraiberg, Selma. *The Magic Years*. New York: Charles Scribner's Sons, 1959.

Freud, Anna. "Adolescence." In *The Psychoanalytic Study of the Child*, Vol. 13. New York: International Universities Press, 1958.

Freud, Sigmund. "Civilization and Its Discontents" [1929]. In *The Standard Edition of the Complete Psychological Works of Sigmund Freud* (hereafter referred to as *Standard Edition*), Vol. 21, edited by James Strachey. London: Hogarth Press, 1961.

———. "The Dissolution of the Oedipus Complex" [1924]. In *Standard Edition*, Vol. 19, edited by James Strachey. London: Hogarth Press, 1961.

———. "The Ego and the Id" [1923]. In *Standard Edition*, Vol. 19, edited by James Strachey. London: Hogarth Press, 1961.

———. "The Interpretation of Dreams" [1900]. In *Standard Edition*, Vols. 4 and 5, edited by James Strachey. London: Hogarth Press, 1953.

———. "Introductory Lectures on Psycho-Analysis, Parts I and II" [1915–1917]. In *Standard Edition*, Vol. 16, edited by James Strachey. London: Hogarth Press, 1961.

———. "New Introductory Lectures on Psycho-Analysis" [1932]. In *Standard Edition*, Vol. 22, edited by James Strachey. London: Hogarth Press, 1964.

———. "The Psychogenesis of a Case of Homosexuality in a Woman" [1920]. In *Standard Edition*, Vol. 18, edited by James Strachey. London: Hogarth Press, 1955.

———. "Some Psychical Consequences of the Anatomical Distinction Between the Sexes" [1925]. In *Standard Edition*, Vol. 19, edited by James Strachey. London: Hogarth Press, 1961.

———. "Three Essays on the Theory of Sexuality" [1905]. In *Standard Edition*, Vol. 7, edited by James Strachey. London: Hogarth Press, 1953.

Frost, Robert. *The Poetry of Robert Frost*. New York: Henry Holt, 1979.

Furman, Erna. *Helping Young Children Grow*. Madison, Conn.: International Universities Press, 1987.

Furman, Robert. "Some Vicissitudes of the Transition into Latency." In *The Course of Life*, Vol. 2, edited by Greenspan and Pollock, 1980.

Galinsky, Ellen. *Between Generations*. New York: Times Books, 1981.

Gallagher, Winifred. "How We Become What We Are." *The Atlantic Monthly*, September 1994, pp. 39–55.

———. *I.D.* New York: Random House, 1996.

Geer, James H.; Gerald C. Davison; and Robert I. Gatchel. "Reduction of Stress in Humans Through Nonveridical Perceived Control of Aversive Stimulation." *Journal of Personality and Social Psychology* 16, no. 4 (1970): pp. 731–38.

Gelman, David. "Born or Bred?" *Newsweek*, February 24, 1992, pp. 46–53.

Gibran, Kahlil. *The Prophet*. New York: Alfred A. Knopf, 1923, 1951, 1988.

Gilbert, Sandra M.; Susan Gubar; and Diana O'Hehir, eds. *Mother-Songs*. New York: W. W. Norton, 1995.

Gilligan, Carol. *In a Different Voice*. Cambridge, Mass.: Harvard University Press, 1982.

Glück, Louise. *The First Four Books of Poems*. Hopewell, N.J.: Ecco Press, 1968.

Goleman, Daniel. *Emotional Intelligence*. New York: Bantam Books, 1995.

Goodman, Lisl Marburg. *Death and the Creative Life*. New York: Penguin Books, 1981, 1983.

Gottman, John. *Why Marriages Succeed or Fail*. New York: Simon & Schuster, 1994.

Gray-Little, Bernadette, and Nancy Burks. "Power and Satisfaction in Marriage: A Review and Critique." *Psychological Bulletin* 93, no. 3 (1983): pp. 513–38.

Greenspan, Stanley. *The Challenging Child*. New York: Addison-Wesley Publishing, 1995.

Greenspan, Stanley, and George Pollock, eds. *The Course of Life*, Vol. 1: *Infancy and Early Childhood*. Washington, D.C.: Government Printing Office, DHHS Pub. No. (ADM) 80–786, 1980.

———. *The Course of Life*, Vol. 2: *Latency, Adolescence and Youth*. Washington, D.C.: Government Printing Office, DHHS Pub. No. (ADM) 80–999, 1980.

———. *The Course of Life*, Vol. 3: *Adulthood and the Aging Process*. Washington, D.C.: Government Printing Office, DHHS Pub. No. (ADM) 81–1000, 1981.

Griffin, William, ed. *Endtime*. New York: Collier Books, 1979.

Grotstein, James. "The Psychology of Powerlessness; Disorders of Self-Regulation and Interactional Regulation as a Newer Paradigm for Psychopathology." *Psychoanalytic Inquiry* 6, no. 1 (1986): p. 95.

Group for the Advancement of Psychiatry (GAP). *Psychotherapy with College Students*. New York: Brunner/Mazel Publishers, 1990.

Hamer, Dean, and Peter Copeland. *The Science of Desire*. New York: Simon & Schuster, 1994.

415

Hendin, Herbert. *Seduced by Death.* New York: W. W. Norton, 1997.

Hochschild, Arlie. *The Second Shift.* New York: Viking, 1989.

Holden, Constance. "A Cautionary Genetic Tale: The Sobering Story of D2." *Science,* June 17, 1994, pp. 1696–97.

Horgan, John. "Eugenics Revisited." *Scientific American,* June 1993, pp. 123–31.

Horner, Althea. *The Wish for Power and the Fear of Having It.* Northvale, N.J.: Jason Aronson, 1989.

Howard, Judith; Philip Blumstein; and Pepper Schwartz. "Sex, Power, and Influence Tactics in Intimate Relationships." *Journal of Personality and Social Psychology* 51, no. 1 (1986): pp. 102–109.

Hutchings, Barry, and Sarnoff A. Mednick. "Criminality in Adoptees and Their Adoptive and Biological Parents: A Pilot Study." In *Biosocial Bases of Criminal Behavior,* edited by Barry Hutchings and K. Christiansen. New York: Gardner, 1977.

Ibsen, Henrik. *A Doll's House and Other Plays.* London: Penguin Books, 1965.

Isay, Richard. *Being Homosexual.* New York: Avon Books, 1989.

———. "Late Adolescence: The Second Separation Stage of Adolescence." In *The Course of Life,* Vol. 2, edited by Greenspan and Pollock, 1980.

James, Henry. *The Turn of the Screw and Other Short Fiction.* New York: Bantam Books, 1981.

Janoff-Bulman, Ronnie, and Philip Brickman. "Expectations and What People Learn from Failure." *Expectations and Actions: Expectancy-Value Models in Psychology.* Hillsdale, N.J.: Lawrence Erlbaum Associates, Publishers, 1982.

Janoff-Bulman, Ronnie, and Irene Hanson Frieze. "A Theoretical Perspective for Understanding Reactions to Victimization." *Journal of Social Issues* 39, no. 2 (1983): pp. 1–17.

Johnson, Craig, and Mary Connors. *The Etiology and Treatment of Bulimia Nervosa.* New York: Basic Books, 1987.

Jong, Erica. *Fear of Flying.* New York: Holt, Rinehart & Winston, 1973.

Joyce, James. *A Portrait of the Artist as a Young Man.* New York: Penguin Books, 1976.

Kagan, Jerome. *Galen's Prophecy.* New York: Basic Books, 1994.

———. *The Nature of the Child.* New York: Basic Books, 1984.

Kagan, Jerome, and Sharon Lamb, eds. *The Emergence of Morality in Young Children.* Chicago: University of Chicago Press, 1990.

Kaplan, Eugene. "Adolescents, Age Fifteen to Eighteen: A Psychoanalytic Developmental View." In *The Course of Life,* Vol. 2, edited by Greenspan and Pollock, 1980.

Kaplan, Louise. *Adolescence: The Farewell to Childhood.* New York: Simon & Schuster, 1984.

Katan, Anny. "Some Thoughts About the Role of Verbalization in Early Childhood." In *The Psychoanalytic Study of the Child,* Vol. 16, pp. 184–88. New York: International Universities Press, 1961.

Kenison, Katrina, and Kathleen Hirsch, eds. *Mothers.* New York: North Point Press, 1996.

Kenyon, Jane. *Otherwise.* St. Paul: Graywolf Press, 1996.

Kestenberg, Judith. "Eleven, Twelve, Thirteen: Years of Transition from the Barrenness of Childhood to the Fertility of Adolescence." In *The Course of Life,* Vol. 2, edited by Greenspan and Pollock, 1980.

Kevles, Daniel J. "The X Factor." *The New Yorker,* April 3, 1995, pp. 85–90.

Kiell, Norman. *The Adolescent Through Fiction.* New York: International Universities Press, 1974.

Kimball, Robert, ed. *The Complete Lyrics of Cole Porter.* New York: Alfred A. Knopf, 1983.

Kipnis, David. "The Use of Power in Organizations and in Interpersonal Settings." In *Applied Social Psychology Annual,* Vol. 5, edited by S. Oskamp. Beverly Hills, Calif.: Sage, 1984.

Kipnis, David; Patricia Castell; Mary Gergen; and Donna Mauch. "Metamorphic Effects of Power." *Journal of Applied Psychology* 61, no. 2 (1976): pp. 127–35.

Kipnis, David; Stuart M. Schmidt; and Ian Wilkinson. "Intraorganizational Influence Tactics: Explorations in Getting One's Way." *Journal of Applied Psychology* 65, no. 4 (1980): pp. 440–52.

Klagsbrun, Francine. *Married People.* New York: Bantam Books, 1985.

Kramer, Peter D. *Listening to Prozac.* New York: Viking, 1993.

Kramer, Selma, and Joseph Rudolph. "The Latency Stage." In *The Course of Life,* Vol. 2, edited by Greenspan and Pollock, 1980.

Landers, Ann. *Wake Up and Smell the Coffee.* New York: Villard, 1996.

Langer, Ellen J., and Judith Rodin. "The Effects of Choice and Enhanced Personal Responsibility for the Aged: A Field Experiment in an Institutional Setting." *Journal of Personality and Social Psychology* 34, no. 2 (1976): pp.191–98.

Lawrence, D. H. *The Complete Poems of D. H. Lawrence.* Edited by Vivian de Sola Pinto and Warren Roberts. New York: Viking Press, 1964, 1971.

———. *Selected Poems.* New York: New Directions, 1947.

Lefcourt, Herbert M. "The Function of the Illusions of Control and Freedom." *American Psychologist,* May 1973, pp. 417–25.

———. *Locus of Control.* Hillsdale, N.J.: Lawrence Erlbaum Associates, Publishers, 1982.

417

Lehman, Darrin R., and Shelley E. Taylor. "Date with an Earthquake: Coping with a Probable, Unpredictable Disaster." *Personality and Social Psychology Bulletin* 13, no. 4 (December 1987): pp. 546–55.

LeShan, Lawrence. *Cancer as a Turning Point.* New York: Plume, 1990.

Levant, Ronald. *Masculinity Reconstructed.* New York: Dutton, 1995.

LeVay, Simon. "A Difference in Hypothalamic Structure Between Heterosexual and Homosexual Men." *Science* 253 (August 30, 1991): pp. 1034–37.

Lewontin, R. C.; Steven Rose; and Leon J. Kamin. *Not in Our Genes.* New York: Pantheon Books, 1994.

Lewy, Ernst. "Responsibility, Free Will, and Ego Psychology." *The International Journal of Psycho-Analysis* 42 (1961): pp. 260–70.

Lidz, Theodore. "The Adolescent and His Family." In *Adolescence: Psychosocial Perspectives*, edited by Gerald Caplan and Serge Lebovici. New York: Basic Books, 1969.

Lobell, John, and Mimi Lobell. *John & Mimi.* New York: St. Martin's Press, 1972.

Loewald, Hans. "The Waning of the Oedipus Complex." *Journal of the American Psychoanalytic Association* 27, no. 4 (1979): pp. 751–75.

Loos, Anita. *Gentlemen Prefer Blondes.* New York: Boni and Liveright, 1925.

Lykken, D. T.; M. McGue; A. Tellegen; and T. J. Bouchard, Jr. "Emergenesis." *American Psychologist*, December 1992, pp. 1565–77.

Mahler, Margaret; Fred Pine; and Anni Bergman. *The Psychological Birth of the Human Infant.* New York: Basic Books, 1975.

Mann, Charles C. "Behavioral Genetics in Transition." *Science* 264 (June 17, 1994): pp. 1686–89.

Marks, Gary; Jean L. Richardson; and John W. Graham. "Role of Health Locus of Control Beliefs and Expectations of Treatment Efficacy in Adjustment to Cancer." *Journal of Personality and Social Psychology* 51, no. 2 (1986): pp. 443–50.

Marwell, Gerald, and David Schmitt. "Dimensions of Compliance-Gaining Behavior: An Empirical Analysis." *Sociometry* 30 (1967): pp. 350–64.

McBride, Angela Barron. *The Secret of a Good Life with Your Teenager.* New York: Times Books, 1987.

McClelland, David C. *Power: The Inner Experience.* New York: Irvington Publishers, 1975.

McDevitt, John, and Margaret Mahler. "Object Constancy, Individuality, and Internalization." In *The Course of Life*, Vol. 1, edited by Greenspan and Pollock, 1980.

McGovern, George. *Terry*. New York: Villard, 1996.

Mendelson, Steven T. "The Dying of the Light." *The Washington Post*, March 19, 1995, pp. F1, F5–F7.

Michael, Robert; John Gagnon; Edward Laumann; and Gina Kolata. *Sex in America*. Boston: Little, Brown, 1994.

Milgram, Stanley. *Obedience to Authority*. New York: Harper & Row, 1974.

Millay, Edna St. Vincent. *Collected Poems*. New York: Harper & Row, 1956.

Miller, Alice. *For Your Own Good*. New York: Noonday Press, 1983, 1984, 1990.

Miller, Dale T., and Carol A. Porter. "Self-Blame in Victims of Violence." *Journal of Social Issues* 39, no. 2 (1983): pp. 139–52.

Miller, Jean Baker. *Toward a New Psychology of Women*. Boston: Beacon Press, 1976, 1986.

Miller, Michael Vincent. *Intimate Terrorism*. New York: W. W. Norton, 1995.

Miller, Suzanne M. "Controllability and Human Stress: Method, Evidence and Theory." *Behaviour Research and Therapy* 17 (1979): pp. 287–304.

Millett, Kate. *Sexual Politics*. New York: Doubleday, 1970.

Montaigne, Michel de. *The Essays: A Selection*. London and New York: Penguin Books, 1987, 1991.

Morgan, Ernest. *Dealing Creatively with Death*. Bayside, N.Y.: Barclay House, 1990.

Morin, Richard. "Mothers and Sons." *The Washington Post*, February 26, 1995, p. C5.

Morowitz, David. "Bagels on Sunday." *The American Scholar* 65, no. 1 (Winter 1996).

Moyers, Bill. *Healing and the Mind*. New York: Doubleday, 1993.

Murchison, Carl, ed. *Psychologies of 1930*. Worcester, Mass.: Clark University Press, 1930.

Murphy, Lois. "Psychoanalytic Views of Infancy." In *The Course of Life*, Vol. 1, edited by Greenspan and Pollock, 1980.

Nabokov, Vladimir. *Pale Fire*. New York: Vintage Books, 1962, 1989.

Neely, Wright. "Freedom and Desire." *Philosophical Review* 83 (1974): pp. 32–54.

Nelson, Randy J.; Gregory E. Demas; Paul L. Huang; Mark C. Fishman; Vallna L. Dawson; Ted M. Dawson; and Solomon H. Snyder. "Behavioral Abnormalities in Male Mice Lacking Neuronal Nitric Oxide Synthase." *Nature* 378 (November 23, 1995): pp. 383–86.

419

Neubauer, Peter. "Phase-Specific Disorders of the Second and Third Years of Life." In *The Course of Life*, Vol. 1, edited by Greenspan and Pollock, 1980.

Nietzsche, Friedrich. *Thus Spoke Zarathustra*. New York: Penguin Books, 1954.

Norman, Jane, and Myron Harris. *The Private Life of the American Teenager*. New York: Rawson, Wade Publishers, 1981.

Noshpitz, Joseph. "Disturbances in Early Adolescent Development." In *The Course of Life*, Vol. 2, edited by Greenspan and Pollock, 1980.

Nuland, Sherwin B. *How We Die*. New York: Alfred A. Knopf, 1994.

Okimoto, Jean Davies, and Phyllis Jackson Stegall. *Boomerang Kids*. Boston: Little, Brown, 1987.

Olsson, Peter A. "In Search of Their Fathers-Themselves: Jim Jones and David Koresh." *Mind and Human Interaction* 5, no. 3 (August 1994): pp. 85–96.

Ostow, Mortimer. "The Control of Human Behavior." *The International Journal of Psychoanalysis* 40, parts 5–6 (1959): pp. 273–86.

Parens, Henri. "Psychic Development During the Second and Third Years of Life." In *The Course of Life*, Vol. 1, edited by Greenspan and Pollock, 1980.

Parker, Dorothy. *The Portable Dorothy Parker*. New York: Viking Press, 1944.

Pattison, E. Mansell. "Religion and Compliance." In *Compliant Behavior*, edited by Max Rosenbaum, pp. 107–34. New York: Human Sciences Press, 1983.

Person, Ethel. "Male Sexuality and Power." *Psychoanalytic Inquiry* 6, no. 1 (1986): pp. 3–25.

Piaget, Gerald. *Control Freaks*. New York: Doubleday, 1991.

Piaget, Jean. "The Intellectual Development of the Adolescent." In *Adolescence: Psychosocial Perspectives*, edited by Gerald Caplan and Serge Lebovici. New York: Basic Books, 1969.

Plomin, Robert. "The Role of Inheritance in Behavior." *Science* 248 (April 13, 1990): pp. 183–88.

Plomin, Robert; Michael J. Owen; and Peter McGuffin. "The Genetic Basis of Complex Human Behaviors." *Science* 264 (June 17, 1994): pp. 1733–39.

Portwood, Doris. *Common Sense Suicide*. Eugene, Ore.: National Hemlock Society, 1978.

Price, Reynolds. *A Whole New Life*. New York: Atheneum, 1994.

Quill, Timothy. "Death and Dignity: A Case of Individualized Decision Making." *The New England Journal of Medicine* 324, no. 10 (March 7, 1991): pp. 691–94.

420

————. *Death and Dignity.* New York: W. W. Norton, 1993.

Rapaport, David. "The Theory of Ego Autonomy: A Generalization." In *The Collected Papers of David Rapaport,* edited by Merton M. Gill. New York: Basic Books, 1967.

Raven, Bertram. "A Taxonomy of Power in Human Relations." *Psychiatric Annals* 16, no. 11 (November 1986): pp. 633–36.

Rodin, Judith, and Ellen J. Langer. "Long-Term Effects of a Control-Relevant Intervention with the Institutionalized Aged." *Journal of Personality and Social Psychology* 35, no. 12 (1977): pp. 897–902.

Rogers, Malcolm P.; Devendra Dubey; and Peter Reich. "The Influence of the Psyche and the Brain on Immunity and Disease Susceptibility: A Critical Review." *Psychosomatic Medicine* 41, no. 2 (March 1979): pp. 147–64.

Roiphe, Anne. *Fruitful.* Boston: Houghton Mifflin, 1996.

————. *Lovingkindness.* New York: Summit Books, 1987.

Roiphe, Katie. *Last Night in Paradise.* Boston: Little, Brown, 1997.

————. *The Morning After.* Boston: Little, Brown, 1993, 1994.

Rose, Phyllis. *Parallel Lives.* New York: Alfred A. Knopf, 1983.

Rosenbaum, Max. "Compliance." In *Compliant Behavior,* edited by Max Rosenbaum, pp. 25–49. New York: Human Sciences Press, 1983.

————. ed. *Compliant Behavior.* New York: Human Sciences Press, 1983.

Ross, John Munder. *The Male Paradox.* New York: Simon & Schuster, 1992.

Ruitenbeek, Hendrik M., ed. *The Interpretation of Death.* New York: Jason Aronson Publishers, 1969, 1973.

Scharff, David. *The Sexual Relationship.* Boston: Routledge & Kegan Paul, 1982.

Schecter, Marshall, and Lee Combrinck-Graham. "The Normal Development of the Seven-to-Ten-Year-Old Child." In *The Course of Life,* Vol. 2, edited by Greenspan and Pollock, 1980.

Scheppele, Kim Lane, and Pauline B. Bart. "Through Women's Eyes: Defining Danger in the Wake of Sexual Assault." *Journal of Social Issues* 39, no. 2 (1983): pp. 63–80.

Schwartz, Amy. *A Teeny Tiny Baby.* New York: Orchard Books, 1994.

Schwartz, Tony. *What Really Matters.* New York: Bantam Books, 1996.

Schwartz, Wynn. "The Two Concepts of Action and Responsibility in Psychoanalysis." *Journal of the American Psychoanalytic Association* 32, no. 3 (1984): pp. 557–72.

Segal, Nancy L. "The Importance of Twin Studies for Individual Differences Research." *Journal of Counseling and Development* 68 (July/August 1990): pp. 612–22.

Seligman, Martin. *Helplessness*. New York: W. H. Freeman, 1975, 1992.

Seuss, Dr. *Oh, the Places You'll Go!* New York: Random House, 1990.

Shapiro, Theodore, and Richard Perry. "Latency Revisited: The Age 7 Plus or Minus 1." In *The Psychoanalytic Study of the Child* 31 (1976): pp. 79–105.

Shields, Carol. *The Stone Diaries*. New York: Penguin Books, 1993.

Siegel, Bernie S. *Love, Medicine & Miracles*. New York: Harper & Row, 1986.

Silver, Roxane L.; Cheryl Boon; and Mary H. Stones. "Searching for Meaning in Misfortune: Making Sense of Incest." *Journal of Social Issues* 39, no. 2 (1983): pp. 81–101.

Sklansky, Morris. "The Pubescent Years: Eleven to Fourteen." In *The Course of Life*, Vol. 2, edited by Greenspan and Pollock, 1980.

Snow, Catherine. "Language and the Beginnings of Moral Understanding." In *The Emergence of Morality in Young Children*, edited by Kagan and Lamb. Chicago: University of Chicago Press, 1990.

Solomon, Andrew. "A Death of One's Own." *The New Yorker*, May 22, 1995, pp. 54–69.

Sontag, Susan. *Illness as Metaphor and AIDS and Its Metaphors*. New York: Anchor Books, 1977, 1978, 1988, 1989.

Spencer, Heidi H. *"Did I Do Something Wrong?"* Far Hills, N.J.: New Horizons Press, 1995.

Spencer, Scott. *Endless Love*. New York: Alfred A. Knopf, 1979.

Staples, Herman, and Erwin Smarr. "Bridge to Adulthood: Years from Eighteen to Twenty-three." In *The Course of Life*, Vol. 2, edited by Greenspan and Pollock, 1980.

Sulloway, Frank J. *Born to Rebel*. New York: Pantheon Books, 1996.

SUPPORT contributors. "A Controlled Trial to Improve Care for the Seriously Ill Hospitalized Patients." *Journal of the American Medical Association* 274, no. 20 (November 22–29, 1995): pp. 1591–98.

Tannen, Deborah. *Talking from 9 to 5*. New York: William Morrow, 1994.

———. *You Just Don't Understand*. New York: Ballantine Books, 1990.

Taylor, Shelley E. *Positive Illusions*. New York: Basic Books, 1989.

Taylor, Shelley E.; Joanne V. Wood; and Rosemary R. Lichtman. "It Could Be Worse: Selective Evaluation as a Response to Victimization." *Journal of Social Issues* 39, no. 2 (1983): pp. 19–40.

Tellegen, Auke; David T. Lykken; Thomas J. Bouchard, Jr.; Kimerly J. Wilcox; Nancy L. Segal; and Stephen Rich. "Personality Similarity in Twins Reared Apart and Together." *Journal of Personality and Social Psychology* 54, no. 8 (June 1988): pp. 1031–39.

Thomas, Dylan. *Selected Writings*. New York: New Directions, 1946.

Thompson, Sharon. *Going All the Way*. New York: Hill & Wang, 1995.

Thompson, Suzanne C. "Will It Hurt Less If I Can Control It? A Complex Answer to a Simple Question." *Psychological Bulletin* 90, no. 1 (1981): pp. 89–101.

Toews, John. "Adolescent Developmental Issues in Marital Therapy." In *Adolescent Psychiatry*, Vol. 8, edited by Sherman C. Feinstein; Peter L. Giovacchini; John G. Looney; Allan Z. Schwartzberg; and Arthur D. Sorosky, pp. 244–52. Chicago: University of Chicago Press, 1980.

Tolins, Jonathan. "A Playwright's Insight—and Warning." *Time,* July 26, 1993, pp. 38–39.

Turkel, Ann Ruth. "Money as a Mirror of Marriage." *Journal of the American Academy of Psychoanalysis* 16, no. 4 (1988): pp. 525–35.

Viorst, Judith. "Are You a Moral Wimp?" *Redbook,* September 1993, pp. 72, 74.

———. *If I Were in Charge of the World and Other Worries.* New York: Atheneum, 1981.

———. "Is Your Child's Personality Set at Birth?" *Redbook,* November 1995, pp. 174, 178.

———. "The Messes, the Stresses, the Strains, the Joys . . . Kids." *Redbook,* June 1976, pp. 89, 141, 143, 144.

———. *Murdering Mr. Monti.* New York: Fawcett Crest, 1994.

———. *Necessary Losses.* New York: Simon & Schuster, 1986.

———. *People and Other Aggravations.* New York: World Publishing, 1971.

———. *Sad Underwear and Other Complications.* New York: Atheneum, 1995.

———. "What's a Good Mommy?" *Redbook,* October 1974, pp. 38, 40.

Waelder, Robert. "Psychic Determinism and the Possibility of Predictions." *The Psychoanalytic Quarterly* 32, no. 1 (January 1963): pp. 15–42.

Wallerstein, Judith S., and Sandra Blakeslee. *The Good Marriage.* Boston: Houghton Mifflin, 1995.

Wallston, Kenneth A., and Barbara Strudler Wallston. "Who Is Responsible for Your Health? The Construct of Health Locus of Control." In *Social Psychology of Health and Illness,* edited by Glenn S. Sanders and Jerry Suls. Hillsdale, N.J.: Lawrence Erlbaum Associates, Publishers, 1982.

Weil, Andrew. *Spontaneous Healing.* New York: Fawcett Columbine, 1995.

Weisz, John. "Understanding the Developing Understanding of Control." *The Minnesota Symposia on Child Psychology,* Vol. 18, edited by Marion Perlmutter. Hillsdale, N.J.: Lawrence Erlbaum Associates, Publishers, 1986.

White, Robert W. "Motivation Reconsidered: The Concept of Competence." *Psychological Review* 66, no. 5 (1959).

Wilder, Thornton. *Our Town.* New York: Harper & Row, 1938, 1957.

Wilson, James Q. *Moral Judgment.* New York: Basic Books, 1997.

———. *The Moral Sense.* New York: The Free Press, 1993.

Wolf, Naomi. *The Beauty Myth.* New York: William Morrow, 1991.

———. *Promiscuities.* New York: Random House, 1997.

Wortman, Camille B. "Coping with Victimization: Conclusions and Implications for Future Research." *Journal of Social Issues* 39, no. 2 (1983): pp. 195–221.

Wortman, Camille B., and Jack W. Brehm. "Responses to Uncontrollable Outcomes: An Integration of Reactance Theory and the Learned Helplessness Model." In *Advances in Experimental Social Psychology,* Vol. 8, edited by L. Berkowitz. New York: Academic Press, 1975.

Wright, Robert. *The Moral Animal.* New York: Pantheon Books, 1994.

Yahraes, Herbert. "Parents as Leaders: The Role of Control and Discipline." In *Families Today,* Vol. 1, edited by Eunice Corfman, pp. 289–97. Washington, D.C.: U.S. Government Printing Office, 1979.

Yourcenar, Marguerite. *Memoirs of Hadrian.* New York: Farrar, Straus & Giroux, 1954.

Zaleznik, Abraham. *Learning Leadership.* Chicago: Bonus Books, 1993.

Zanden, James W. Vander. *Human Development.* New York: McGraw-Hill, 1993.

Acknowledgments

In the course of writing this book, I turned to many, many people for their wisdom and experience and support. There are some whose names I can't mention because I promised them that I would protect their privacy, but I hope that they know they have my enduring gratitude. As for the others, I offer these heartfelt thanks:

I thank the therapists and the psychoanalysts who shared their ideas and expertise with me: Joan Willens Beerman, Ruth Caplin, Robert Gillman, Stanley Greenspan, Arlene Heyman, Joan Krash, Betty Ann Ottinger, Gerald Perman, Harvey Rich, Sheila Rogovin, Earle Silber, and Anne Stephansky.

I thank Cornelia Biddle, Nell Minow, and Larry Ramer for their special insights.

I thank my favorite rabbi, Leonard Beerman, and my favorite internist, David Morowitz, and the remarkable people connected with Hospice of Washington and other hospices, all of whom helped me think about death, surrender, and control: Carol Atkins, Sister Barbara Marie C.S.C., Jane Corrigan, Fran Dunphy, Susan Johnson, Karen Jones, Dorothy Kavanaugh, Helen Lindsey, Rita Paddack, Molly Sherwood, Mary Wassman, Les Whitten, and other good men and women—far too many to mention.

I thank Nicholas Viorst, who critiqued the first draft with his fine editorial eye and his usual combination of rigor and tact; and Ira Pastan, who so helpfully read the first chapter; and Barbara and Lou Breger, whose thoughtful comments on the manuscript were invaluable; and Lisbeth Schorr, who made major conceptual contributions.

I thank my agent-for-life Robert Lescher and his terrific associate Michael Choate. I thank the golden editorial team of Fred Hills and Burton Beals for their caring, constructive nagging—and for almost always being right. And I thank Sheila Bétit, of the Washington Psychoanalytic Foundation, who tracked down research materials for me with a graciousness that was surpassed only by her competence.

I thank my sons, Anthony and Nick and Alexander; my daughter-in-law, Hyla; and my wonderful women friends—including, but surely not limited to, Hanna Altman, Sunny Aurelio, Phyllis Hersh, Elinor Horwitz, Silvia Koner, Elaine Konigsburg, Leslie Oberdorfer, Sally Pitofsky, Shay Rieger, Barbara Rosenfeld, and Judy Silber—for their encouragement and sustaining goodwill.

Finally, I thank my husband, Milton, for his love, unflagging confidence, patience, and support during the three intense years I worked on this book.

Index

About the Author

Judith Viorst is the author of eight collections of poetry and five books of prose, including the best-seller *Necessary Losses* and her comic novel, *Murdering Mr. Monti.* She has also written twelve children's books, among them the classic *Alexander and the Terrible, Horrible, No Good, Very Bad Day.* A graduate of the Washington Psychoanalytic Institute, she is the recipient of various awards for her journalism and psychological writings. She lives in Washington, D.C., with her husband, political writer Milton Viorst. They have three sons.